T0319931

UNWITTING ARCHITECT

Emerging Frontiers in the Global Economy

EDITOR   J.P. Singh

Unwitting Architect

German Primacy and the Origins of Neoliberalism

Julian Germann

STANFORD UNIVERSITY PRESS

Stanford, California

STANFORD UNIVERSITY PRESS
Stanford, California

© 2021 by the Board of Trustees of the Leland Stanford Junior University.
All rights reserved.

No part of this book may be reproduced or transmitted in any form or by any means, electronic or mechanical, including photocopying and recording, or in any information storage or retrieval system without the prior written permission of Stanford University Press.

Printed in the United States of America on acid-free, archival-quality paper

Library of Congress Cataloging-in-Publication Data

Names: Germann, Julian, author.
Title: Unwitting architect : German primacy and the origins of neoliberalism / Julian Germann.
Other titles: Emerging frontiers in the global economy.
Description: Stanford, California : Stanford University Press, 2021. | Series: Emerging frontiers in the global economy | Includes bibliographical references and index.
Identifiers: LCCN 2020019976 (print) | LCCN 2020019977 (ebook) | ISBN 9781503609846 (cloth) | ISBN 9781503614291 (epub)
Subjects: LCSH: European Union—Germany. | Monetary policy—Germany (West)—History. | Monetary policy—Germany—History. | Neoliberalism—History. | Germany (West)—Economic policy. | Germany—Economic policy—1990– | Germany (West)—Foreign economic relations. | Germany—Foreign economic relations.
Classification: LCC HC286.6 .G4624 2021 (print) | LCC HC286.6 (ebook) | DDC 337.1/420943—dc23
LC record available at https://lccn.loc.gov/2020019976
LC ebook record available at https://lccn.loc.gov/2020019977

Book design: Kevin Barrett Kane

Typeset at Stanford University Press in 10/14 ITC Galliard Pro

Contents

Abbreviations and Acronyms

BDA—Bundesvereinigung der Deutschen Arbeitgeberverbände (Confederation of German Employers' Associations)

BDI—Bundesverband der Deutschen Industrie (Federation of German Industries)

BdL—Bank deutscher Länder (Bank of German States)

CAP—Common Agricultural Policy

CRU—collective reserve unit

CIA—Central Intelligence Agency

DC—Democrazia Cristiana (Christian Democratic Party, Italy)

DIHK—Deutscher Industrie- und Handelskammertag (Association of German Chambers of Commerce and Industry)

DM—deutsche mark

ECB—European Central Bank

EEC—European Economic Community

EMU—Economic and Monetary Union

EMS—European Monetary System

ERM—European Exchange Rate Mechanism

ESM—European Stability Mechanism

EU—European Union

FDI—foreign direct investment

FOMC—Federal Open Market Committee

FRG—Federal Republic of Germany

G5—Group of Five (France, Germany, United Kingdom, United States, Japan)

G7—Group of Seven (Canada, France, Germany, Italy, Japan, United Kingdom, United States)

GDP—gross domestic product

IMF—International Monetary Fund

IPE—International Political Economy

IR—International Relations

MIP—Macroeconomic Imbalance Procedure

NATO—North Atlantic Treaty Organization

NIEO—New International Economic Order

OECD—Organisation for Economic Co-Operation and Development

OEEC—Organisation for European Economic Co-Operation

OPEC—Organization of the Petroleum Exporting Countries

PCI—Partito Comunista Italiano (Italian Communist Party)

SDR—Special Drawing Right

SPD—Sozialdemokratische Partei Deutschlands (Social Democratic Party of Germany)

U&CD—uneven and combined development

VEBA—Vereinigte Elektrizitäts und Bergwerks Aktiengesellschaft (United Electricity and Mining Corporation)

Acknowledgments

This book owes its existence to more people than I can acknowledge here. Its archival research was funded by a Pierre Elliott Trudeau Fellowship from York University and a grant from the Gerald R. Ford Presidential Foundation. I would like to thank the custodians of the institutions that supported and hosted me during this research: Jlenya Sarra-De Meo, Marlene Quesenberry, and Judy Matadial at my *alma mater*; Kerstin Schenke, Kurt Braband, and Philip Möckel at the German Federal Archives; Sven Harman and Christoph Stamm at the Archive of Social Democracy of the Friedrich Ebert Foundation; Karin Fitzner, Rolf Herget, and Gerd-Christian Wannovius at the Historical Archives of the German Federal Bank; and Mark Fischer and Jeremy Schmidt at the Gerald R. Ford Presidential Library. I would also like to thank Helmut Schmidt, posthumously, for permission to access his personal papers, and Daniel Kinderman for generously sharing some of his hard-won archival data from the German central bank with me. Richard Sylla helped me interpret some quantitative evidence, and Barbara Würtz deciphered some stenographic protocols for me.

Many of the ideas that inform this book sprang from my doctoral dissertation. They first evolved in the vibrant graduate community at York University and benefited greatly from the stimulating discussions in our Historical Materialism & International Relations reading group, hosted by my supervisor and friend Hannes Lacher. To name but a few from a brilliant cohort of doctoral researchers whose comradeship and scholarship supported and inspired me, I would like to thank Christopher Bailey, Joseph Baines, Robert Batarseh, Timothy David Clark, Eren Duzgun, Jessica Evans, Paul Foley, Jeremy Green, Sandy Brian Hager, Geoffrey McCormack, Dermot O'Connor, Ingar Solty, and Sean Kenji Starrs. Among these, I owe a special thanks to Olivia Sultanescu for her friendship and support with preparing and submitting the dissertation from which this book was extensively developed. And last, but certainly not least, the dissertation would never have seen the light of day without the guidance of my supervisors Hannes Lacher, Leo Panitch, and Stephen Gill, and without the generous and constructive engagement of my external examiner Eric Helleiner.

From these early beginnings, this book has matured into its full and final form over my last eight years at Sussex University. The Research in Progress seminar series organized by the Department of International Relations allowed me to present my ideas soon after I arrived, and since then many of my colleagues have helped me develop them further. Some of the archival material and the arguments of this book have been published in different forms and other outlets. I am grateful for the editors and anonymous reviewers of *New Political Economy*, *International Studies Quarterly*, and *European Journal of International Relations* for their helpful comments and suggestions. In the process of finishing the book and finding a publisher, I have accumulated more debts of gratitude. Mareike Beck, Lara Coleman, Samuel Knafo, Justin Rosenberg, Jan Selby, Benjamin Selwyn, and Benno Teschke have given invaluable feedback on the proposal and the manuscript, and Beate Jahn, Patricia Owens, and Rorden Wilkinson provided very helpful publishing advice.

I would like to thank my editors, Steve Catalano and J.P. Singh, and their team at Stanford University Press, for working so hard to bring this book to print. I am also grateful to the two anonymous reviewers for their supportive comments and helpful suggestions.

I am deeply grateful to the friends and loved ones who supported me in many different ways throughout the years. Among them, I would like to mention Henning Schmitz, who provided valuable creative support, and Ana Maria Sanchez Molina, who helped me keep perspective and reminded me of what matters most. The book has had a long journey to publication, and my family has been there for me every step of the way. I owe everything to them, and I dedicate this book to the memory of my dear grandmother, Maria Germann.

UNWITTING ARCHITECT

Introduction

GERMAN PRIMACY IN EUROPE—four words that once conjured up a continent's dark past now seem to presage its future. The European fallout from the global financial meltdown of 2008 cast the Federal Republic into an unrivaled position of regional influence at the same time that it threw the European Union (EU) into existential crisis.[1] The divergence in fortunes since the devastation wreaked by this so-called "eurocrisis" is astounding. Most of the eurozone has suffered from economic stagnation, rising debt, and financial instability over the past decade. At the start of the 2020s, it faces an even deeper depression, brought on by the coronavirus outbreak. The German economy, by contrast, has been set on a record-beating path of high growth, low unemployment, and sound finances, and is expected to rebound more quickly from the virus-induced slump (Fleming and Khan 2020). Since 2014, the German state has run budget surpluses and significantly reduced its debt (FAZ 2017). Since 2016, it has been able in principle to borrow at negative yields—meaning that investors are *paying* the German government to borrow from them. And in 2019, Germany posted the world's largest current-account surplus for the fourth year in a row (Wagner 2020), while its exports in goods alone accounted for a staggering 38.6 percent of its gross domestic product (GDP).[2] These indicators of economic strength are mirrored in the political ascendancy of Germany in the EU. As the EU's largest creditor and leading contributor to the European Stability Mechanism (ESM) (Sinn 2016), the German state quickly established itself as the principal manager of the eurocrisis (for example, Bulmer and Paterson 2013: 1392). With its payments into and hold over the next seven-year budget of the EU (2021–2027) set to increase after Brexit, the German government is likely to play an equally prominent role in defining the EU's economic response to the virus. And with France in domestic turmoil, Britain on its way out of the EU, and the US incapacitated by the Trump presidency, Germany finds itself in an unprecedented position to shape the European project after the pandemic.

Judging by how it handled the eurocrisis, however, the German state is unlikely to use this growing weight to address the deep divisions that continue to threaten the EU. It long hesitated to offer support for its financially distressed partners, refused to boost domestic demand to provide a market for their exports, and blocked several proposals to contain the crisis by spreading the risk and sharing the costs more evenly. Instead, it demanded painful reforms involving deep budget cuts, the fire sale of public assets, and the restructuring of labor markets in exchange for financial assistance (for example, Lapavitsas and Flassbeck 2015). The German insistence on a program of crushing austerity for European debtors during the eurocrisis does not bode well for the future, and it has baffled sympathetic observers and infuriated its critics ever since.[3] Many have asked why a country they took to be fully committed to the European idea has failed to provide enlightened leadership at such a crucial juncture (for example, Maull 2013). Others point out that its response has exacerbated rather than contained the centrifugal forces that endanger the EU (such as Wolf 2016). And some, in fact, go so far as to see in Germany's imperious imposition of fiscal retrenchment and structural reforms on its Southern partners the ugly image of a zero-sum politics that is bound to return in the face of the pandemic (for example, Kundnani 2011: 40; Kluth 2020). In short, while few can imagine the EU surviving without a strong Germany at its center,[4] others ponder whether "German domination [is] compatible with further European integration or [whether it] will . . . prove a fracturing force" (Cohen 2015).

Given the importance of this new German question for the region's destiny and the future of the world economy, it is surprising to see that the historical horizon that informs this debate has been remarkably limited. References to Germany's imperial or fascist past or, more favorably, to the peculiar legacy of its postwar development, are aplenty in today's political commentary and scholarly analysis. Overall, however, there is hardly any sustained inquiry into the sources of Germany's newfound power and purpose that reaches back further than the 1990s.[5] In the overwhelming majority of accounts, Germany's reunification after the Cold War and its reformed position within Europe's new Economic and Monetary Union (EMU) are taken as the unquestioned parameters that supposedly explain its predominance today.

This book argues that outside of this limited field of vision lies an earlier strategic turning point that profoundly shaped Germany's political economy, the European project it presides over, and the broader global context in which its attempts to manage the eurocrisis and its aftermath converge and conflict with those of others. This turning point is the turbulent crisis decade of the 1970s, when monetary turmoil, rampant inflation, rising unemployment, and a generalized recession conspired to tear the "embedded" liberal international economic order (Ruggie 1982) asunder. Marked by macroeconomic imbalances and financial instabilities, the end of the long postwar boom raised questions about the responsibilities of surplus countries and deficit countries that closely resemble those today. More fundamentally, it confronted German and other North Atlantic policymakers with the problem of how to sustain social peace, economic growth, and a liberal international order. The search for ways out of the crisis was marked by significant domestic tensions, painful trade-offs, and transatlantic frictions. And the "solution" that Anglo-American elites ultimately hit upon—to attack the organized power, institutionalized protection, and guaranteed rights of labor in favor of capital and to dismantle welfare state regulation in favor of market forces and individualized self-help—inaugurated a new global era infamously known as "neoliberalism."[6]

The global rise of neoliberalism is widely seen as a dynamic originating in the United States and the United Kingdom at the end of the 1970s and sweeping across the world in the decades that followed. From this Anglocentric perspective, Germany's emergence at the center of neoliberal restructuring in contemporary Europe seems perplexing. The consensus since the 1980s holds that Germany has been reluctant to embrace Anglo-American "free market" capitalism and presents—in practice or at least in principle—a more coordinated and socially balanced alternative.[7] But how then could this supposed stalwart of a social market economy turn into the vanguard of neoliberal reform in Europe? The only available answer is to emphasize the erosion of the German model under the pressures of neoliberal globalization since the 1990s. But this reading assumes that Germany's lead role in the neoliberal restructuring of the eurozone results from the same forces conventionally associated with the Anglo-American pioneer.

This book challenges this ruling narrative empirically and conceptually. Drawing on original archival research, it argues that Germany emerged as the *unwitting architect* of neoliberal globalization in the 1970s. It was an *architect* because it contributed to the grand shift from embedded to neoliberal capitalism in crucial respects. The German decision to float the deutsche mark (DM) for the sake of domestic price stability destabilized the Bretton Woods regime, and the regional currency bloc it organized in its stead tied participants to its restrictive monetary policy. Together with their US counterparts, German policymakers used their financial muscle to counter eurocommunism in Italy and the Bennite Labour left in the United Kingdom, and to support the French technocratic Barre government against the left alliance led by Mitterrand. The German government also frustrated efforts of the Group of Seven (G7) countries to coordinate a Keynesian reflation of the world economy, and, finally, it used the DM as leverage to steer the United States toward a radical course of deflation that broke the capital-labor compromise. In short, Germany's anti-inflationary policies and monetary power unsettled the embedded liberal world order, prevented its partners' attempts to restore or progressively transcend it, and narrowed down the options so that an attack on organized labor—the font of the neoliberal revolution—won out as the only path out of the crisis.

This contribution to the global rise of neoliberalism has gone unnoticed in part because it was *unwitting*. German officials did not intend to set the world on a neoliberal path. On the contrary, they sought above all to sustain the domestic compact between capital and labor. But because its embedded liberal compromise had been built on Germany's success in global markets, it was exposed to the crisis responses of others. German officials thus actively opposed the interventionist and expansionary remedies discussed and pursued in Europe and the United States—not because they favored a neoliberal solution, but because they feared that protectionism and imported inflation would erode the basis of Germany's export success and social peace. Though not guided by neoliberal ideas or interests, Germany's actions had unintended neoliberal consequences. Its attempts to maintain open markets and stable prices—while aimed at preserving embedded liberalism at home—precluded left-wing and centrist Keynesian alternatives and provided the external impetus that launched the neoliberal counteroffensive in the United States and the United Kingdom.

Revealing German policymakers as proactive, if peculiar, agents of neo-liberalism from the very beginning furnishes the coordinates we need to locate Germany's place in a crisis-ridden and virus-hit Europe today. For, although initially successful in safeguarding the embedded liberal class compromise, Germany's attempts to commit Europe and the United States to monetary and fiscal discipline ultimately turned out to be self-defeating. In triggering a neoliberal response, German officials helped create a socially regressive but internationally competitive form of capitalism that has put significant pressures on the German model since the 1980s. The painful "Hartz IV" labor market and social security reforms introduced in the early 2000s marked the culmination of a decade-long process of adjustment to this new Anglo-American variety.[8] And yet the longer-run perspective taken in this study reveals that, far from a story of convergence on an Anglo-American model, the German state still seeks to preserve a shrinking core of its social market economy, now critically dependent on global demand and European supply chains. From this vantage point, the book illuminates the very different rationale behind the painful reforms German state managers have demanded of their indebted eurozone partners. In the context of a regional manufacturing network centered on Germany and extending across the old and new members of the EU, German policymakers see neoliberal austerity as a way to create an attractive low-cost environment for German capital. In as far as their ability to regionalize production, supply, and investment allows German manufacturers to compete in global markets and rewards skilled workers in the major exporting industries, removing what remains of the burdensome postwar settlement across Europe serves to sustain what is left of the embedded liberal compromise in Germany. German policymakers, in short, promote neoliberalism abroad so as not to practice it at home. By tracing the origins of German crisis management back to the 1970s, this book provides a fuller picture than is currently available of the wider vision of the EU as a subordinate supply zone that guides them, and the potentially broader appeal of their actions to some European intermediate producers.

The book argues that the role played by Germany makes it an outlier from existing theory: it diverges dramatically from what we think we know about the origins of neoliberalism. Therefore, it both calls for a different approach and produces new theoretical insights. The prevailing accounts of neoliberal globalization center on the United States and the United Kingdom, and derive from their experience a general model of neoliberal change. The relative strength or weakness of similar attributes in other societies determines the weight they are given in the overall story: countries in which neoliberally minded elites or free market ideas are strong are said to have played an active role; countries in which these are weak are relegated to the sidelines. The German state, however, was guided by neither neoliberal ideology or social forces, nor was it pushed against its will by states that were. Because Germany does not fit this model and yet played a demonstrably central role in the rise of neoliberalism, this book calls for a break with the established Anglocentric perspective. To do so, it draws on insights from the alternative framework of uneven and combined development (U&CD). Rather than generalize from the dominant actor in the system, this approach holds that world order change is driven by the interaction of multiple states and the developmental differences between them. The book argues that we can use this wider lens to reintegrate seemingly deviant cases such as Germany into our explanation of neoliberal globalization. It traces how Germany's postwar capitalism combined a new social compromise pioneered in the US with its traditional world market orientation. It examines how this distinctive version of embedded liberalism, dependent on competitive prices and open borders for its exports, led Germany's policymakers in the 1970s to prioritize low inflation and free trade. And it argues that this crisis response restructured the international environment to deny others the chance to democratize capitalism or revive growth by Keynesian means, thus creating the conditions in which a specifically neoliberal solution—the confrontation with organized labor under Reagan and Thatcher—was devised and successfully tried.

Because the German case defies the Anglocentric master story, it also points toward a more nuanced appreciation of neoliberalism as a world-historic phenomenon: rather than an Anglo-American *project* rolled out across the globe, it is better approached as a cross-national and open-ended *process* driven by a plenitude of actors whose interests and ideas appear to be idiosyncratic but become intelligible when located in a wider international context. This expanded view also changes how we think about the future of neoliberalism. Existing predictions of what will come "after" neoliberalism are bound to be misleading because they rest on a false analogy with how neoliberalism emerged in the 1970s. The German experience demonstrates that neoliberalism was never a singular movement that, once fully formulated, conquered the world in one fell swoop. Instead, the making of neoliberalism depended from the start on the contingent and interdependent decisions of multiple actors, many of whom were guided by economic ideas, social interests, and international constraints that diverged significantly from those attributed to the US and the UK. It is the same sensitivity that this book argues needs to be brought to bear on the current conjuncture. Seeing neoliberalism as a uniform project has made us search in vain for some comprehensive equivalent that might replace it, only to find, in the absence of such an alternative, confirmation that neoliberalism is here to stay. This book argues that neoliberalism is better understood as a new era of capitalism that has shattered the central political question of the postwar West—how to organize mass consent—into a myriad of practices that seek to reverse and remold the rights that working people had won in this process of reconstruction. Leaving behind the notion of neoliberalism as a full-fledged market program frees us to attend to the pragmatic and counterintuitive choices of agents neither fully wedded nor fundamentally opposed to it who—as the Janus-faced character of Germany's eurocrisis management demonstrates—may be more likely to shape the future of the European and global political economy.

Structure of the Argument

The presentation of the argument in this book is as follows. Taking up the preceding discussion, Chapter 1 reviews the three most prominent explanations of the global rise of neoliberalism provided within the International Relations (IR) subfield of International Political Economy (IPE) and its critical tradition, which the chapter argues contrasts favorably with conventional liberal and realist approaches. The first account argues that neoliberalism arose primarily from the geopolitics of an ailing US hegemon that, in the turbulent 1970s, invented and imposed free market capitalism on its core allies and developing countries in order to stave off its decline. A second account argues that neoliberalism was the political project of business elites, who sought to reassert their power by attacking the welfare state gains and political representation of the labor movement. A third account presents the return of free market capitalism since the 1970s as a change of economic paradigms, brought about by a network of intellectuals that successfully injected neoliberal ideas into policy discourse. The chapter argues that these state-centered, class-based, and ideational approaches differ in emphasis but suffer from the same weakness: they generalize from the dominant state in the system. Other actors do not enter the story, unless and until they can be shown to be subject to ideas, societal pressures, or hegemonic interests similar to those of the United States. Because they pivot unduly on the Anglo-American world, these accounts are unable to capture the peculiar German contribution to the origins of neoliberalism. And as a result, they misread the rise of Germany to the apex of a neoliberal Europe as a belated repetition of the same global movement spearheaded by the US and the UK.

To overcome this debilitating Anglocentrism, Chapter 2 outlines a conceptual framework through which the role of Germany in the making of neoliberal globalization can be brought into focus. The solution, the chapter argues, is to eschew a comparative approach and interrogate the German political economy as not only different from but entwined with other national political economies in fundamental ways. The lens of uneven and combined development sheds light on this interconnectedness: it emphasizes the coevolution of national capitalisms, the systemic pressures that arise from their coexistence, and the interactive context of foreign economic decision making. Rather than viewing the neoliberal shift as an endogenous Anglo-American development that was subsequently globalized, I argue that this heuristic allows us to approach the "disembedding" of the liberal world economy as a cross-national and, in important respects, "conflict-driven" sequence of policy action and reaction. Not only does this broaden the inquiry into the origins of neoliberalism beyond the putative Anglo-American pioneer, but by focusing on the specific configurations of social *and* international forces that act upon policymakers, we are able to appreciate the potentially counterintuitive interests and idiosyncratic ideas that guide their actions.

Chapter 3 traces the long-term development of German capitalism across the liberal world orders of the late nineteenth and early twentieth centuries. It argues that Germany's postwar social market economy was built upon an externally oriented developmental model inherited from its belated but accelerated insertion into the world market and used to enroll capital and labor in a global export offensive. The influence of "ordoliberalism"—Germany's variant of free market ideology—in the making of this German model has been exaggerated.[9] Its proponents were opposed to many of the social reforms necessary to establish this distinctive version of the embedded liberal compromise, and had little to say about its critical international supports: an undervalued DM held in place by the fixed-exchange-rate regime of Bretton Woods, and continuous trade surpluses facilitated by comparative price stability, which policy elites saw not as an ordoliberally prescribed end in itself but as a benchmark of social peace and international success. The underlying vision of Germany as the workshop of an advanced industrial and newly industrializing world coincided with the postwar plans of the United States for an open, multilateral global economy. And yet the prevailing image of Germany as a liberal "trading state" (*Handelsstaat*) that had traded power for wealth as its prime objective fails to capture the novel ways in which the German state, from the crisis of the 1970s onward, has come to exert its influence internationally to sustain this export-led growth model.[10]

Moving on to the end of the postwar boom, Chapter 4 challenges the prevailing view that Bretton Woods died at the hands of a declining hegemon. Instead, it argues that the demise of the monetary architecture of embedded liberalism was driven in large part by the actions of the United States's allies: while French attempts to push the US toward monetary reform destroyed the golden anchor of Bretton Woods as early as March 1968, German efforts to protect themselves from the abuse of *dollar seigniorage* "floated the system" five years later (Gray 2007). Zooming in on the German decision to float the DM and adopt monetarism after the collapse of the fixed-exchange-rate regime, the chapter argues that the prevailing state-centered, ideational, and class-based models of neoliberal change cannot help explain the German policy shift. Rather than submit to US pressures, German policymakers chose to float in order to shield their own economy from the inflationary consequences of American fiscal and monetary indiscipline. Rather than being guided by free market beliefs, the German government and central bank sought to more effectively intervene in the distributive struggle between capital and labor. And last, I argue that floating enabled the German state to reorganize its relationship with the dominant export bloc and pursue a monetarist policy that recommitted both social partners to reciprocal, and mutually beneficial, wage and price restraint—a constellation of interests very different from the multinational corporations and banks that are said to have promoted floating in the United States. Uniquely among the industrialized countries, the chapter concludes, Germany's fight against inflation stabilized the embedded liberal compromise domestically, even as the breakdown of the fixed-exchange-rate regime unsettled it elsewhere in the advanced capitalist world.

Having argued that German policymakers had found a way to cope with the 1970s crisis domestically, in Chapter 5 I examine the international extension of German "stability politics." Because their efforts to stabilize the domestic consensus depended on the continued price advantage and world market access of its exports, Germany's state elites sought to defeat the twin threats of protectionism and imported inflation. To keep the world economy open and to shore up their competitive position, German policymakers mobilized their monetary and financial power in order to contain the interventionist and expansionary responses of the European left in particular. Although seriously considered at the highest echelons of German policymaking, proposals for a global Keynesianism that could have aligned the redistributive demands of the Global South with a recovery of the industrialized countries were discarded in favor of a self-interested anti-inflationary path. The strategic decisions that have come to define the German approach to the eurocrisis—eschewing responsibility for macroeconomic rebalancing and imposing adjustment costs onto its partners—were made at this earlier juncture. Although far from seeking to impose neoliberal change directly at that time, Germany's anti-inflationary bias undermined alternative resolutions of the 1970s crisis and tilted the balance in favor of the neoliberal counteroffensive of Thatcher and Reagan at the turn of the decade.

Chapter 6 argues that in order to protect its export model from the dangers of imported inflation, Germany strove above all to commit the United States to monetary and fiscal rigor. To this end, German state managers blocked the attempts of the Carter administration to organize a global Keynesian expansion, and scaled back their foreign exchange interventions in support of a weakening dollar. Both actions helped push the US into the Volcker interest rate shock that radically disinflated the world economy and launched the attack on the organized power of labor. The chapter concludes that the neoliberal experiment in the United States, paralleled and reinforced by similar attempts in the UK, was late and lucky. Rather than the outcome of a decade-long domestic shift—seamless and sealed off from the world outside the Anglo-American heartland—the making of neoliberalism was driven in part by the external impetus of German crisis management. In a similar way, it was then sustained by a bout of global investment, primarily from Japan. Drawn in by a peculiar mix of monetary restraint and fiscal latitude, this investment helped finance Reagan's massive tax cuts and military expenditures, and thus shored up the political, economic, and especially financial success of neoliberalism after the global recession of the early 1980s.

Chapter 7, finally, draws out the empirical and theoretical payoff of this investigation and applies these insights to the conundrum of German primacy in contemporary Europe. The first part investigates the social and geographical recomposition of the German political economy and the corresponding reorientation of its governmental and corporate elites under the neoliberalizing pressures of the past three decades. Rather than attribute a neoliberal outlook to Germany's state managers on the assumption that their society has undergone a transformation similar to those of the US and the UK before it, the chapter casts the erosion of the German model as a governance problem that builds on the distinctive experiences and practices of Germany's crisis managers in the 1970s. Concerned with preserving a crumbling class compromise and attracted by the massive demand for German exports in emerging markets, managers of both the German state and businesses see the neoliberal transformation of the EU into a subordinate production and supply zone as an opportunity to shore up the economic success and social stability of the German model. Despite this nascent grand strategy and its elite support, however, German officials are vulnerable to a rise in US interest rates, to which they fell victim during the Volcker Shock and which has led them to push austerity beyond what German business (or other social groups) could hope to gain from these reforms. This combination of long-term vision and short-term necessity resolves the paradox of German power, which has endangered the very existence of the EU while taking the process of European integration into unprecedented directions.

The Conclusion places Germany's current position in the EU within a global context and draws out the wider implications of this study. It advances a conception of neoliberalism as a multifaceted process in which actors draw upon, and contribute to, an ever-wider array of available techniques to deconstruct or reconfigure the social, economic, and political gains working people had wrought from capital and invested in the postwar welfare state. While in this respect neoliberalism is the indispensable marker for a new era of capitalism, it is too amorphous a term to serve as a guide to the emerging frontiers and faultlines of the global political economy.

A Note on the Archival Method

This book is based on primary research conducted at the Archive of Social Democracy of the Friedrich Ebert Foundation, the Federal Archives (Bundesarchiv) in Koblenz, and the Historical Archives of the German Federal Bank. The research was supplemented by a visit to the Gerald R. Ford Presidential Library in Ann Arbor, Michigan, and draws extensively on the government records published online and made available through the *Foreign Relations of the United States* series.[11]

Much of this evidentiary basis is drawn from archival sources that have only recently become declassified and accessible. This book is not the first to unearth this material, but it approaches it with a set of questions and concerns that are rarely brought to the government record. Diplomatic and international historians tend to take the wider processes of international and societal change that concern this book as the unquestioned backdrop to the events and personalities they focus on. Scholars interested in the structural transformations of global capitalism, by contrast, do not usually consult the national archives themselves. With the passing of the thirty-year embargo in Germany and other advanced industrialized countries, however, we are now in a unique position to test our theoretical knowledge about the global rise of neoliberalism since the 1970s against this new material. Adding an archival method of investigation to the repertoire of critical IPE is thus an enormously fruitful exercise, as long as a number of potential problems are recognized and addressed.

The first limitation is that the archival evidence is almost certainly incomplete. Some documents are irretrievable or still classified, and some sensitive information may never have been committed to the record in the first place. By itself, then, this material cannot tell the full story. But when read against three decades of scholarship on the origins of neoliberal globalization, it can offer valuable insights that confirm, clarify, complicate, or confound what we thought we knew.

The public records of the chancellery, the obvious starting point for this research, illustrate these limitations and the ways in which they can be addressed. The Federal Archives publish the minutes of the weekly cabinet meetings in book form and online.[12] With very few exceptions, however, this edition only contains an official log of the cabinet meetings rather than a detailed or verbatim record of the conversations. This means that we do not know what was said when policymakers made their final decisions. But by consulting the internal briefs and memoranda of the chancellor's office, as well as the top-level communications with the major ministries and the central bank, we can still go some of the distance—enough, at any rate, to offer a fuller sense of the policy debate than has previously been available. In this respect, the archival method offers an important advantage over accounts that simply "read back from ultimate policy outputs to hypotheses about policy goals" (Gowan 1999: x). This technique of "backward mapping" is unavoidable where access to the executive decision-making process is restricted. The obvious shortcoming is that it can only shed light on those decisions that were ultimately taken.

Because the policy outcome is the point of departure and the aim is to infer the factors that produced it, backward mapping is bound to miss out on, and indeed tends to underestimate, the plurality of policy options under discussion. In light of the new documentary evidence, it is now possible to distinguish alternatives that were seriously considered from those that were ruled out *a priori*. To do so is to explore what may be "crucial 'non-decisions' . . . often neglected in histories of the globalization process" (Helleiner 1995: 325; see also Strange 1986: 26).

A second caveat is raised by Barry Eichengreen's (2004: 1543) review of an archive-based book in international monetary history: Can we take the realist language in many of these government documents at face value? To put it bluntly, what may read like cunning maneuvers on the geopolitical chessboard may be little more than the impotent great power fancies of mid-level bureaucrats. To correct for such a bias, the memoranda from the foreign office or embassies that routinely use the language of *realpolitik* in their situational analyses have been treated with particular caution. The principal focal point of this study is instead on actionable information produced and discussed by the German chancellor's office, the finance and economics ministries, and the central bank—the neuralgic center of foreign economic policy and the strategic site where Germany's power has been rethought and deployed.

The ministerial bureaucracies have produced an overabundance of material that has yet to be fully categorized. As a result, the most valuable sources of documentation have been the personal files of chancellor Helmut Schmidt and his key economic advisor, Horst Schulmann (involved in the construction of the European Monetary System [EMS] and the preparation of the G7 meetings), placed at the Archives of Social Democracy, as well as the correspondence and collections of the central bank governors Karl Klasen, Otmar Emminger, and Karl Otto Pöhl located at the Historical Archives of the Bundesbank. Another major source of information are the bimonthly meetings of the Central Bank Council (Zentralbankrat). This supreme body of the Bundesbank, consisting of the presidents of the central banks of the *Länder* (federal states), is a key forum of macroeconomic deliberation and monetary decision making that is regularly attended by government representatives from the chancellor's office and the economics and finance ministers. The meeting protocols and verbatim records of these discussions, located at the Historical Archives of the Bundesbank in Frankfurt, have been comprehensively reviewed for this study.

This method is also open to the charge that it simply trades the statism of realist IPE for that of diplomatic history. The former is theoretically preordained. States are posited as the most important actors in the international political economy. The latter, by contrast, is empirically induced. It emerges from a self-imposed restriction to the public record. The effect, however, is the same. The state, embodied by its officials whose every decision is so amply documented, appears outsized in relation to societal actors whose power and influence seem elusive to the point of mere conjecture.

To counter this potential objection, the book gears its archival research to the question of how social forces act upon decision-making elites. Particular attention has therefore been given to the interactions of the core executive and major private-sector interests. The written correspondence of leading state personnel with private economic actors, as well as the informal and institutionalized contacts between them, has been closely studied. Chief among these are the meetings of the Foreign Trade Advisory Council (renamed Foreign Economic Advisory Council in mid-1974) hosted by the Ministry of Economics, which brings together key government officials with representatives of the export industry, private banks, and affiliated trade unions. The composition of the council aims at a regional and sectoral balance, but in practice large exporters and their financiers predominated for most of the postwar period and throughout the 1970s. With over forty council members, the Advisory Council was rather large and unwieldy. Only some members participated regularly and contributed to the work of the council and its ad hoc committees, however. In practice, therefore, the affairs of the Advisory Council were steered by a handful of influential personalities over long stretches of time. The track record of the Advisory Council is mixed. Sometimes it simply duplicated the lobbying activities of the peak business associations; at other times, it effectively mediated between the articulation of interests and the making of economic policy. Members were called upon not to represent individual firms or sectors but to offer independent, expert advice to the ministry. In principle, therefore, and sometimes in practice, this is the committee tasked with coordinating the general interest of Germany's export industry with the policy objectives of the state bureaucracy.

Last, some may object that to present these findings in terms of German "crisis managers" or "policy elites" is to give a false sense of uniformity across the German state and government. This homogeneity clearly dissolves at a closer level of inspection, where various ministries and departments with different ideas and interests come into play. Given that the archival research of this book opens up the proverbial "black box" of national interest formation, why use a language that closes it up again?

To an extent, such shorthand is unavoidable for a study that investigates the changing contours of German foreign economic policy across several governments and ministerial reorganizations, as well as the state transformations engendered by German reunification and European integration. But this narrative choice is also theoretically guided. Because the book aims to situate key German policy decisions within a wider international context of capitalist crisis and transformation, it often highlights Germany's external relations rather than its internal politics. Indeed, my archival research reveals a surprising level of policy conflict between states supposedly bound by US hegemony. Because this loosens the traditional US-dominated view, it carries more theoretical weight for my argument than the divisions within the German state that undoubtedly existed. Similarly, because one important explanation of the global rise of neoliberalism stresses the lead role of think tanks and business groups, my archival research focuses on the nexus of public policy and private interests rather than bureaucratic rivalries. Here again, the resilience of the postwar social consensus as the basis for German foreign economic policy is more important for my book to explore than the different preferences of particular government agencies. Of course, wherever they do carry theoretical significance, internal policy divisions are scrutinized in detail: for instance regarding the "two-level game" supposedly played by the Schmidt government at the G7 Bonn summit to outflank domestic opposition to a Keynesian stimulus, or the putative role of the German central bank as the carrier of ordoliberal ideas, set over and against the preferences of successive governments from Schmidt to Merkel (Chapters 4 and 6).

In sum, this book uses the new evidence from the government records in tandem with, rather than in place of, the methods and insights of critical IPE scholarship. This window into the official mind of the German state offers new insights into the economic and political determinants of German foreign economic policy during the pivotal crisis of the 1970s; it yields a richer understanding of the origins of neoliberal globalization; and it brings us one crucial step closer to unlocking the puzzle of German primacy in Europe today.

CHAPTER 1

The Origins of Neoliberalism
and the Role of the German State

IN THIS BOOK, I investigate how German policymakers have been implicated in the crisis and transformation of the embedded liberal world order since the 1970s. I do so from within the discipline of International Political Economy (IPE), designed specifically to reflect on this crucial conjuncture. I argue that critical IPE, though a broad church,[1] is best suited to this task of historical and conceptual revision. The reason is that it is guided by three assumptions that separate it from conventional realist and liberal approaches. The first is that its inquiries are driven not by the search for general laws that hold true for all times and places, but by a concern to produce historically specific explanations of particular social and international orders. The second is that it focuses on the struggles of social forces over the definition of state power, social purpose, and the "national interest" rather than rely on an abstract calculus of power or utility (Cox 1981; Gill 1993a; Bieler and Morton 2001). And last, as a consequence of highlighting both social agency and historical variability, critical IPE recognizes that something important occurred in the 1970s that could have happened differently.[2] In other words, it is able to recover an element of contingency that is lost in the prevailing accounts that see the outcome of this crisis decade as preordained either by the incessant pressures of the interstate system or the globalizing forces of market integration.

But while the critical tradition of IPE forms the most promising vantage point for this study, it also confronts an enormous intellectual distortion.

From its outset, IPE debated the crisis of embedded liberalism and its likely consequences in terms of a "crisis of US hegemony." The trauma of the Vietnam War, social unrest, and labor militancy at home; the mounting challenge from the Global South; and the rise of Western Europe and Japan as major economic competitors—all these events were read as a loss of American global power that coincided with a profound destabilization of liberal multilateralism. In the face of the breakdown of Bretton Woods and the oil shock and economic recession of 1973–1974, as well as transatlantic dissension over how to respond to these challenges, the specter of the 1930s had returned. Starting with Charles Kindleberger (1973), hegemony was devised as a term to capture the *status quo ante* of a stable and prosperous postwar order that seemed to be eroding, and to predict the future on the basis of a historical comparison with Britain's rise and fall in the late nineteenth and early twentieth centuries. The ensuing debate therefore focused on whether the advanced capitalist world would experience a replay of the Great Depression, as realist scholars predicted, or whether the system could survive without a hegemon, as some liberal scholars objected (compare Krasner 1976: 343; Gilpin 1975: 72; 1981: 239; 1987: 351, 394–408; Ruggie 1982: 384; Keohane 1984a). Building on the thought of Antonio Gramsci (1971) to deepen the analysis of the emerging world order, critical approaches made a lasting inroad into the mainstream debate and what is arguably their most important intellectual contribution to the discipline (Cox 1981; 1983). But in framing their investigation in terms of a hegemonic transition, they too placed the emphasis squarely on the United States and its apparent decline (Overbeek 2008: 184).[3] In short, the focus on the country that had rebuilt the postwar liberal economic order, but no longer seemed willing or able to maintain it, provided the impetus behind the development of the discipline in both its mainstream and critical guises. Forty years on, we still find iterations of the same debate, cast around the term of hegemony which has come to be *the* master concept of International Relations (IR) and IPE.

In many respects, the outcome of this turbulent decade was the opposite of what the pioneers of IPE predicted. Rather than decline and turn inward, the United States assumed an even more prominent role in steering global capitalism (Panitch and Gindin 2012). And the neoliberal resolution it embraced led to increasing openness rather than economic closure, an extension of markets rather than a resurgence of state control, and intensified international cooperation rather than economic nationalism. And yet the original focus on the American hegemon has persisted and, as this chapter argues, dominates the scholarly imagination of how neoliberalism came into this world. To bring Germany into the picture thus requires more than an empirical shift in focus. It also means that we need to overcome an Anglocentrism that stands at the very heart of the discipline and skews our explorations of other actors and forces involved in this world-historical transformation. To do this, this chapter reviews the critical IPE literature on the origins of neoliberal globalization, and asks how Germany fits into the story. I propose that one can usefully distinguish three models of explanation: (1) a *state-centered* argument, which holds that neoliberalism was imposed by the United States in a bid to reassert its global dominance; (2) a *class-based* argument, which sees neoliberalism as the outcome of business or financial elites who sought to restore their corporate profits and power vis-à-vis organized labor; and (3) an *ideational* argument, which approaches the displacement of Keynesianism by neoliberalism as a paradigmatic shift in economic ideas.[4]

The next three sections interrogate each of these models in turn. Each section starts off by reconstructing the specific explanation of the genesis of neoliberal globalization that they provide. I demonstrate that each of these interpretations suffers from a particular form of Anglocentrism that limits a fuller appreciation of Germany as a protagonist. Apart from being one-sided, I argue that each of these accounts is problematic even on its own terms. The purpose of the next chapter then is to build a conceptual framework that can overcome both their individual inadequacies and their common bias.

State-Centered Interpretations

The first interpretative model locates the origins of neoliberalism in the arena of power politics and attributes it to the hegemonic agency of the United States. In this view, the United States is said to have dismantled the embedded liberal order and deregulated markets in order to stave off its economic decline and restore its political power. What has made this interpretation so appealing is that it builds directly on the first paradigmatic debate within IPE over the hegemonic decline of the United States. On one side stood realists who predicted the geopolitical fragmentation of the Cold War West. On the other side were liberals who argued that economic interdependence would ensure cooperation even "after hegemony." The state-centered narrative can claim to overcome the disciplinary deadlock that emerged once these expectations turned out to be wide of the mark (Cohen 2008: 76–77). For if realists had to concede that the collapse of the Cold War West they predicted had not (yet) materialized, liberal scholars had erred on the side of continuity. This oversight is most apparent in John Gerard Ruggie's groundbreaking work on embedded liberalism. Designed to defuse the declinist scenario, his account missed out on what was most decisive about the 1970s: the profound "disembedding," rather than preservation, of the postwar international economic order, and the radical redefinition, rather than retention, of the social purpose to which state power was now to be put.[5]

Accounts that see neoliberalism as the product of US statecraft close the gap between predicted and actual outcomes that a new generation of IPE scholars chose to gloss over rather than address. They take seriously the economic difficulties and political tensions dividing the United States and its allies in the 1970s. And rather than simply acknowledging that American power globalized rather than receded despite these challenges, they ask how the United States was able to accomplish this feat. Its military superiority, though important in its standoff with the Soviet Union, is seen as only one of the instruments in a wider arsenal deployed by the United States to manage this situation (Gilpin 1987; Gilpin 2000; Layne 2006; Mastanduno 2009).[6] Shifting the focus to the politico-economic terrain, a number of scholars have argued that some of the most decisive global economic changes of the 1970s—from President Richard Nixon's closing of the gold window in August 1971 to Federal Reserve Chairman Paul Volcker's war on inflation in October 1979—need to be placed in the strategic context of hegemonic restoration. In this view, neoliberalism, seen as the purposive deregulation and globalization of markets, is read as a bid by the American hegemon to reverse its economic fortunes and to reestablish its political leadership (for example, Helleiner 1994; Spiro 1999; Gowan 1999; Arrighi 2005a; 2005b; Basosi 2006).

The most explicit and provocative account in this regard comes from Peter Gowan (1999; 2003). For him, the 1970s are indeed a period of intensified economic competition as well as "[s]erious inter-state tensions pitting groups of protectorates against the US" (2003: 4). While crisis and conflict opened up an array of possible trajectories, the United States, Gowan argues, was able not only to constrain but to decide these struggles in its favor. Although "[t]here were a range of options for the leading capitalist powers to choose from," the United States ultimately succeeded in imposing its preferred solution. Neoliberal globalization, Gowan concludes, was "the outcome of international political conflicts won by the American government" (1999: 4–5). Enforced over and above the interests of Western Europe and Japan, and then rolled out across the Global South, neoliberalism is said to have benefitted the economic and financial position of the United States and reinforced its global hegemony (Arrighi 2005a; 2005b).[7]

There is much to like about this state-centered explanation. In hindsight, much of realist and liberal IPE dismisses these intra-West tensions as insignificant, supplanted either by the superordinate conflict with the Soviet Union or the globalizing drive of markets (Webb and Krasner 1989; Keohane and Nye 1977; Rosecrance 1986: 141–2). In contrast to these *post hoc* rationalizations, the critical IPE perspective articulated by Gowan and others recognizes the openness of this historical situation and a variety of possible pathways, and links the policy disagreements that surfaced in this period directly to the neoliberal form of capitalism that ultimately triumphed.

And yet attempts to include Germany in this story confront a massive empirical imbalance. Despite the emphasis on a contest between states, the attention has rested almost exclusively on the role of the United States in shaping this transition. There may, of course, be sound reasons for this Anglocentrism. The enormous economic and military resources at its disposal, and their purposive deployment in reconstructing and integrating its capitalist allies and former rivals into a liberalizing and expanding world economy, were truly unprecedented. Given that the US played a central role in the reconstitution of global capitalism after 1945, and given the reassertion of US power in the 1980s, it makes sense to assume that it also decisively shaped its evolution during the turbulent 1970s. And yet recognizing the centrality of the American state does not, in itself, warrant the conclusion that neoliberal globalization depended solely on US policy decisions (for example, Abdelal 2007: 25). Too narrow a focus on American foreign economic strategy might lead to a selection bias: the agency of the US in shaping the evolution of the world economic order appears so overwhelming simply because other actors are excluded from view (Eichengreen 2004: 1543). And indeed, while Britain is seen by some as an accomplice in this project, courtesy of its former hegemonic status (for example, Helleiner 1994: 14), other core powers such as France, Germany, and Japan are almost entirely absent from the picture. While the initiative lies with the United States, they are seen as reactive and defensive: assumed to be heavily invested in the embedded liberal order but unable to prevent its destruction at the hand of American strategists (Gowan 1999: 44–48).

Accordingly, the German state hardly features in these state-centered accounts of the rise of neoliberalism. Defeated, divided, and occupied, West Germany is widely regarded as a "semi-sovereign" frontline state firmly under Western tutelage, inhibited by its fascist past and vulnerable to Soviet encroachment from the East (Strange 1980: 46; Eichengreen 2011: 71; Lippert 2011: 4) A major recipient of Marshall aid and US foreign direct investment, moreover, its export-led economy was also most vitally dependent on the open and expanding world market that had been reconstructed by the United States. In many respects, then, Germany seems to be the country most securely incorporated into America's world hegemonic order and most susceptible to American pressure. But does it follow from this that Germany, in the end, could do little else than accept the neoliberal agenda imposed by the United States? In some respects, at least, Germany also had perhaps the greatest "counter-hegemonic" capacity. Unlike the mostly symbolic defiance of a militarily independent but industrially laggard France, it formed the hub of a regional and potentially rival pole of accumulation. Unlike an economically ascendant but demilitarized and isolated Japan, Germany had rebuilt its military capabilities and assumed lead roles in Western European integration and Eastern détente. And while Germany's "social market economy" is often juxtaposed to the "free market" capitalism that emerged from the crisis of the 1970s (Crouch and Streeck 1997; Hall and Soskice 2001; Amable 2003; Abelshauser 2006), it also eschewed the Keynesian and dirigiste orientations of many of its postwar allies (Allen 1989). Curiously, therefore, Germany seems to be at once firmly integrated into and most capable of challenging US hegemony, with some interests rooted in but others pointing beyond the embedded liberal order.

The problem is that as long as we approach this period as one of hegemonic crisis and renewal, we create exaggerated expectations of power-political contestation that, as we know in hindsight, never actually came to pass. Framed in this way, the German state can only ever appear as an aspiring but ultimately frustrated rival. And this, in turn, sets the bar too high for what the German state actually did to register. Too quickly, the fact that German policy elites did not successfully challenge the American hegemon is taken as evidence that they had no significant input into the transition toward neoliberalism. And yet, unless we shift focus and zoom in on their actions and intentions, we cannot rule out that they never actually tried to contest American power in this way, and that the reasons for why neoliberal solutions emerged victorious reach deeper than the ability of the US to impress its will.

By marshaling new evidence from the government records, this book challenges the view that Germany was little more than a pliant Cold War ally or a peaceful "trading state," unable to oppose the neoliberal transformation favored by the United States. The more fundamental task, however, undertaken in the next chapter, is to break with the assumption of a hegemonic power politics at the heart of neoliberal globalization. For this does not only deprive the German state of strategic agency in the pivotal decade of the 1970s. Assumed to be a recurring feature of international relations, the concept of "hegemony" also invites profoundly misleading comparisons between the United States in the postwar era and Germany in the wake of the eurocrisis of the 2010s (Matthijs and Blyth 2011; Bulmer and Paterson 2013: 1388; Kundnani 2014: 108). The German choice for neoliberal austerity, according to this popular view, derives from Germany's standing as a frustrated regional hegemon that is unable or unwilling to provide the sort of benevolent leadership exercised by the United States (Kundnani 2014: 108; Cafruny 2015: 67; Streeck 2015).

Because it proceeds by analogy rather than historical inquiry, such a reading risks missing out on the longer-term transformation that—starting with the crisis of embedded liberalism—has profoundly reshaped the global political economy, the international policy environment, and the strategic context of Germany's contemporary crisis management. Accordingly, this book eschews the notion of successive hegemonies that informs parallels between such superficially similar but decontextualized episodes "then" and "now." It reconceptualizes the postwar historical process through the lens of uneven and combined development, which yields a very different understanding of what the regime and policy conflicts of the 1970s were about. And last, by tracing how the German state helped shape the global rise of neoliberalism from the outset and has since been affected by it, this book casts an alternative and longer-run perspective on its power and purpose in Europe today.

Class-Based Interpretations

The second camp shifts the focus from the interstate to the societal conflicts that fueled the global rise of neoliberalism. It encompasses a broad range of critical pluralist, elite-theoretical, and Marxist perspectives. The argument, at its most basic, is that neoliberalism was the product of a collective effort on the part of business to restore its profitability and authority in the midst of an economic and social crisis that threatened to undermine both (compare Duménil and Lévy 2004; Epstein and Jayadev 2005; Harvey 2005; Stein 2010; Streeck 2014). The social agents behind this project are conceptualized variously as capitalist elites, organized business interests, a rentier class, or multinational firms and banks (Hawley 1984: 163); the shared assumption is that these actors, through various direct and indirect channels of influence, were able to translate their preferences into neoliberal policies that advanced their interests at the expense of the embedded liberal compromise with organized labor.

This literature has focused on the United States and the United Kingdom as the most compelling cases for the influential role of business and financial elites in the making of neoliberal capitalism. But while there is a broad consensus on the importance of business in the emergence of neoliberalism in these two countries, "the ways in which neoliberalism has asserted itself on a global level" (Duménil and Lévy 2004: 212–213) remain subject to divergent interpretations.

One strand of scholarship has conjoined a class-based account of neoliberalism with the state-centered accounts introduced earlier. The works of Giovanni Arrighi (1994: 323) establish an explicit, if conceptually and empirically undeveloped, link between the influence of financial interests and the reassertion of American dominance. Gowan (1999: 68–69), too, argues that the internationalization of neoliberalism by the United States served the interests of its dominant class fractions. And Gérard Duménil and Dominique Lévy (2004: 210) argue, rather vaguely, that "financial hegemony and American power combined into one dynamic." Seeing neoliberal globalization as a joint project of state and class domination, needless to say, is subject to the same limitations outlined in the previous section. An additional drawback of these formulations is that the agency of social forces, not only in the recipient societies but also in the United States itself, remains largely unexplored. The potential advantage of class-theoretic over statist analyses that treat the state as a "black box" remains unrealized in accounts that simply assume the interests of these social forces to be coextensive with the state as their external representative. In Gowan's formulation, for instance, states are rather unproblematically posited as pursuing the "national *capitalist* interest" of their dominant oligopolies (Gowan 1999: 63, 65).[8] Because their interests are assumed to be commensurate with those of the state, the agency of dominant social forces drops out of the subsequent analysis. As Greta Krippner (2011: 13) aptly summarizes the problem, "[T]here is a kind of instrumentalism lurking in some of these accounts that supplants the interests of the financial sector for the interests of the state or simply assumes these interests to be identical."

By far the most prominent and conceptually distinctive reading of the global rise of neoliberalism is to approach it as a transnational class project instead. Although its starkest formulations replicate the problems of instrumentalism by positing a globally unified capitalist class governing through an international state apparatus (Robinson 2001; 2004; Sklair 2001), this strand of critical IPE scholarship tells a very different and potentially more fruitful story of the making of neoliberalism than the state-centered accounts introduced earlier.

Within critical IPE, this line of investigation has been pursued most systematically, if somewhat idiosyncratically, by the so-called Amsterdam School (Overbeek and Jessop 2019). Its students have based their investigation on the functional distinction between the roles of finance and production in Marx's analysis of capitalism, said to translate into two different broad orientations of the capitalist class. Located in the abstract sphere of circulation, the "money capital" interest of, most notably, bankers and investors espouses the greatest possible movement of capital, goods, and services. By contrast, the "productive capital" perspective of, say, the classical factory owner is grounded in the sphere of production and thus tied to a specific (although progressively expanding) geographic location. Because its reproduction takes place in a specific social and political setting, productive capital depends on bargains with labor and the support of the state. Its owners display a greater affinity to principles of social protection as well as economic protectionism (van der Pijl 1984: 10; Overbeek 1990: 26; Overbeek and van der Pijl 1993: 4: van Apeldoorn 2002: 28–29).

The approach has been criticized for a reductionism that derives social interests from Marx's abstract schema rather than empirical inquiry (Teschke 2008), but the broad contours of the social and world order change they develop on this basis have become a staple of critical IPE. After 1945, the embedded liberal world order and the political economies of its core states were based on the primacy of "productive capital," which involved the suppression of financial and rentier interests and the integration of organized labor. By contrast, the gradual erosion of embedded liberalism has been associated with the reassertion of a "money capital" perspective:

large investment banks and multinational corporations came to push for the removal of restrictions on their domestic operations and international expansion. In a collective effort to rid themselves of the regulatory burden and the increasing social demands placed upon them from the late 1960s onward, the owners, investors, and speculators of "money capital" rebelled against and ultimately achieved the repeal of the New Deal and social-democratic bargains (Overbeek 1990: 20). This has resulted in the widely observed exorbitant growth of financial markets and the growing predominance of speculative over productive activity over the past three decades (for example, Stein 2010; Madrick 2011).

While the leadership of Anglo-American elites is recognized in this strand of scholarship, the effort to free capital from social regulations and restrictions is seen as a collective endeavor rather than a one-sided imposition. And while disagreements between and within different fractions (and regions) of capital are analyzed to a large extent (van der Pijl [2006] goes furthest), the emphasis is nevertheless on the formation of a neoliberal elite consensus, envisioned and implemented through a range of public and private policy forums such as the Group of Seven or the Trilateral Commission.

The endeavor to capture a broader shift in the internal balance of power in the advanced industrialized countries and the coordination and convergence of ruling-class strategies is a valuable contribution to understanding the global rise of neoliberalism. Conceptualizing the specific part played by Germany in these terms turns out to be more cumbersome, however. To be sure, scholars writing in this vein have generally recognized that neoliberalism has spread unevenly across the capitalist core, differing in speed and intensity and producing a considerable range of national variations (compare Harvey 2005: 116; Duménil and Lévy 2004: 213; van der Pijl 1989: 12–13). Accordingly, Germany has been cited by proponents as a case-in-point for a country that—given a social-democratic government and strong labor movement—remained wedded to the principles of embedded liberalism. Unable and unwilling "to turn the wheel drastically in the 1970s" (Overbeek 1993: 16), Germany's turn toward neoliberalism is an immensely protracted story of partial convergence that only fully takes off with the so-called "Hartz IV" reforms in the early 2000s. Whether the image of a temporally differentiated and socially variegated convergence on a neoliberal form of capitalism provides a helpful guide to the changing parameters of Germany's political economy and European policy remains to be seen. But even if this ideal-type approximation could capture the *subsequent* transformation of the capitalist core in the 1980s and 1990s, it would still be of limited use in analyzing the *initial* responses to the postwar crisis of those states and social forces outside the Anglo-American heartland. For it ultimately relies on an assumption of sameness—in this case that, at least in principle, it is the same elite fraction of capital that favors neoliberalism in every country, even as their ability to implement this shared vision is then impeded and inflected by the national rigidities and peculiarities they encounter (Overbeek and van der Pijl 1993: 15–16).

And yet when turning to Germany, we find that the basic distinction between productive and money capital that informs Amsterdam School accounts of systemic change does not seem to apply. Industry and finance have historically been integrated into a unified bloc of the "big three" universal banks that own, finance, and supervise the largest industrial corporations (van der Wurff 1993: 182). This unified export bloc of finance and industry, I argue, did not push for neoliberal reforms. Throughout the 1970s, it fought a defensive struggle against the revaluation and flotation of the DM, the tax burden imposed by the extension of social provisions under chancellor Brandt's social-liberal coalition, and the more radical proposals for extended codetermination and investment controls emanating from the trade unions and the youth organization and left wing of the Sozialdemokratische Partei Deutschlands (SPD, Social Democratic Party of Germany). The social balance of power, corporate elites understood, was unfavorable to a more comprehensive and forward-looking mobilization of capitalist class power.[9] Even the "moderate German form of Thatcherism"[10] that shone through in the reform proposals of the infamous Lambsdorff Paper that toppled the social-liberal coalition in 1982 never fully materialized until the "third way" social-democratic government of Gerhard Schröder took office some fifteen years later. As Richard van der Wurff (1993: 182) sums up this situation, "[T]he changes in the political landscape taking place in the early 1980s cannot be explained by a changing balance of forces between different fractions of capital."

Given the unbroken unity of industry and finance in the German political economy throughout the crisis decade of the 1970s, the question arises as to how else to explain shifts in German foreign economic policy—from floating the DM and targeting the money supply to negotiating multilateral financial assistance or dollar support programs. The key conceptual move here, the next chapter explains, is to relax the instrumentalist assumptions about how private interests shape public policy and to anchor the relative autonomy of governing elites in a richer conception of the international context of decision making. Equally important is to consider what difference some of these key policy decisions made. The upshot of attributing the emergence of neoliberalism to a particular class fraction is to cast Germany—and other leading "state-society complexes" (Cox 1981: 134) such as France and Japan—as passive spectators that share in the global rise of neoliberalism only once, and in so far as they undergo a regrouping of dominant social forces similar to the US and the UK somewhere down the line. By contrast, this book details how, despite the absence of a dominant class coalition that actively promoted neoliberalism, German state managers nevertheless contributed significantly, if indirectly, to its global emergence.

Ideational Interpretations

The final set of interpretations for the global rise of neoliberalism, and the most promising approach to Germany's role within it, centers on the power of ideas. The classical formulation, written from a historical-institutionalist perspective and centered on the Anglo-American world, has been provided by Peter Hall (1989; 1992; 1993). Later adaptations and applications, including to Germany and the eurocrisis, have been advanced primarily from the constructivist school of IPE (Blyth 2002; 2013a; 2013b; Matthijs 2011; 2016). What these ideational accounts have in common is that they conceptualize the crisis and transformation of the embedded liberal world order in the 1970s as an intellectual contestation between rival economic paradigms.

According to Hall (1992: 91–92), policy paradigms provide interpretative frameworks that help policymakers define problems, the possible solutions, and the means to achieve these goals. Hall described the displacement of Keynesianism as a learning process on the part of state managers that was provoked by economic crisis, characterized by an associated loss of confidence in established economic thought, and guided by the search for alternatives. His argument is that the stagflationary decade posed intractable problems that the predominant Keynesian macroeconomic framework proved unable either to explain or to resolve. This situation of intellectual disillusionment and economic turbulence provided an opening for neoliberal ideas to regain currency within academic and policy circles after being discredited by the Great Depression. The shift from Keynesianism to what Hall (1992: 95) called monetarism "is ultimately a story about the movement of ideas." It is also a story that centers on civil society rather than the state, conceptualized by Hall as providing "an outside *marketplace in economic ideas*" (1992: 104) that policymakers could turn to. Neoliberalism, in this view, began as an experiment with new policy instruments (monetary targeting, supply-side reforms) and culminated in the radical redefinition of the means and ends of state policy under Thatcher and Reagan. It emerged not from the narrow self-interest of state actors or social forces but "in response to an evolving societal debate" (Hall 1993: 288) in which parts of the media, certain think tanks, and sections of political parties offered new economic ideas to counter the inadequacies of Keynesianism (288–289).

Building on this groundbreaking work, the global rise of neoliberalism has come to be associated with the sustained endeavor of a small group of intellectuals, led most prominently by Friedrich Hayek and Milton Friedman, who had preserved, developed, and disseminated free market ideas after 1945 and gradually shaped the opinions of wider circles of intellectuals, entrepreneurs, journalists, technocrats, and decision makers. Similar to the Keynesian paradigm shift half a century earlier, a transatlantic advocacy network stood ready to seize upon the crisis of capitalism and established economic thought (Burgin 2012; Jones 2012). Proponents of an ideas-based account emphasize the avant-garde and educational role of neoliberal thinkers and eschew a "simplistic class analysis" that reduces neoliberalism to the self-interest of capitalist or state elites. Their argument is that neither of them "knew precisely what sort of political economy would prove to coincide with their interests; rather, they had to be taught what it was they wanted" (Mirowski 2008: 117). It thus fell on a network of neoliberal intellectuals to seize the moment and educate state managers, business owners, and the public about the virtues of the free market.[11]

Similar to the state-centered and class-based readings of neoliberalism discussed earlier, this paradigm shift occurred first and foremost in the United Kingdom and the United States, where it "foreshadowed a similar change that would take place throughout the advanced industrial world in the 1970s and 1980s" (Helleiner 1994: 122). Nevertheless, Germany makes a promising candidate for the extension of this ideational account. First, some scholars have argued that key German policymakers in the course of the 1970s—such as chancellor Helmut Schmidt; his economic advisor, Karl-Otto Pöhl; or the head of the Bundesbank, Otmar Emminger—had started to question the embedded liberal framework of thought that had prescribed an interventionist role for the state, countercyclical demand management, and the vital importance of fixed exchange rates (Helleiner 1994:

126). Second, Kathleen McNamara (1988) in particular has developed a "diffusionist" model of ideational change in which Germany emerged as one of the centers of dissemination. Where Hall focuses on the United Kingdom, McNamara adds that policymakers across Europe also learned from each other, and from Germany in particular. Rather than each state going through its own separate cycle of policy failure and paradigmatic innovation, Germany offered a prime example of how monetary restraint could more aptly manage the stagflationary crisis of the mid-1970s. Through a process of policy emulation, she concludes, its European partners converged on a neoliberal consensus that prioritized low inflation over full employment and underpinned European monetary integration from the late 1970s onward (McNamara 1998: 69, 152–154).

Last, some have gone so far as to emphasize an independent German path toward neoliberalism that does not seem to posit an Anglo-American epicenter. The economic culture and political philosophy of German society, it is argued, had itself developed a peculiar and influential version of neoliberalism. The new liberal economic doctrine, developed in the 1920s by a circle of economists led by Walter Eucken at the University of Freiburg, outlined an explicitly non-Keynesian approach to macroeconomic policy. At the center of this "ordoliberalism" lay the conviction that the state had to play a critical and yet closely circumscribed role in economic life (Ptak 2009: 100). The purpose of economic policy was to create and maintain a constitutional framework in which market forces could operate freely and efficiently. This required a strong and proactive state with the foresight and capacity to prevent concentrations of private economic power, to ward off attempts by special interest groups to conspire against the price-finding mechanism of the market, and to resist the temptation to use the public purse in order to meet the demands of mass democracy (Ptak 2009: 102; Bonefeld 2012: 5; Biebricher 2013: 341–342).

After 1945, ordoliberals presented their version of neoliberalism as the sound alternative to *laissez-faire* capitalism and a tendentially totalitarian economic planning (Nicholls 1994). Under the Christian-democratic chancellor Konrad Adenauer and his economics minister, Ludwig Erhard, ordoliberal ideas are said to have served as a blueprint in the reconstruction of German capitalism after 1945.[12] The postwar success of the social market economy, premised on ordoliberal foundations, meant that German state managers only belatedly and hesitatingly turned to Keynesian ideas (Allen 2005: 199–201). It explains why, in the subsequent crisis of

postwar capitalism, they were quick to revert back to an economic orthodoxy of price stability, monetary restraint, and financial rectitude (Allen
1989; Bonefeld 2012).

This narrative recasts the German political economy as an intellectual kin
rather than an institutional opposite to free market capitalism. It can thus
claim to capture what appears to be a distinctive German contribution to the
ascendancy of the neoliberal worldview. Alongside the Austrian or Chicago
School, the Freiburg ordoliberals have been cited as "a second source of
neoliberal inspiration" (Jones 2012: 121). To many scholars of economic
thought it constitutes a precursor or at least addition to the Anglo-American
version that conquered the globe from the 1980s onward, with some even
arguing that it influenced Thatcher's neoliberal program (Bonefeld 2013:
235; Gamble 1979: 5; Ptak 2009: 99; Jones 2012: 125–126).

Most important, the newfound appeal of this ideational account lies in
its perceived ability to speak to the exigencies of the present. Numerous
authors have argued in recent years that the ways in which German policymakers have interpreted and responded to the eurocrisis are (mis)guided
by an ordoliberal paradigm (Dyson 2010; Dullien and Guérot 2012; Blyth
2013a; Art 2015). The German reading of the crisis as a problem of Southern profligacy to be solved through painful austerity, structural reforms,
and unmitigated competition, in this view, reflects a deep-rooted economic
culture. Not only does this ordoliberal worldview set Germany apart from
most other countries, including their Anglo-American partners, for the
many critics who argue that Germany's policy prescriptions have worsened
the problems of indebtedness and instability within the eurozone, its ordoliberal commitments seem to trump even its own national self-interest
in preserving the European Union (Blyth 2013a; Matthijs 2016).

Despite this allure, this book argues that the efforts to construe ordoliberalism as a meta-narrative of the German political economy are historically
unconvincing. Drawing a straight line between the writings of the Freiburg
School in the 1920s and German crisis management in the 1970s or the
2010s is bound to miss out on significant discontinuities and transformations. Its adaptation to the new realities of the postwar world and its fading
intellectual presence during Germany's boom years had rendered it largely
irrelevant by the time the embedded liberal order began to crumble (for example, Nützenadel 2005; Rittershausen 2007: 20). There is no evidence that
it shaped the outlook of German state managers during the crisis decade of
the 1970s—not even Germany's Bundesbankers, whose fixation with sound

finances and a stable currency is often considered to be ordoliberally inspired. The reason German policy elites decided to let the DM float, for instance, had nothing to do with a belief in the market as a superior determinant of currency values. The reason they chose monetarism to curb inflation was to more effectively intervene in the distributive conflict between capital and labor. And the reason they singled out price stability was that it offered export opportunities that could help secure social peace.

Apart from being historically flawed, these ideational accounts are also conceptually problematic. For even though some of them claim to capture a uniquely German economic culture, their conception of when and how ideas came to matter nevertheless derives from an Anglo-American model. The content of these ideas—free markets *and* a strong state—may well be specific, but the role they play is assumed to be the same in both contexts. They are said to serve as orientating devices to state managers who, disillusioned with or inoculated against Keynesianism, return to the foundational truths revealed by Hayek or Eucken and kept "alive and available" by their disciples—as Milton Friedman (quoted in Matthijs 2011: 10) put it—until the openings of a crisis (Hien and Joerges 2018: 10; Ötsch, Pühringer, and Hirte 2018). The questionable assumption here is not only that this crisis model of ideational change can travel easily outside of the Anglo-American world, but that it can be based on the self-perceptions of key intellectuals who thought in terms of, and sought to bring about, such a paradigm shift.

John Maynard Keynes, of course, famously declared "that the power of vested interests is vastly exaggerated compared with the gradual encroachment of ideas" (quoted in Jones 2012: 1). At least on this point he seems to have convinced Hayek, who modeled the Mont Pelerin Society—considered by many a "neoliberal thought collective" (for example, Mirowski and Plehwe 2009)—on precisely this insight (Burgin 2012: 217). And Friedman, too, believed that ideas have the power to shape the opinions of policymakers in the long run. While taking his cue from the British constitutional lawyer Albert Venn Dicey rather than Keynes, Friedman argued that previously marginalized ideas gradually radiate outward from a small core of true believers to a new generation of scholars and, when circumstances call for action, to society at large (Burgin 2012: 219–221). For Friedman, "only a crisis—actual or perceived—produces real change. When that crisis occurs, the actions that are taken depend on the ideas that are lying around" (quoted in Blyth 2013a: 103). Clearly, the notion of a change in paradigms, led by intellectuals who painstakingly reshape the ideological environment in which policymakers make their decisions, reflects what both Keynesian and neoliberal thinkers thought they were doing (Helleiner 1994: 145).

The question, however, is whether we are well-advised to derive our mode of explanation of how economic thought shapes social reality from the self-understanding of those agents actively engaged in propagating these ideas (compare Burgin 2012: 217–222). Ideological entrepreneurs, in the heat of the moment or in nostalgic retrospective, may well overstate the intellectual coherence and the causal efficacy of the paradigms they promote. And policymakers may find it convenient to associate themselves with a particular tradition of thought without actually being guided by it.[13] Taking these representations at face value is to miss that, as Monica Prasad (2006: 21) has argued, "even quite narrowly defined economic ideas are polyvalent and even self-contradictory, so that the same idea may come to mean quite different things at different times or to different audiences." Open to multiple interpretations, ideas do not unproblematically translate into policy; they are shaped, and frequently twisted out of recognition, by the circumstances of the time. Political opportunism or economic expediency may determine which ideas get selected and how they are defined.

This does not mean that a story of ordoliberalism in postwar Germany cannot be told. But it is to insist that it cannot be neatly mapped onto, and much less explain, the key conjunctures in the German or global political economy. And while much may be learned by comparing German ordo-liberalism to Anglo-American neoliberalism, it is misleading to assume that they were of equivalent, paradigmatic importance for policymakers who sought to formulate responses to the critical turning points of the 1970s or the eurocrisis.

Conclusion

The explanatory models examined in this chapter differ according to the causal weight they ascribe to the factors of state power, social interests, and economic ideas. In the final analysis, however, they suffer from a similar deficiency: their accounts of neoliberal transformation tend to extrapolate from the properties and dynamics of the dominant state-society complex in the system. Whether the emphasis is on a hegemonic imposition, a parallelism of social forces, or the diffusion of ideas, the US is considered to be the prime mover in a neoliberal direction. Other social formations partake in this systemic change to the extent that they possess comparable characteristics. Decision-making elites may have been exposed to similar ideas, been subject to the same societal pressures, or stood at the receiving end of the hegemonic relationship (or have hegemonic interests of their own). Those societies with a different ideological environment, domestic balance of forces, or geopolitical situation can converge on the Anglo-American model, but they are precluded conceptually from adding to this transformation. In each of these explanations, differences are confined to varying tempos and gradations of the same general movement from the crisis of embedded liberalism to its neoliberal resolution.[14]

To arrive at a fuller appreciation of the specific ideas, interests, and power politics that have informed the neoliberal agenda of the German state in contemporary Europe, we need to let go of this Anglo-American standard. Rather than assume that Germany, in the end, traveled along a similar path, we need to ask how its policy elites may have been involved in the global rise of neoliberalism from the very beginning, and for very different reasons. To assist this archive-based reinterpretation, the next chapter outlines an alternative conceptual framework that is sensitive not only to the diversity of national political economies, but also to the creative agency and strategic interaction of their decision-making elites across an interdependent world economy.

CHAPTER 2

Foreign Economic Policy
and Advanced Unevenness

THE PREVIOUS CHAPTER argued that the field of IPE has approached the crisis of the 1970s primarily through the lens of an ailing American hegemon. The result, first and foremost, is that the available state-centered, class-based, and ideational accounts of how the embedded liberal order gave way to neoliberal capitalism tend to pay insufficient attention to the actual and potential contributions of other states and social forces. And even when and where their actions and intentions are considered, they are bound to be misread because they are either implicitly or explicitly compared to an Anglo-American standard.

Using this baseline to inquire how Germany has come to occupy a central position within a neoliberal Europe is either unhelpful or misleading. Ideational accounts divert our attention to the Freiburg School thinkers that are said to have provided an endogenous "ordoliberal" paradigm for German policymakers—peculiar in its substance but equivalent in function to the free market ideas disseminated from Chicago. Class-based interpretations have left us waiting for over two decades for the emergence of a German counterpart to Anglo-American elites that would be able and willing to implement a neoliberal program under the Hartz IV reforms—an account that, we suspect, misses out on important, earlier developments.[1] And state-centered explanations throw us back onto the structural and direct power of the United States to command allegiance from its principal anchor state to its neoliberal master plan. The implication here is that present-day

Germany—a frustrated rather than ailing and regional rather than global hegemon—imposes a version of this on the rest of Europe.

In light of this Anglocentrism and the explanatory inadequacies it produces, it would seem sensible to abandon the search for similarities and instead home in on the differences that distinguish Germany from the putative pioneer of neoliberalism. And indeed, there is an extensive body of scholarship, rooted within *comparative* rather than international political economy, that has been dedicated to precisely this task. Within this literature, Germany appears not as a neoliberal laggard but as a paradigmatic other to Anglo-American "free market" capitalism—endowed with distinctive institutions that govern its polity and economy in fundamentally different ways. Could this literature provide the resources needed to illuminate the role of the German state in the crises of the 1970s and 2010s?

The first section of this chapter rejects this proposition on methodological grounds. It argues that the comparative method deployed by this scholarship suffers from three limitations: its ideal-type approach lacks a dynamic conception of change, its comparative setup artificially isolates national political economies from one another, and its search for cross-case generalizations marginalizes the agency of decision-making elites. The result is a stylized and decontextualized German model that only further removes the German state from the global rise of neoliberalism.

The chapter argues that the solution to the problem of Anglocentrism lies in the opposite direction: rather than withdrawing into national varieties of capitalism, we need a richer conception of their international interconnectedness. To this end, the second section of this chapter outlines the conceptual framework of uneven and combined development (U&CD). This heuristic offers an alternative to the comparative approach by integrating an international dimension into its analysis of social and world order change. It therefore allows us to approach the making of neoliberalism as an *interactive process* involving several states, and diverse interests and ideas, rather than as an Anglo-American project writ large.

To examine the role of the German state in this, the third section of this chapter draws on these insights in order to analyze foreign economic policy in a world of similarly "advanced" but differentially constituted and positioned capitalist states. The specific condition of this "advanced unevenness" varies for each state and across time; it generates causal forces beyond the domestic context; and it produces distinctive forms of political economy, social forces, and ruling ideas that cannot be comprehended comparatively. When applied to Germany, this lens yields a dramatically different story from the prevailing state-centered, class-based, and ideational accounts of the rise of neoliberalism that focus on the United States. It explains how Germany's postwar political economy came to diverge from that of the United States; how this difference shaped the outlook and interests of German policymakers once the postwar "catch up" boom lost its momentum in the 1970s; and how the response of the German state to the crisis of embedded liberalism was both shaped by the actions of its foreign counterparts and in turn narrowed the choices available to them. Neoliberalism, in this view, did not arise from the domestic conditions prevailing in the US or the UK alone, but within a wider international environment structured by the German state for particular reasons that precede the Anglo-American turn and continue to shape its crisis management to this day.

The Limits of the Comparative Method

As the previous chapter has established, the existing explanations of the global rise of neoliberalism center on what is assumed to be the Anglo-American experience and then falsely elevated to a general model of neoliberal change. Read against this Anglocentric standard, the German case appears as a perplexing outlier: a country that for decades was held to be a laggard that embraced Anglo-American neoliberalism belatedly and partially, if at all—only to emerge as the vanguard of neoliberal restructuring in the wake of the eurocrisis.

Given these limitations, why not eschew the presumption of sameness that characterizes these accounts? Rather than posit the same direction of travel, why not start instead from the long-standing and persistent national varieties of capitalism? After all, there exists a vast and varied tradition of comparative political economy that has documented and distilled the specificities of the German political economy into a paradigmatic model of organized, nonliberal, coordinated or Rhineland capitalism. Germany here is no longer trailing behind, but archetypically different from, Anglo-American, free market, (neo)liberal capitalism (for example, Coates 2000; Hall and Soskice 2001; Hancké 2009; Streeck 2009; Hollingsworth and Boyer 1997). And instead of searching in vain for state strategies, social forces, or economic ideas that mirror those of the United States, this literature centers on distinct institutions—formal and informal rules, norms, customs, and conventions—as the key variables that differentiate national systems of production and shape political-economic processes (Bruff 2011).

There is no doubt that we need to inquire into the distinctiveness of the German political economy—an endeavor that is rightly considered to be the hallmark of this strand of scholarship. And yet when it comes to the object of this book—to understand a moment of profound social and world order change, and the hand of German policy elites in it—the comparative approach at the heart of this literature suffers from a number of conceptual strictures.[2]

The first problem is the tendency within the comparative literature to rely on "ideal types" in order to frame the analysis. This technique singles out distinctive features of national political economies and organizes them into abstract thought constructs that can be taken to different contexts and systematically compared to each other. The drawback is that while this can illuminate the institutional differences between, for instance, German and US capitalism, it also freezes each of them in time. Not only does the historical process that produced these national varieties escape attention,[3] any future development threatens to burst the explanatory bounds of the ideal types built to capture their essence (Teschke 2003: 50–51). The bias that inheres in this method is thus to emphasize reproduction over transformation (Streeck and Thelen 2005; for more comprehensive assessments, see Holmwood and Stewart 1991: 63–88; Bruun 2007: 41–47, 207–238). In the case of Germany, this tendency has been reinforced by the desire to present a viable alternative to free market capitalism (Panitch and Gindin 2003). In as much as change is admitted, it tends to be limited to the level of individual institutions, without calling into question the validity of its ideal-type representation.[4] Broader transformations, while not ruled out entirely, become difficult to grasp: they are registered as deviations of the concrete case from the posited ideal type. But while their growing distance can be measured, it cannot be fully accounted for—unless we posit a second ideal type that the concrete case is said to approximate. Change then is conceived as the passage from one ideal type to another.[5]

The second problem is that these national varieties of capitalism, singled out and juxtaposed to each other, are cut off from the international environment they inhabit (Panitch and Gindin 2003: 10; Nölke 2016: 146).[6] External influences are admitted as carefully controlled "stimuli" only, but they are denied any generative power. The responses they trigger are said to be conditioned by the internal makeup of the societies under consideration, following logics inscribed in the institutional models that typify them (Henning 1994: 8). The comparative method, to be sure, promises to drill down into the details of each case. But the intellectual cost is high. By holding them apart and considering them in separation, any possibility that the development of one conditions the development of the other is categorically ruled out (McMichael 1990; 2000).

The system of which both are a part forms a static backdrop only. It cannot reach deeper into the constitution and evolution of these national varieties, or else the comparative setup is jeopardized (McMichael 2000). Change—if and when it is recognized—remains *internal* to each case. As a result, the system can be no more than the exact sum of its individual parts, rather than the product of their interactions. We may hope to better understand how the German state and society responded to the neoliberal transition. But we cannot build a bigger, richer picture of the overall shape of the process.

Third, and last, the focus on models of capitalism, defined and governed by specific institutions, often carries with it a deductive logic that neglects agency in two respects. First, it derives the group interests said to characterize particular countries or industries from abstract economic models applied to the case at hand, often before any substantive engagement with the empirical material occurs. In principle, of course, these general models are based on systematized empirical observations or the simplification of market operations. And yet there is a risk that the stylized facts which provide the pool of independent variables and the basis for conditional "if x then y" statements can miss out on critically important nuances. To use the example of a "bank-based" financial system that informs much of the earlier literature on the German political economy (Katzenstein 1978; Zysman 1984; Henning 1994), the relationship between banks and industry in France and Germany, or in Germany in the 1900s and the 1950s, may be described as similarly "close" as opposed to the arms-length relationship of "market-based" financial systems, and yet turn out to be qualitatively different in ways that matter for what interests are formed and how they are pursued.

A closely associated risk is that the focus on institutions as the principal intervening variables that mediate between societal preferences and policy outcomes reduces policy formation to a mechanistic procedure. Not only do actors act out interests attributed to them *a priori*, their chances of success are decided even before the policy process begins by political institutions that determine the relative weight of competing interests in a given issue area (Hiscox 2005: 65). Hidden from view here is a significant part of the actual *politics* of (foreign) economic decision making: the competing and oftentimes creative strategies that, Samuel Knafo (2010) argues, agents employ in pursuit of their interests. To get what they want, actors do not take the existing institutional infrastructure and the associated opportunities and constraints as a given. Not only do they seek to reinforce institutions that are favorable to them or to leverage them in new ways, they also try to bypass, short-circuit, or replace institutions that are opposed to their interests. Institutions may constrain certain agents and enable their opponents, but they do not exhaust the repertoire either side has at its disposal, and even less do they determine the end result.

In sum, the promise of greater specificity through formal comparison comes at the hidden cost of agency, interactivity, and historical openness. First, the specification of national varieties of capitalism tends to involve a disabling structuralism, which reduces the social and political actors to passive bearers of interests rather than authors of their own story. Second, the context of national and foreign economic decision making is confined to the particular national model, with little systematic attention to how the presence of other such models shapes these parameters. And last, the overall outcome of the policymaking process—continued reproduction or change conceived as convergence—is predetermined by the ideal types that frame the analysis. Because the general direction is already known, the difference that agents make is difficult to discern.

On the whole then, a comparative focus on the institutional specificities of German capitalism offers some valuable empirical insights but does not help us conceptually to overcome the problem of Anglocentrism. Deracinated from history and its wider context, Germany, even if no longer a latecomer, remains an outsider to the story of neoliberal globalization. Rather than retreat to national particularities, the remainder of this chapter argues, we need to reconceptualize the international environment in which Germany and other advanced capitalist states responded to the postwar crisis of embedded liberalism, and in which neoliberalism ultimately emerged. By placing the German political economy alongside others, and by interrogating the causal significance of this co-presence, we can trace its development over time, understand the specific interests and ideas that guided its decision-making elites, and more fully appreciate the systemic consequences of their actions.

Uneven and Combined Development

To meet the task of reconceptualization, this book proposes an alternative framework centered on the idea of uneven and combined development. U&CD was first devised by the Russian revolutionary Leon Trotsky (1969; 1992; 2016) to grapple with an impossible anachronism. Where Marx's laws of history predicted the working classes would rise in the most advanced capitalist countries, it was in the deeply autocratic state and semi-feudal society of Czarist Russia that a small-sized proletariat led the world's first socialist transformation. To reground historical materialism and reorient political praxis in light of this anomaly, Trotsky broke with its unilinear conception of capitalist development and insisted that it was *uneven* and *combined* instead (Rosenberg 2017: 226). Born into a world made up of many different societies, he reasoned, capitalism could not be expected to unfold according to a singular logic. The fact that countries would industrialize *unevenly*—at different times and thus under different circumstances—meant that history could not repeat itself. External pressures—such as military threats, commercial competition, cultural imperialism, and so on—would compel latecomers to try to bridge the enormous gap in power and wealth that separated them from societies in which industrial capitalism had already taken root. And in their search for ways to overcome their experience of "backwardness," they could learn from their more "advanced" predecessors and, if they mastered the task, skip over rather than repeat the steps taken by them. Whether successful or not, the result of these catch-up attempts would never be carbon copies of the capitalist pioneers, but a rich tapestry of "hybrid" societies that *combined* preexisting with newly imported forms of social organization, technologies, and ideas. These national particularities, in Trotsky's view, were "nothing else but the most general product of the unevenness of historical development." And they, in turn, would "enter as component parts and in increasing measure into the higher reality which is called world economy" (1969: 148). Ultimately, then, Trotsky envisioned a globalizing capitalism that would itself be continuously reshaped by the multiple and diverse societies upon which it encroached.

For Trotsky, the primary point of this radical revision of historical materialism was to oppose first the disabling "stagism" of orthodox Marxism and then the Stalinist doctrine of "socialism in one country." But his basic insight—that the coexistence of multiple societies changes the ways in which any one of them would develop if they were on their own—had far-reaching implications that have only recently been recovered (for example, Rosenberg 2006; Matin 2013; Anievas 2014; Anievas and Nişancõğlu 2015).[7] For our purposes, his dialectical view of national and global development as mutually constitutive holds out three distinct advantages over the comparative approach.

The first is that this framework allows us to retrace the historical process through which national varieties of capitalism emerged without reifying them into timeless ideal types. This task, undertaken for the German political economy in the next chapter, might seem repetitive given that it reaffirms a number of well-established characteristics—although it also highlights the critical importance of exports for the German social model. Yet the importance of this exercise is revealed when we turn our gaze toward the future. Germany's social market economy fused traditions derived from its belated industrialization and particular insertion into the world market with new social relations of production disseminated from the United States. Because the German model was a peculiar amalgamation from the start, its subsequent development ought not to be reduced to the stark choice between the *reproduction* of its institutional features or the *convergence* on a neoliberal archetype. Once we think of the dynamics of change and continuity as not purely internal and not simply institutionally derived, a multiplicity of pathways moves into sight.

The second, and closely related, advantage is that we no longer need to shut out external influences in order to preserve the integrity of the "national models" we have constructed. On the contrary, if we take their coexistence as our basic premise rather than suppress it for the sake of comparison (McMichael 1990; 2000), we are able to integrate an intersocietal dimension into our inquiry of social and international change. Not only do national varieties of capitalism change over time, they also develop in conjunction with others. This changes their individual paths of development and produces systemic outcomes that cannot be derived from any one of them. Here, the heuristic of U&CD offers an alternative to the comparative method. *Differences* between societies form not the end but the starting point of the investigation. Rather than simply registered, they are brought into play as distinct causal forces with the potential to reshape developments in each individual case, as well as at the global level. This last point is of particular importance for loosening the Anglocentric hold over our historical imagination. It follows that systemic changes, such as the demise of the embedded liberal order and the rise of neoliberal globalization, no longer simply emerge from the internal characteristics of particular societies such as the United States and the United Kingdom (Rosenberg 2017: 224). Rather than locating the origins of neoliberalism in the Anglo-American world, we can approach this world-historical transformation as an interactive process driven by multiple, different state-society complexes. This provides an open-ended frame of analysis in which an otherwise truncated Anglo-American experience can be reinserted, and through which the specific German contribution can be more fully appreciated.

Last, the insight that "[n]ational capitalism cannot be even understood, let alone reconstructed, except as a part of world economy" (Trotsky 1969: 148) also matters for rethinking state elites as purposive human agents. They formulate foreign and domestic economic policies not only on the basis of national varieties that can be institutionally mapped out but also with a view to the developmental differences that arise between them. This involves cross-national comparisons that establish contrasts and similarities with their capitalist contemporaries, discern opportunities and contradictions posed by their national particularities and international position, and draw out lessons about which examples to follow and which mistakes to avoid. In short, because state elites engage reflectively with a dynamic international environment, their actions may be inexplicable from a single national model. The decisions they reach cannot be neatly derived from the institutional aggregation of societal interests, but need to be placed in a wider international context. U&CD serves as a framing device that allows us to investigate the particular pressures and incentives that emerge from the uneven character of capitalist development and shape the strategic remit of policymakers, and which are often ignored or introduced as *ad hoc* and extraneous factors and events. The corresponding methodological move taken in this book is to focus on this internationally embedded elite agency, and to use the archival method in order to empirically reconstruct—from the viewpoint of policymakers themselves—which of these lateral determinations registered in their deliberations and decisions.[8]

Advanced Unevenness

As appealing as the advantages of U&CD sound in principle, the critical objection is whether that frame can in fact be taken forward to meet the object of this study, or whether the phenomena and processes it describes are instead confined to the experience of capitalist late industrialization (compare Barker 2006: 75).[9] After all, Germany and the other states that form the focus of this book have long developed into structurally similar, capitalistically "advanced" economies. There is little doubt then that the question of how to overcome (or sustain) the gap between early industrializers and relative latecomers has lost its vital significance. And yet, there are several reasons why the uneven and combined development of capitalism is of continuing relevance for the advanced capitalist countries.

The first is that while the locus of capitalist late industrialization shifted from North America and Western Europe toward other regions of the world after 1945, the states it has left behind still bear the imprint of this experience. They have accumulated distinctive characteristics on their individual paths toward capitalist "maturity." Even after their industrial revolutions, and despite their postwar integration into a US-led bloc, they continue to differ in terms of economic specializations, social arrangements, and governance regimes. Viewed side-by-side, these national particularities—detailed but disconnected in the comparative political economy literature—continue to render intracore relations uneven (Bruff 2015). The fact of any one of these societies "being contemporary with others" (Pollard 1981: 30) constitutes a powerful force that reaches into the present. It introduces an additional layer of causality that would go unnoticed were we to focus on the domestic properties of only one of them.

Second, even with the original transition completed in most parts of the West by the first half of the century, the postwar golden age of capitalism involved another, more concentrated and coordinated process of uneven and combined development in which Western Europe and Japan were encouraged to borrow from the United States in order to rebuild their political economies on similar material and cultural foundations. The unparalleled wave of growth powered by the "catch-up" convergence around Fordist patterns of mass production and consumption, and the slowdown that ensued once it had been completed, forms the international context in which the rise, demise, and displacement of embedded liberalism needs to be situated (Rosenberg and Boyle 2019).

Moreover, while the drama of capitalist late development no longer centers on the North Atlantic, its knock-on consequences reverberate through the old core. Throughout the twentieth century, the globalization of capitalism, and the forced insertion or voluntary arrival of newcomers, reshaped the capitalist world market in ways that mattered profoundly for the subsequent development of earlier entrants. In the twenty-first century, this has found its most powerful expression in the rapid economic rise of the Asian giants. Their massive and compressed catch-up development, hugely important in its own right, is experienced differently by the advanced capitalist states—ranging from heightened competition for some to new market opportunities for others. And, as Chapter 7 will argue with regard to Germany's role in the European Union, it also holds the potential to reshape the relations between them (Rosenberg and Boyle 2019).

The advanced capitalist states also continually diverge in another crucial respect. While they have reached similar "end points" in their industrial transformation (though not, of course, in their development as a whole), they undergo recurring cycles of economic growth, stagnation, and recession. What causes these rhythms is an enduring enigma of political economy (compare Sewell 2012). What matters here is that these upswings and downturns are not perfectly synchronized. Although closely connected, they differ across countries and regions in terms of their timing, depth, and duration. Together, these varying growth patterns form a moving landscape of overlapping peaks and troughs that policymakers need to traverse. They constitute another vector of unevenness that holds actual and potential spillover effects, and exerts an influence over economic decision makers that cannot be reduced to their domestic situation. They formulate policy not only according to their own position, but with a view to the fluctuating fortunes experienced by other economies.

And last, while the relations among the advanced capitalist states are no longer shaped by the imperative of catch-up development, the fundamental problem of unevenness remains. The basic fact that the world consists of *many* states means that the governing of global capitalism needs to be coordinated and negotiated between several of them. This plurilateral management—in which the US plays by far the most prominent role (for example, Bromley 2003; Panitch and Gindin 2012)—involves a distinct set of governance problems that have no parallel at the national level. Because they emerge from the mismatch between political multiplicity and the transnational reach of capital, they need to be theorized in their own right.

In sum, this book proposes that policymakers in the North Atlantic core continue to confront an international system marked out by differences in the historical structures and growth cycles of their capitalist contemporaries—what may be termed "advanced unevenness." At any one point, the co-presence of differently constituted and situated national political economies, with nonconcurring sequences of growth, recession, and recovery, presents a matrix of constraints and complementarities to which political operators respond strategically and creatively. This set of lateral determinations emanates from outside the domestic context and escapes the comparative purview. But once this intersocietal dimension is taken into consideration, the remainder of this chapter argues, it changes fundamentally how we think about the projection of state power, the influence of social interests, and the importance of ideas—the now familiar building blocks used to construct the prevailing Anglocentric narratives of the rise of neoliberalism (Chapter 1).

State Power

The first implication of the U&CD framework is that we need to rethink the hegemonic power politics said to have led to the rise of neoliberalism in the 1970s. The prevailing accounts see hegemony as a recurrent phenomenon—a concept applicable to dominant states that temporarily stabilize the interstate system and world economy, and the decline or desertion of which lead to struggles over succession. It is this reading, we will remember from the previous chapter, that informs the state-centered argument that the United States decided to disembed the liberal world order in order to defeat prospective contenders and reassert its global power. Neoliberalism, simply put, arose from a series of American power plays that cajoled and coerced US allies into submitting to free markets.

By contrast, the longer-term view of U&CD allows us to fully historicize America's postwar hegemony and gain a better sense of what the policy conflicts of the 1970s were actually about. The starting point is the recognition—fleshed out in the next chapter—of the radical differences between the liberal world orders presided over by Britain and the United States in the nineteenth and twentieth centuries. The classical era of free trade and *laissez-faire* centered on an international division of labor between the world's "first industrial nation" and the agrarian interests of its would-be rivals, made possible by the temporally uneven spread of capitalist social relations. In contrast to this organic but transient complementarity of interests, the embedded liberal order constructed by the United States involved the active equalization of developmental patterns in the capitalist core. Based on two distinct moments in the uneven and combined development of capitalism, the forms of international rule exercised by Britain and the United States cannot be subsumed under the same rubric. Hegemony, in short, no longer appears as a general, and indeed *the* principal, world order concept of IPE. Instead, it is turned into a historical category that captures a singular form of international rule, strictly limited in time and place (Lacher and Germann 2012). Once we dispense with the idea of international history as successive hegemonic orders, we are better able to see the truly novel features of American hegemony and the qualitative transformation of intracore relations it involved.

Contrary to Britain's imperial rule, US hegemony did not simply balance against but actively included other great powers in its sphere of influence—with the notable exception of the Soviet Union. And rather than simply rule over them, the US set out to reconstruct its allies and former enemies in the image of its own state-society relations and indeed in the interest of their native ruling elites, who sought to restore their legitimacy after thirty years marked by economic crises and political upheaval and bookended by two world wars. American hegemony, therefore, was founded on the dual organization of consent. Domestically, it sought to establish mass support for a liberal polity and capitalist economy through Marshall Aid, the import of Fordist patterns of production and consumption, a "politics of productivity" (Maier 1977) that rewarded labor discipline, and an interventionist and redistributive welfare state. And internationally, American hegemony rested on a range of multilateral organizations through which its members could coordinate their efforts of economic reconstruction, world market reintegration, and military buildup.

The social dimension that underpinned US hegemony—the embedded liberal compromises struck between capital and labor—came under strain in the 1970s and, with the advent of neoliberalism, has been either outright terminated or significantly eroded. And yet the symbiosis of social and international order under US hegemony had far-reaching consequences for how states would approach this pivotal turning point. In contrast to the interwar period, their attempts to stabilize capitalist social relations and contain working-class unrest did not spill over into geopolitical or geoeconomic contestation. A breakup of the capitalist world into hostile trading and monetary blocs analogous to the 1930s, while on the minds of some political elites and foreign policy intellectuals in the 1970s (most prominently the German chancellor Helmut Schmidt), was never actually in the cards. For, nestled within an open world economy and a collective security alliance pivoting on the US, state elites in the advanced capitalist heartland had ceased to see each other as existential threats to their survival. The security dilemma that realist IPE elevates to a timeless principle of international relations belongs to the long nineteenth century of capitalist late industrialization and mass conscripted and mechanized warfare among the great powers (for example, Buzan and Lawson 2015: 265; Tooze 2015). And even then, it was driven not by the superordinate sphere of power politics that realists posit, but by the contradictions and tensions between early industrializers and relative latecomers. The interimperial rivalries that shattered the liberal world economy, and which classical theorists such as Lenin mistook for the essence of capitalism, were in reality generated by a conjuncture in its uneven and combined development that has since been surpassed.[10] Under the aegis of the United States, the developmental differences that had locked the great powers into this downward spiral were evened out. American hegemony and the golden age of capitalism were based on a US-led process of "catch-up" development that reconstituted the economic basis, social balance of power, and state forms of its allies—most directly in Germany and Japan, which the United States occupied militarily. It amounts to a profound integration and internal pacification of the Northern core that outlasted the exhaustion of the growth dynamic it had unleashed (Rosenberg and Boyle 2019).

American hegemony, then, did far more than simply arrest great power politics for a period of time; in North America and Western Europe, it positively transcended it. It follows that the crisis of the 1970s cannot be framed as a struggle over hegemony, whether rooted in security competition or commercial rivalries. Neither the pressures of systemic anarchy that realists invoke, nor the imperatives of capitalism that neo-Leninists still see at work, can serve as a compass to understand the regime and policy disputes in this critical period (for example, Callinicos 2009). Under US hegemony, the permissive environment that potentially pits the core states against one another emerges neither from the absence of central authority as such nor from capitalist competition writ large but from "advanced unevenness": the co-presence of differently organized and positioned national political economies with intersecting growth cycles. This condition complicates the task of managing capitalism immensely. For even states confronting similar issues such as unemployment or inflation may do so from standpoints that are opposed rather than complementary to one another. Situated within this force-field, states may find their respective policy objectives to be at cross purposes, and to find their own policy choices foreclosed by the decisions of others.

States therefore seek to influence one another's policies and promote their favored solutions—unilaterally as well as in cooperation, and inside and outside the established channels. Under America's postwar hegemony, an elaborate apparatus of interconnected state agencies, international organizations, and public and private coordinating mechanisms has been constructed to manage this unevenness: to resolve the tensions between economic interdependence and political sovereignty and to foster cooperative forms of leadership and crisis management (van der Pijl 1984; Gill 1990; Panitch 1994). And yet governing global capitalism through a multiplicity of economically and politically integrated but formally independent states places limits on the extraterritorial reach even of the leading state and the unity of globalized forms of rule. The territorial constitution of the global political economy renders the international rule of law incomplete and, at least in principle, exposes it to the partial interests of individual states that have to reconcile domestic and international responsibilities (Gill 1992: 270) and may seek to advance the particular interests of capital invested or originating from within their borders in ways that differ from the balancing roles they perform domestically (Lacher 2002: 160–161; Lacher 2006).

At the same time, to say that intercapitalist relations have been profoundly demilitarized under American hegemony is not to dismiss the policy disagreements that do arise as irrelevant. In this respect, liberal approaches are mistaken to see global economic exchange as mutually beneficial in principle, and to reduce the incompatibilities and tensions to mere technical problems of collective action under conditions of anarchy. Capitalist globalization does constitute an important source of instability, as well as competition among the major firms and their home or host countries (Gowan 2013). And yet the differential pursuit of state interests under these conditions need not itself be destabilizing (Trachtenberg 2003). The trick is to take them seriously without, however, exaggerating their hostile character or disintegrative consequences. In other words, these interstate conflicts, in a strictly limited and demilitarized sense of the term, are neither subordinate nor antithetical but *integral* to the form and direction of capitalist globalization. Therefore they must form the focal point of our interrogation over how neoliberalism emerged.

It would be wrong, however, to conclude from the continuing dominance of the United States that these policy conflicts were decided in its favor and unilaterally steered toward a neoliberal resolution. They need to be detached from the moot question of hegemonic succession and placed within a conjuncture of advanced unevenness that had generated the postwar boom but by the 1970s was drawing to a close. Seen from this viewpoint, they can be examined for what they were actually about: the question of how states could sustain capital accumulation and mass consent individually and collectively, and how they could ensure that their counterparts would adopt solutions broadly supportive of their domestic priorities. How these priorities are formulated is the subject of the following section, as we move from the *conduct*, and possible collision, of foreign economic policies to the wider social forces involved in their *formation*.

Societal Interests

The causal implications of societal multiplicity are also present once we step down from the international to the domestic level of analysis. Explanations of neoliberalism located at the level of society, the previous chapter has argued, approach it as a project pursued by globalizing financial or business elites—emanating from the Anglosphere and extending to kindred social forces in other parts of the world. The heuristic of advanced unevenness allows us to pluralize the state-theoretic insights that underpin these accounts (Miliband 1973; Poulantzas 1973). We can recognize the power and influence of business elites without succumbing to the instrumentalism or functionalism that has been associated with this tradition of thought. By regrounding the "relative autonomy" of state elites from their domestic contexts in a dynamic and integrated world economy, we gain a richer understanding of their creative agency in mediating internal and external pressures. And this, in turn, leads to a more nuanced conception of the varying circumstances and constellations of interest that may lead policymakers to favor neoliberal solutions even without comparable elite interests.

In its classical formulation, the essential dilemma policy elites confront under capitalism is that in order to maintain a healthy tax base, to access capital markets, and—in liberal democracies—to secure their reelection, they depend on a privatized economy over which they do not have authoritative control (Block 1978; Offe 1984: 166; Isaac 1987: 180; Przeworski and Wallerstein 1988; Luger 2000: 25; Barrow 2008: 98–99). This structural dependence is often seen as a backstop which ensures that political operators will seek to manage capitalism in ways that advance or at least do not oppose the "general will" of the capitalist class (Block 1977: 15). It also gives business owners—who have first-hand access to and leverage over the economy and who can in principle penalize policies by withdrawing or withholding investment—a privileged position within the political process even where they do not govern directly themselves (Lindblom 1977).

That this structural power and direct influence do not neatly translate into favorable policy decisions is a point well established within the critical literature on the capitalist state. States have been thought to retain "relative autonomy" for several reasons. First, policymakers need to take into account competing social interests and mediate the antagonism between capital and labor in order to secure the legitimacy of their rule and the stability of their economies (Wolfe 1977; Carnoy 1984). In capitalist societies where the power to rule has been made subject to limited forms of representative democracy, governing elites need to create a measure of popular support in order to ensure their short-term political survival and the long-term cohesion of their societies (O'Connor 1973; Wood 1981).

The second reason for why even dominant groups are unable to dictate state policy is that the capitalist class as a whole tends to be disunited by economic competition and divergent political interests (Carnoy 1984: 213–214). In fact, as carefully excavated by Hawley and corroborated in Chapter 5, the same elites may hold incompatible views. State managers therefore not only face competing societal demands or rival business factions (Hawley 1984: 162; Hawley 1983), they may also confront contradictory interests of the same social group (Hawley 1987: 145). Germany's dominant export bloc, Chapter 4 explains, was united in its opposition to both an appreciating DM and comprehensive capital controls. Even if we were to assume that the operators of capitalist states may be structurally predisposed to prioritize capital over other social constituents (Lindblom 1982), such incompatibilities require policymakers to make independent and proactive decisions (Hawley 1987: 145).

The lens of advanced unevenness helps to foreground a third dimension of state autonomy, arising from the fact that capitalist states exist "in the plural" (Barker 1978). Some critical theorists have sought to take the systemic forces generated by this political multiplicity into consideration. But they have conceptualized the international sphere primarily as an arena of political-military and/or commercial rivalry (Hawley 1983; Block 1978; 1980). This view of international relations as the quest for power and plenty, whether ordained by anarchy or shaped by capitalism, neglects the qualitative transformation of intracore relations that occurred under the aegis of the American hegemon.

The heuristic of advanced unevenness focuses instead on the continuing differences in the historical structures and national growth cycles of the advanced capitalist countries. These differences, to repeat, add a second layer of pressures and incentives that act upon policymakers, and may increase their distance from their domestic coalitions and contexts (Lacher 2005: 41). For not only do state managers receive competing demands and mixed signals from within their own societies, they are also exposed to international pressures and incentives that frequently intervene to widen the gap between what dominant groups want and what state elites do. For example, once the United States Federal Reserve pushed up interest rates to record heights in 1979, many of the world's central banks were compelled to follow suit and close the interest rate differential even in economies where inflation did not need to be squeezed out and where the recessionary impact of these actions went against business interests (see Chapter 6).

This historical precedent and the problem of "spillover" it describes are well-known empirically and—as Chapter 7 explains—are of acute concern to German policymakers today. But they are also of major theoretical import. For this lateral exposure amounts to more than contingent factors that occasionally complicate the picture. As a general condition of coexistence, it frustrates any attempt to theorize the capitalist state, let alone world order change, from the standpoint of a single society writ large. State action, especially when outwardly directed, cannot be derived from the domestic balance of forces or the functional tasks required by the capitalist system. Because foreign economic policy cannot be reduced to either its domestic or international context, both dimensions need to form an integral part of the framework and to be given equal weight in our investigation.

The conventional way of bringing these two dimensions together is to map a second layer of (power) political bargaining onto the domestic decision-making process (Putnam 1988; Guerrieri and Padoan 1988: 4–5). In this view of policy formation as a "two-level game," state actors are subject to internal and external influences, engaged in parallel negotiations with their domestic constituents and foreign counterparts and seeking to reach compromises with both. The focus on strategic interaction, though laudable, is negated by the game-theoretical frame of the analysis, which tends to reduce political agency to a sequence of scripted moves of actors according to a fixed preference set. In practice, moreover, a balanced engagement with both spheres of action has been difficult to sustain. To reduce empirical complexity so that it can yield generalizable insights, the analysis often prioritizes one of the two levels while reducing the other to an analytical appendage. One survey rightly concluded that "[w]e clearly need a better two-level mouse trap: a model that incorporates a fuller representation of organized interests and lobbying at the domestic level, while also allowing for the ways in which incentives and constraints are generated at the international level" (Hiscox 2005: 79).

The heuristic of advanced unevenness provides the basis for such a richer framework. It locates these incentives and constraints not in abstract categories such as anarchy or interdependence that (dis)incline states to cooperate, but in a concrete place in a wider world economy, structured by multiple coexisting societies. To be sure, the precise content of these lateral determinations, and their efficacy, has to be established anew in each case. If Miliband was right to insist that "the relationship between the state and the capitalist class has to be specified with historical and empirical precision" (Miliband 1969: 55, cited in Barrow 2008: 88; see also Panitch 2002), the same goes for its particular international situation. The "relative autonomy" of state elites, in this view, emerges from domestic and international determinations which inflect each other in specific ways that can be comprehended retrospectively and projected forward tentatively, but that defy law-like generalizations. Nor can the outcome of these determinations be prespecified with complete certainty, for they ultimately depend on the capacity of agents to reflect and decide and also to err on which steps will take them in a desired direction. This probabilistic rather than deterministic view of causality yields a conception of policymakers as being, in a way, structurally compelled to make creative choices. If the pressures and incentives that confront them at the domestic and international levels are pushing and pulling them in opposite directions, they have to reach decisions that, while conditioned by both, are irreducible to either of these contexts. In cases when they cannot go down either route, they need to forge their own path. And this may well involve creative recombinations, on the part of policy elites, of internal and external forces so that they reinforce or cancel each other out (Teschke and Cemgil 2014; Teschke and Wyn Jones 2017). There is, then, an undeniable element of human agency at work. By situating these decisions in a wider, more dynamic force-field, we gain a better sense of where, when, and how it comes to matter.

The upshot of all of this is not only that state officials retain a significant degree of autonomy and that powerful social groups do not always get what they want. It also loosens the presumption, inherent in many class-based explanations of neoliberalism, that it must be the same elite forces who drive policies in a neoliberal direction wherever they capture the state. If state action cannot be reduced to its domestic context, the global transition toward neoliberalism cannot be explained as a series of shifts, initiated by the US and the UK, in favor of internationally oriented business or financial interests. Once "the international" is integrated into our analysis, we may well find that policymakers promote neoliberal reforms domestically or internationally for reasons that do not reflect the interests, nor even presuppose the presence, of such neoliberally minded elites.

Ideas

The final contribution of the lens of "advanced unevenness" is that it allows us to reinterpret the significance of economic ideas in the shift from embedded to neoliberal capitalism and in the global political economy more broadly. The ideational explanations we have encountered in the previous chapter invariably present the global rise of neoliberalism as the triumph of free market beliefs. Some of them see a role for Germany in this paradigm shift given its supposed tradition of ordoliberalism. But while this ideological variant of neoliberalism is considered particular to Germany, the model of how it mattered is lifted from the Anglo-American experience. In moments of crisis like the 1970s and or the 2010s, economic ideas serve as guides to action on the part of policymakers who are no longer certain of how best to proceed. Whether they come from Chicago or Freiburg, they act as antidotes to Keynesianism and feed into what decades of scholarship have seen to be a global neoliberal agenda.

The lens of advanced unevenness helps us to approach the role of ideas in the perceptions and decisions of policymakers in a more nuanced way. There is no doubt that policy elites may be guided by overarching visions of world order and their country's place within it, and that they devise grand strategies to realize them. In this respect, ideas deserve to be taken seriously. And yet some important reservations are in order. The first is that these geopolitical or geoeconomic imaginaries need to be translated into policies in order to be rendered effective. This moment of implementation is critical because there may well be several policies for state elites to choose from. If so, the "meso-level" ideas that help select the most efficacious options are at least as significant as—but may well differ from—the ideas that define the desired goals. Second, whatever else these imaginaries may involve, they require some form of material support. Unless and until they reach for a postcapitalist future, their realization depends on the ability of policymakers to maintain business confidence and economic growth. This does not mean that ideas simply reflect or rationalize objective interests.

In fact, the problem is the exact opposite. It is because the relationship is imprecise rather than straightforward that actors have to search for some sort of fit between them.

For while capitalism may establish outer bounds of what states can do without facing significant economic consequences (compare Thompson 1978: 48; Skocpol 1980: 200), it does not select the course of action they ought to take instead (Knafo 2010: 507). Apart from a clear-cut *quid pro quo* (such as campaign contributions in exchange for legislative action), what capital wants and needs is not always unequivocally clear (Barrow 1993: 62; Luger 2000: 28; Barrow 2008: 100). This is so not only because capital speaks with many voices but because the structures of accumulation are essentially silent. The structural power of capital tends to be proscriptive rather than prescriptive; it may delineate which policies cannot be taken without significant sacrifices, but it rarely offers guidelines for positive state actions. On the contrary, it is precisely this structural indeterminacy that poses a critical dilemma for state elites, who depend on a functioning and flourishing economy without being able to know in advance which actions they need to take to (re)create these conditions. The issue, as Blyth (2002: 10) has argued, is that capitalism does not come with a manual.

In moments of crisis in particular, therefore, the agencies of the state and the representatives of capital and other social groups are engaged in an interpretative effort to find the most appropriate policy responses. This search for solutions may be marked by indecision as well as creativity, as actors frequently probe and push "the limits of the limits" (Teschke and Cemgil 2014: 611) of what is supposed to be structurally possible (Knafo 2010). This contested endeavor—contingent but not wholly indeterminate—increases the possibility for independent state action, as well as for misguided policy decisions.

In principle, of course, this search for solutions allows for a panoply of values, norms, and conventions to inform the actions of policymakers. The constructivist IPE scholarship that inspires most of the ordoliberal readings of German crisis management clearly has a point in insisting that actors' interests are not structurally predetermined. In a world of uncertainty rather than calculable risk, aggravated in moments of crisis, agents do not pursue interests according to a fixed and maximal program that corresponds to the structural position they occupy; they are looking for rule-of-thumb guidance as to what is "good enough" (Katzenstein and Nelson 2013: 233–235).

And yet the environment that agents are in principle "free to interpret" is structured not only by the national economy they seek to decipher but also by those of their capitalist contemporaries. The problems of legibility that leave policymakers uncertain as to how to respond to crises run parallel. In lieu of an absolute and objective measure, state officials tend to take the performance of their foreign counterparts as their point of reference. Such comparison presupposes differentiation in two respects captured by the concept of unevenness. The division of the world into multiple units creates the conditions of possibility for comparisons to be made, and the coexistence in the world of *unlike* societies gives substance to what is being compared and why (Rosenberg 2017: 18). In the contemporary core, capitalism has emerged as the great comparator. It provides a series of relational benchmarks—growth, exchange and inflation rates, export volumes, stock market indices or market shares—that allow independent decision makers to "size up" one another, see what others are doing and how they are faring, and define their interests flexibly and in comparison with one another. For German policymakers, and for reasons that will be explored in subsequent chapters, exports have emerged as the critical metric of success.

Realist scholars have been the first to recognize the relational context in which states define their interests (Waltz 1979). Where they identify systemic anarchy and the imperative of state survival as the matrix of strategic calculation, critical analysts have suggested that in matters of political economy state action is guided by the competitive and thus inherently comparative nature of capitalism (Gowan 2002; 2013; Nitzan and Bichler 2009). Neither of them is quite right. In a world of advanced unevenness, state operators think "relationally" not because they are worried about the survival of their nation-state, as realists would have it, nor because they have been enlisted in or internalized a capitalist profit motive, as some critical scholars propose. They do so because they routinely encounter a series of equally viable policy options they need to choose between, with no clear guidance on which option is the most preferable. Because policy elites find their national political economy difficult to decode, their eyes wander over to their peers. Hence the comparative and competitive concerns of states to do better (or less badly) than their partners are not driven by an existential struggle over either power or wealth, but by the search for a decision-making compass.

In this way, advanced unevenness shapes the subject position of policymakers and enters into how crises are perceived and what solutions are formulated. It allows us to recognize the intersubjective constitution of the global political economy without having to accept a disembodied idealism as the only alternative to a "vulgar" materialism.

This does not rule out that more far-reaching visions of national and world economy may come to matter for how policy elites read, and respond to, the problems they face. But they are subject to too many vagaries to carry the weight that ideational explanations put on them. Not only are they shaped by political struggles and economic exigencies, they are contingent on the actions of others and the imponderables of the international system. In short, they are themselves the product of processes that need to be interrogated, rather than solid devices that can be deployed to explain why states converged on neoliberalism.

To posit ordoliberalism as the lens through which German policymakers make sense of their situation is to ignore "the international" as a source of inspiration and frustration in its own right, something that policymakers themselves can hardly afford to do. And, indeed, the next chapter shows that some of the elements usually attributed to ordoliberalism—monetary and fiscal restraint, price stability, a disinclination to incur debt, market-conforming interventions—owed far more to pragmatic considerations of how the German economy could best recover under the American postwar order. After considerable debate, they were selectively included or discarded in pursuit of an overarching strategy that—revisited and reformulated at the critical junctures of the 1970s and 2010s—is far broader than what one could possibly derive from the tradition of the Freiburg School.

Conclusion

This chapter has developed the tools we need to break out of the Anglo-centric mold and recover the German state as a historical actor in the crisis and transformation of the embedded liberal world order. The first section has argued that a comparative approach cannot assist in this task because its conceptual horizon is too narrow. While it sheds precious light on the institutional varieties of national capitalisms, it cannot comprehend their structural interdependence. To explore this condition of coexistence and its causal significance, the chapter has drawn on the alternative framework of uneven and combined development. Using the lens of "advanced unevenness," it has highlighted the creative autonomy of decision-making elites from their domestic contexts and their strategic interaction across an international system of capitalistically developed but variegated national political economies.

In this way, this chapter has established a base from which to approach the global rise of neoliberalism as a cross-national sequence of events rather than an Anglo-American invention. At any given point, and especially in times of crisis, the operators of the core capitalist states face difficult choices between a number of policy options; state managers settle on a course of action on the basis of the particular domestic and international circumstances of their state and economy, and often in direct comparison to the policies of others. The choices they make feed back into and reshape the international context in which other state administrators have to make theirs. The search for global and national remedies, then, is shaped not only by uncertainty but also by tensions and contradictions, as the solutions adopted by some may pose problems to others, and as states seek to project their power and influence internationally in order to advance their objectives and structure one another's choices.

In short, the neoliberal transformation of the postwar order is best understood as an interactive and constructive process, driven by several states whose actions, interests, and ideas—refracted through the prism of "the international"—need not correspond to those of the Anglo-American "pioneer" in order to register as significant.

The remainder of this book mobilizes the heuristic of uneven and combined development to generate new insights into the German deliberations and decisions at the twilight of the embedded liberal order and—in extension—at the apex of the neoliberal restructuring of post-2008 Europe. Starting from the *unevenness* of capitalist world development, we can see how Germany's postwar social market economy came to play on, but also differ from, the Keynesian and Fordist means of restoring growth and integrating the working class pioneered by the United States (Chapter 3). This difference, deriving from Germany's traditional export orientation, informed, and rewarded, its decision to double down on domestic price stability in order to cope with the exhaustion of the postwar "catch-up" boom in the 1970s (Chapter 4). A focus on *interactivity* illuminates how a "grand economic strategy" was formulated in response to Germany's European and American partners, whose protectionist, interventionist, and reflationary solutions threatened the open markets and stable prices on which the German export model depended (Chapter 5).[11] An emphasis on *combination* reveals how the pursuit of this strategy radically reshaped the international environment and compounded the domestic forces that prompted the United States to openly renounce the embedded liberal compromise and demolish the material aspirations and organizational strength of the working class (Chapter 6). Last, globalized through a worldwide recession and debt crisis triggered by the Volcker Shock, this new form of capitalism has *renewed uneveness* in the core and created neoliberal pressures that German policy makers have sought to deflect across contemporary Europe, in view of a gigantic wave of capitalist late industrialization led by China (Chapter 7).

CHAPTER 3

Embedding Liberalism

The German Social Model and Its International Supports

THE PURPOSE OF THIS CHAPTER is to draw out the distinctiveness of the German political economy from the vantage point of uneven and combined development (U&CD). The first section highlights the fundamental differences between the two spectacular waves of capitalist globalization in the nineteenth and twentieth century. It fleshes out the argument presented in the first chapter that the ebb and flow of these tidal movements cannot be explained in terms of successive hegemonies. Because Britain and the United States did not perform equivalent roles of global ordering, the term hegemony fails as a meta-concept that can be projected backward and forward. Instead, it denotes a singular form of international and social order the nature and future of which need to be understood on their own terms, and preferably through the eyes of America's allies. The second section traces the late development of German capitalism across these two liberal world orders. Building on a developmental model oriented toward the world market from its inception, Germany's embedded liberal compromise was constructed around a positive balance of payments that depended on wage moderation, price stability, an undervalued DM, and the promotion of exports. Ordoliberal ideas, the third section contends, had little influence on the making of this "social market economy" even as it differed from the Fordist, Keynesian, and statist techniques used to generate mass consent in other advanced industrialized countries. Foundational to this project was the vision that German manufacturers could supply an already developed and newly industrializing world with customized capital goods. While this vision of Germany as the workshop of the world, embodied by Ludwig Erhard's economics ministry, broadly corresponded to America's globalizing designs, the final section argues that it also ran up against the Cold War division of the world market and the inward-looking character of European integration. The notion of Germany as a docile "trading state" passes over these latent conflicts, and ignores that German policymakers were prepared to find new ways to project their power once the economic expansion and openness of the embedded liberal world order seemed seriously at risk.

The Uneven and Combined Development of Liberal World Order

The two great cycles of global expansion and integration over the past two centuries are only outwardly similar. Viewed through the lens of U&CD, we can see that they revolved around two distinct sets of social and geopolitical relations. The liberal cosmopolitan world order of the middle decades of the nineteenth century was based upon the developmental difference and passing complementarity between an industrial-capitalist and liberal-constitutional Britain on the one hand and the still predominately agricultural and aristocratic regimes in Prussia and Continental Europe on the other (Lacher and Germann 2012). Free trade and *laissez faire*, in other words, rested on the supplementary integration of Germany and other potential rivals as agricultural and raw material producers into a rapidly expanding, British-centered world market. This temporary symbiosis between differently constituted societies and ruling-class projects—one premised on the industrial revolution and the other on neofeudal restoration—was short-lived for two reasons. First, the onset of a global depression in commodity prices in the 1870s, marked by the entrance of cheap North American grains, destroyed the competitive advantage of Prussia's landed elites as subsidiary suppliers and their ability to sustain their power in this way. Their acceptance of economic liberalism, as famously argued by Gustav Stolper (1940: 63–65; see also Wehler 1985: 36–37), vanished with it. Under the notorious coalition of "iron and rye" between Junker agrarians and Ruhr industrialists, Imperial Germany—alongside other *anciens régimes* of Europe—embarked on protectionist projects of late industrialization that paralleled and rivaled that of Britain. Second, the ruling elites of the German Reich and other late developers confronted as the inevitable by-product of these efforts an industrial working class rapidly growing in numbers and strength. To absorb and deflect demands for popular sovereignty, they resorted to broadly similar measures that sought to contain and externalize class tensions through conservative social and chauvinist foreign policies (Deppe, Salomon, and Solty 2011: 27–41). Toward the end of the nineteenth century, therefore, the great powers converged upon broadly similar nationalist-imperialist forms of rule and development that stabilized these societies internally at the cost of pitting them against one another in the international arena. The combined effect of social stabilization and catch-up industrialization at home was to externalize social contradictions into colonial conquest, to militarize the relations between the great powers, and to prompt societies to turn their backs on free trade and march toward total war (Polanyi 1957).

The American architects of the postwar liberal order could not ignore the carnage and crises produced by the first wave of capitalist globalization. Capitalism had been delegitimized in many parts of Europe and the world, and for the market economy to again become accepted as the organizing principle of society, a major social and international reconfiguration was necessary. This required not only substantial social and material concessions to subordinate forces, but a concerted effort by governing elites to ensure that national projects of "domesticating" the working classes would not come into conflict with one another again. In this view, what happened in the West after 1945 is truly exceptional. By exporting Fordist methods of production and consumption and encouraging equivalent compromises between organized labor and corporate capital, the United States set out to recast its allies and former enemies in the image of its own society (Maier 1977; Milward 1984; Rupert 1995). Unlike the British system of imperial governance—inherently fragile as it excluded those core states with the power to challenge it (Darwin 2009: 5)[1]—the US incorporated its imperialist rivals into a multilateral framework of security, trade, and investment designed to manage social and economic contradictions (Gill 2008: 59–61). And in contrast to the fleeting coincidence of industrial and agricultural export interests that had formed around British free trade in the mid-nineteenth century, a new system of public and private international organizations was put in place to forge a durable transatlantic consensus among governing elites, internationally oriented capitalist owners, and reformist trade union leaders (Gill 1990: 126).

In sum, under the postwar leadership of the United States, there was both a top-down leveling of societal unevenness and an unprecedented, and transnationally mediated, harmonization of social and world orders.

When situated in the wider frame of U&CD, the uniquely consensual character of American hegemony comes into view. It follows that the rise and demise of the embedded liberal world order over which it presided is perhaps best approached from the opposite end: those allied states and classes, to borrow from Geir Lundestad (1986), that had welcomed, or at least accepted, this peculiar empire after the war and that would face the choice to renew or revoke their invitation when its economic foundations unraveled in the 1970s. Germany features prominently in this inverted image, not only because it had transformed from principal rival to a key "anchor state" of American power (while retaining significant counter-hegemonic potential), but also because its developmental model differed from Anglo-American capitalism both before and after the neoliberal turn of the 1980s.

Embedded Liberalism, Made in Germany

The German variety of capitalism emerged from what contemporaries and later historians saw as a "special path" (*Sonderweg*) of modernization that clashed brutally with the liberal West in the first half of the twentieth century (Berghahn 2006: 35; Blackbourn and Eley 1984; Kocka 1988; 1998; Abelshauser 1987). From the standpoint of U&CD and its emphasis on multilinearity, we can reject the notion of a "normal road" from which only Germany deviated. At the same time, it is clear that "its ability to generate a fascist response to the world economic crisis after 1929" (Blackbourn and Eley 1984: 91) makes it the most momentous of pathways in Europe to consider. And, in fact, returning to the moment of Germany's entrance into the capitalist world market holds importance for understanding its postwar trajectory as well. Once we widen our conception of the challenges of industrial "catch-up" beyond the purely technical task of mobilizing adequate resources and realizing sufficient scales,[2] some remarkable continuities in the basic structure of German capitalism move into view (Berghahn 2006: 41; Abelshauser 2001).[3]

As intimated earlier, the full-scale industrial transformation of German society took place against the backdrop of a prolonged world economic downturn that imperiled the Junker elites who owned the land and staffed the state as well as industrialists who faced British competition at home and in global markets.[4] It also called forth an increasingly organized working class with political and economic demands that were incompatible with the conservative-authoritarian regime and the capitalist development to which it aspired (Green 2012; Blyth 2013a: 134–135). Britain, with its seemingly corrosive and obsolete form of liberal capitalism, could not present a viable blueprint for how to marry economic success and social stability. In often explicit contradistinction, businesses turned to cartels and banks to syndicates in order to manage competition and organize accumulation (Trebilcock 1981: 65–68, 99; Wehler 1985: 42). And the conservative bureaucracy selectively integrated skilled workers into a stratified social insurance system that staggered benefits according to the incomes and contributions of workers and was carried over into the postwar era (Manow 2001a: 95, 110). The result was a corporatist model of societal organization. In lieu of political liberties, it offered particularistic social status and protection. And in place of unmitigated competition, it massively concentrated and tightly integrated industry and banking (Abelshauser 2001: 515; Streeck 2001: 11–12).

While overshadowed by the long depression, Germany's industrialization drive also coincided with a series of technological innovations that supplanted the lead industries on which Britain had based its industrial supremacy (Allen 2010: 137; Braun 1990). New opportunities opened up for the German latecomer in the emerging growth sectors of chemical and electrical engineering and motor construction. Together with ready access to the agrarian economies to its East and South, they quickly transformed Germany from a mere intermediary between the British core and continental periphery to a major high-technology exporter (Pollard 1981: 174, 178, 182).

The historical timing and geographical position predisposed the German political economy toward exports. Its social organization, however, turned these incentives into an imperative, as the protectionist bargain of "iron and rye" limited the possibilities for domestic expansion. Agricultural protection raised wage costs and kept workers in the countryside (Gerschenkron 1966: 45). And the cartels that formed behind industrial tariff walls constrained competition and inflated prices (Gerschenkron 1966: 45; Trebilcock 1981: 71–72). Given the lack of sales markets and productive outlets at home, international trade came to be seen as indispensable for Germany's industrial development (Kemp 1985: 108; Braun 1990: 58, 66; Abelshauser 2001: 511).

Accompanied by a government-led export offensive that undercut the infant industries of its European neighbors (Trebilcock 1981: 73), Germany after 1900 emerged as the premier provider of a range of capital goods—machinery, transport equipment, and chemicals—that fueled the "second industrial revolution" across continental Europe and elsewhere (Lindlar and Holtfrerich 1997: 221). Between 1880 and 1913, Germany surpassed France and Britain to gain second place among the leading exporters, behind the United States (Stolper 1940: 52). On the eve of the First World War, its manufacturers held a world market share of 13 percent—a position that its product portfolio allowed it to quickly recover and maintain after 1945 (Braun 1990: 22, 238).

According to Volker Berghahn (2006: 34–35), this developmental path reached its economic extremes in the runup to the Second World War, when the totalitarian vision of a state-directed, cartelized, authoritarian, and autarkic world region was being rolled out over the German-occupied parts of Western and Eastern Europe. Seen as the radicalization of the corporatist, patriarchal, centralized, and nonliberal industrial order of the late nineteenth century, this *Großraumwirtschaft* (greater economic area) differed paradigmatically from the free enterprise and free trading, multilateral, and global system envisioned by the United States in the Atlantic Charter.

The degree to which the original elements of this German model of capitalism have been retained or withered away under the pressures and incentives of postwar Americanization is subject to a continuing debate, overshadowed only by the concomitant controversy over how sustainable this model will prove in an era of neoliberal globalization.[5] Taking the cue from Berghahn, the most productive vista is to see the German model as a unique combination of indigenous elements that can be traced back to the political unification and economic transformation of the *Kaiserzeit* (imperial era) and to elements that disseminated from the American reformation of capitalism after 1945.

This brief history suggests that the development of the German political economy has been driven to an exceptional degree by worldwide over domestic demand, especially for the capital goods needed to launch and sustain capitalist industrialization elsewhere. In this way, Germany stood at one remove and yet benefitted from the internationalization of Fordism under American hegemony. Mediated through its exports, it could partake in the golden age of capitalist growth without absorbing Fordist principles wholesale. In addition to producing standardized goods in large volumes, companies from the German *Mittelstand* and the southern provinces in particular retained and deepened aspects of "diversified quality production" (Streeck 1991; Herrigel 1996; Abelshauser 2005: 30–34; Beck 2015: 219 fn. 152, 220; Fratzscher 2018: 41). By focusing on specialized, custom-made, and income-elastic goods, German exporters were able to corner specific segments of the world market and avoid price competition in the first two postwar decades (Delhaes-Guenther 2003: 47–51; Beck 2015: 223).

Stefan Beck (2015: 230–231, fn. 166) suggests that a portion of the higher profits realized abroad were used as side payments to incentivize and remunerate skilled labor in the export industry. The Fordist cycle of mutually reinforcing mass production and mass consumption, therefore, was only partially realized. In important respects, it looped through the world market. Its postwar expansion, more than internal demand spurred by higher wages, generated the corporate profits and productivity-enhancing investments that rebuilt the German economy (Hirsch 1995: 112–113; Beck 2015: 161, citing Eicker-Wolf 2003: 80; Shonfield 1965: 288; Dickhaus 1996). Organized labor was rewarded only after and as long as this export offensive yielded success. Wherever German manufacturers faced low-cost competitors, wage restraint was demanded (Beck 2015: 223). That it could generally be expected owed in part to the decimation and decapitation of the working-class movement under German fascism. Their weak political position was aggravated in the economic sphere by the slow decline of unemployment due to a constant influx of workers from the Eastern parts of the former German Reich (Beck 2015: 166–167). And indeed, wages did not keep up with productivity gains until the late 1960s.

A far less favorable legacy of fascism for business was the delegitimization of the patriarchal and authoritarian forms of labor control that had characterized many German companies.[6] Instead, the embedded liberal compromise made in Germany incorporated the working class on different terms, partly inherited from the past (Rhenisch 1999: 70, Cesaratto and Stirati 2010: 73, Becker 2015: 240), and partly mediated by Marshall planners, Christian reformers, and a small circle of progressive managers (Booth, Melling, and Dartmann 1997; Fear 2006). The fierce confrontation between corporate owners and organized labor over the commanding heights of the German economy was channeled into "codetermination" legislation. Far-reaching demands by trade unionists and socialists for economic democracy were traded in for a seat at the table: parity representation on the supervisory boards of companies, in coal and steel since 1951, and, after 1976, for all companies with more than two thousand employees.

Recognized as a stakeholder in the performance and governance of the firm, and enlisted in a common export drive that provided stable employment and (non)wage compensation, organized labor was included in an enduring, if more recently eroding, system of macroeconomic coordination and crisis management (Esser 1982; Urban 2012; Solty 2016: 39–40). Since the late nineteenth century this system had involved a small number of universal banks and large industrial firms that held shares and took an interest in one another's business. It also extended to state agencies, research institutes, and other nongovernmental organizations that had long been concerned with promoting and mobilizing Germany's industrial power for a range of geopolitical and geoeconomic purposes (for example, Berghahn 1996; Gross 2015).

The world market orientation of the German political economy is therefore rightly considered a constant running through its entire late capitalist development (Abelshauser 2016: 483). But as this world market expanded and contracted across a dynamic interstate system, the problems it posed and the solutions it offered changed continuously. Hotly debated and contested in German society, many different answers were given to the questions thrown up by each turning point: how to compete in the commercial and military rivalry with Britain, how to break out of the political and economic isolation after the First World War, how to carve out a protected sphere in response to the Great Depression, how to violently overturn the liberal world order, and finally, how to prepare for a postwar order dominated by the US once the desired *Endsieg* had moved positively out of reach.

The Social Market Economy and the Irrelevance of Ordoliberalism

Regarding the question most important for our purposes, that of preparing for a new postwar order, one increasingly popular view is to see Germany's postwar capitalism as rebuilt around an ordoliberal paradigm. Ordoliberalism prescribes a carefully delineated role for the state in the construction of a competitive market order with stringent rules, clear price signals, and full liability for its participants (James 2017: 26–27; see Chapter 1). Its advocates, trained at or affiliated with Freiburg University, defined themselves in opposition to the planned economies of Hitler

Germany, Stalinist Russia, and—after 1945—the Keynesian persuasion. Said to be involved in postwar planning circles, and closely connected to Ludwig Erhard and his economics ministry, ordoliberals are considered by supporters and critics alike as having injected free market principles into the postwar constitution of the German economy (Ptak 2004).

The notion of a homegrown "neoliberalism"—serving as an antidote to the Keynesian turn in other advanced capitalist countries—seems to offer a tempting shortcut. Its promise is that we can understand the character and contradictions of Germany's European policy today without having to work our way through its postwar history. In this view, ordoliberalism serves "as the ideational source of Germany's crisis politics" (Hien and Joerges 2018: i; Art 2015: 187). And yet, the effort to connect the present to a supposedly ordoliberal past is deeply flawed in several respects.

A closer look at the intellectual origins of ordoliberalism raises serious questions about the liberal commitments of its Freiburg founders. Philip Manow (2001b) has built a compelling argument that the works of some of the most prominent ordoliberal thinkers were inspired by a protestant inflection of the wider conservative reaction against Weimar democracy. The vision of social reform that guided ordoliberal thinkers was based on a skeptical view of human nature as sinful and in need of moral correction. A market economy of small-scale farmers and artisans, supervised by the strong moral authority of the state, was conceived as a counter-project to a "massified" industrial society. According to this vision, the forces of supply and demand were to be left alone not in order to guarantee the efficient allocation of resources but in order to reward the disciplined and keep the weak-minded in check (Manow 2001b: 192).

More important still than the antiliberal sentiments and protofascist exonerations of the state that shine through in works of some of the most prominent ordoliberals in the 1920s and 1930s is the profound adaptation that their economic ideas had to undergo in order to fit in with the exigencies of Germany's postwar reconstruction. Rebuilding capitalism required a compromise between the market organization envisioned by ordoliberals and the social protection that had been afforded by the nationalist welfare state established by Bismarck and extended during the Weimar Republic (Hien 2013: 350; Blyth 2013a: 113). The welfare state and redistributive designs by Alfred Müller-Armack clearly broke with ordoliberal orthodoxy, and his hopes that the interventionist and stabilizing measures taken to establish the "social market economy" would be temporary remained illusory (Berghahn and Young 2013: 772). But the ordoliberal vision remained unfulfilled in other important respects as well. The ideal of a competitive system of private property dispersed among a large number of small and medium-sized producers was utopian. It ran counter to Germany's highly concentrated and centralized ownership structure, and far exceeded the oligopolistic competition that American postwar planners had in mind (Berghahn 2010a: 5–6; Berghahn and Young 2013: 771). Even the less ambitious plans for the German state to check dangerous concentrations of market power, proposed by Walter Eucken and Franz Böhm, failed to translate into legislation; they were long delayed and significantly watered down by the opposition of organized capital (Nicholls 1994: 335–336; Neebe 2004: 327). Last, the principle of codetermination, while forming the cornerstone of German corporatism, amounted to a conspiracy against the market that ordoliberals would clearly have rejected (Nicholls 1994: 338–339).

In sum, for a new market economy to succeed, it needed to be rendered *social* in ways that significantly deviated from ordoliberal prescriptions. This German model, to be sure, would differ in crucial respects from many of its Western partners. But the aversion to Keynesian interventionism and the empowerment of organized labor as the key driver of demand reached far beyond ordoliberal circles. It encompassed wide sections of Germany's conservative and liberal elites, who feared a far-reaching socialization of German industry advocated by socialists and initially supported by the occupying powers.

Most important, there is very little in ordoliberal writings that would prescribe the specific world market solution which German policymakers came to favor instead. Ordoliberals like Eucken rejected a manipulation of the external value of money (Biebricher and Vogelmann 2017: 6). But German macroeconomic policy sought to sustain an undervalued DM until the collapse of Bretton Woods in 1973. Ordoliberals like Wilhelm Röpke looked back to the gold standard as the equilibrator of trade and investment flows (Biebricher and Vogelmann 2017: 6). But German state elites elevated to a strategic priority the balance-of-payments surpluses the German economy would regularly post (Herr and Voy 1990: 53–54). Ordoliberals are said to have "welcomed free trade as an additional source of competitive pressures for domestic producers" (Wolf 1995: 329). But Erhard's economics ministry explicitly sanctioned export cartels, precisely in order to avoid "ruinous price competition,"[7] and argued that export promotion by the state was unavoidable given that "the international order of exchange rates and price relations is disturbed" (quoted in Abelshauser 2016: 513).

The German emphasis on stable prices, balanced budgets, and monetary restraint—rather than ordoliberally inspired—has to be seen in this international context. From the early 1950s onward, the German state, led by Erhard's economics ministry and the Bank deutscher Länder (BdL, Bank of German States) headed by Wilhelm Vocke, embarked on a form of "monetary mercantilism" (Holtfrerich 1999; 2008) that substituted for protectionism in an age when Germany stood to benefit from worldwide liberalization. The central idea was that restrictive monetary and fiscal measures would keep price and wage levels below those of Germany's major competitors. With exchange rates among national currencies being fixed under Bretton Woods, and with the convertibility of currencies and movement of capital still restricted, these lower levels of inflation allowed German exports to be more competitively priced or to reap super profits (Holtfrerich 2008: 35; Cesaratto and Stirati 2010: 69; Wadbrook 1972: 61–63). As Erhard explained to Vocke on 2 August 1950: "A great opportunity for the future of German exports has arisen out of the current situation. If, namely, through internal discipline we are able to maintain the price level to a greater extent than other countries, our exports' strength will increase in the long run and our currency will become stronger and more healthy, both internally and with respect to the dollar" (Holtfrerich 1999: 345; quoted in Cesaratto and Stireti 2010: 72). Vocke agreed that "to strengthen exports, things need to be kept tight inside" (quoted in Dickhaus 1996: 70). But as one of the Reichsbank's deflationists[8] under the Brüning government, which had "sought to overcome the world economic depression by strict household consolidation and mandated wage and price reductions" (Young 2017: 232), Vocke took the austere view that "full employment equals full inflation" (quoted in Dickhaus 1996: 72, fn. 96). Erhard, by contrast, had come to realize that "Germany's return to the world market"—as he titled a coauthored book published in 1953 in parts in the left-liberal weekly *Die Zeit*—could offer a distinctly non-Keynesian route toward welfare capitalism (Cesaratto and Stirati 2010: 73).

As anticipated by Erhard in a secret working paper written in 1943–1944,[9] the currency reform of 1948 had wiped out the enormous public and private debt of the Nazi era, sparing property owners and employers at the expense of workers and savers. It also decontrolled most consumer goods, which brought them back to stores but also hiked prices. But with trade unions ready "to accept a 15 per cent increase in wages despite a 25 per cent rise in prices" (Tipton 2003: 513), a basic dynamic was created in which labor discipline and wage moderation boosted German exports and generated profits that would drive investment at home and, as long as this outward expansion continued, deliver full employment and other material benefits without the need for state intervention. It is in this sense that foreign trade was championed by Erhard as "the very core and even precondition of our economic and social order" (Cesaratto and Stirati 2010: 73). And it is for this end that German fiscal and monetary policy was to be used.

By itself, a politics of deflation, as advocated by many national economists within and outside the Freiburg School (Ptak 2004: 142), could never have been successful. While Erhard "never considered himself an exponent of the Freiburg School or as the executor of their ideas" (Wigger 2017: 168; Wünsche 2015), his 1944 memorandum, too, had remained moot on the question of how the majority of the population could be made to carry this burden (Brackmann 1993: 164). And yet in contrast to those who stuck to their austerity position, expressed in the ill-fated mantra *Mut zur Armut* (Yes to poverty) (Roth 1999b: 521), Erhard came to see a global export offensive as the vital complement to a social market economy that realized *Wohlstand für Alle* (Prosperity for all) at home (Neebe 2004: 17–18; Abelshauser 2016: 508; Wigger 2017: 168).

Integration into a rapidly expanding world economy—reconstructed and superintended by the American hegemon—provided the missing link between the rigid internal consolidation that favored capitalist property owners and employers, and popular demands for far-reaching reforms or at least a significant rise in material living standards (for example, Brackmann 1993: 285). It could provide the source for what Erhard considered "a wealth that all create and share in," and which he saw as "the only possibility to avoid social tensions and to paralyze the always and everywhere latent and virulent class struggle" (Erhard, paraphrased in Wünsche 2015: 74).

Rethinking the German *Handelsstaat*

American hegemony presided over a period of rapid catch-up development in which the capitalist states of Western Europe and Japan were enabled and encouraged to adopt production techniques, consumption habits, and organizational models pioneered in the United States in the 1930s. This process of "Americanization," and the massive postwar expansion it unleashed, propelled the advanced industrialized states toward structurally similar "high points" in their late developmental trajectories. But, as our focus on the German social market economy has established, they continued to differ in terms of how the class compromise of embedded liberalism was institutionalized. Moreover, even though the sources of interimperialist rivalry were abolished, the grounds of contestation shifted toward a new policy terrain: the problem of how to manage global capitalism and sustain social peace as the distance between the US and its follower economies narrowed and the postwar boom came to a close.

American plans for a global and national reorganization of capitalism, premised upon a regime of rising productivity and redistribution, coincided with German plans for a social market economy and an open trading system as the most promising road to prosperity, power, and prestige. Where other countries resorted to Keynesian-style intervention and protectionism, Germany's postwar settlement with organized labor was most directly sustained by seizing upon the export opportunities provided by the US-centered liberal world economy (Rhenisch 1999: 70; Cesaratto and Stirati 2010: 73).

Comparatively speaking, then, the reintegration of America's erstwhile rival proved to be fraught with fewer tensions than the parallel plans to dismantle the colonial empires of its former allies. Opening up the colonial dependencies pitted American policymakers against British and French attempts to preserve these preferential monetary and trading zones, and the unraveling of the British Empire proved to be particularly cumbersome, posing perhaps as much of a challenge to America's global designs as Soviet "expansionism" (Smith 2004: 379). Whereas Britain and France only hesitatingly surrendered to American designs, West German economic planners came to see the liberal multilateralism championed by the United States as the road to political rehabilitation and economic reintegration (Neebe 1996: 99). An open global trading system offered the best possible chance of gaining access to technology, investment, and raw materials, and of regaining a foothold in markets that had been lost during the war.

These economic interests were coupled with the strongly felt political imperative of submitting to the American military and political leadership of the West. Its proximity to the Soviet sphere of influence and the exposed position of its former capital made West Germany depend on the American military apparatus and the continued presence of its forces in Berlin, Germany, and Europe (Zimmermann 2002: 228). This military dependence gave the US considerable political leverage. West German policymakers were clearly aware that they had to avoid open confrontation with the

United States at any cost. And US officials learned to use the tacit threat of a withdrawal of US troops to exact important political and economic concessions—most explicitly through a series of "offset negotiations" that linked America's commitment of troops to German financial and monetary support (Zimmermann 2002; Gavin 2004).[10] These alliance pressures ought not to be overstated, however. The image of Germany as America's "obedient ally" neglects that this geopolitical vulnerability worked in both directions. Precisely because it made West Germany so dependent on the military and political leadership of the United States, it compelled policymakers to strive toward a greater degree of flexibility and autonomy: through a closer military alliance with Gaullist France considered under Adenauer, and a far-reaching new Eastern Policy (*Ostpolitik*) advanced under Brand (Granieri 2004; Geiger 2008; Lippert 2011).[11] There is little doubt that the particular mode of integration of Germany into the liberal international economic order and the subordination to American politico-military leadership had profound and lasting consequences. It removed once and for all the material basis of what were now ideologically discredited autarky or *Großraum* conceptions, and diminished the influence of the archconservative, illiberal, antidemocratic, and authoritarian forces that had supported them. The most reactionary remnants of the nobility and political elites inside and outside of the West German government were now left to cultivate their distaste for American materialism and liberal democracy in the cultural and spiritual sphere rather than the political and economic sphere (Conze 2005a). The Europe that they continued to imagine as a Christian *Abendland* (Occident) free from both Eastern barbarism and Western decadence had little to do with the political and economic union that was actually being constructed.[12]

And yet however irreversible, Germany's "long road to the West" (Winkler 2000) ought not to be mistaken for the total transcendence of power politics and the complete congruence of American and German interests. In this respect, the binary distinction between a cooperative "trading" and conflictive "territorial" state developed by Richard Rosecrance (1986) and adopted by scholars such as Hans-Peter Schwarz (1994: 130–132), Michael Staack (2000), and Richard Neebe (2004)[13] is bound to fail as a guide to Germany's foreign economic policy. In their writings, West Germany's turn toward liberal multilateralism after 1945 constitutes a paradigmatic shift away from the obsolete categories of nation-state and territorial power and toward accepting the economic rationality of an effective, functional, and

unimpeded worldwide division of labor. Britain, it is said, had already accomplished this transition with the repeal of the Corn Laws in 1846 and
the shift to an "imperialism of free trade" (Gallagher and Robinson 1953).
By contrast, the ideological and military mobilization of German society,
which in the early twentieth century sought twice to win territorial control
over the European continent, is said to indicate that Germany had not yet
accepted global markets as the arbiter of policy choices. German political
and economic elites, in this view, remained caught in the territorial logic of
"the military-political world" of the preindustrial era that measured success in
terms of the size of territory, military might, and population and that strove
for closed empire and largest possible degree of autarky. According to this
account, it is only after 1945 that German policymakers caught up with the
realities of global interconnectedness, embraced their status as a "trading
state," and henceforth identified their national interests with an open world
market and peaceful international cooperation (Neebe 2004: 33–34).

The problem with this reading is that it presents the German choice in
favor of multilateral trade as the only economically rational one. What is
lost here is the specificity of what was being constructed and consented to.
The postwar order of "embedded liberalism," after all, deviated in important
respects from the ideal of the unimpeded reign of market forces that had
prevailed in the mid-nineteenth century. Because the new order redrew the
balance between states and markets, and national and global regulation,
the German commitment to it involved more than a mere subordination
of foreign (economic) policy to global economic interdependence.

The flip side of this line of argument, moreover, is that any policy option or opinion that diverges from liberal multilateralism is ascribed to an
antiquated, territorial mode of thought. This residual category presents as
a Manichean choice what ought to be seen as a spectrum of possibilities of
how political power can be exercised within a globalizing capitalism. In fact,
the famous contribution by John Gallagher and Ronald Robinson (1953) on
which this dualism is based recognized the subtle continuities, as opposed
to the stark contrast, between formal imperial rule and an informal empire
of free trade. Between these two poles lie numerous forms of political and
economic organization and influence that need to be investigated. Indeed,
this framework has been fruitfully applied to the debate among Germany's
elites over its place in Europe between the two world wars (Berghahn 1996:
3–5; Gross 2015). The same needs to be done for the postwar period, and
indeed for the role of Germany in contemporary Europe.

To equate skepticism and opposition vis-à-vis the liberal multilateral world established by the US with an inherited and hopelessly anachronistic way of thinking is to fundamentally underestimate the contingency of the situation and the range of options. In short, there may have been reasons why Germany's political and economic elites were concerned about the type of incorporation envisioned by US planners that had little to do with being trapped in an outdated mindset. That some German strategists envisioned the postwar economy in terms of regional blocs, for instance, does not seem particularly backward-looking if one takes into account the bifurcation of the world economy by the Cold War, the uncertain prospects of America's drive toward world market integration, and the still undecided fate of the British Empire.

The issue therefore is not simply that some of Germany's postfascist elites had to be compelled to accept an economically and politically liberal capitalism. The point is rather that even those state officials and business representatives who came to look favorably upon the ambitious American vision of an integrated world market raised questions as to the likely success, the appropriate pace and scope, and the optimal means of liberalization. How effective and durable would American globalism be? Could US demands that Germany act as a trailblazer of economic liberalism backfire? And wasn't German industrial prowess best brought to bear in direct bilateral bargaining rather than in large and unwieldy multilateral negotiations (compare Berghahn 1986; Bührer 1990: 149–150, 154; Erker 1999: 14, 16; Grunenberg 2008: 159)?

Erhard's idea to build a social market economy on genuinely open global free trade thus met with considerable skepticism on political and economic grounds. For his plans to succeed, Erhard insisted that Germany had to become the "workshop of the world" rather than simply the engine of European reconstruction, as its allies had had in mind (Abelshauser 2016: 508). Most business elites agreed with his stance that the European Economic Community (EEC)—favored by Adenauer to deepen Franco-German cooperation—constituted a dangerous diversion from the global orientations of German capital (Neebe 1996: 121; Milward 1986: 239).[14] At the same time, however, they also attacked Erhard's plans to decartelize the domestic economy (Grunenberg 2008: 159). In contrast to Erhard, Müller-Armack, section chief of the economics ministry's policy department and cofounder of the social market economy, conceded that integration into a liberal international system "despite all orientation towards global organizations, needs after all the initiative of a close European circle" (quoted in Warneke 2013: 186; Rhenisch 1999: 85).[15] And last, the Foreign Office offered an intriguing economic rationale against the wider European free trade area that Erhard supported:

> The federal minster of economics is of the belief that the integration of the free world will proceed in the form of an ever further liberalization of the movement of goods, services and capital, a reduction of tariffs and other protectionist barriers, i.e. corresponding to the OEEC. If one thinks this way one has indeed to see in the integration of the Six "an island of dis-integration in a by now more open world." In that case, Germany would indeed be impeded in its freedom of movement and threatened in its vitally important linkages to the other world powers by the burdensome marriage with a protectionist France. The Foreign Office does not entirely share the federal economic minister's *economic plan for conquering the world* because such a vehement and extensive thrust into free space has to encounter its limits at one point, be it an economic crisis or another shock. Then only that which is politically organized will endure, namely the Community of the Six or, after the accession of Britain, that of the Seven, or else German economic expansion will fall back onto itself" (the memo, dated 4 October 1956, is quoted in Neebe 2004: 301–302).

Pace Reinhard Neebe, who reads this passage as proof that some of Germany's foreign economic planners continued to think in outdated territorial terms, I find little in this excerpt that is particularly archaic. Fast forward to today, or even just a decade and a half, and the concerns that economic growth might not continue indefinitely, that liberal multilateralism could come up for revision, and that a politically integrated European core would prove to the best possible guarantee against national retreat seem surprisingly prescient.

But even where the outlook of German elites coincided with American globalism, the convergence emerged at least in part out of potentially conflicting motivations (Neebe 1990: 166). While the United States wanted to firmly anchor Germany within Western Europe and the transatlantic alliance in order to foreclose an independent path of economic development and political sovereignty, German policymakers and business elites sought above all to reestablish the global economic position that Germany had enjoyed before the two world wars. Under the slogan of an open global trade policy,

Erhard's ministry reached for markets far beyond the North Atlantic and across the emerging Cold War divide (Abelshauser 2016: 508; Bernardini 2018). Given Germany's long-run specialization in customized machine construction and plant engineering, the economics ministry concentrated on countries that seemed at the cusp of a "new epoch" of industrialization and thus in need of German capital goods (Abelshauser 2016: 508–509).

The postwar economic offensive of German business also *exceeded* the transatlantic area—and transatlanticism—in important respects. It comprised German ventures into Latin America, which seemed to offer markets that could easily be penetrated by German exports due to the disinterest of the US and the lower quality of British products (Neebe 1991: 22). It also involved plans of a number of influential German industrialists for a joint Franco-German advance into a newly decolonizing world (Rhenisch 1999: 79–80).[16] And it involved, most critically, sustained efforts on the part of German industry to revive its traditional markets in the European east and southeast (Spaulding 1996; Rudolph 2004)—seen as "a fallback should the Western world economy for some reason not function as predicted or lapse into another 1930s-style crisis" (Berghahn 1996: 27). Thus some of the most internationalized segments of German capital and parts of the German state found themselves in opposition to the United States, which sought "to instrumentalize foreign trade for the purpose of waging economic warfare against the Soviet Union and its satellites" (Neebe 1996: 121).

From the late 1940s onward, the United States sought not only to rebuild global capitalism but also to confront an explicitly anticapitalist model of social organization and development (Neebe 1996). This meant that "the liberal world economic order could at best be semiglobal" (Stokes 1988: 625). It introduced geopolitical considerations that collided with, and often superseded, the economic case for the largest and freest possible flow of trade and investment (Smith 2005: 96)—an important precedent for the conflict of interests the German state confronts in the escalating US trade war against China today.

To ameliorate these tensions, German policymakers sought to dissociate their global economic interests from their foreign policy commitments to the Western alliance (Rudolph 2004: 34; Neebe 2004: 509). Germany's avowal of global free trade and liberal multilateralism has to be seen in this context. It was meant to isolate its foreign economic relations from the intrusion of alliance politics and the painful concessions that this might entail. Rather than indicating a paradigmatic shift from world politics to world economy, this depoliticization of international economic relations is best understood as a pragmatic and self-interested move. Our analysis of German foreign economic policy ought to look behind this "divorce of convenience," rather than reify it by casting Germany as a thoroughly integrated and unconditionally cooperative *Handelsstaat*, categorically outside the world of power politics.

Conclusion

This chapter has traced the long-term development of the German political economy across two episodes of capitalist globalization with dynamics of cooperation and conflict that were fundamentally different. Free trade in the Victorian era was made possible by the developmental differences between the British pioneer and capitalist latecomers such as Germany. Its belated but accelerated industrialization destroyed this harmonious international division of labor, and its attempts to pacify the working class gave rise to geopolitical tensions that escalated into global war. Out of this chaos and destruction, a new and uniquely consensual world order was constructed around Fordist mass production, Keynesian macroeconomics, and welfare state intervention. This relative equalization of developmental patterns within the capitalist core uprooted the sources of interimperial rivalries. Once we realize this singular accomplishment of American postwar hegemony, the crisis decade of the 1970s emerges in an entirely different light. The concern of the United States and its European and Japanese allies was not to hasten, manage, or reverse yet another cycle of hegemonic decline but to shape the future direction of an era of global capitalism that seemed to have reached its limits.

Germany's version of the embedded liberal compromise modified the template provided by the American hegemon in some notable respects. It was driven by global rather than simply domestic demand, based on diversified quality production in addition to Fordist economies of scale, and dependent on price stability rather than economic stimulus. Built on Germany's long-standing world market orientation rather than ordoliberal prescriptions, this social market economy elevated trade surpluses to a strategic priority and enlisted organized labor in a sustained export offensive that required and—when and where successful—also materially rewarded work discipline and wage restraint.

The fact that Germany's governing elites—led by Erhard and his ministry—embraced the globalizing designs of the US does not mean that

Germany had become a pliant cold war ally or a docile trading state. To view Germany's commitment to the embedded liberal world economy as the *complete* separation of economic rationality from *any* (geo)political considerations makes us blind to the new ways in which German statecraft would be brought to bear once this order began to crumble in the 1960s and 1970s. Unless we zoom in on these policy disputes and strategic questions, we miss out on the deeper continuities and changes that connect that crisis episode to today, and confront what falsely appears to be a complete *volte face* in the exercise of German power in contemporary Europe (for example, Maull 2013).

CHAPTER 4

Unwinding Bretton Woods
The Deutsche Mark Float and the Renewal of Stability Politics

THIS CHAPTER ASKS how German policy elites responded to the monetary turbulences that signaled the end of the golden age of capitalism from the mid-1960s onward. To address this question, the chapter challenges the popular view that the United States unilaterally and deliberately brought down Bretton Woods—the monetary system put in place in 1944 to help Western states rebuild their economies around embedded liberal welfare compacts between capital and labor. By contrast, the chapter argues that the demise of Bretton Woods was driven by allied attempts to revise its terms in order to address the United States's privileged but increasingly problematic position within it. While France had pushed the world toward a *de facto* dollar standard three years before the so-called "Nixon Shock" of 1971, the German decisions to float the DM unilaterally in October 1969 and May 1971, and together with other European currencies in March 1973, upended the regime of fixed exchange rates and removed another central pillar of the embedded liberal world order.[1]

The takeaway from this chapter is that the transition from embedded toward neoliberal capitalism was not simply the product of US statecraft but is best understood as an interactive process. Its more specific task is therefore to explain how and why German policymakers moved toward a floating "nonsystem" that introduced the volatile exchange rates and exacerbated the erratic capital movements that states had to contend with in that crisis decade. The chapter argues that neither pressure from the United States nor the influence of neoliberal ideas or interests drove this shift. Instead, the decision to float an undervalued DM sought to curtail the external sources of inflation and enable the central bank to attend to its internal sources: a wage-price spiral that the bank thought could be broken by visibly limiting the money supply. In marked contrast to its European and American partners, whose currencies weakened under the floating "nonsystem" and who moved toward monetarism much later, unwinding Bretton Woods and doubling down on price stability did not undermine but sustained the embedded liberal compromise in Germany—insofar, and as long as, their markets would remain open to its export-led model.

The Embedded Liberal Order of Bretton Woods

The monetary system of Bretton Woods was at the center of attempts to ensure the external compatibility and internal stability of the newly reconstructed capitalist economies after the catastrophic collapse of the world economy in the 1930s. To prevent competitive devaluations and create stable conditions for multilateral trade, US and British postwar planners chose a regime of fixed exchange rates centered on the dollar and anchored in gold. At the same time, the new system would depart in important respects from the principles of the classical gold standard, which had required that any debt that one country owed to another was to be settled through a transfer of gold.[2] Because national currencies had to be exchangeable for gold, an outflow of the auric metal would reduce the money supply and induce a contraction of the economy. The Bretton Woods arrangement sought to shield national economies from these painful adjustments. To relieve deficit countries of the pressure of having to deflate prices and wages in order to restore balance-of-payments equilibrium, a new international organization—the International Monetary Fund (IMF)—was created that could provide short-term financial assistance and permit parity changes under conditions of "fundamental disequilibrium" (Quote from IMF 2020, sched. C, par. 6; see also Obstfeld and Taylor 2004: 37–38; Eichengreen 2008: 91–92, 95). Moreover, the Bretton Woods arrangement also imposed restrictions on the international flows of capital that were feared to circumscribe macroeconomic authority, destabilize exchange-rate parities, and upset liberal trading patterns (Helleiner 1994: 5, 33–35; Eichengreen 2008: 3, 92–93; Frieden 2006).[3]

By softening the rigidities of the classical gold standard within a stable and rule-based exchange-rate regime, the Bretton Woods system sought to free governments from the imperative of achieving *external* at the expense of *internal* stability. The aim, in short, was to synchronize global and national forms of capitalist regulation, which had previously worked at cross purposes. According to Ruggie (1982: 393), this balance was "the essence of the embedded liberalism compromise: unlike the economic nationalism of the thirties, it would be multilateral in character; unlike the liberalism of the gold standard and free trade, its multilateralism would be predicated upon domestic interventionism."[4]

Crucially, the independent policy space thus created was to be used for a specific social purpose: the construction of an internationally compatible *and* socially legitimate form of capitalism that could reconcile private ownership with widespread demands for social protection (Schmelzer 2010: 41–42). It is in this sense that the embedded liberal order of Bretton Woods came to be based on the internationally mediated organization of a series of social compacts between capital and labor, broadly along the lines of the New Deal and Fordism (Keohane 1984b: 19; Ruggie 1991: 203; Streeck 2011: 10).

Launched on the basis of an enormous productivity gap that separated the United States from the war-torn economies of Western Europe and Japan, the long boom involved a process of catch-up development that undermined the stability of Bretton Woods. As Germany and Japan launched their economic miracles as the world's major exporters, they accumulated ever more dollars, the value of which, though nominally tied to gold at $35 an ounce, came increasingly into question. One problem was that by 1960, the amount of dollars held abroad had outstripped the gold reserves of the United States (Eichengreen 2011: 49–50). The other problem was that the diminishing lead of the United States opened its macroeconomic policies to the scrutiny of foreign dollar holders. Unwilling to raise interest rates and cut spending in order to restore confidence, the US compared less favorably to countries such as Germany that posted balance-of-payments surpluses, exercised greater monetary and fiscal constraint, and offered a higher return on investment. Despite the use of foreign exchange controls under Bretton Woods, the dollar's exchange rate to hard currencies such as the DM came under enormous pressure as the relative economic weight of Western Europe and Japan increased. There was little doubt from the early 1960s onward that the current system of exchange rates fixed around a dollar-gold standard was in need of fundamental reform. And yet a devaluation of the dollar would uproot the golden anchor of the system. A revaluation of other major currencies was politically contested. And domestic deflation seemed out of reach as the Johnson administration embarked on deficit spending to finance its promise of a "Great Society" while waging war in Vietnam.

Closing the Gold Window

The conventional view holds that the collapse of Bretton Woods was the product of American unilateralism (Gowa 1984). Originally seen as a sign of decline (Hudson 1972; Calleo 1982), the decisions to delink the dollar from gold in 1971—the infamous Nixon Shock—and to shift toward a floating "nonsystem" in 1973 have come to be seen by some as the first step in a successful bid to renew US hegemony.[5] By disembedding the postwar economic order and liberating global markets, the United States is said to have restored its economic competitiveness and political dominance over its main allies and prospective rivals (Arrighi 1994; Helleiner 1994: 21, 202; Gowan 1999; Spiro 1999; Sobel 2012: 185).[6]

Against this reading, it should be noted that throughout the 1960s, the monetary strategy of the US was essentially *conservative*. Using the whole arsenal of statecraft, the United States sought to preserve rather than transform a system with cracks that were becoming increasingly apparent (Zimmermann 2002; Matusow 2003: 769; Gavin 2004). Its efforts were focused on trying to slow down the outflow of gold and improve its balance of payments. In doing so, the United States sought to avoid a deflation of its domestic economy that it could not afford. And it sought to avoid more far-reaching monetary reforms that it might not be able to control.

The incentive for change, by contrast, rested principally with the Europeans. While the US tried to prop up a failing system for most of the 1960s, France in particular emerged as its principal adversary. *Dollar seigniorage*—the ability to issue a national currency that foreigners had little choice but to accumulate—afforded what Charles de Gaulle and his finance minister Giscard d'Estaing called "exorbitant privileges" to the US while undermining the international monetary system. In response, France launched a series of rhetorical attacks on the dollar-gold standard, backed by systematic conversions of dollars into gold. Indeed, evidence from the German archives suggests that France was responsible for the collapse of the London Gold Pool—the *de facto* end of the dollar-gold standard three years before Nixon notoriously ended it. Created by the United States and European central banks in 1961, the gold pool had sought to defend the official rate of $35 per ounce of gold in the private market. Not only did France withdraw from the pool in June 1967, in secret, it also placed large demands for gold that forced British authorities to suspend gold pool interventions in March 1968.[7] Henceforth, the US restricted dollar to gold convertibility to official transactions among central banks. Because monetary officials understood that the United States would renounce even this limited guarantee when confronted with substantial demands for gold, the gold window had effectively been shut.

The aggressive gold conversion policies of de Gaulle are, of course, a staple of hegemonic stability theory, and the argument that France brought down the dollar-gold standard seems to fit well with its description as the classical case of a "spoiler." Too weak to offer a monetary alternative, yet too strong to be a passive regime-taker, France is said to have squeezed the United States for side payments until the monetary system of Bretton Woods collapsed (Kindleberger 1976: 21–22; Kirshner 1997: 192–203). Yet what is missing in this abstract designation of France is the crucial distinction between the aim and (unintended) outcome of policy action. In reality, France was no more the system's spoiler than the US was its hegemon in decline.[8] The notion of France as the antagonist of an ailing hegemon neglects the prospect that the ultimate objective of French actions was to *reform* the world monetary system rather than hold it to ransom. Drawing on a long-standing series of reform proposals developed since the 1920s, France sought to create a more symmetrical monetary arrangement under which no single national currency would enjoy the privileges of *seigniorage* (Bordo, Simard, and White 1994: 11). That these plans never came to fruition, and that the pressure France applied backfired,[9] does not change the fact that it sought to revise the terms rather than destroy the foundations of Bretton Woods.

The corresponding view that Germany was an "obedient ally" in monetary matters because it depended on the United States for its security is equally unhelpful (Strange 1980: 46; Eichengreen 2011: 71; Lippert 2011: 4; Mastanduno 2009: 132). It is certainly true that the German state provided the critical support that allowed the United States to put off monetary reform despite France's attacks on the dollar-gold link. Beginning in 1961, German officials agreed to buy US military material and Treasury bonds in exchange for security guarantees (Zimmermann 2002: 242). The official theme of these "offset negotiations" was to help cover the costs of stationing US troops in Germany, but the real motif of the American counterparts was to earn back dollars and reduce their balance-of-payments deficit. German collaboration with the US in maintaining the Bretton Woods system culminated in March 1967, when central bank president Karl Blessing pledged in a note to the Americans that the Bundesbank would refrain from converting its dollar holdings into gold.[10] With the highly controversial nonconversion commitment, the Bundesbank is said to have acquired a major stake in the defense of the dollar and its golden linchpin: any devaluation or delinking of the dollar from gold would lead to an effective loss of German reserves (Zimmermann 2002: 226).

Rather than assume an identity of interests, however, we need to ask in what ways German monetary policy converged with American preferences for different reasons. Oriented toward the world market, Germany's macroeconomic policy sought above all to shore up the international competitiveness of German exports. To do this, the German central bank bought up foreign currencies and built up its reserves in order to "sterilize" capital inflows and contain imported inflation, and pursued a restrictive policy at home in order to contain wage demands and maintain price stability (Herr and Voy 1990: 16). An integral part of this strategy was that the German finance ministry, in charge of setting the exchange rate, resisted demands for a revaluation of the DM in order to maintain the competitive advantage afforded by its comparatively lower inflation rates. And last, the German government also sought to deflect international pressures to reduce the consistent trade and balance-of-payments surpluses that critics came to see as the mirror image to America's deficits and a source of macroeconomic instabilities.[11] In as much as the DM continued to be undervalued, the German economy was shielded from global inflation, and the Bundesbank was free to pursue a restrictive monetary policy, German officials had good reasons of their own to support the attempts of the United States to maintain Bretton Woods even as they grew concerned about its irresponsible fiscal and monetary policies.

The notion that they were forced to go along with American monetary designs thus needs to be seriously qualified. Threats to reduce or withdraw US troops could not easily be mobilized to place demands on German authorities—excessive pressure, the Americans feared, might strengthen the Gaullist fraction within the German government and push it into the arms of France. The offset negotiations therefore involved compromises rather than one-sided concessions (Zimmermann 2002: 242). In exchange for dollar support, most notably, the US refrained from asking for a revaluation of the DM in the early 1960s. For the US, moreover, the monetary support provided by Germany as part of the offset agreements was a double-edged sword. While it helped stabilize monetary relations in the short term, it also increased the disruptive ability of a potential Franco-German monetary bloc in the long run (Gavin 2004: 66).[12]

Last, the very vulnerability of West Germany to US Cold War policy led to the formulation of a novel and independent security policy vis-à-vis the Soviet sphere that would have repercussions for Germany's monetary stance. Brandt's *Ostpolitik* traded traditional military for political-economic instruments and incentives and committed to the EEC as the way forward for the continent as a whole. The promotion of the European project in the late 1960s and early 1970s rested squarely on efforts to move toward economic and monetary union. This, it was explicitly acknowledged, was a requirement for a successful *Ostpolitik* (Gray 2010: 151). And for such a common position to emerge, an agreement with France was seen as key. "After all," one policy document noted, "the pressure for a European breakthrough in monetary matters can only increase further during a phase of successful Eastern policy activities. This means, first and foremost, that the courting of France needs to be intensified."[13] From this perspective, then, German state managers were increasingly inclined to make concessions to France rather than continue to cater to the United States. Thus when Brandt embarked on his *Ostpolitik*, he was "not particularly disposed to make a strong effort in order to save the transatlantic bargain" that had hitherto characterized German monetary relations with the US (Zimmermann 2001: 68). This newly gained autonomy was exemplified by the fact that Brandt was unprepared to make substantial monetary concessions to the US during the offset negotiations of 1971 and quite willing to risk, or rather call the bluff regarding, its "continued military presence in Europe" (Lippert 2011: 94).[14]

In sum, the distinction between a French spoiler and German supporter may reflect the instrumental viewpoint of US policymakers, but it seriously underestimates the extent to which the German state was able to pursue a more independent monetary policy (Kreile 2006: 157). Once we drop this schematic representation, we can see more clearly that Germany, too, pursued ends broadly similar to those of France, albeit with a different set of instruments.

Anxious to avoid the charge of anti-Americanism, the rhetoric that underpinned de Gaulle's attack on the dollar as an instrument of American dominance was hardly palatable to German officials.[15] How to respond to this overture in practical terms was a different matter, however.[16] In fact, in 1965 German officials seriously considered joining de Gaulle in asking for an increase in the price of gold (Zimmermann 2002: 226). Even the possibility of joining France in converting dollar surpluses into gold—raised most prominently by the former president of the Bank deutscher Länder (BdL), Wilhelm Vocke—was discussed (compare Eichengreen 2011: 53). The decision not to follow de Gaulle's lead was based on pragmatic considerations rather than a sense of loyalty toward the US. At the least, Germany would need more time to stock up its gold reserves before taking any radical steps.[17] Furthermore, even without an official proclamation to convert future dollar surpluses into gold, it was concluded, the Bundesbank would be able to convert part of its dollar reserves into assets denominated in DM or gold. In fact, as one document pointed out, the Bundesbank had done so previously. In 1964—despite a commitment not to convert dollars into *US Treasury* gold—it had been able to reduce its dollar reserves from 12.6 to 8.6 billion DM (see also similar figures in Loriaux 1991: 185). An official commitment to use gold for international settlements, as demanded by de Gaulle, would only make it more difficult to use previously accumulated dollars in order to settle deficits.[18] In light of these sober calculations, the decision to forego a confrontational stance is less an indication of a lack of solidarity with France or any particular wartime "debt" to the United States than the evident limits of this strategic move.[19]

While the persistent pressure, though not the anti-American overtones, of France on the United States was appreciated, it was understood that it could not be generalized. As early as 1965—two years before the Bundesbank supposedly tied its hands with the "Blessing letter"[20]—its officials had concluded that any concerted attempt to convert dollars into gold would simply prompt the US to suspend convertibility.[21] Because dollar holdings still accounted for 40 percent of official Bundesbank reserves at that time, a US gold embargo would put the Federal Republic in an unfavorable position.[22] German officials were not alone in expecting this outcome. British monetary authorities had begun contingency planning after the gold crisis of March 1968, including several scenarios for floating the pound (Hamilton and Oliver 2007: 496–497, 503–506). And France had anticipated and prepared for the closing of the gold window by the United States at least since the sterling devaluation of 1966.[23]

Given that the closing of the gold pool made the end of the dollar-gold system a practical inevitability, there is at least some indication that America's allies knew what they were doing when they started to convert dollars into gold *en masse* in the spring and summer of 1971. In a meeting of European economics and finance ministers in July 1971, the Commission and Community members considered "actions in reserve policy" that would prompt the US to change the financing of its balance-of-payments deficit. One may surmise that these steps included breaking with the gentlemen's agreement reached after the collapse of the gold pool, whereby central banks had agreed not to convert existing dollar holdings into gold but remained free to cash in any additional dollars acquired since 1968 (Eichengreen 2000: 217). Notably, the German delegation did not comment on this topic, citing "particular political difficulties."[24] The possibility of an intensified and coordinated conversion policy of EEC member states was rejected, not simply because it would burden the offset negotiations with the United States, but because it was considered ineffective. Because it would prompt the US to close the gold window, it was dismissed as "not an appropriate means to force the US to improve its balance of payments."[25]

And yet when—in response to Nixon's refusal to stem the speculative move out of the dollar in 1970–1971—the central banks of Belgium and the Netherlands turned in $140 million dollars for gold (Hudson 2003: 334), Germany expressed its intention to do the same (Eichengreen 2007: 18).[26] France cashed in $282 million dollars, which it used to pay back the loan from the IMF received in the wake of May 1968 (Hudson 2003: 334). And on 13 August 1971, the Bank of England asked for a guarantee on an additional three billion dollars' worth of gold (Nichter 2008: 112–113; Gray 2007: 312; Eichengreen 2011: 60).[27] Faced with such massive demands for gold, the Nixon administration felt under tremendous pressure to move as quickly as possible in order to prevent any further losses of gold. Two days later, the gold embargo was imposed, and "one of the most accurately and generally predicted of major economic events" (Garber 1993: 461) had finally occurred. Whether a coordinated action or a matter of *sauve qui peut*, it was the combined pressure of European states that forced the Nixon administration to resort to this final option and draw from a range of contingency plans that had been developed within the state bureaucracy in previous years.

Although Germany significantly extended the lifeline of Bretton Woods throughout the 1960s and doubted the rationale of intensified gold conversions (Kreile 2006: 156, 161; Zimmermann 2002: 239), its overall assessment of the monetary situation was very similar to that of its European allies.

"The fundamental problem," as one policy document spelled it out most clearly, "consists in the fact that in the current monetary system the US assumes a position which allows it to force the rest of the world to give almost unlimited credit to finance its balance-of-payments deficit."[28] While the United States enjoyed the benefits of this position, the responsibility for maintaining stable exchange rates was relegated to the Europeans and Japanese.[29]

The remainder of this chapter shows that German policymakers in the 1970s reluctantly, but repeatedly, resorted to floating in order to extricate themselves from this situation—not in response to America's putative hegemonic decline but in order to insulate their domestic economy from the inflationary impact of its fiscal and monetary indiscipline. In keeping with the three interpretative models introduced in Chapter 1, it first discards such a (counter)hegemonic reading of German monetary policy and then moves on to consider the influence of neoliberal ideas or business elites.

Floating the Deutsche Mark

If German state officials were relatively free from direct American tutelage, the structural pressures they faced were undeniably real. German officials in the government and central bank had embraced the world market opportunities afforded by a low dollar-DM exchange rate encased in Bretton Woods. As long as they could guarantee greater price stability at home, exporters would maintain a competitive advantage over spendthrift economies. And yet, with the par value system strained by growing imbalances between surplus and deficit countries, the German finance ministry came under repeated pressure either to revalue or to find other ways to address its country's growing trade surplus. The Bundesbank, meanwhile, was required to take in as much foreign currency as necessary in order to maintain the parity of the DM, which was increasingly seen as a safe haven and speculative object. Unable to prevent these ever larger inflows from raising domestic price levels, the recurring monetary crises that beset Bretton Woods and raised the attractiveness of the DM threatened to undermine the very basis on which German export success and social peace had been built. Germany's financial and monetary officials faced the choice between a rock and a hard place. An upward adjustment of the DM peg to the dollar might ease the pressure in principle, but any rumors of such a step would feed a speculative frenzy. Worse still, it was widely believed that a higher-valued DM would harm German export interests. The only alternative to ward off speculative inflows was to impose exchange and capital controls that, if escalated and generalized, would threaten the open trading order on which Germany's postwar prosperity had rested.[30]

Faced with this trilemma, and through much trial and error, German finance and monetary officials gradually came to favor an internationally floating DM in order to control this inflationary influx, while seeking to bring the currencies of their European partners into close alignment (see Chapter 5). Although their corrosive effect on Bretton Woods was the same, each of the three decisions to float owed to a different combination of internal and external pressures and opportunities. In September 1969, a political deadlock within the cabinet prompted officials to let the DM float for some time. The Bundesbank would simply withdraw from foreign exchange markets, thus leaving open the controversial question of what the new exchange rate to the dollar ought to be (Gray 2007: 302–303). In May 1971, strategic considerations—widely shared across several agencies of the German state—figured prominently in the decision: a floating DM would redirect "hot money" to Germany's European partners, put further pressure on the US dollar, and thus bolster the case for monetary reform. "It is a somewhat nasty technique," the vice-president of the Bundesbank, Otmar Emminger, said in describing his preference for a temporary float, given the speculative pressures that would now shift toward the franc. The foreign ministry, more diplomatically, agreed that a limited float would "exert a healthy pressure on [German] [EEC] partners to agree on a common stability policy."[31] The head of one of the German *Landesbanken*, Ludwig Poullain, hoped that it might demonstrate to US officials just how frail the dollar had become.[32] And even Emminger's opponent and superior at the Bundesbank, Karl Klasen, who favored capital controls over floating, recognized that "we will not get out of this predicament unless the others are forced to do something, too."[33] Thus, twice before the United States decided to "free" the dollar from gold, German policymakers had violated the rules of Bretton Woods by unilaterally floating the DM (Gray 2007: 296; Panitch and Gindin 2012: 388, fn. 49). And finally, in March 1973, when the US still did not know what kind of monetary system it wanted (for example, Odell 1982: 311, fn. 23), Germany sealed the fate of the fixed-exchange-rate regime by pressuring its European allies into a joint float and under the veiled threat of moving ahead alone (Johnson 1998: 83; Gray 2007: 321).

None of these steps was in keeping with American designs. Although it mobilized contingency plans developed since 1966 (Gavin 2004: 169–170), the Nixon administration had not yet decided to end the par value system of

Bretton Woods, and this indecision would continue until its eventual collapse in 1973. Floating, one policy document suggested, was instead to be used as a bargaining and "fall back" position in subsequent negotiations. The US should indicate that it is "prepared to live with the floating rate system indefinitely."[34] But this was still aimed at improving the trade balance and protecting American jobs in order to secure Nixon's reelection in 1972 (compare Gowa 1983; Williamson 1977: 77; Matusow 1998: 132–137).

When Germany first floated the DM, US officials complained that there was "no reason to jettison the Bretton Woods system"[35] (Volcker and Gyohten 1992: 74, cited in Zimmermann 2008: 168, fn. 57); leaned on their German counterparts to stay within the fixed-exchange-rate regime and use capital controls instead (Schmidt 1996: 174; Moravcsik 1998: 250–251; Hetzel 2002: 41–42, fn. 19); and objected to a European block float on political grounds (Trachtenberg 2011: 20–23). To be sure, in the wake of the Nixon Shock, when it seemed clear that monetary concessions would have to be made, German policymakers were keen to convince their American partners that by floating the DM Germany had already made a significant advance contribution. Yet an earlier report had concluded pessimistically that German monetary policy—from the nonconversion pledge to DM revaluation and floating—could hardly be sold to the Americans as an act of goodwill, as it was evident that "it promises to be to our own trade and monetary advantage."[36]

This is not to say that the German state aspired to a genuinely counter-hegemonic project by organizing a European currency float. This position, most strongly articulated by Erik Hoffmeyer, the former governor of the Danish central bank (1965–1994), holds that "the decisive change in the international monetary system after 1971 was the outcome of a German desire to unwind US influence and regain their own political independence" (Hoffmeyer 1993: 82; compare Zimmermann 2008: 156–157). While Hoffmeyer rightly assesses the weight of Germany's monetary decisions, he misinterprets the overall objective. Rather than contest US monetary power for (geo)political purposes, German policymakers primarily sought to limit its misuse or at least to protect themselves from the monetary fallout.[37] As one position paper by the finance and economics ministry put it, "The dollar will retain its importance as an intervention currency; but it will be important to abolish, as far as possible, the special advantages that the US has derived from this role of the dollar, and the dangers that result for the other countries (expansion of international liquidity)."[38] In the short run, German officials sought to shield their economy from the inflationary pressures that flowed from the US abusing its dollar privilege to finance its budget and trade deficits. And in the long run, they sought to make US monetary hegemony serve the general (or at least German) interest rather than that of the United States alone (Kreile 2006: 161).

Having revisited and rejected the notion that Germany was either an acquiescent Cold War client or an unruly rival making a bid for regional hegemony, how else can the change in German monetary policy be explained? The next section asks to what extent neoliberal beliefs—homegrown or imported—may have influenced officials in the German government and central bank to float the DM and target the money supply.

Floating Ideas?

The most promising ideas-based explanation of the German shift to floating and monetary targeting centers on the Bundesbank as the principal, ordoliberal, protagonist in the breakdown of Bretton Woods and—in extension—the global rise of neoliberalism. Few scholars would deny that ordoliberalism lost whatever hold it may have had on German postwar policymakers in the course of the 1960s. And yet it might be argued that ordoliberalism found an intellectual habitat in the fiercely independent and stability-oriented Bundesbank (Art 2015: 190; for a critique, see Young 2017: 225). Resisting the Keynesian "half-turn" of the German economic policy establishment in the late 1960s and early 1970s, and inspired by their neoliberal brethren in Chicago, Germany's central bankers may have stood ready to offer policy alternatives as the principles of the embedded liberal order—state-led macroeconomic management, stable exchange rates, and exchange controls—were thrown into question.

And indeed, in some respects, the Bundesbank did lead the way. It was by far the most significant central bank to shed the obligation to sustain the par value of its currency. Letting the forces of supply and demand determine the external value of the DM seems to have offered a market-conforming solution more favorable to the continuous foreign exchange interventions and, between 1969 and 1973, the ever more rigid administrative controls that had been necessary to sustain the par value of the DM. Freed from having to take in unwanted dollars, the Bundesbank was also the first to heed to the minimalist focus on the quantity of money that neoliberals such as Milton Friedman had recommended. And assisted by these new monetarist techniques, the Bundesbank launched a restrictive monetary policy that was unprecedented in the first half of the 1970s and which reasserted the primacy of price stability (Herr and Voy 1990: 26)—over the goal of full employment and, as is generally assumed in the literature, against the preferences of the social-democratic chancellery and majority ruling party (Scharpf 1991; Marsh 1992; 2009). Though short of the radical turn of Thatcher and Reagan, monetarism "implies a desire to strengthen the power of market forces and to minimize state interference" (Leaman 2001: 157). Such a reading links up neatly with contemporary perspectives in which the Bundesbank is presented as a bastion of ordoliberalism that shaped European monetary integration and provided a blueprint for the construction of the European Central Bank (ECB) (Beck and Kotz 2017: 19; Art 2015: 190).

The critical role of the German central bank, and its interplay with the German government and its economics and finance ministries, certainly deserves consideration. And yet to cast "the *Bundesbank* . . . as the epitome of the ordoliberal tradition" (Young 2017: 225) is to grossly exaggerate the influence of ordoliberalism on the monetary architecture, culture, and policy of the German central bank (Johnson 1998: 56; Bibow 2009).

To be sure, the founding father of ordoliberalism, Walter Eucken, had stressed "the primacy of currency policy" as one of the foundational principles of a market order (Feld, Köhler, and Nientiedt 2015: 2). And yet, for the very same reason, he had also rejected the idea of an independent central bank in both principle and practice (Feld, Köhler, and Nientiedt 2017: 42). His ordoliberal credo that only market-conforming state regulation was permissible militated against the practice of central banks (independent or otherwise) to set the rate of interest. To do so, in his view, was to constantly interfere with the price-finding mechanism of the market (Bibow 2009: 169).[39] On political grounds, too, Eucken opposed central bank autonomy as introducing a dangerous "'pluralism' that would jeopardize the unity of state policy" (quoted in Bibow 2009: 170). That Germany's central bank emerged as formally independent from government directives owes little to ordoliberal precepts but rather to historical happenstance and complex political battles (Leaman 2001: 112; Bibow 2004: 30; 2009). When the Bundesbank's precursor, the BdL, was established in 1948, a federal state did not yet exist (Buchheim 1999; 2001; Marsh 1992: 144–145; Bibow 2009: 158). And in the power struggle over the Bundesbank Act of 1957, Erhard's advisory council, which included a number of high-profile ordoliberals, "designed and recommended a model . . . that was essentially

Keynesian in spirit" and that would have tightly linked the Bundesbank to the government (Bibow 2009: 184; 2004: 23–26). The Bundesbank has been widely assumed to resist any encroachment of its authority. Curiously, however, most of its officials were disposed to restrict its legal independence when confronted with the great inflation of the late 1960s and early 1970s (Johnson 1998: 24).

Nor can ordoliberalism be credited for the Bundesbank's monetary conduct (Johnson 1998: 56; Richter 1999: 24; Spahn 2005: 19; Bibow 2009: 155; Feld, Köhler, and Nientiedt 2015: 6–7). The Bundesbank has certainly been keen to present itself as the guardian of the DM, acting out of a sense of historical responsibility to the German population, which, it has been repeatedly argued by policymakers and academics, has been haunted by the collective memories of hyperinflation in the 1920s (Leaman 2001). The reality was far more mundane. Equally important to the German public and policymaking elites, and thus just as likely to have influenced monetary policy, was the fear of economic recession and mass unemployment that had brought Hitler to power (Johnson 1998: 24–25). The postwar solution, Chapter 3 has argued, was seen to lie in an expanding trade surplus, assisted through an undervalued DM and shored up by monetary and fiscal discipline. Price stability mattered a great deal—but principally in so far as it cheapened Germany's exports relative to those of its core competitors. It was never an end in itself but one of several closely related goals, including full employment, which Germany's monetary authorities sought to realize (Richter 1999: 23–24). And indeed, when price stability came into conflict with Germany's return to the world market, it had to cede. For instance, Germany's export industry was exempted from the monetary restrictions imposed by the BdL in the late 1940s. As its president, Vocke, explained, "In one respect we will safely disregard the general orthodox rules of a central bank, that is to say, where the promotion of exports is concerned, we begin with long-term and medium-term credits" (quoted in Dickhaus 1996: 70).

The Bundesbank's strict adherence to price stability, then, does not unequivocally emerge from the historical experience of hyperinflation. And less still was it inspired by ordoliberalism. In hindsight, of course, numerous invocations of the ordoliberal creed and Eucken's *Grundsätze der Wirtschaftspolitik* can be found (Dyson 2017: 89). But even if we were to assume that postwar monetary officials looked to Eucken, his work lacked a compelling theory of money that could ground monetary policy. His endorsement of a commodity money and full reserve banking system in the immediate postwar years had pushed him to the margins of the monetary debates at the time. Ordoliberals, to be sure, had stressed price stability as the essential precondition for a functioning market economy. But then Keynes, too, argued that the productive and financial sectors "cannot work properly if the money, which they assume as a stable measuring-rod, is undependable" (quoted in Bibow 2009: 170). Moreover, the Bundesbank officials that sought to defeat the great inflation in the early 1970s adopted a series of highly interventionist measures—opposed, it should be noted, by the devoutly Keynesian economics and finance minister Karl Schiller—that would have been anathema to ordoliberals (Johnson 1998: 24).[40]

If a homegrown tradition of ordoliberalism does not offer an explanation for the shift toward floating, could neoliberal ideas have been brought in from the outside? Indeed, in the Bundesbank debates of the early 1970s, vice-president Otmar Emminger borrowed the arguments of Friedman and other neoliberals that relying on market forces to establish the exchange values between currencies would allow the Bundesbank to concentrate on the internal stability of the DM (Johnson 1998: 70). Similarly, the subsequent turn of the Bundesbank toward monetarism—ostensibly "one of the most uncompromising free market doctrines" (Johnson 1998: ix)—has been said to have been inspired by an Anglo-American debate (Richter 1999: 74; Spahn 2005: 19; Feld, Köhler, and Nientiedt 2015: 9–10).

There was indeed a sense of intellectual backwardness that led a minority within the economics profession to turn to Chicago (Richter 1999; Spahn 2005: 19). But the practice of monetary targeting that the Bundesbank finally and cautiously adopted diverged in important respects from the original prescriptions—focusing, for instance, on the smaller, more manageable aggregate of "central bank money" and combining it with inflation targeting (Spahn 1990: 58; Bernanke and Mihov 1997). Its embrace of monetarism, then, was of a pragmatic rather than paradigmatic nature, concerned with how to reposition itself and signal a credible commitment to price stability after the collapse of Bretton Woods (Spahn 1990: 55; Johnson 1998: 57). Moreover, as others have observed and as we will discuss at the end of this chapter, monetarism was adapted to a novel social purpose. It was meant to set clear monetary limits to the distributive conflict between capital and labor (Spahn 2005: 26; Johnson 1998; Iversen 1999).

As far as the neoliberal case for floating is concerned, Emminger remained a lone voice within the Bundesbank's Central Bank Council (Henning 1994: 183). Most of the council's members remained committed to the par value system of Bretton Woods until its collapse in March 1973 (Heisenberg 1999: 29–33; Johnson 1998: 73). On the contrary, they experimented with an ever more tightly knit system of exchange controls in order to defend the external and internal value of the DM (Johnson 1998: 74–75; Henning 1994: 184).

The decision to float, in the end, lay not with the Bundesbank but with the German government. And here its most vocal proponent was the social-democratic, and staunch Keynesian, finance minister Karl Schiller, hardly a neoliberal sympathizer. In May 1971, Schiller convinced the cabinet to temporarily float the mark rather than impose the regulatory controls that the Bundesbank had recommended (Johnson 1998: 74). Since 1969, moreover, he had championed a movement to revalue the DM in order to rebalance the German economy away from exports (Henning 1994: 183; Gray 2007: 301). For him, and the social-democratic left and trade unions, which supported a higher-valued DM, greater exchange-rate flexibility meant a step toward Keynesian demand management rather than a departure from it. Schiller stepped down in June 1972 when the cabinet chose administrative measures over his plea for a DM float, and after alienating his peers by insisting that the government run a deficit only to counter a recession, rather than to win elections (Johnson 1998: 78). On the issue of countercyclical spending, his successor, Helmut Schmidt, would prove politically more savvy and less wedded to Keynesian orthodoxy than Schiller. Unlike him, moreover, Schmidt favored tighter controls until illness removed him and Klasen from the discussions that led to the DM float in March 1973 (von Hagen 1999: 412; Johnson 1998: 79, 83; Panitch and Gindin 2012: 145–146).

Neither the cabinet nor the Bundesbank ever supported floating because they saw the market as the better arbiter of currency prices but instead because they feared the corrosive impact of imported inflation on the embedded liberal compromise. In this regard, Friedman was under no illusion that governments had ever accepted his argument (compare Jones 2012: 220). And even Emminger (1986: 251), who had drawn on Friedman, discounted the importance of ideas when he concluded that "[i]n reality the transition to floating was forced upon us by events, whatever rational considerations and expectations we had with regards to a float."[41] The emphasis on price stability, we have seen, was rooted neither in ordoliberal doctrine nor in the trauma of hyperinflation, but in a postwar settlement constructed around Germany's export performance and now in need of revision.

Dominant Interests?

The chapter thus far has considered the German experience of floating and, on the whole, discarded the idea that Germany either followed or challenged the American hegemon. It has also rejected the notion that ordoliberal or neoliberal ideas influenced the German decision to float. Returning to the threefold interpretation of state-centered, ideational, and class-based accounts introduced in Chapter 1, this section asks whether private economic interests may have prevailed on German state managers. With regard to the United States, the dominant interpretation is that the postwar alliance of state and business elites which had preferred stable exchange rates over free capital movement came undone in the 1960s (Helleiner 1994: 100). As US corporations and investment banks expanded abroad, they came up against the financial regulations put in place by US officials to maintain the par value of the dollar (Hawley 1987: 107; Helleiner 1994: 119). As the dollar came under increasing downward pressure, banks and businesses chose flexible exchange rates over tighter regulations.[42] Keen to capitalize on the rapidly growing foreign exchange and eurodollar markets, moreover, some financial actors advocated floating exchange rates as the financial counterpart to a liberal trading order (Aronson 1977: 142–149; Schmelzer 2010: 56, 174–175, 181).

In Germany, however, the constellation of social interests that favored flexible exchange rates was radically different. It consisted of a broad and diverse alliance led by economics minister Karl Schiller, the left wing of the Sozialdemokratische Partei Deutschlands (SPD), and trade unionists who, from 1969 onward, championed DM revaluation as a means to reorient Germany's overly export-dependent economy toward domestic production and consumption and render it receptive to a Keynesian "global steering" (Gray 2007: 301). Support for a higher-valued DM also came from the economics profession, research institutes, and the print media, and extended to savers and homeowners, the *Mittelstand*, and importers (Lankowski 1982a: 280, 282–283; Johnson 1998: 10).

Although the coalition of interests fractured quickly, and the ambitious project of lessening the export orientation of German capitalism in favor of a Keynesian demand management was never accomplished (Lankowski 1982a: 285), it managed to place greater exchange-rate flexibility firmly on the policy agenda.

German exporters and their financiers, meanwhile, vigorously opposed any upward adjustment of the DM, let alone the wider rebalancing of the German economy that Schiller and other Keynesians sought to achieve. Having lost an important battle with the Adenauer government in 1961 that saw a modest increase in the par value of the DM, the peak business associations had warned incessantly that any further move to revalue the DM would destroy the competitive strength of the German economy.[43] So averse were dominant export interests to a higher-valued DM that they had accepted administrative measures to contain the upward pressure on the DM in the early and late 1960s (Crotty and Epstein 1996: 124).

By the end of the decade, however, the united front of industrial, financial, and agricultural interests that had supported an undervalued DM began to show some cracks. When the grand coalition government of Kiesinger refused to yield to international pressures for a stronger DM in November 1968 and instead opted for a 4 percent tax on exports (and a corresponding 4 percent subsidy on imports) in order to diminish its balance-of-payments surplus, it came under surprising criticism from the very export interests it had sought to defend. Much to the chagrin of policymakers, who observed that "the attitude of business to the revaluation of the DM had visibly changed," some business members of the Foreign Trade Advisory Council pointed out that they would have preferred a one-off revaluation to the more intrusive provisions of the *Absicherungsgesetz* (External Financial Stability Act).[44]

On the whole, however, the dominant export bloc remained firmly committed to the fixed-exchange-rate regime that secured its international competitiveness. Shaken out of complacency and stiffened in its opposition by the government's decision to temporarily float the DM one year later, the pressure it brought to bear on German policymakers, and the extent to which the latter took account of its interests, is nothing short of extraordinary (Kinderman 2008).

Unable to block a renewed float in May 1971, its representatives in the economic ministry's Foreign Trade Advisory Council accepted limited capital controls in the hope of a swift return to prefloating, fixed parities.[45] Capital restrictions, though far from desirable, were considered to be "the lesser evil"[46] as long as they were not too rigid—and arguably because corporate and financial actors knew they could find ways to circumvent them.[47]

Meanwhile, the specter of *permanent* float, feared to push the DM ever further upward, was to be fought tooth and nail.[48] With the personal endorsement of the "who is who" of Germany's industrial elite,[49] the peak business associations ran a campaign in four leading newspapers to reject the case for greater flexibility, to criticize the forces behind it, and to call for a return to fixed exchange rates.[50]

Could an elite fraction of German capital—similar to the American multinationals and investment banks held to have militated against the strictures of Bretton Woods—have embraced flexible or floating exchange rates? Perhaps the largest German companies, with operations across several national jurisdictions with different currencies, found it easy to hedge against exchange-rate risks (Kinderman 2008: 854; Helleiner 2005: 26)? Or perhaps the Bundesbank, as Holtfrerich (2008: 39) suggests—in supporting a float and focusing on domestic price stability—broke allegiance with export industry and instead came to champion "the interests of the internationally active financial sector" in a strong and attractive DM?

Dissenting voices were certainly to be found—but they remained too isolated or timid for the thesis of an elite fraction to be sustainable. The Hanseatic private banker Joachim Willink, for instance, pleaded with Bundesbank president Klasen to let the DM float upward for an extended period of time. But his proposal was conscious of the fundamental opposition of the financial and industrial community to such a plan.[51] In hindsight, the head of one of Germany's regionally owned and most internationally engaged *Landesbanken*—Ludwig Poullain of the WestLB—recognized that the May 1971 float had served to hammer home the need for monetary reform. Yet he refused to see floating as anything other than a tactical device to gather international support.[52]

Opposition to floating also extended into the innermost circles of German industry, which regularly brought together the chief financial officers of its top twenty corporations to exchange information and views.[53] Little is known about these informal meetings, but central bankers were sometimes invited and thus a thin paper trail exists.[54] As far as we know, these captains of industry, with one foot in finance, were deeply concerned about a DM float and warned of the serious repercussions for the German economy.[55] The private contacts of chancellor Schmidt confirm that floating won elite approval only *after* facts had been created. In the wake of the joint European float of 12 March 1973, Ernst Wolf Mommsen, who liaised with financial and industrial elites and organized social gatherings with the chancellor, reported that "there is now after all almost a consensus that the attained result was optimal with regards to all other alternatives."[56]

All this goes to suggest that the societal constellation surrounding the collapse of this part of Bretton Woods was different from that in the US, and far more complicated than an instrumentalist reading of class power would suggest. Corporate elites did not proactively shape German monetary policy. In fact, they held mutually opposed interests: they completely rejected the idea of floating and yet were equally opposed to the comprehensive exchange controls that would have been required to shield the German economy from continued dollar influx. In this contradictory situation, German policymakers needed to decide for them (Hawley 1987: 145). But even so, the choice was not that simple.

The question remains why they turned against the interests of the German export bloc in the way they did. The first section of this chapter has already considered and, on the whole, discounted the view that German state managers acted "on orders" from the United States. A more plausible variation of this argument may be that German policymakers accepted the burden of adjustment imposed by a higher-valued DM. Moving toward a more realistic and sustainable set of exchange rates may have been seen as necessary in order to correct the global imbalances that were threatening Bretton Woods—even if this meant hurting Germany's export industry (compare Gray 2007: 296).[57]

There is some evidence to suggest that, in the wake of the Nixon Shock, German state managers had come to realize that the times when their manufacturers had registered record exports while the US balance of trade deteriorated were over. As one state official told representatives of the export industry, "every country had to sacrifice part of its competitiveness in favor of the US."[58] And the German chancellor concluded in his "Political-Economic Paper" in April 1974 that "in the interest of the whole, then, the adjustments and sacrifices associated with appreciation had—and still have to!—be asked of individual branches."[59] Internally, however, the economics and finance ministry had come to the conclusion that the incessant complaints about the catastrophic consequences of a stronger DM had been greatly exaggerated.[60] The lessons they drew from the revaluation of 1961 and the 1969 and 1971 floats were that despite the doom and gloom, German exporters had fared remarkably well.[61] In the decisive years of 1971–1973 at least, it seemed that their competitive position had anything but suffered. In fact, the ministry observed that German exporters had been able to pass on the costs of a more valuable DM to their customers abroad[62]—confirming the long-standing assumption within the comparative-institutionalist literature that German manufacturers tend to compete through specialization rather than through price alone (Streeck 1991). Rather than indicating a serious sacrifice on the part of German policymakers, it is more likely that their talk of "concessions" to their American partners was meant to justify a prolonged float vis-à-vis the export sector.[63]

State Capacity, Capital Accumulation, and Structured Choices

Outside such geopolitical considerations, however, how else can this growing independence of German policy elites from the dominant export bloc be explained? To find the answer to this question, a twofold conceptual shift is in order. First, we need to move from interallied relations toward the world market as the source of the constraints and compulsions under which policymakers operate. And second, we need to shift from the direct political power that private economic actors wield over policymakers toward the indirect ways in which their economic actions shape the terrain of public policy options. This structural power of capital used to be the subject of considerable controversy and conceptual advances before it was expelled from "reputable" social science in the course of the 1980s (for example, Gill and Law 1989)—only to be rediscovered, three decades later, in the wake of the global financial crisis (for example, Culpepper 2015). A notion of structural power is indispensable in order to situate state policy within the full gamut of social relations that permeate the ostensibly distinct arenas of "politics" and "economics." Yet rather than seeing this structural power as the product of abstract market forces or a logic inherent in capitalism, we need to zoom in on the concrete corporate actors hidden behind it. German exporters and their financiers shaped German monetary policy not only through their considerable political clout but also in the very way they did business. The same actors who lobbied so successfully against revaluation and floating were also responsible for most of the disruptive capital flows that frustrated the attempts of German policymakers to adhere to their wishes.

The German export machine, in short, was undermined by its own success rather than destabilized by speculative attacks from the outside. The greater the trade surplus, the higher the sums that German manufacturers brought back from abroad (Lankowski 1982a: 276–277). The further they extended their global reach through production facilities and sales outlets, they more they had to assume the foreign exchange risks previously absorbed by independent importers.[64] Borrowing abroad also enabled German corporations and banks to avoid the credit restrictions of the German central bank (Kreile 1977: 794; Spahn 2005: 25, 28). And finally, in a self-reinforcing spiral, the more the dollar came under pressure and the fixed-exchange-rate regime under strain, the keener German (and other transnational) companies became to convert their dollar holdings into the hard currency of the DM.[65] Overall, such transactions made up between one-half and two-thirds of the dollars that flooded the Bundesbank and undermined its attempts not only to maintain DM parity but also to limit inflation.[66]

Policymakers across the state and central bank were well aware that German exporters and their financiers themselves had created this untenable situation. Though not for a lack of trying, they ultimately shied away from the ever more intrusive capital controls that would have been required to separate purely speculative from economically necessary capital flows.[67] Short of such dirigiste and politically explosive measures, the Bundesbank sought the collaboration of the "decisive economic circles" to stem further dollar inflows.[68] Its officials asked German banks to persuade their corporate clients—between eighty and one hundred industrial companies, according to one memorandum[69]—to cease borrowing from abroad and to repay their foreign debts. In return, the Bundesbank promised in a meeting with the ten leading industrial companies to help hedge against exchange-rate fluctuations.[70]

The highly concentrated and closely coordinated nature of German capitalism revealed by these concerted efforts is nothing short of remarkable. Nevertheless, the attempt to reach an understanding through these corporatist channels was destined to fail. German banks, both private and state-owned, continued to funnel foreign funds to German borrowers, violating the spirit and sometimes the letter of the Foreign Trade and Payments Act (*Außenwirtschaftsgesetz*).[71] German industry, meanwhile, certainly had a collective interest in preventing or at least adhering to the ever more restrictive measures that monetary authorities adopted from March 1972 onward in order to stem these inflows—not least because the only alternative to tighter regulation was a DM float. And yet the pressures on individual firms to gain favorable access to international financial markets, or at least not to be the last to hold the dollar bag if the par value of DM changed, proved irresistible.

The increasing frustration on the part of policymakers was aptly expressed by central bank governor Karl Klasen, who replied to protestation by his former associates at Deutsche Bank, "We would surely not have needed [the *Bardepot* or cash deposit system], had those in whose interest we've tried to prevent revaluations not made such a countercyclical measure necessary by borrowing too heavily abroad."[72] As Bundesbankers found that capital restrictions penalized small and medium-sized enterprises while large companies and their banks continued to circumvent them, they came to see floating as the only viable option to limit these inflationary pressures (Lankowski 1982a: 276–277).[73]

In sum, there is little doubt that the structural power of capital had forced the hands of German policymakers—but paradoxically, and contrary to how it is usually understood, it operated "behind the backs" (Marx 1990: 135) and against the interest of those who wielded it. German exporters, their financiers, and even some of the public *Landesbanken* had found ever new ways to subvert the credit restrictions that the Bundesbank had imposed. But in doing so, they only amplified the pressures that in the end prompted German officials to permanently float the DM.

The profoundly political dimension of this decision, rather than the mere technical fix it provided, is hinted at in Emminger's assessment that "[w]e called a halt to that particular game on March 2 and began 'floating,' not because of any lack of funds—a central bank can create its own money without limit in order to buy up dollars—but because the inflationary effect of these dollar inflows on our monetary system had become intolerable."[74] Given that German corporations and banks were clearly understood to be the principal perpetrators, the strategy of domestic stabilization that the Bundesbank would pursue was also aimed at them.

Liberated by the German government from the obligation to absorb unwanted dollars in order to sustain the parity of the DM, the Bundesbank regained a critical measure of control over the creation of money. It used this new room for maneuver to embark on the most intensive phase of monetary contraction in German postwar history (Herr and Voy 1990: 26). And, as discussed earlier, it also introduced a "pragmatic monetarism" that announced annual growth targets for the money supply (Scharpf 1991). Contrary to monetarist doctrine, however, the Bundesbank did not see inflation as "always and everywhere a monetary phenomenon," as Friedman (1963: 17) had argued. Echoing a sentiment widely shared across the chancellery and federal ministries—and informed by the foreign exchange pressures that German officials had traced to a handful of banks and firms—the Bundesbank approached inflation as a distributive conflict driven by capital and labor.[75] The purpose of monetarism was not to limit central bank intervention to a steady money supply but to place highly visible limits on the scope for this inflationary struggle (Spahn 2005: 26, 33). Accordingly, the fact that the Bundesbank consistently missed these monetary targets was considered of secondary importance.

Thus, along with inflation, the commercial banks and exporters that had been seen to put pressures on the domestic price level moved into the crosshairs. Rising interest rates and an upward floating DM limited the euromarket access to cheap credit that German banks and businesses had previously exploited (Johnson 1998: 85). They also aimed at the excessive profit margins that German exporters had enjoyed for much of the 1960s, courtesy of an undervalued DM. In 1969, record profits had spurred calls for higher wages and set off a wave of unparalleled wildcat strikes. Their formidable speed and success called both trade union control and the firmness of employers into question, and continued to hang over future bargaining rounds (Johnson 1998: 72). The German *Mittelstand* complained that large firms were altogether too quick to surrender to labor's demands so as not to risk a replay.[76] Their market power enabled them to shift the higher wage bill onto clients and consumers at home and abroad. The danger in the eyes of the German government and central bank officials was that this would set off an inflationary spiral of rising prices and wages. Restabilizing the embedded liberal compromise demanded renewed moderation from both sides. Thus the threat of high interest rates did not aim only at organized labor (compare Franzese and Hall 2000: 182). It was also meant to steel the resolve of employers to resist these wage pressures and to desist from simply raising prices in response.[77] Years later still, when the stabilization efforts had already proven successful, Schmidt was to point out to the executive committee of the Bundesverband der Deutschen Industrie (BDI) that their members' pricing policy would be decisive for union discipline in the upcoming round of bargaining. "[N]o one," the chancellor was advised to tell this exclusive audience, "can have an interest in encouraging wild wage movements à la summer 1969."[78]

Within the par value system of Bretton Woods, the German Council of Economic Experts (Sachverständigenrat) had concluded, wage moderation would simply reimport inflation through higher export profits (Spahn 2005: 21). In the new context of a floating DM, however, driven upward by German monetary restraint, exporters could no longer simply pass on wage costs to their customers without the risk of pricing their products out of international markets (compare Franzese and Hall 2000: 183).

That the German state was relatively more successful in reining in inflation did not rest only on the Bundesbank's renewed capacity for "moral suasion." Nor did it flow directly from the ability of Germany's organized capitalism to deliver price and wage restraint (Iversen 1999). While its corporatist institutions facilitated dialogue and compromise between capital and labor, any agreement ultimately depended on the benefits each side could derive as long as Germany's export surplus could continue to grow. And indeed—although it presumably narrowed corporate profit margins, a higher-valued DM had had little impact on the growth (or direction) of German trade, as one Bundesbank official told the Foreign Economic Advisory Council one year after the shift toward floating.[79] The postwar emphasis on external expansion through internal price stability thus outlasted Bretton Woods and brought both social partners together. To employers, a stronger DM meant cheaper imports of primary products (Lankowski 1982a: 36). More important, maintaining lower levels of inflation turned out to shore up their international competitiveness even as the competitive advantage of an undervalued currency had been abolished (Webber 1983: 71). Addressing the Foreign Economic Advisory Council, the state secretary of the economics ministry Otto Schlecht argued that "[t]he effects of DM appreciation from 1972 to 1976 had been more than compensated by the lower increases in the rates of inflation".[80] And to the trade unions, internally divided into export-oriented winners and domestically oriented losers (Markovits 1982: 5), a growing trade surplus promised to shore up "export rents" and associated wage and employment gains in a time of economic crisis.

Conclusion

The breakdown of Bretton Woods is often presented as the deliberate product of American statecraft. In hindsight, it has come to be read by some as the opening gambit by the US to restore its hegemony by removing the embedded liberal strictures of the capitalist world economy (for example, Gowan 1999; Basosi 2006). This chapter contends that the end of Bretton Woods is better understood as a collective and complex process of unwinding—a process in which France, and most important for this book, Germany, played key roles that had little to do with either the defense or demise of US hegemony. The leadership of the United States

in managing global capitalism was too structurally entrenched and institutionally reinforced to come up for revision in this period (Panitch and
Gindin 2012). What the policy conflicts revolved around instead were the
terms and conditions attached to its global power. Given that "the American state had embarked on an uncharted voyage through the 'stagflationary' crisis decade of the 1970s" with the closing of the gold window
(Panitch and Gindin 2012: 13), German policymakers sought to influence
the course that the US would take in the long run, and to protect themselves from its inflationary fallout in the short term.

The case of Bretton Woods suggests that the story of how the embedded
liberal order gave way to neoliberal globalization cannot be told in terms
of a single dramatic arc that pivots on the United States and extends from
the Nixon Shock to the Volcker Shock. But neither can it be presented as
a single economic paradigm or set of elite interests that led policymakers in
other countries in the same direction. The German shift toward floating and
monetarism owed little to the neoliberal conviction that the exchange rates
or the cost of capital are best set by market forces. And although German
policymakers were beholden to business to a remarkable degree, its interests
lay squarely in sustaining the comparative advantage of an undervalued DM
for as long as possible. The relative autonomy of the German state emerged
instead from the incompatibility of these societal demands with the realities of the postwar recovery. As the German economy closed the distance
and compared more favorably to that of the United States in the eyes of
investors, resisting the upward pressure on the DM came into conflict with
the goal of price stability, which, though never an end in itself, was seen as
foundational to taming the distributive struggle between capital and labor.
Once German policymakers realized that the corporate interests they had
sought to protect had exaggerated the negative effects of revaluation and
accounted for a large portion of the inflationary capital inflows, they chose
to float the DM vis-à-vis the dollar to foreclose this option. On the eve of
a new era of economic malaise, the German shift toward a floating regime
and the attendant turn toward monetarism in the course of 1973 and 1974
enabled the German state to restabilize the relationship between capital and
labor (Beyer and others 2008: 12). To a remarkable degree, though not
without frictions, German state elites succeeded in preserving the embedded liberal compromise domestically. Paradoxically, however, their ability
to do so would contribute to the dissolution and indeed termination of
the compromise elsewhere in the capitalist world in the decade to follow.

For not only did the collapse of the fixed-exchange-rate system exacerbate the volatile capital movements that states confronted in the late 1970s and early 1980s (Helleiner 1994: 121). "[O]pting out of the great inflation" (Beyer and others 2008) also required extending Germany's stabilization efforts internationally. And this outward projection, we will see, involved a far more conflictual process than previously recognized (for example, McNamara 1998)—one in which German power was conceptualized and exercised in new ways and for new ends.

CHAPTER 5

Defeating Alternatives

German Grand Strategy and the European Left

THE PREVIOUS CHAPTER analyzed Germany's role in the peculiarly "confrontation-driven" fragmentation of Bretton Woods into a fiat money and floating-exchange-rate system. These monetary turbulences and attendant policy disputes had been thrown up as the German and Japanese "laggards" closed in on the American "lead" economy. The end result of this catch-up development was an evening out and slowing down of growth and productivity rates across the advanced capitalist world (Brenner 2006; Rosenberg and Boyle 2019). While this deceleration has continued until today, it first took on systemic proportions with the OPEC oil shock in October 1973. For the rest of the decade, it was experienced as "stagflation"—an ugly word[1] that aptly describes the grim reality for millions of working people whose livelihoods, barely sheltered for more than a generation from the calamities of capitalism, were unsettled by a perplexing combination of mass unemployment and rapidly rising costs of living. Amidst growing social tensions over how to respond to a widening economic rather than simply monetary crisis, cooperation among the advanced capitalist states also reached new lows "as every country sought individual solutions to the economic challenges of the time" (Basosi 2010: 8).

The present chapter explores the strategic choices made by German policymakers in the face of divergent national responses that seemed fundamentally at odds with their own attempts to manage the crisis of embedded liberalism. First called into action by the import surcharge levied by the Nixon administration, German state officials debated how best to deal with a decelerating as well as potentially disintegrating liberal world economy—a dangerous development that they attributed not only to the irresponsible actions of the US hegemon but also to the solutions proposed by their fellow socialists and rival communists across Europe. In Italy, the ever more popular Partito Comunista Italiano (PCI) demanded to enter into government on a platform of eurocommunism, which German and other Western elites feared could undermine NATO and infect other Mediterranean countries. In the United Kingdom, the Alternative Economic Strategy demanded by the Labour left led by Tony Benn threatened to increase the role of the state at the expense of an integrated European and world economy. And in France, the specter of an alliance between socialists and communists, barely held at bay by the Barre government, materialized with the electoral victory of Mitterrand.

The first section argues that these and other protectionist, interventionist, and inflationary threats led the German state to discard two alternative pathways afforded by its relative economic strength. German policymakers chose neither to shield their national economy from the vagaries of the world market, nor—despite serious consideration—to generously assist their trading partners in solving their domestic problems. Instead, they used their country's considerable monetary and financial power to tilt the crisis responses of their partners in directions that were thought to complement their own attempts to secure internal price stability and external market opportunities. The second part analyzes the two principal channels through which this influence was brought to bear in the mid-1970s: the disciplining effect of a block of European currencies orbiting the DM, and the multilateral loans and conditionalities organized under a German-American "entente" (Parboni 1981: 138; Basosi 2011: 109). German policymakers were neither willing nor able to impose neoliberalism from above in either of the three country cases—Italy, Britain, and France—that constitute the final section of this chapter. But their opposition to the radical and progressive possibilities that briefly emerged across Europe, and their insistence on monetary and fiscal restraint, created the inhospitable environment in which these national and global alternatives to neoliberalism were defeated.

German Crisis Management and the Roads Not Taken

The previous chapter has argued that the Nixon Shock only formalized the widely expected end of the dollar-gold standard. But what was truly shocking was the 10 percent surcharge on imports that Nixon imposed in the same breath (Meltzer 2009: 771; Zimmermann 2010: 137). To German state and corporate elites, these and other protectionist measures demanded by forces inside and outside of Congress seemed capable of spiraling into an all-out trade war.[2]

Under the multilateral order constructed by the United States, Germany had been able to chart a hugely successful course of economic expansion and social stabilization. But with this golden age coming to an end, America's liberal commitments in doubt, and class contestation on the horizon, it seemed that a decisive crossroads had been reached. In a confidential memorandum written in 1974, the German chancellor Helmut Schmidt warned that the collapse of Bretton Woods might only be the prologue to a drama that could prompt a relapse into economic nationalism and culminate in the collapse of the democratic structures of industrial societies.[3] What is remarkable is that in this paper, not at all designed for public consumption, Schmidt was adamant that "this is not an apocalyptic vision but a real possibility of the world economy."[4] Given how central Germany's long-standing and deepening export dependence had been to the institutionalization of the embedded liberal compromise after the Second World War, its policy elites felt highly vulnerable to these threats. But by the middle of the decade the German state also seemed to be in a far better position to weather the storm than its American and European partners. Despite a global economic slowdown, it had posted lower inflation rates, recorded growing trade and financial surpluses, amassed the world's largest foreign exchange reserves, and secured highly favorable financing conditions (Gray 2007: 307–308).[5] The key question that arose was how these considerable capacities could be used to cope with economic stagnation and social conflict at home and abroad. Numerous ideas of how to draw on these resources for a range of inward-looking to wider transformative objectives circulated within the state bureaucracy, and some of them found their way into the highest echelons of policymaking—attesting to the fact that by the mid-1970s, German crisis management had reached a watershed moment.[6]

Overall, two very different sets of policy responses were seriously considered, hotly debated, and eventually dismissed: the first was reflective of a territorially bounded economic rationality, while the second was bound up with a more globally oriented, social-democratic politics of solidarity. Analyzing why German policymakers ultimately decided against both strategic possibilities reveals the structural parameters that delimited Germany's foreign economic choices and yet inspired a novel appreciation and subsequent deployment of its economic power.

A Farewell to Economic Nationalism

For the better part of a century, petroleum has been the vital source of energy of the capitalist world economy, rendering the Middle Eastern region in particular a decisive theater of confrontation of rival imperialisms and giving rise to countless power-political ploys and intrigues, covert operations, and military interventions. The controversial thesis that the US government conspired with the major oil companies to quadruple the price of oil in October 1973 (compare Engdahl 2004; Petersen 2009) thus deserves to be taken seriously—even if, to date, it finds no conclusive support in the relevant government archives (Garavini and Petrini 2011: 219–221). The more recent, and near exhaustive, release of US documents paints a more nuanced picture. According to one reviewer, the American state encouraged the oil majors to accept higher prices for oil out of concern that OPEC might turn to more radical measures of nationalization, and partly because the US was less dependent upon foreign imports than its European and Japanese partners (McFarland 2012: 2). There clearly was an understanding that the US would be harmed less than its competitors, but there is no evidence of a plot to sabotage their industrial capacities (compare Gowan 1999: 21). What the records do indicate is just how deeply the mutual suspicions among the allies ran. Far from being confined to conspiracy theories and sensationalist journalism, they extended to the very people in charge of policy.[7] French circles had warned as early as April 1973 that the US might exploit its lesser dependence on foreign oil by precipitating an energy crisis (Garavini and Petrini 2011: 220, fn. 24). And in the wake of the oil shock, German officials observed with concern that behind the facade of Western solidarity, "the French as well as the British are currently involved in more than dubious dealings with Arab countries for the long-term safeguarding of their oil supply"—information that Schmidt noted to be of "great significance for foreign and European policy."[8]

Fueled by the 1973 oil shock, the threat of similar producer cartels, and mutual distrust, one group of German policy proposals suggested that the state draw on its foreign exchange reserves to build up raw material stocks. Rather than simply holding gold or dollars, why not have the Bundesbank diversify into other, economically more vital, resources?[9] Alternatively, the

German government could either itself acquire and store raw materials, or at least provide financial support to industry so that they could entertain their own reserves.[10] With energy sources being the most critical of these resources, these proposals form part of a more comprehensive plan that included deals with the Soviet Union (Lippert 2011), bilateral supply contracts with Middle Eastern countries, and the creation of a national energy corporation (through the state-sponsored merger of VEBA and Gelsenberg in 1974–1975) that some political elites hoped might be able to balance against the big multinationals (van der Pijl 2006: 121).[11]

In these contingency preparations, one can detect the contours of a more economically self-reliant national strategy. Indeed, one memorandum traced the idea of raw material stockpiles to the proposals of the bankers Hjalmar Schacht and Rudolf Münemann in the 1950s (whom the memo referred to sardonically as "financial geniuses"). As former president of the Reichsbank and Reich Minister of Economics under Hitler, Schacht of course provides the much more significant link to the autarky designs of German fascism.[12] Although one can surmise that in case of an acute emergency the state might have taken a more central role and similar plans might have been acted upon, Germany's postwar dependence on a cooperative and free-trading world economy rendered such a unilateral course of action undesirable as well as unlikely (Deubner 1984: 506, 511, 532).

The available evidence suggests that any more determined plans of national energy independence were seen as unviable in the face of the monopolistic control of the Anglo-American multinational giants. A direct confrontation, it was feared, might lead to a cutoff from supplies.[13] Plans to build a national energy giant were formally buried by the controversial acquisition of the oil company Gelsenberg by Deutsche BP in 1979.[14] Pushed through against the veto of the German cartel office by means of veiled threats of an investment stop[15] as well as the personal intervention of Prime Minister Callaghan (Matthiesen 1987: 63),[16] the deal symbolizes that a central aspect of economic sovereignty had been surrendered after 1945 and irretrievably lost by the 1970s. America's postwar planners had sought to reestablish Germany as Europe's engine of growth while precluding a reprise of militarism and autarky (Painter 2012: 30). The reorientation of German industry from self-sufficiency to overseas supplies of cheap energy sources controlled by Anglo-American firms and their states restored German economic power while firmly integrating it into global markets (Stokes 1988: 629–630). Alongside Japan, West Germany had become the advanced industrial country most reliant on imports of energy sources and other raw materials.[17] From this perspective, the trend toward the conclusion of bilateral agreements posed a particular danger that those capitalist economies that were themselves raw material exporters—principally the US, Canada, Australia, and South Africa—did not face. Lacking a raw material economy integrated with its industry, the Foreign Trade Advisory Council concluded, Germany could not embrace bilateralism without amplifying tendencies that were comparatively less favorable to its own economy.[18] Careful not to add to existing tendencies toward economic bloc formation, German policymakers eschewed politically administered, self-help measures in favor of world market solutions (compare Rosecrance 1986: 16).

By discarding isolationism and bilateralism even as a contingency, German policy planners broke decisively with the designs for formal or informal empire that had circulated among German elites in the interwar period (Gross 2015). Under fascism, Germany had withdrawn from a crumbling world market and sought to carve out an exclusive greater economic sphere in Europe. The defeat of these aggressive ambitions in the Second World War established an integrated global economy as the preferred path to power and prosperity. Some of Germany's postfascist elites, to be sure, had raised questions about how sustainable America's liberal-globalist designs would be (Neebe 2004: 506). And yet the benefits of a rapidly expanding world economy were undeniable. Not only did they persuade Germany's government officials and corporate leaders to embrace free trade and multilateralism in the course of the 1950s and 1960s, they also convinced their main trading partners to open their markets voluntarily. Under these conditions, Germany no longer needed to exercise political authority to secure export opportunities. Instead, as we saw in Chapter 3, German policymakers sought consciously to insulate global free trade—which Germany would dominate by virtue of its economic weight—from the power-political realities of the Cold War and the concessions that a defeated and occupied Germany would have to make (compare Rudolph 2004: 34; Neebe 2004: 509).

And yet, with the slowdown of the 1970s, German attempts to "depoliticize" global market relations no longer worked. It is at this juncture already—rather than in the eurocrisis three decades later—that readings of Germany as a liberal "trading state" whose "primary concern is with wealth, rather than with power" go awry (Maull 2015: 415; see also Rosecrance 1986; Schwarz 1994; Neebe 2004). Its postwar political rulers, to be sure, had internalized and sought to sustain liberal multilateralism. But in the inhospitable global climate of the 1970s, this commitment was no longer enough. The royal road to prosperity through an open and integrated world market now seemed imperiled by the actions of others. German policymakers not only needed to resist a relapse into economic nationalism themselves, but to arrest similar tendencies elsewhere (Kreile 1977: 782). And this, in turn, demanded a significant reorientation of German foreign economic strategy that surpasses Rosecrance's distinction of a cooperative trading and conflictive territorial mode of international relations. "[I]n this dangerous catharsis of the world economy," Schmidt's Political-Economic Paper had asserted, "the strategy and foreign policy of states ought not to be limited to their classical fields."[19]

In the face of interallied disputes over how to resolve economic turmoil and class tensions, German officials in the Bundesbank, chancellery, and finance and economics ministries strove to convert their country's economic and financial weight into political power. The principal aim of the "grand economic strategy" that emerged from these efforts was to defeat the protectionist pressures and mercantilist tendencies that emanated from other countries.[20] Its main target, the next sections explain, was the political spectrum left of Germany's social-democratic government and its radically transformative proposals of how to deal with the capitalist crisis. And the unforeseen consequence of this strategy, which was not neoliberally motivated itself, was to tip the scales in favor of the ideologically driven counteroffensive under Thatcher and Reagan at the turn of the decade.

Germany's *Nein* to Global Keynesianism

The deceleration of the great cycle of postwar expansion dissolved the uneasy marriage of market economy and social democracy and defined the political problem of the crisis decade: that one might have to give way to the other (Devine 2007; Streeck 2011, 2014). The new political economy launched at the end of the 1970s shifted the balance vigorously toward the rule of private property. But in the beginning of the decade, the governments of the center countries faced the task of mediating between the interests of capital and a range of radical forces and reform proposals that sought to broaden the scope of social welfare and extend democratic control to the economic sphere (van der Pijl 2006: 109; Panitch and Gindin 2012: 143; Gill and Solty 2013: 57).

German policymakers concluded that the centrifugal forces threatening the liberal world economy emanated primarily from the interventionist economic programs of socialist and social-democratic forces.[21] They were far from alone in this assessment. Already in the 1960s, wage-push inflation had been identified by the Organisation for Economic Co-Operation and Development (OECD) as a central problem affecting the industrial world; the broader issue of "too much democracy" (Gill and Solty 2013) was raised by dominant forces from across the advanced capitalist bloc since at least the middle of the 1970s. The elite deliberations of the Trilateral Commission infamously warned that the demands of "strong industrial and labor lobbies" and other "new self-assertive groups" rendered advanced capitalist societies "internally more turbulent and externally less responsive to each other's needs" (Duchêne, Mushakoji, and Owen 1974: 17; Crozier, Huntington, and Watanuki 1975: 116, 165). There was even an understanding that a new politics of austerity, imposing what one dissenter described as "a little more unemployment, a little less education, a little more deliberate discipline, and a little less freedom of expression" could offer a significant corrective if not a panacea (Crozier, Huntington, and Watanuki 1975: 194). And yet the global balance in the mid-1970s rendered a direct confrontation with the forces of social and economic democracy an enormous gamble that few among the ruling elites were willing to risk. The organized strength and political representation of the working classes and their domestic and international allies was reflected in the considerations of policymakers of what could and could not be done. In this situation of stalemate, we shall see, Germany's crisis managers came to play a crucial role in charting the way forward. On the one hand, the external vulnerability of Germany's export-driven economy raised the costs of indecision. But more important still was that, uniquely among the major capitalist powers, a program of monetary orthodoxy and reciprocal wage and price restraint could sustain a competitive edge for its dominant export sector and thus prove stabilizing rather than punitive.

Because the success of their crisis response depended on continued access to global markets, German policymakers were anxious not to add wind to the sails of left-wing demands for a greater role of the state in steering investments, nationalizing industries, or extending worker control. It was in part for these reasons that they ultimately refrained from using the Bundesbank's vast reserve assets to align national self-interest with international solidarity. The original proposal championed by the chancellor's and foreign offices in the mid-1970s was to lend out a fraction of foreign exchange reserves to financially distressed countries in Western and Eastern Europe as well as the Global South. This would provide a massive stimulus to global demand

and pull the advanced industrialized countries, and Germany in particular, out of the recession.[22] These plans were in part a response to the explosive and uncertain international context of widespread redistributive demands from within and from outside of the capitalist core. The calls for the New International Economic Order (NIEO), backed up by the OPEC oil embargo, had sown considerable disharmony within the Western camp and posed the threat of similar producer cartels (Cox 1983: 171; Krasner 1985: 92; Overbeek 2008: 183).[23] In this respect, the proposal connected to social-democratic plans for what the Austrian chancellor Bruno Kreisky had called a "Marshall Plan" for the developing world and held out the possibility of a far-reaching and progressive reorganization of the world economic order. Had Germany's policymakers followed through with their plans to recycle parts of its balance-of-payments surplus in such an outward-oriented fashion, it may have allowed both surplus and deficit countries to sustain (or construct) the embedded liberal compromise through a combination of financial assistance and export promotion.

And yet such a benevolent hegemonic strategy was rejected by the Bundesbank and finance and economics ministries. The counterargument that swayed its proponents was that this scheme was bound to endanger Germany's stabilization strategy. Most advanced capitalist states had tried to "paper over" the societal faultlines that opened up in the wake of the economic recession with the help of the printing press. "For governments facing conflicting demands from workers and capital in a world of declining growth rates," Wolfgang Streeck (2011: 12) recalls, "an accommodating monetary policy was a convenient *ersatz* method for avoiding zero-sum social conflict." The by-product of this coping strategy, which postponed rather than resolved the clash of distributive claims, was escalating inflation as both capitalists and workers sought to raise their relative income shares (for example, Devine 2007: 37). The particular solution that German policymakers had found in the wake of the DM float was unique. The Bundesbank had used a nonaccommodating monetary policy to recommit capital and labor to wage and price restraint, and to keep inflation levels below those of Germany's major trading rivals (Beyer, Gaspar, Gerberding, and Issing 2008: 12; Franzese and Hall 2000: 182–183). Greater price stability offset an appreciating DM and translated into competitive advantage in international markets, and mutual benefits to both social partners (Herr and Voy 1990: 57; Webber 1983: 71). To a remarkable extent, Germany's stabilization policy was able to sustain the embedded liberal compromise domestically by preserving differential opportunities for the dominant export bloc around which it had originally been constructed. Just as important as continued access to world markets, however, was the construction of a wider zone of stability that could shield the German economy from global inflationary pressures.[24] The proposal to tap into and lend out central bank reserves would have the opposite effect. Although it was recognized that an expansion of international liquidity would stimulate global demand and benefit German exports in particular, the inflationary dangers were considered to outweigh these advantages.[25] German monetary officials were concerned that the additional funds created through the extension of German credit to deficit countries would only encourage further spendthrift behavior—an argument very similar to their public defense of Germany's austerity agenda since the eurocrisis. Worse still, the Bundesbank feared that these funds would circle back into the German economy and raise domestic price levels. The conclusion that the Bundesbank reached is important in this regard. To serve as "a lever of international stabilization efforts," financial support ought to be channeled through international financial institutions and to be given only on condition of monetary and fiscal restraint.[26]

Overall, then, the continued capacity of German policymakers to pursue an anti-inflationary program militated against attempts to sustain the embedded liberal compromise outside Germany, let alone globalize it beyond the North Atlantic. Success, after all, was defined in relative rather than absolute terms: the remarkable ability, as Schmidt's Marbella Paper had pointed out, to maintain lower inflation and unemployment rates, to sustain higher per capita income rates, and even to afford larger military expenditures (relative to its GDP) than the rest of the capitalist world.[27] From this differential point of view, German self-interest trumped collective and progressive solutions. Without Germany's full support, Chapter 6 will show, the locomotive approach of coordinating a global economic stimulus was doomed from the start. Any concerted efforts to restabilize embedded liberalism on an international scale were subordinated to the narrow goal of German state elites to maintain internal order.

Germany's Grand Economic Strategy

Our review of German crisis planning and the two poles of possible actions it evolved around has found that state managers, in the event, decided neither to retreat from nor to reflate the world economy. In the eyes of decision makers, both economic nationalism and global Keynesianism were held to set dangerous precedents: other countries might follow the German lead and gear their raw material procurement or lending policies to the purpose of export promotion,[28] and financial assistance to some countries would prompt further demands from others, leading to an unacceptable expansion of credit.[29] In short, therefore, the limits to national self-reliance were set by the fear of an escalating protectionism, while the limits to international solidarity were set by the fear of global inflation.

Instead, a third and, no less important, strategy took precedence. What remained of the reflationary and redistributive proposals was the recognition that Germany could best pursue its political and economic interests by relying on its monetary power and working through international financial institutions. Echoing the Marbella Paper's famously cited assessment of the historical limits of West German foreign policy after 1945, one report noted that "[o]ur particular political circumstances and our interests continue to bar us from demonstrating our capacity, e.g. by delivering weapons, sending troops as international peace forces, accepting border guarantees, etc." "In point of fact," the memo concluded, "the real instrument with which we can bring our strength, namely our economic and financial strength, to bear in our foreign policy lies in the sphere of financial assistance. . . . Only in terms of foreign exchange reserves are we stronger than most others, without foreign policy considerations proscribing the use of this means a priori."[30]

The social purpose to which Germany's financial and monetary strength was henceforth to be put was radically different. In the midst of the 1970s crisis, German policymakers adhered to these instructions in order to defeat the forces of protectionism and inflation—first, vis-à-vis its European neighbors, and second, as Chapter 6 explains, vis-à-vis the United States. To sustain open markets and its comparative advantage, the German state set out to counter the interventionist and expansionary remedies of the European left. In a sense, the social-liberal government of Schmidt tried to extend internationally what had started in the early 1970s as an internal attempt to discipline militant labor, the insubordinate youth organization, and the left wing of the Social Democratic Party (Sozialdemokratische Partei Deutschlands, SPD). To project power across politically bounded space rather than from the top down was of course a much more problematic undertaking. While far from successful in every case, German policy elites sought to use their financial clout to shift the balance of social forces away from radicals whose proposals were seen to foreclose access to European and global markets, and toward moderates prepared to follow Germany's anti-inflationary path (Lankowski 1982a: 344).[31] Yet German policymakers, far from seeking to impose neoliberal change, sought merely to preserve the export model that had secured the embedded liberal compromise at home.

European Monetary Integration
and the Deutsche Mark Block

While the disintegration of Bretton Woods into a floating regime increased the macroeconomic scope of the Bundesbank, the erratic exchange rates also posed significant problems for the coherence of the European Economic Community (EEC). To limit internal fluctuations, Germany and its EEC partners resurrected plans to accelerate the monetary integration of Europe. In late 1972, they concluded the European Exchange Rate Agreement, or "currency snake," which stipulated that members maintain the exchange value of their currencies within a margin of +/–2.25 percent. The long-term consequences of the currency snake and its more durable successor—the European Monetary System (EMS) created in 1979—were to propel the European project toward monetary union and to give it a distinctly neoliberal inflection (for example, Cafruny and Ryner 2003: 233). From the German point of view, the immediate objectives were to protect this vital European market for German industry against exchange-rate risks, a loss of price competitiveness, and the threat of import controls and competitive devaluations (Lankowski 1982a: 344). The concern that underpinned these more ambitious plans was to create a zone of stability amidst global inflation.[32] At a minimum, the snake was meant to pull together and single out states that could strengthen their currencies by embracing the monetary and fiscal restraint demonstrated and demanded by Frankfurt and Bonn.[33] The argument that the snake failed because Italy left early on and France dropped out several times is only partially true (compare Kaltenthaler 1998: 45). Its German architects accepted that countries unable or unwilling to follow Germany's direction ought best to be kept out. A smaller core of hard-currency countries was preferred to the extensive financial assistance that wider EEC membership would require.[34] And in fact, Swiss participation, briefly considered in 1975, was welcomed as a means to harden the snake and keep France and Italy at bay until a more serious commitment to monetary and fiscal prudence could be expected.[35]

The modalities and implications of removing a country like Greece from today's Economic and Monetary Union (EMU) are of course infinitely more complex. And yet as Chapter 7 explains, it is from a similar standpoint that a minority faction within the German government led by finance minister Wolfgang Schäuble came down in favor of a temporary "time out" for countries that are unwilling or unable to adopt the structural reforms necessary to remain a productive member of the eurozone.

Adhering to the narrow bands of the snake was no easy task for its small members either, however (Jones 2005).[36] Similar to the larger states of the EEC, they faced a trade-off: would they accept wage demands and risk higher inflation, or take a nonaccommodating stance at the expense of growth and employment (Scharpf 1984: 259; Straumann 2010: 187–188)? Unlike with the larger states, however, the choice between flexible and fixed exchange rates was shaped less by domestic conditions. External constraints such as EEC membership, trade integration, and financial openness, new research shows, played a far more determining role than the comparative-institutionalist literature has recognized (Straumann 2010: 15–17). Uncertainty about the future shape of the world monetary order and the inability to exert much influence over its direction (exemplified in their exclusion from top-level monetary discussions of the major capitalist countries in the G7 summit and finance minister meetings), coupled with the fear that their smaller economies would be particularly vulnerable to exchange-rate fluctuations, convinced them of the necessity of a fixed-exchange-rate regime (Straumann 2010: 206, 210).

The peg to the DM, however, linked countries such as Belgium, the Netherlands, and Denmark to Germany's restrictive monetary policy. The result was a form of "imported monetarism" in which the Bundesbank made the choice between unemployment and inflation for them (Scharpf 2000: 33; Straumann 2010: 223, 234, 239). In these cases, then, monetary restraint was imposed rather than emulated.[37]

German policymakers knew full well that the currency alignment with a strong DM compelled their European partners to adjust their macroeconomic policies to Germany's anti-inflationary program.[38] The political-economic paper concluded that "[i]t is politically necessary not to have the snake appear as a currency block led by Bonn. In reality, however, we need to maintain our efforts to coordinate the general economic policies of the snake countries."[39]

It was with a similar disciplinary intent that German policymakers chose to replace the currency snake with the EMS in 1979. The insightful study of Carl Lankowski (1982b: 98) argues that the EMS was "a cover for demanding that the other [EEC] governments adopt policies that would adjust their economic performance to that of West Germany; the West German government was actually asking for the initiation of austerity policies throughout Europe. . . . Under these circumstances, the West German government was willing to support the external value of the currencies of its [EEC] partners with its enormous foreign exchange and gold reserves."[40] Compared to Germany's smaller economic satellites, however, the extension of monetary rigor to the larger EEC countries depended to a far greater extent on internal shifts in political objectives and social power relations. Through financial (dis)incentives and institutional mechanisms such as the EMS and the IMF, German policymakers certainly sought to extract and lock in similar commitments, but they could not dictate terms. If and when German state managers came close to outlining the solution, it was due to an important convergence of American and German economic thinking in the second half of the 1970s.

The Limits of "Benign Neglect" and the German-American Entente[41]

The events surrounding the breakdown of the fixed-exchange-rate regime between 1971 and 1973 have been discussed earlier and need no recounting here. As Germany readied its European partners to float against the dollar in March 1973, the US formalized its policy of nonintervention—not because the case for floating had won the economic argument, but because Nixon and Kissinger concluded that "European unity will not be in our interest"[42] and sought to "create conditions in which the Common float is as hard to work as possible."[43] By refusing to stabilize a declining dollar, the US put pressures on the currency snake and frustrated efforts to negotiate a new monetary system (Hudson 1977: 95–96; Trachtenberg 2011: 23). But by early 1976, the drawbacks of this monetary *laissez faire* approach could no longer be ignored.

The decision of the Bank of Italy to withdraw from foreign exchange markets at the start of the year had seen the lira-dollar exchange rate drop by 20 percent in three months.[44] The British authorities, too, were believed to have forced a drop in the sterling exchange rate in early March. US officials observed that "[b]oth Italy and Britain, plagued by domestic inflation, are unlikely to achieve in coming months the domestic economic stability required to stabilize their exchange rates."[45] Japan, too, was suspected of practicing a "dirty float" (Biven 2002: 108). And it was feared that France, which had left the snake on March 15, would join in the race of competitive devaluation. Evidently, the freedom to float had undermined whatever rules of the game had remained intact. "The principal danger in this situation involves the types of adjustment efforts that could be taken," one memo warned.[46] Rather than address the root causes of the problem, it seemed that countries would resort to beggar-thy-neighbor policies or protectionist measures.

US policymakers realized that even if floating exchange rates might accurately reflect "market fundamentals," as its academic proponents had promised, by themselves market forces would do little to encourage responsible economic policy (compare Helleiner 1994: 15). On the contrary, as Schmidt had told William Simon (now treasury secretary) and Fed chairman Arthur Burns, floating exchange rates might lessen the disciplinary pressure on countries to control domestic inflation.[47] Worse still, in the absence of serious efforts to address underlying imbalances, gyrating exchange rates were bound to have profoundly destabilizing effects domestically and systemically. Clearly, the pressures of floating exchange rates and capital flows did not lead to economic discipline but to disintegration. Under these circumstances, the US came to accept what German economic strategists had argued early on: that to prevent the system from collapse, *benign neglect* was insufficient.[48] Rather than relying on free markets, the exercise of political influence was necessary to encourage system-conforming adjustments.[49] American policymakers concluded that "[t]he United States, for the first time in years now has the capacity, particularly in cooperation with the West Germans, to do something about this."[50] The success of German state elites in managing the capitalist crisis by way of monetary and fiscal prudence, and their efforts to impose macroeconomic restraint via the currency snake, rendered Germany the most important ally in preventing a downward spiral of import controls and competitive devaluation (Ludlow 2013: 144).[51]

While most scholarly attention has focused on the Nixon Shock and the Volcker Shock as the two decisive moments in the constitution of neoliberal globalization, it was during the much neglected Ford administration that some of the most important programmatic and institutional changes took place. Under Ford, a new market-centered paradigm emerged that prioritized the fight against inflation through reducing the levels of taxation, public expenditure, and state intervention (Moran 2011: 59, 61). At the international level, US policymakers began to develop a program of economic stabilization that specified conditions for financial assistance and to create an institutional mechanism for enforcing adjustments. The most lasting effect of this endeavor was to reinvigorate the International Monetary Fund, which seemed moribund when the par value system of Bretton Woods collapsed. And the litmus test was to jointly use the new instrument to induce structural adjustment in Britain and (to a lesser extent) Italy (James 1996: 285). "US/FRG cooperation," it was noted, "will be essential in any solution."[52]

That the roots of the problem and their possible solution contained a class dimension is brought out very clearly in the remarks by William Simon that "[d]eep divisions on the distribution of income have in Italy and the United Kingdom, for example, been obscured by efforts to manufacture solutions through policies which would assure rapid economic expansion."[53] The efforts to defer class struggle by Keynesian means, characteristic of the whole of the postwar era and applicable to the United States itself, had issued in runaway inflation. Having lived beyond their means, the welfare states and working classes of Western capitalism now had to accept major concessions.

And yet, no matter how astute this diagnosis, neither Germany nor the US were able or willing to prescribe a comprehensive solution to these ills. The German government struggled to keep at bay the radical elements of the European labor movement, the alternative economic programs of which threatened the German export model and the domestic social compact sustained by it. While hoping to contain these interventionist and expansionary policies, German policymakers were in no position to reverse the balance of forces. For such a class realignment to occur across the regions of advanced capitalism, and for a neoliberal program to prevail, American policymakers needed first to apply internally the economic and political lessons they had drawn from the example of the European deficit countries (Panitch and Gindin 2012: 159). In short, whereas the German state still acted to defend its embedded liberal compact at home, the US had yet to prove to the world that a full-frontal attack on the organized power of labor was feasible. It was only after Carter's final bid for a coordinated Keynesian reflation, and indeed under pressure from Germany, that this could be tried (Ludlow 2013: 159). And when it was, the neoliberal experiment departed from the fiscal conservatism of balanced budgets that had guided the Ford administration. Its success came instead to rest on the enormous tax cuts and deficit spending of the Reagan administration (Moran 2011: 60; Prasad 2012: 352; see Chapter 6).

At the midpoint of the decade, then, the capitalist world was still far away from this neoliberal resolution. The looming election of the

Italian communists into power, the danger that British Labour might opt for the statist Alternative Economic Strategy, and the menacing alliance of the French socialists and communists—all these were scenarios that German and US officials sought to influence but that they could not fully control. German policies and prescriptions, we shall see, narrowed the range of possible pathways out of the crisis, and in this respect Germany came to matter as much for what it did as for what it didn't do. It is entirely plausible to hold that the course chosen was in the last instance determined by the social forces on the ground, the convictions that guided them, and the access to the power of the state they enjoyed. The key analytical point is that these ideas and interests, formulated under specific domestic and international circumstances, did not follow a neoliberal template derived from the American hegemon. And the empirical question that follows from this is how the German state shaped this external environment.

Though unlikely in retrospect, each of these three cases had the potential of recasting the European and international order in terms detrimental to liberal capitalism and more favorable to organized labor and social welfare. Their failure, in turn, laid the groundwork for and undermined the capabilities of progressive forces to resist the neoliberal counterrevolution of the late 1970s and 1980s. And yet the fact that these alternatives never came to pass cannot itself be attributed solely to the growing strength of neoliberalism as a state, class, or ideological project.

Italy was most vulnerable to external pressures, but it was geostrategic concerns that guided the financial interventions of the US and Germany. And the Italian Communist Party, which was the main target of foreign interference but also the key auxiliary of an internationally negotiated politics of *austerità*, can hardly be accused of a neoliberal orientation. British state managers were confronted with a full-fledged neoliberal project and constituency, but the Labour government departed from the postwar consensus selectively and sought Germany's help in avoiding IMF austerity. The lack of political alternatives, rather than the force of the neoliberal argument or the pressure of the market, best explains its actions. Finally, the French state bureaucracy under Raymond Barre sought to emulate the German model in the absence of domestic support for neoliberalism. Its trial run of *rigueur*, made possible by its exceptional degree of insulation from wider social interests, cannot be generalized into an ideas-based account of neoliberal change.

Italy: Communist Austerity

Italy was one of the countries hit hardest by the capitalist crisis and attendant social and political upheavals. Suffering from some of the highest unemployment and inflation rates in the OECD, a deteriorating current account, and mounting public debt, Italy became heavily dependent on international borrowing and a major test case for conditional financial assistance (Sassoon 1996: 588; Bernardini 2011: 330).

The reliance on foreign credit alone meant that the path toward austerity capitalism would be influenced by external forces. But the situation was further complicated by the peculiar geopolitical position that Italy occupied by virtue of having the strongest communist movement in the Cold War West. In the mid-1970s, the Italian Communist Party seemed destined to take over the reins of power from the Christian Democratic Party (Democrazia Cristiana, DC) and its centrist coalition just as the crisis came to a head. The postwar objective of the United States and its NATO partners of keeping the communists out of government and Italy firmly within the Alliance played an important role in shaping the economic "stabilization efforts" of Italy's creditors.[54]

The German SPD leadership sought to prevent the emergence of a credible anticapitalist and eurocommunist alternative to social democracy (Bernardini 2011: 321), and urged its socialist brother party and the ruling Christian Democrats not to enter into the "historic compromise" proposed by the PCI. In mid-1974, the Schmidt government tried for the first time to use financial aid to commit its Italian partners to keeping the PCI out of government and continuing a restrictive monetary policy. The plan backfired, and a scandal ensued (Bernardini 2011: 325–327).[55] Prime Minister Mariano Rumor was replaced by Aldo Moro soon after, and an inclusion of the PCI seemed unavoidable as the economic situation continued to deteriorate. In 1975, the Italian state tried to promote economic growth by expansionary fiscal and monetary measures but proved unable to stem the downward pressure on the lira and inflationary repercussions this entailed. Efforts to stabilize the lira depleted the resources of the Bank of Italy, which withdrew from foreign exchange markets between January and March 1976 (McNamara 1998: 133). The confluence of economic and political considerations is aptly described in a German foreign office memo: "Italy is sick; an effective long-term therapy should be provided. Its Western partners have an important role to play. But coping with the present crisis is also a matter of urgency:

for the first time in 30 years a fundamental change in the balance of forces has become possible."[56]

The Americans likewise considered the situation in Italy to hold "significance for the future of the European Community, the Western economic system, and the Western political and security system."[57] German and American policymakers agreed that "unless they put their own house in order external financial assistance would be money down the drain."[58] In the first half of 1976, they settled on the IMF as the appropriate mechanism to supply these funds and enforce adjustments, and in secret meetings with Britain and France developed the economic and political conditions to be attached to a new financial package. Most central, once again, was the vow not to include the PCI in a new Italian government (Bernardini 2011: 335; Ludlow 2013: 153). The economic dimension of the program followed the monetary and fiscal policies that had proven successful in Germany. But the backlash against German interference in 1974 had made clear that the impression of direct influence had to be avoided. Accordingly, the US side concluded that "[t]he best institutional arrangement for producing conditional financing is the IMF. It . . . cloaks the conditionality in a multinational mantle that dilutes opposition within a borrowing country to conditions imposed by the US or other outsiders."[59]

The newly formed minority government of the DC welcomed the "recommendations" of the Quad (US, Germany, France, and Britain) as a way of keeping the communists at bay. The international negotiations enabled the DC to short-circuit parliamentary debate and to enlist the support of the PCI to the economic conditions tied to the financial assistance (Bernardini 2011: 336). The issue of why the Italian communists were willing to impose austerity on their working-class electorate falls outside of the scope of this book, but may have involved a peculiarly anticapitalist rather than neoliberal critique of Keynesianism.[60] The outcome, in any case, was to discredit the PCI, which had little influence over the economic program but was held responsible for its adverse impact on the working class. The entry of Italy into the EMS in 1979, opposed by the PCI, was used by the DC as an excuse to terminate the national solidarity government (Simonazzi and Vianello 1998: 109; Abse 2005: 255–256).

Having joined at least in part because, as the political aide to Schmidt's predecessor reported, "[Andreotti] thinks it is more dangerous for Italy to stay outside,"[61] Italy continued to chart an erratic course between expansion and deflation rather than set out on a clear-cut neoliberal path. But what was significant was the demolition—assisted, though of course not directed, by German-American financial pressures—of the prospects for a distinctly communist and potentially European-wide alternative to capitalism embodied by the PCI.

Britain and the IMF

From their early blunders in Italy, German policymakers drew two conclusions. First, rather than risk the exposure of bilateral negotiations, the terms and conditions of financial assistance were best determined in a nominally multilateral setting. And second, within the recipient country some political faction needed to be found that was amenable to the pressures brought to bear upon it.[62] Both lessons were followed in the infamous episode of Britain turning to the IMF in 1976. There is no doubt that behind the IMF stood Germany and the United States. As the two largest creditors to the General Agreement to Borrow, it was they who shaped the conditions under which Britain would be allowed to access emergency financing. But even though they wielded considerable influence, the IMF crisis does not amount to an outside-in displacement of the Keynesian compromise.[63]

In important respects, the British Labour government had already departed from the Keynesian policy consensus before it turned to the IMF in 1976 (Ludlam 1992; Hickson 2005: 222). Elected in 1974 on the campaign promise of bringing about "a fundamental and irreversible shift in the balance of power and wealth in favor of working people and their families" (quoted in Rogers 2013: 9), the party leadership had to contend with an ambitious "Alternative Economic Strategy" put forth by Tony Benn and the Labour left that emphasized the extension of public ownership, investment control, and industrial and workplace democracy (Hickson 2005: 50–53). Its proponents argued that in an age of transnational corporations and global financial flows, building socialism required a degree of national policy autonomy that could only be established through interventionist and protectionist measures (Hickson 2005: 171).

On the side of capital, the Labour government confronted not simply the opposition of conservatives but a forcefully articulated critique of Keynesian demand management, an ostensibly superior interpretation of the causes of stagflation, and a handy set of tools and techniques for addressing them (Jones 2012: 216). In contrast to Germany, where ordoliberal ideas mattered little in the economic policy discourse (Johnson 1998: 56), in Britain we find think tanks, the business press, and the City of London that espoused the free-market fundamentalism of Hayek and Friedman (Hall 1993; Cockett 1995; Dixon 2000; Hickson 2005: 186; Jones 2012).

Rather than fully converting to neoliberal ideology, however, the Labour party would "pick and choose from a menu of neoliberal offerings" (Jones 2012: 18, 246–247; Hickson 2005: 223–224; 226; Ludlam 1992: 716–724; 727)—exhibiting a pragmatism that, as Chris Rogers (2013: 4) has pointed out, does not sit well with the notion of a fundamental contestation of economic paradigms.

By 1976, to be sure, British macroeconomic policy had moved on from the core Keynesian belief that the state could deficit-finance its way out of a recession. In a moment of economic crisis, Callaghan told the Labour Party Congress in September, the fight against inflation would have to take precedence over full employment (Hickson 2005: 104). But while drawing on neoliberal policies such as "cash limits" on public expenditures and monetary targets, the Callaghan government still sought to achieve full employment in the long run (Hickson 2005: 212)—a far cry from the objective of Thatcher and Reagan to induce a recession in order to squeeze out inflation and target the labor movement. Peter Jay, Callaghan's son-in-law and advisor as well as a monetarist advocate, who had written the passage of Callaghan's speech (Hickson 2005: 104), rightly cautions that "the attempt to tell the story as though it were a kind of story of ideological evolution, revolution or counter-revolution or something, seems to me to do great violence to the actual detail and particularity of history which is much more messy than that" (quoted in Jones 2012: 247).

The departure of the Wilson and Callaghan governments from embedded liberalism cannot be rooted in the realm of ideas alone. Nor can it be reduced to a simple shift in the social balance of power. For while Thatcher would indeed launch a class offensive, her predecessors still steered a centrist course between calls for extending public authority over capital on the one hand and calls for freeing the market from an encroaching state on the other (Clarke 1987: 396–397). Though only one part in a long-winded story, the IMF crisis marks the culmination of years of external constraints on Labour to follow this middle ground.

To British policymakers, the decision to float the pound in June 1972 had promised to restore macroeconomic autonomy without the need for administrative controls. A downward floating pound, it was hoped, would automatically correct balance-of-payments imbalances. By improving the competitiveness of British exports and reducing the trade deficit, a lower exchange rate would lessen the need to borrow abroad or attract short-term and potentially volatile sterling inflows. In this way, the two major and—from a centrist position—undesirable alternatives of either import and exchange controls or deflationary measures might be avoided (Wass 2008: 57, 96, 146–147).

While the Treasury favored devaluation, its overseas finance section and the Bank of England expressed the concerns of overseas sterling holders and the City of London about the future value and international role of the pound (Wass 2008: 333). Unable to agree on an active depreciation policy, it was decided to rely on downward market pressure and, at most, to limit the countervailing interventions of the Bank of England. The resulting impasse, and the stubbornly stable exchange rate of the pound between 1974 and 1976, foreclosed the possibility of charting a middle course via depreciation. The choice faced by the Labour government was thus limited to the protectionist measures advocated by the left as a means of achieving a balance-of-payments surplus, and the painful but more manageable course of deflation. It is this latter route on which the Labour leadership embarked with the budget cuts of 15 April 1975, and which culminated in the IMF agreement in December 1976 (Hickson 2005: 57).

The Treasury got what it wanted when the Bank of England—by accident or design—set off a fall in the exchange rate by selling sterling on 4 March 1976 and reducing interest rates on the following day. Douglas Wass, who was the permanent secretary to the Treasury at the time, insists this was "fortuitous" (2008: 179; see also Hickson 2005: 74–78), but the German records suggest that the key actors thought otherwise. At a meeting of the Group of Four (France, Germany, United Kingdom, United States) financial deputies on 23 March 1976, Derek Mitchell, head of the overseas section of the Treasury, argued that a devaluation of the pound had been necessary because of strong pressures of British industry and the Trades Union Congress. The alternative, he explained, would have been to adopt import controls.[64] US Undersecretary of the Treasury for Monetary Affairs Edwin Yeo protested that "the way in which the pound had been floated downward constituted a clear violation of the new IMF regulations that expressly prohibit an 'aggressive floating.'" Speaking to Pöhl in private, Yeo left little doubt that Britain was pursuing a policy of competitive devaluation.[65]

Either way, the Treasury welcomed the decline and therefore did not see the need to take any active measures to support sterling until its near collapse of June 1976 (Wass 2008: 346), when Britain was forced to rely on support from the Bank for International Settlements (Helleiner 1994: 125). In this situation of an international loss of confidence, the middling course no longer worked. British policymakers realized even before accepting the stricter IMF conditions that in order to restore market confidence, deflationary measures would be necessary.

And yet these market pressures should not be overemphasized either. Rogers (2013; 2009a; 2009b) has argued that the British state also shaped the "impression of crisis" in order to legitimate its policy choices against the opposition and alternative proposals of the Labour left. The devaluation of the pound in particular was used by the chancellor to convince his cabinet colleagues, the party base, and the trade unions of the necessity of harsh anti-inflationary measures (Rogers 2013: 14–15; 2009a: 635, 643–644; 2009b: 979–982; Wass 2008: 347).

Second, as in the German case of floating discussed in Chapter 4, it is important here again to disaggregate the structural power of capital and to look at the particular agents that made up "the markets" and outlined the contours of the crisis for the British state. One of the problems certainly was that investors in the gilt-edged market in the summer of 1976 were "refusing to purchase public sector debt as it feared rising inflation and expected interest rates to rise in early-September" (Hickson 2005: 99). This undoubtedly entered the official mind as a problem of market confidence that needed to be addressed (Burk and Cairncross 1992: 52). These two problems continued until October, when the decision of Healey to tighten monetary policy (raising the minimum lending rate by 2 percent to 15 percent and increasing the ratio of sterling deposits by 2 percent) stabilized the pound and boosted demand for gilts. From then on, the sterling rate was the only remaining concern (Hickson 2005: 116). And here it is important to point out that the sterling troubles of 1975 and 1976 were primarily caused by a group of four major official holders of sterling (among them Kuwait, Nigeria, and Saudi Arabia) (Wass 2008: 133, 135, 336). As Wass (337) notes, "during the course of 1976 . . . the main selling came from official holders, and non-official holders scarcely moved their holdings even during periods of intense uncertainty."

This insight is extraordinarily important in order to assess the role of Germany. Given that the predominant pressures on the pound at the height of the IMF crisis came from a small number of central banks rather than a myriad of unruly market operators, a negotiated resolution seems to have been feasible. British policymakers certainly believed as much, as they repeatedly asked for German financial assistance in offering a guarantee for sterling deposits.[66] The considerable concessions they were willing to make in exchange for Germany's support in setting up a "safety net" for sterling balances goes to show that they still hoped to avoid the IMF rather than simply use it as a pretext for a course of austerity they had planned to pursue all along. In this crucial respect, neoliberal ideas had not yet triumphed. The problem, however, was that the German side refused to play along. Asked by a desperate Callaghan to at least offer an assurance that a safety net would be forthcoming *after* an IMF agreement had been reached, Schmidt replied that the US would not accept this.[67] But while Schmidt blamed the Americans, German policymakers were keen to avoid an agreement on sterling that might sideline the prospective role of the IMF as an enforcement mechanism (Hickson 2005: 124; for more on this see Burk and Cairncross 1992: 66–67).

The successful conclusion of a sterling "safety net" might have solved a large part of the confidence problem besetting British society and saved it from the strictures of IMF adjustment. This counterfactual is important to consider for two reasons. It implies that the structural power of financial markets did not fully force the hands of powerless policymakers. Austerity was not unavoidable but was adopted because the political alternatives had been rejected. And second, Germany precluded a less painful settlement and, once again, swung the balance against the embedded liberal compromise of one of its neighbors.

From the German point of view, the IMF negotiations with Britain would set a crucial international precedent.[68] This certainly meant that the conditions ought not to be too generous, as this would prompt further calls from other countries for the provision of international liquidity.[69] At the same time, Schmidt warned deficit hawks in the Ford administration, whom he suspected to be influenced by the Tory opposition,[70] not to ask for more than Callaghan could deliver.[71] The conditions, to be sure, ought to have been stringent enough for him to overcome the opposition from his party and the unions to his reform agenda.[72] But a breakdown of negotiations or change in leadership might have given support to the radical proposals of Tony Benn, who had taken the position "that Britain should introduce overall import quotas for manufactures, enforce exchange controls, introduce a Capital Investments Committee to channel investment to priority areas, and take reserve powers to introduce planning agreements through the National Enterprise Board" (Rogers 2009b: 986). Indeed, looking back a few months later, economics minister Schlecht concluded that "had the conditions been excessive, Great Britain would have instituted direct import controls."[73]

The IMF negotiations, then, rather than a one-sided imposition, were a delicate balancing act for all parties involved. The British Labour government, having failed to bypass the IMF, needed it for two reasons. IMF approval would consecrate its existing economic strategy of fiscal cuts and monetary restraint that, short of an alternative "safety net," was considered crucial in order to restore confidence in sterling (Clift and Tomlinson 2008: 546, 566; Burk and Cairncross 1992: 225). Furthermore, IMF negotiations and conditions would also help overcome internal opposition to this course of action and help to externalize the blame for politically unpopular measures.[74] From the perspective of the Fund and the two major creditors that sought to reconstruct it, "[t]he 1976 crisis was to be a major test case to see if the IMF still had a function that it could perform" (Hickson 2005: 62). The differences between the US and German sides in the negotiations was more of a matter of emphasis rather than a question of fundamentally different strategies. As Yeo put it, "The Germans will be SOBs, but with us one step ahead."[75]

Both sides clearly believed that the stakes were vital. The German concerns were mirrored by the assessment, relayed by the former secretary of state William Rogers, that

> It was a choice between Britain remaining in the liberal financial system of the West as opposed to a radical change of course, because we were concerned about Tony Benn precipitating a policy decision by Britain to turn its back on the IMF. I think if that had happened the whole system would have come apart. God knows what Italy might have done; then France might have taken a radical change in the same direction. It would not only have had consequences for the economic recovery, it would have had great political consequences. So we tended to see it in cosmic terms" (quoted in Burk and Cairncross 1992: 77).

The difference in negotiating positions therefore did not change the close cooperation and cordial relations between US and German authorities. When William Simon left the Treasury with the outgoing Ford government, Emminger commended him for his "role in the biggest international financing operation ever . . . particularly as regards the economic policy conditions that have been attached to the IMF standby arrangement."[76] At the same time, it was not a neoliberal consensus that brought the two states together. The key point is that policymakers did not need to share Simon's free market fundamentalism to be concerned about a potential breakaway of Britain and the chain reaction to which this might lead. For the US-German entente, the IMF crisis was not about the imposition of a particular neoliberal solution but rather about preventing the protectionist scenario of currency devaluation and import controls.

Inside Britain, too, the IMF crisis meant not the triumph of neoliberal ideology but the decisive break between the Labour leadership, its party base, and the working-class movement. It was this schism that the Letter of Intent symbolized and "locked in," that erupted into the Winter of Discontent in 1978–1979, and that the rapprochement within the party after the election of Thatcher would do little to mend.

France and the EMS

The year 1976 also marked a turning point of sorts for France. The dramatic break with embedded liberalism, to be sure, would only come with the defeat of the socialist program of President François Mitterrand in 1983, when the neoliberal sea-change in the United States and United Kingdom was already well under way (Sassoon 1996: 561). But the prime ministerial appointment of Raymond Barre by Mitterrand's centrist predecessor seven years earlier initiated a peculiar and precocious shift toward neoliberalism that was both modeled on and assisted by the German state (Prasad 2006: 258–259).

A political outsider hailing from the European Commission and drawing on his monetary expertise, Barre rejected Keynesian recipes of reflation and devaluation (Howarth 2016: 77). Instead, he sought to curb inflation through monetary, fiscal, and wage restraint and to boost international competitiveness by extricating the state from industry and the market economy (Moss 2005: 131; Prasad 2006: 271, 272). The Barre program, which included the removal of state subsidies and price and capital controls, proved so unpopular that it had to be abandoned (McNamara 1998: 156; Prasad 2006: 239, 272–273). Its lasting impact, however, was to significantly roll back the traditionally interventionist role of the French state (Duménil and Lévy 2005: 37; Fourcade-Gourinchas and Babb 2002: 565).

The early French departure from embedded liberalism was peculiar in that it was free from either external diktat or an internal lobby (Fourcade-Gourinchas and Babb 2002: 567; Sassoon 1996: 547). To be sure, a politics of *austerité* was possible in principle because the French labor movement was weak and fragmented and its political representation split into socialist and communist camps (McNamara 1998: 132). At the same time that there was little opposition, however, there was also practically no business support for the punitive Barre Plan either (Fourcade-Gourinchas and Babb 2002: 567).[77] As premier and, from 1976 to 1978 finance minister, Barre was placed at the helm of a centralized state bureaucracy insulated from particular societal interests, capable of imposing solutions by administrative fiat, and thus at liberty to "search for the most successful practices among neighboring states" (Prasad 2006: 276, see also 23; Fourcade-Gourinchas and Babb 2002: 562).

Given that in 1976 the United Kingdom and the United States hardly embodied an attractive, let alone economically conservative, alternative, this search focused on the German state in particular (Moss 2005: 131; Prasad 2006: 239; Howarth 2016: 90). Germany, after all, called for close attention not only because of the relative success of its crisis management at keeping down inflation and unemployment, but also because of the competitive challenge posed by its industry. French policymakers focused on Germany as the font of these "best practices" in terms of monetary targeting and restriction, an anti-inflationary zeal, and a strong currency (McNamara 1998: 155–156).

Though France under Barre seems the ideal student in what some describe as a "transnational learning process" (McNamara 1998: 152; see also Mourlon-Druol 2010; 2012), Germany did more than instruct by example. Concerned that the French left and its cross-party *programme commun* might win a majority in the next elections, the German state sought actively to support the Barre government and its efforts to copy the German model (McNamara 1998: 69–71; Moss 2005: 131; Prasad 2006: 239).[78]

The move toward further European monetary integration needs to be seen in this context. There is no doubt that the EMS promised some important economic advantages to Germany. An extension of the more limited European currency "snake" to France and Britain (and the *de facto* association of Austria and Switzerland) would "create a 'zone of relative monetary stability' for almost half of German exports," Emminger concluded.[79] This would meet the interests of small and medium-sized exporters that found

it difficult to hedge against exchange-rate fluctuations.[80] It would also promote the use of other reserve, transaction, and investment currencies[81] and
spread the upward pressure on the DM.[82] Above all, however, the pursuit
of what Schmidt called a "grand strategy for integrating Europe" (Schmidt,
quoted in Marsh 1992: 233) was meant to overcome the centrifugal forces
of the political left, which seemed to threaten the common market not only
in Italy and Britain, but also in France.[83]

Having crashed out of the currency snake twice already, France's commitment to a strong franc was no longer credible[84]—most important, in the
eyes of its trade unions, who believed that the government would sooner
revalue than push through its ambitious plans to cut spending and reduce
the wage bill.[85] A new monetary agreement with Germany offered a powerful symbol that France would stay on course (Gruber 2000: 177–178).
Materially, too, the EMS was seen as a "crucial external constraint . . . to
keep inflation down and public spending under control" (Howarth 2016:
90). The long-term vision of French officials may well have been to balance
German monetary power in a symmetrical exchange-rate system before Eu-
ropeanizing it through a monetary union. For Barre, however, the immediate aim was not to limit the excess of German monetarism but to emulate
its success (Howarth 2016: 89–90). Conversely, for the German chancellor,
the point of the EMS was to renew the disciplining device of the currency
snake and to put it in the service of political forces who were serious about
monetary and fiscal restraint (Parboni 1981: 131; Putnam and Henning
1989: 53; Gruber 2000: 177).[86] It was this core element of the EMS that,
as the common denominator of German grand strategy, survived the policy
conflicts between Schmidt and the Bundesbank (Kaltenthaler 1998: 54).
The opposition of the Bundesbank to a symmetrical exchange-rate regime,
the opt-out it obtained, and its insistence that downward adjustments be
accompanied by measures to curb inflation, created a currency block more
akin to the gold standard and "tilted in a strongly anti-Keynesian direction"
(Halevi 2019: 3; see also Ryner and Cafruny 2017: 88; Kurzer 1993: 221).

Some have highlighted the enormous political costs involved in the
socially and internationally negotiated, and frequently contested, par value
changes under the new European Exchange Rate Mechanism (ERM)
(Höpner and Spielau 2018). From the German vantage point at the outset of the EMS, these conflicts between domestic winners and losers, and
between hard-currency and soft-currency countries, were less a by-product than a key part of the original design. The new ERM, the chancellor

explained in his bid for the Bundesbank's endorsement in his November 1978 address, would bring par values changes back into the political domain and the public eye. This would expose governments to social and political pressures by lobby groups and media outlets, as well as the influence of the German state and central bank.[87] Rather than "a drawback of discretionary flexible regimes" (Höpner and Spielau 2018: 168), the chancellor considered its politicized nature an advantage over exchange rates determined by market forces and discreet central bank interventions.

These considerations would pay off only three years later. The last Keynesian experiment under President Mitterrand and Prime Minister Mauroy foundered in an inhospitable international environment structured by the Volcker interest rate shock and the weight of the DM within the EMS. The highly restrictive monetary policy of the United States, discussed in the next chapter, pushed up the value of the dollar and sucked in capital from abroad. The relative strength of the DM and German economy, meanwhile, compelled France to maintain even higher interest rates than the Bundesbank (Reichart 2015: 18–19; 39). The need to stem capital flight and keep the franc in the narrow bands of the ERM curtailed the macroeconomic space available to the socialist government once Mitterrand's bid for an alternative "European social space" had been rejected by the German state and central bank (Henning 1994: 197, fn. 39; 1998: 560).

Adjusting through devaluing the franc was not possible within the ERM. Changing the rates required unanimity (Höpner and Spielau 2018: 162), and the German government opposed a large devaluation (Cameron 1996: 62, 64). Only if France left would it be free to devalue the franc as it saw fit. In principle, this path was open to Mitterrand when he assumed office (Cameron 1996). But as the economic fundamentals of the two countries diverged further, this window of opportunity closed, and the political and economic costs of crashing out of the EMS increased at the same time that the constraints of membership tightened (Dyson and Featherstone 1999: 128, 137).

The currency adjustments that France had to negotiate inside the EMS, meanwhile, were too moderate to restore competitiveness. And in return for a realignment of currencies, the German government asked that France commit to deflationary measures. In the run-up to the currency realignment of June 1982, German officials discussed a package of wage and price freezes and fiscal and monetary restraints with their French counterparts (Cameron 1996: 67). The Bundesbank, meanwhile, offered bilateral assistance to keep France inside the EMS. But it categorically refused to soften the terms of the EMS, arguing instead that "[t]here ought to be an offensive tactic. We want a certain hardening."[88] In March 1983, finally, the German negotiators tied another currency adjustment to a program that involved deep fiscal cuts and that consecrated the French turn toward austerity (Cameron 1996: 71–72; Moss 2005: 135; 2000: 262).

Without discounting the internal politics that drove Mitterrand's *volte face*, it should be clear that Germany had exerted consistent external pressure—vilified by the left as a form of imperialism (Dyson and Featherstone 1999: 129), yet welcomed by those within the French state and bureaucracy who championed a program of competitive disinflation. This influence went far beyond simply providing a model for others to follow (compare McNamara 1998: 70). Nor was it limited to a form of structural power that diffused the Bundesbank's anti-inflationary policies. The smaller European countries, to be sure, had been drawn into Germany's monetary orbit since the snake and almost by default. The new ERM placed the burden on countries with weaker currencies and compelled them to align their interest rates with the Bundesbank's (Kurzer 1993: 221). But as far as France under Mitterrand was concerned, it was Schmidt's idea to "repoliticise" exchange-rate policy that opened the door to German influence and empowered "a loose coalition of pro-EMS partisans of *rigueur*" who invoked a stark choice between austerity or a chaotic exit (Cameron 1996: 67).

Within the confines of the EMS, Mitterrand's promise to improve the livelihoods of working people was effectively abandoned in favor of controlling inflation, if rhetorically projected onto the wider plane of European integration. And yet the idea of a Social Europe, we now know, never entered into the Franco-German compromise that led to the creation of the EMU, and that managed to curb the power of the Bundesbank only by enshrining its stability preferences.

Conclusion

This chapter has examined the development of a grand economic strategy broadly shared by the major agencies of the German state from the middle of the 1970s crisis decade onward. Its primary objective was to shore up the domestic compact between capital and labor internationally. To its political operators, this meant that Germany could not afford to turn inward, or to expend its resources on lofty visions of European integration or global solidarity. Rather than "pay the bill for the economic indiscipline of other [EEC] countries," the German state sought to make its partners adopt monetary and fiscal policies congruent with its anti-inflationary program, even when this came to the detriment of the embedded liberal promise of full employment and welfare expansion.[89] In a situation of stalemate between capital and labor in the advanced industrial core, the German state had effectively taken sides, even as it sought to balance these opposing interests domestically. The result was to close down the policy space for a progressive reform agenda and move the world one step closer toward the neoliberal counterrevolution.

CHAPTER 6

Disciplining the Hegemon

German Monetary Power and the Volcker Shock

THE PREVIOUS CHAPTER explored a grand economic strategy with which the German state sought to defeat the protectionist and inflationary forces that were held to endanger the liberal world economy, and that were seen to emanate primarily from the crisis responses of the European left. Under the Ford presidency, this objective had been broadly shared with the United States, and by the end of 1976, significant progress had been made in turning the British Labour government to the IMF and locking the Italian communists out of office but into an unpopular austerity program. With the election of Carter, however, this German-American entente ended abruptly. As the balance in the US administration shifted from conservative "stabilizers" to Keynesian "stimulators" (Sargent 2015: 195), the present chapter argues, German attention returned to the United States as the principal offender whose negligence regarding the internal and external stability of the world's major currency was seen to lie at the heart of the stagflationary crisis of the 1970s.

German policymakers had known from the outset of Bretton Woods that the preeminent status of the dollar had served the interests of the United States first and foremost. Under Adenauer, the chancellor's office had floated a proposal through which this power imbalance could be, if not rectified, then at least rendered more transparent. By converting some central bank dollar holdings into bilateral loans, the financial support that Germany and other surplus countries routinely provided to the United States might be brought into political negotiations and linked to other issues and demands.[1] Although this plan was never followed through, the reallocation of reserve assets away from US Treasury bills resurfaced in discussions—explored in the previous chapter—over whether the Bundesbank's reserves could be repurposed to provide financial assistance to deficit and developing countries or to stockpile vital raw materials.[2]

Having charted a third way between these progressive and retrograde uses, the question for the Schmidt government was "[w]hether the Bundes-bank's currency reserves invested in the US could be used as leverage" to commit the United States itself to a more accountable and austere "global management."[3] If the Bundesbank diversified away from Treasury bills, the United States would have to turn to capital markets to finance its debt and, Schmidt reasoned, assume greater fiscal and monetary responsibility in order to attract the necessary funds.[4] An interagency tussle between the chancellery and Bundesbank followed that lasted until 1979. The chancel-lor was adamant that the Bundesbank's foreign exchange holdings should not be seen as "tied up in the US as a matter of course." The Bundesbank pointed out that its statutes obliged it to invest in safe and freely and quickly exchangeable assets. Measured in these terms, there was hardly a substi-tute for the dollar, and little room for moving foreign exchange reserves *en masse* into longer-term and potentially riskier investments. At the same time, the Bundesbank conceded that, in practice and unofficially, political considerations had been taken into account in the past and might again be given precedence on a case-by-case basis.[5] Aside from political and legal issues, the Bundesbank objected, divesting from the US was simply unlikely to produce the desired results. The US would find it relatively easy to find other buyers for its debt and thus break free from the limits the chancellery sought to put on its macroeconomic policies.[6]

The fact that such plans were debated at the highest levels of policy-making is in itself significant. This episode matters less as an indication of bureaucratic rivalry, but more because of a shared understanding among German policy elites, that, though not for a lack of trying, there was no escape from the American center of gravity. The refusal of the Bundesbank, and its ability to sway the chancellor's office, did not emerge from its much vaunted institutional autonomy, but from a sober assessment of the struc-tural power of the United States within global capitalism. And yet, as the rest of this chapter makes clear, the German government, in tandem with the Bundesbank, would search for other ways in which to continue, as Helmut Schmidt put it, "the fight against an administration that had come into power believing that inflation could cure the world."[7]

Derailing the Global Growth Locomotive

The presidency of Jimmy Carter epitomizes the confusion, hesitation, and errors of policymakers as they stumbled toward neoliberalism. Carter and his Keynesian advisors had been elected into the White House on the promise of putting together an internationally coordinated economic program that included prounion labor legislation, job creation schemes, and a fiscal stimulus (Biven 2002). Within two years, the progressive rhetoric of restoring the New Deal coalition with organized labor had vanished (Cowie 2010). When Carter left office at the end of 1980, he had instead initiated a process of deregulation that extended to the financial sector, adopted social spending cuts, and above all sanctioned what turned out to be an excessive policy of monetary tightening known as the Volcker Shock (Prasad 2006: 62; Basosi 2010: 14; Jones 2012: 216–217, 248–249).[8]

Whatever caused this policy reversal, compared to the transformative schemes put forth by parts of the European left, there was little that was particularly radical about the program of the incoming Carter administration. Amidst an increasingly unfavorable social balance of power and international economic environment, Carter would attempt one last push to overcome the domestic limitations of Keynesian demand management through a process of international policy coordination that was aimed, at most, at the conservation of the *status quo*. In this it was supported, most notably, by British policymakers, who had not yet fully embraced the logic of neoliberal austerity. For even though the Labour government had recognized the failure of an expansionary policy in their own country, they were keen to pass on the burden of an economic stimulus to the countries that posted large trade surpluses and seemed poised to pull the world economy out of recession (James 1996: 290; Baker 1999: 84). The main reason why the attempts to coordinate an international macroeconomic expansion at the G7 summits in London and Bonn in 1977 and 1978 failed, and why a neoliberal alternative was subsequently tried, has to do with the intransigence of Germany—the single most important economy where monetarism, far from an ideology of class war, had proven effective in ameliorating distributive conflict and in sustaining the postwar consensus (Johnson 1998).

The Carter administration came to power with a two-pronged international program. On the one hand, it sought to realize the proposals developed by the influential Trilateral Commission—a private policy-planning group established in 1973—to create a multilateral system of governance in which the US, Western Europe, and Japan would jointly manage economic and political interdependence (Gill 1990). And on the other hand, the Carter administration sought to solicit international support for a Keynesian program of demand management that had been developed by the OECD in 1975 and that was supported by many Trilateral Commission members (Biven 2002).

The newly established G7 summits became the focal point of the efforts of the Carter administration both to multilateralize the making of foreign economic policy and to organize an internationally coordinated macroeconomic expansion. The most influential account of economic summitry has been provided by Putnam and Henning (1989: 133, fn. 114), who conducted high-level interviews with almost all of the key individuals involved in the London and Bonn summits. Their main argument, informed by a model of "two-level games" (Putnam 1988), holds that the international negotiations allowed a small faction within the German government that favored macroeconomic expansion—individuals in the economics ministry and chancellery and leadership in the trade unions and left wing of the SPD—to link up with their Keynesian counterparts in the US and Japanese governments and to use the leverage of the negotiating process to overcome the opposition of the Free Democratic Party, the Bundesbank, and the majority of economic officials, as well as banking and industry (Putnam and Henning 1989: 107). Schmidt, in short, is said to have harnessed the external pressure from the US toward the adoption of a fiscal stimulus for which he would otherwise have had little domestic support (Putnam and Henning 1989: 67; Biven 2002: 151).

Paradoxically, even though the Bonn summit has since been "heralded as a paradigmatic case of international economic cooperation" (Bryant and Hodgkinson 1989: 2), most observers agree that the substantive outcome of the summit was a failure (Putnam and Henning 1989: 19). As Gerald Holtham (1989: 141) has demonstrated, there are two divergent and politically motivated interpretations as to why. Some suggest that trilateral macroeconomic coordination, though well-intended and a step in the right direction, was counteracted by events such as the Iranian revolution and the second oil crisis that changed the global parameters in unexpected ways and rendered the stimulus ineffective (Holtham 1989: 141; Bergsten and Henning 1996: 57). Had these external shocks and, from the problem-solving perspective of world economic management, "unfortunate events," not occurred, this position implies, a global reflation might have proven successful. The prevailing view today is that the overall approach was not simply badly timed but inherently flawed (Bergsten and Henning 1996: 57). From this perspective, a hesitant Germany had been drawn into an ill-fated Keynesian experiment of demand management that negatively affected domestic price levels and Germany's balance-of-payments position (compare Giersch, Paqué, and Schmieding 1992: 240–243). Having learned their lesson the hard way, German policymakers supposedly resolved "never again" to depart from their anti-inflationary program (compare Allen 2005: 214). In essence, this is not a debate about the historical record but an interpretive struggle between Keynesian and neoclassical economists that centers on different conceptions of appropriate macroeconomic policy. In the heat of the debate, the actual events of the Bonn summit and the larger context have been lost, and the triumph of the latter over the former created a lasting myth that, Holtham rightly feared, would be impossible to correct.

Critical approaches have argued that German policymakers refused to do very much to begin with (Parboni 1981: 125; Lankowski 1982b: 100; Parboni 1988: 48). As Gill (1999: 132) points out, previous summit communiqués had already articulated an anti-inflationary perspective. Putnam and Henning (1989: 42) admit that this reflected the monetarist perspective of Germany, which was opposed to the expansionary plans that British prime minister Callaghan had raised as early as 1975 (Biven 2002: 98). At the 1976 Puerto Rico summit, Schmidt insisted that "[o]ur priority must be to check price increases and to strengthen confidence among investors. . . . If we have an inflationary environment there is less confidence. Increases in inflation increase risk, and make it seem prohibitively expensive to undertake large investments. Expansion requires that prices be held in check. And employment increases are not possible in the face of growing rates of inflation." And he warned that "[i]f we again lapse into inflation, we could again find ourselves back at square one in less than two years."[9] In London in the following year, Schmidt and his summit "sherpa" Karl Otto Pöhl reiterated their strong anti-inflationary stance, managing to insert into the final communiqué the phrase "inflation does not reduce unemployment. On the contrary, it is one of its major causes" (Putnam and Henning 1989: 42).

On the whole, German policymakers had been extremely concerned about the inflationary effects of the stimulus package prepared by the incoming Carter administration and its attempt to enlist the surplus economies in this endeavor (Biven 2002: 99; Stein 2010: 160). Together with Japan, the German delegation refused American pressures at the London summit. The leaders of the two countries rejected binding growth targets and merely restated the going economic predictions, even though it was already clear that these would not be met (Biven 2002: 112; Stein 2010: 161).

It should also be noted that the Americans, rather than counting on Schmidt's commitment, sought to apply pressures outside the bargaining table in order to get Germany to reflate. To increase the pressure on Germany and Japan, the US announced it was going to expand no matter what. If Germany and Japan chose not to follow suit, they would have to tolerate the appreciating DM and yen and associated loss in export competitiveness that would result from the American trade deficit. Throughout 1977, the United States abstained from foreign exchange interventions in favor of a declining dollar in the hope that Germany and Japan would choose to stimulate their economies (Biven 2002: 108, citing Putnam and Henning 1989: 36–37). And indeed there is at least one documented occasion (one of the presummit meetings of the Group of Five (G5) deputies (France, Germany, Japan, United States, United Kingdom), on 16 June 1978) when the Americans intimated that the US would cause difficulty through its foreign exchange policy if their German counterparts were too obstinate.[10] In addition, they threatened they would not attend the Bonn summit unless Germany committed to a stimulus, thus ruining a public relations opportunity for Schmidt (Biven 2002: 146–147).

Because of these threats, the bargaining process that led up to the Bonn agreement was fraught with considerable tensions and shrouded in uncertainty. German policymakers entered the negotiations convinced that what was to be negotiated was a "quid pro quo" that sought to commit the US to an anti-inflationary monetary policy and an energy-saving program[11] and that assumed that Germany had already done its part.[12] Emminger summed up the view that "because of international obligations, something has to be done in order to increase the pressures on the others."[13]

At the Bonn summit, Germany rejected an explicit economic growth target but agreed to a considerable fiscal stimulus of "up to 1%" of its GDP (Stein 2010: 170). Although German policymakers honored this commitment, the devil is in the detail. The stimulus overwhelmingly took the form of tax cuts that were meant to offset "bracket creep," a process whereby inflation pushes taxpayers into higher income brackets, increases the overall tax burden, and limits aggregate demand. Such compensating measures, Holtham (1989: 147–148) notes, had been repeatedly used in the past and had again been made necessary by the record tax revenues of 1977. Germany's summit commitment was therefore nothing out of the ordinary. In fact, one of the political participants at the time concluded that "one can dispute whether . . . the German decision would not have been taken without the summit" (Tietmeyer 1988: 137, quoted in Truman 2004: 283, fn. 9). It may be fair to say that the summit determined the scope and timing of these measures, but, as Holtham (1989: 147) concludes, this is "a far cry . . . from the claim that the German government reluctantly but altruistically agreed to something at the summit that was contrary to its interests." Clearly, then, Germany's was not an exceptional experiment in macroeconomic demand management. Emminger (1986: 428), who opposed the fiscal stimulus from the outset, criticized the prevailing view that the German state "was pumping 1% of GDP into the economy" as giving the false impression of some deficit-financed job creation scheme.

The claim by Putnam and Henning (1989: 36) that Schmidt signaled informally that he preferred to be pushed in an expansionary direction, and used the negotiations to build a Keynesian coalition, is also questionable. Indicative of the uncertainty of German economic policy, he had toyed with reflationary proposals in 1973–1974, but since 1976 had come down on the side of anti-inflation (Putnam and Henning 1989: 35; Biven 2002: 149–150; Bernardini 2017). Although Schmidt asked Emminger for the Bundesbank's support in implementing the German commitment on the final day of the summit (presumably by refraining from tightening monetary policy), he soon distanced himself from the Bonn agreement.[14] Addressing the Bundesbankers four months after the summit and *before* the tax cuts came into effect, he dismissed as "nonsense" the notion that Germany ought to act as a locomotive and noted that, just as the Americans hadn't lived up to their commitments, Germany had only done half of what it was supposed to do.[15]

Last, the fiscal measures implemented after Bonn were offset by the restrictive monetary stance taken by the Bundesbank at the end of 1978 and throughout 1979 (Marsh 2009: 90; Truman 2004: 285–286; Holtham 1989: 151, 152). Encouraged to continue its stability course by the economics ministry, the Bundesbank had already committed to monetary restraint in mid-December 1978 when it decided to announce an ambitious monetary target of 6 percent to 9 percent, which, it was clearly understood and explicitly stated at the time, would make restrictive measures inevitable.[16]

Though primarily with a view to setting the tone for the new EMS rather than as an explicit countermeasure to the summit decision (compare Holtham 1989: 152–153),[17] Germany's monetary tightening cancelled out whatever "stimulus" the tax measures (which were really more of a "demand-neutral" equalizer) provided. Taken together, "overall German macroeconomic policy in 1979 was anti-inflationary" rather than expansionary (Holtham 1989: 143, 159). The second oil shock was only an afterthought in this, and served primarily as a means of justifying the anti-inflationary stance of the Bundesbank internationally.[18]

German policymakers, rather than being caught out by unforeseen economic developments (Kreile 2006: 165), had already turned their backs on the locomotive approach prior to the spike in oil prices. It was Japanese rather than German officials, for whom "[t]he idea of an expansionary policy was not as inherently unacceptable" (Biven 2002: 102), who now found their macroeconomic leeway curtailed by a newly inflationary environment.[19] The international outlook of German authorities, and the common denominator for the government and central bank, was the same as in 1973–1974.[20] This was especially so as the Bundesbank observed that German business seemed prepared to use the oil shock as an excuse to raise prices.[21] The implication for economic policy, the Central Bank Council concluded, was that the room for price increases needed to be narrowed down as much as possible. Only then could a devastating wage-price spiral be prevented. An expansion of domestic demand that Keynesian proponents asked for would only accelerate inflation, increase balance-of-payments problems, and fuel social conflict across the advanced industrial world.[22]

On the whole, therefore, there is scant evidence that the Carter administration had coaxed German policymakers into a failed Keynesian experiment (compare Giersch, Paqué, and Schmieding 1992: 242; Kreile 2006: 165). In fact, as the next section demonstrates, the exact opposite was the case. Having resisted American calls for macroeconomic expansion, German policymakers now pushed the US into a "successful" neoliberal experiment.[23]

From Benign Neglect to the Volcker Shock

Far more important than the package deal reached at the Bonn summit, it was the structural weakness of the dollar that called the United States into action. American officials had remained indifferent to its declining exchange rate after the termination of Bretton Woods. For most of 1977, US policymakers had hoped that an appreciating DM would get Germany to stimulate its economy (Putnam and Bayne 1984: 70–71). But in December 1977 and January 1978, it was feared the downward slide of the greenback would turn into a free fall (Parboni 1981: 130–131; Biven 2002: 119–120). To stabilize it, US monetary officials abandoned their policy of "benign neglect" and returned to foreign exchange interventions (Truman 2005: 353)—with little success. After the dollar declined by 18 percent vis-à-vis the DM between August and October 1978 and a panic loomed, the US announced a dollar rescue package that included monetary tightening and the procurement of foreign currency to finance foreign exchange interventions (Biven 2002: 169–170).

Bundesbank officials gloated that they had followed the Swiss example of waiting out their American counterparts.[24] While the chancellor lauded Germany's hard-line stance at the Bonn summit for this change of course,[25] Emminger argued that it owed to the Bundesbank's limited interventions in foreign exchange markets (Emminger 1986: 382, 384). Added to this, one of Germany's Central Bank Council members believed, was the threat that OPEC countries might raise the price of oil or cease to quote it in dollars altogether.[26] The claim made in one Central Intelligence Agency (CIA) report that "[t]he anti-inflation and dollar support programs adopted by the United States in the fall of 1978 were the result in great part of allied pressure"[27] was premature in that the real showdown was to come in the following year, but is much closer to the truth. For even as Germany signed up to a dollar support program in November 1978 (Bordo, Humpage, and Schwartz 2010: 19), it now saw a chance to tighten the screws and extract a firm anti-inflationary commitment from the US (Truman 2005: 354).

In his November speech before the Bundesbank's Central Bank Council, Schmidt was keen to align the proposed European Monetary System with this strategy. In his bid to convince central bank officials, he argued that "something like a zone of stable currencies in [our] area" would add "a very strong additional psychological pressure on the American politicians to give up the policy of 'benign neglect' on their side."[28] It is indeed true that the Carter administration, despite official support, was highly skeptical about the EMS and a joint European position toward the dollar (Biven 2002: 168; Basosi 2010).[29] And more than a matter of psychology, US monetary officials had complained to their German counterparts that the dollar interventions needed to keep European currencies within the snake were "unnecessarily exacerbating the weakness of the dollar."[30]

The EMS, in Schmidt's view, was also to rally Europe behind Germany in its coming confrontation with the United States.[31] Echoing the Bundesbank's sentiments, Schmidt insisted that there was a clear limit to how far Germany was prepared to go to support the dollar. For Germany to state unequivocally that "this is the end of the line" and then hold firm against American pressures and protestations, a united European front was needed.[32]

And indeed, just as the United States had returned to foreign exchange markets, the Bundesbank had started to reduce its interventions (Emminger 1986: 392). Whereas in November 1977 the Bundesbank still bought ten dollars for every one dollar purchased by the US Federal Reserve, by September 1979 the monthly ratio had reversed to five to one.[33] Following Schmidt's speech in support of the EMS, the economics ministry concluded that the onus of stabilizing the dollar had to be put firmly on the United States and achieved principally through domestic deflation.[34] Within limits, the Bundesbank at times even sold dollars to prevent too strong a devaluation of the DM and to protect itself against inflation.[35]

This reversal of German foreign exchange interventions was critically important because of the growing counterweight of the mark to the dollar. Given the DM's status as the world's second and Europe's principal anchor currency, the Fed mainly targeted the dollar-DM exchange rate in order to stabilize the dollar (Bordo, Humpage, and Schwartz 2010: 12). Alarmed by German complacency, Fed officials demanded that the Bundesbank intervene more forcefully and even accused their counterpart of letting the dollar slide on purpose.[36] Worse still was that, short of any substantial foreign currency reserves of their own, they had to rely primarily on the Bundesbank to lend them the marks needed for their dollar support interventions (Bordo, Humpage, and Schwartz 2010: 12, 19, 21, 29). But here, too, the Bundesbank put up opposition, and "grew increasingly reluctant to extend further credits without changes in U.S. macroeconomic policies" (19, see also 25, 30, 40).[37]

In the second half of 1979, these tensions finally escalated. Although the dollar came under renewed attack, the Bundesbank dragged its feet, leaving the Federal Reserve to try in vain to stabilize the exchange rate.[38] By July, the dollar had lost all the ground gained against the mark since its international rescue in November 1978. The new Fed chairman, Paul Volcker, appointed in August, worried, "If the market gets in its head that the dollar is really going down [against the DM], would we be able to stop it without spending a lot more money than we're already spending?"[39] And indeed, despite massive interventions, the dollar continued its downward trajectory, and US monetary officials drew down their DM reserves (Silber 2012: 166). In the two months from when Volcker took office to the Fed's radical change of course on October 6, the Fed's DM holdings dropped from \$1,485 million to \$138 million (\$72 million in October). At the same time, the Treasury's DM reserves decreased from \$2,208 to \$759 million (\$435 million in October).[40] Its undersecretary for monetary affairs, Anthony Solomon, was alarmed that "we face . . . a situation that could quickly degenerate into a full-blown destructive crisis" and that "we are being bled to death and will have to let go."[41] And on the other side of the Atlantic, just days before the start of the infamous Volcker Shock, the Bundesbank's president noted that "if the Americans continued to intervene in this vein as over the last days, they would be finished very quickly."[42]

The decisive meeting between the two sides had taken place during the previous weekend. On his way to the IMF meeting in Belgrade, Volcker stopped in Hamburg to plead with Schmidt for further dollar support measures. The chancellor flat out refused and—as he had signaled in his speech to the Central Bank Council a year earlier—sided with the Bundesbank's hard-line stance. Any attempt to put a floor under the dollar would not only fail to impress markets but go against German interests. Selling DM to buy dollars had expanded the money supply and risked bringing back inflation, forcing the bank to raise interest rates and drawing the ire of trade unions—an unacceptable cost in the upcoming election year. "The United States," Schmidt told Volcker, "could not demand from us that we ruin our economy for their sake."[43] Without restoring the underlying political and economic fundamentals, the chancellor concluded, the downward pressure on the dollar would continue, and any stabilization efforts would come to naught.[44]

Informed by the image of a two-level game as discussed earlier, some practitioners and academics have argued that Volcker availed himself of German pressure at Hamburg in order to push through his monetarist plans (compare Volcker and Gyohten 1992: 168; Truman 2004: 286). Edwin Truman, who worked for the Federal Reserve Board in this period, speaks of a "pro forma effort by the U.S. Treasury officials to enlist additional German support" (2004: 286) and explains that it was important "to have done so in order to bring [Treasury and the Council of Economic Advisors] around to accepting the need for fundamental monetary policy action" (2005: 353). This reading suggests that a transgovernmental coalition emerged that was intent on circumventing the bureaucratic inertia that stood in the way of a radical change of course. While worthy of further investigation beyond the scope of this book, the issue with this interpretation, as it stands, is that it fails to account for the considerable tensions between German and US policymakers. The archival records confirm significant external economic and political pressures behind the formulation of the Volcker program (Woolley 1984: 103–104). To reduce them to being "part of an international policy coordination process" (Truman 2005: 353) is suspect of intentionally glossing over these frictions. It is highly unlikely, for instance, that the heavy criticism Volcker himself came under at Hamburg when he asked for additional support measures to flank his anti-inflationary program was merely scripted.

The more plausible explanation, provided by one of his biographers, is that Volcker, too, only opted in favor of a monetarist shift in the week between the Hamburg meeting and his abrupt departure from the IMF conference in Belgrade (Silber 2012: 166). Emminger's admission to the Central Bank Council that "we have made a theoretical contribution [to Volcker's program of 6 October] by illuminating policy in Hamburg" points in this direction.[45] Of course, rather than either simply inspire or embolden Volcker, the Hamburg meeting had curtailed the options available to him in a decisive moment. In this respect, the notion that Volcker let himself be pushed ignores the fact that Hamburg capped off a decade-long, crisis-ridden and conflict-driven process in which the German state had sought to direct the efforts of US policymakers toward domestic economic measures.

The emergency meeting of the Federal Open Market Committee (FOMC) that Volcker convened after his return to Washington further confirms this reading. The decisive passage is missing from the transcript because Volcker stopped the tape recorder (Stein 2010: 230)—a likely indication of just how contentious "the views of foreign officials regarding a coordinated package" had been.[46] The bottom line, Volcker concluded, was that a reprise of the 1978 dollar rescue program could not be expected without serious action by the Fed.[47] This put the US in an extremely vulnerable position because market rumors had it that such a package was forthcoming (Stein 2010: 230).[48] Yet with "no specific swaps, SDRs, or IMF drawings [under consideration]" and "no desire to solidify any of that at this point,"[49] the Fed could not hope to calm markets with the conventional instruments at its disposal. The German refusal to rescue the dollar at Hamburg, probably in conjunction with broader European opposition at Belgrade (Greider 1987: 118; Stein 2010: 230), had removed the last remaining alternative to the monetarist turn now favored by Volcker and adopted by the Fed.

While its principal objective was to quell domestic inflation, the declining dollar had been the chief catalyst of this paradigm shift (Treaster 2004: 53, 68).[50] Its external and internal weakness were two sides of the same problem, and the lack of German assistance with the exchange rate of the dollar—as Schmidt and Emminger had intended and as Volcker recognized—only intensified the pressures on the Fed to achieve domestic price stability (Bordo, Humpage, and Schwartz 2010: 24–25). In theory, both the external and internal value of the dollar could be strengthened with a bold move on interest rates, and in practice a drastic 2 percent rise in the discount rate was on the table at the 6 October FOMC meeting. The problem, however, was that the credibility of the Federal Reserve's commitment to tighten monetary policy as long as necessary in order to quell inflation had vanished over the preceding decade (Axilrod 2005: 238; Lindsey, Orphanides, and Rasche 2005: 210). To restore confidence in the dollar and the Fed, Volcker saw the dramatic shift toward monetary targets as a "comprehensive symbol" that the Fed would stay on an anti-inflationary course no matter the consequences (Panitch and Gindin 2012: 167; Hetzel 2008: 150).

The German welfare state was soon to become one of the many casualties of the Volcker program and its calculated disregard for the social and global ramifications of escalating interest rates and a deepening world recession. In an important sense, however, these negative repercussions need to be seen as the blowback of Germany's strategy. German state elites, for much of the 1970s, had sought to impel the United States toward fiscal and monetary discipline, and from the Bonn summit onward had focused on the DM-dollar exchange rate as the vehicle for bringing this pressure to bear on their American counterparts. By scaling back their currency interventions, limiting American access to DM, and, finally, refusing any additional dollar support measures, German policymakers had helped bring about a radical experiment in US monetary policy that pushed interest rates to unprecedented levels, induced a global recession, and ultimately broke the strength of organized labor.

In this sense, the German state was a critical force of neoliberal change against the will of its administrators, who had sought myopically to maintain an international environment conducive to preserving peace and prosperity within their own society. And yet their successes at defending the domestic compact from the global forces of protectionism and inflation frustrated attempts to transform the Keynesian truce in the interest of the working class or at least refurbish it in the service of the existing state of affairs. By precluding potentially more progressive alternatives and committing the United States to monetary rigor, German state elites had helped to inaugurate the neoliberal counterrevolution.

Volcker Shocked: *Haute Finance* and the "Faustian Bid" Reconsidered

A comprehensive rereading of the Anglo-American history of neoliberalism through the inverted lens of Volcker "shocked" is a task that is largely outside of the scope of this book. And yet the argument that German state operators both frustrated Carter's attempts to fuel global demand and limited Volcker's options to global deflation means that some aspects of the ideational, statist, and class-based accounts we have encountered are in need of immediate revision. Most important, in light of the evidence presented earlier, the Volcker turn can no longer be seen as either a coup of international *haute finance* (compare Greider 1987: 118; Duménil and Lévy 2004: 165; Harvey 2005: 45; Stein 2010: 227) or as the final step in a "Faustian bid" to reassert American power over and against the interests of its core country rivals and a disobedient periphery (Gowan 1999: 40; 2001: 366).

The first point that follows from the argument above is that the Fed's monetarist turn was driven by material circumstances more than any particular belief system. Volcker, after all, was never particularly enamored with the Chicago School (McNally 2011: 33; Madrick 2011: 160; Panitch and Gindin 2012: 167), and although his job certainly put him in close contact with free market fundamentalists, he did not belong to this movement himself. Volcker had rejected monetarist proposals in the past, and the excessively tight monetary policy that the Fed followed under his leadership departed radically from the slow and steady rate of growth of the money supply that Friedman had prescribed (Neikirk 1987: 66–67; Treaster 2004: 149). His relationship with Friedman and other monetarists was less than amicable (Silber 2012: 150). While Volcker disapproved of the inflexible recommendations of the monetarists, Friedman and Meltzer harshly criticized the track record of the Fed (Neikirk 1987: 92). In the depths of the recession that was to follow, Friedman was keen to distance himself from a policy he had followed with a mixture of goodwill and skepticism (Silber 2012: 148–149). In a speech to the Mont Pelerin Society, he was adamant that "[i]n October 1979, the Federal Reserve in desperation adopted monetarist rhetoric. It did not then and has not since adopted a monetarist policy" (Friedman 1983: 1). Both the modifications of monetarism adopted by Volcker in 1979 and their denunciation by Friedman three years later are perfect examples of the plasticity of ideas in the face of changing economic and political circumstances and considerations.

Volcker's former jobs at Chase Manhattan and the New York Fed certainly exposed him to the strongly anti-inflationary views that prevailed in the international banking community in the late 1970s. At the same time, his active membership as North American Director in the Trilateral Commission also means that he was familiar with the concerns of those international elites who, in 1979 still, feared the political costs of curing wage-push inflation and labor insubordination through a prolonged recession (Gill 1990: 227).[51] The reasons why Volcker chose to do precisely that, I argue, cannot be reduced to the persuasive power of ideas, nor can it be explained in terms of his allegiance to the financial rather than the productive interests of society.

The fight against inflation, after all, was not advocated by high finance alone, but supported by a broad coalition of industry, the trade union leadership, middle-class tax payers, property holders, and small savers (Panitch and Gindin 2012: 170). Moreover, the Volcker program involved a painful adjustment process not only for uncompetitive industries but also for globalizing finance. Stein (2010: 265) notes that "[h]igh and volatile interest rates caused the biggest collapse of financial institutions since the Great Depression, as more than a thousand thrifts with assets over $500 billion failed." Even some of the largest US banks were pushed to the brink of bankruptcy by the record interest rates and the default of developing countries on their loans (266). The international debt crisis not only threatened the stability of the global financial system but also undermined the dominant position that multinational banks had acquired as the intermediaries of petrodollar loans to the Global South. The new regulatory regime adopted under Reagan promoted the rise of nonbank financial firms that increasingly rivaled the transnational commercial banks (Sassen 2008: 157; 1991: 66, 71). The fact that new financial actors emerged from the fallout of the Volcker Shock and benefitted from the subsequent liberalization drive casts further doubt on the story of a "financial coup" (compare Duménil and Lévy 2004; Stein 2010: 227). Because they involved serious shocks and invited new competition, it is unlikely that these policies emanated from the established financial circles, even if these reforms subsequently strengthened *rentier* interests and deepened the structural power of internationally mobile capital (Epstein and Jayadev 2005; Gill 1990: 213, 217).

Nor can the Volcker turn be understood as the reassertion of American supremacy over its allies (Duménil and Lévy 2004: 210; Gowan 1999: 68–69; Arrighi 1994: 323). Long-term interest rates had been rising since the mid-1970s, and at the time Volcker took office an economic downturn already loomed on the horizon. The problem, as summarized by representatives of the German export bloc, was that inflation would continue if the recession was too mild and too short.[52] And the possible solution, Stein has argued, was just as widely shared. "Everybody knew that you could get rid of inflation by producing a steep recession. What was different after 1979 was that the people in power were willing to accept the costs" (Stein 2010: 267). Rather than taking the final step in a series of ingenious moves on the geostrategic chessboard, the Volcker Shock followed a well-known recipe that other countries expected of the United States but feared to apply at home.

Moreover, the monetary program of the Fed, rather than unilaterally imposed, sought to enlist the cooperation of the major central banks and the multinational financial institutions under their authority.[53] To fully enforce the special marginal reserve requirements that flanked his anti-inflationary strategy, Volcker had to rely on the goodwill of American banks not to circumvent the new rules (Helleiner 1994: 136). And to prevent US corporations from avoiding these restraints by borrowing offshore, Volcker asked Emminger and other central bankers "by whatever means you consider appropriate to urge the principal banks in your country, whether or not they have branches and agencies in the United States, to support our program while these temporary measures are in effect." As he explained, "[I]t is an important condition for the success of our program that banks, foreign as well as domestic, avoid taking advantage of possible special opportunities that almost inevitably tend to develop under the circumstances."[54] Whether or not this appeal bore fruit, and whether the informal influence of other central banks over market operators reached further than the limited success of the US (Greider 1987: 143–145) is a different question. The key point, however, is that the Fed's program was designed as a multilateral undertaking from the start.

Most important, international central bankers encouraged the Federal Reserve to see the restrictive monetary policy through to its end—even as the prospects of a global economic crisis grew ever larger. The German central bank, in late May 1980, rejected an American proposal to jointly lower interest rates. Markets would read this as the end of the anti-inflationary program and downward pressure on the dollar would recur, Pöhl warned.[55] And the Swiss central bank governor—at an annual international bankers' meeting that unanimously called on the US to maintain its restrictive monetary policy—"went as far as to call a recession necessary in order to break the mentality of inflation."[56]

Overall, then, the notion that the Volcker Shock and Reagan revolution enabled the United States to reassert its dominance misses the fact that American leadership did not need to be enforced internationally in this way. To a large extent, it was already being demanded by the main capitalist states and their leading classes for much of the 1970s. America's partners were quite willing to "renew their invitation." What they required in return was that the US submit to the same sort of economic discipline it had begun to impose on other countries in cooperation with Germany and through the IMF. The German state, thanks to the central role of the DM and the Bundesbank, was the purveyor of this message.

In sum, the fact that German state managers had pushed monetary and fiscal responsibility onto the US for the better part of a decade complicates the notion of neoliberalism as a unilateral master plan on the part of US policymakers. We have also seen that it challenges the notion that a financial or rentier fraction of capital had hijacked the policymaking process to advance its agenda (for example, Greider 1987; Crotty and Epstein 1996; Epstein and Jayadev 2005; Stein 2010). This remains the case even if one were to object that the Volcker Shock would have happened even without German pressure. For the plausibility of such a counterargument rests squarely on the assumption that a broader realignment of social forces and more incremental shift in economic thinking had already occurred in the United States. The notion that Volcker acted on behalf of financial elites is misleading precisely because it abstracts from the broader change in the social balance of power and intellectual climate that had made the neoliberal experiment possible (Duménil and Lévy 2004: 165; Stein 2010: 227).

The counterfactual argument that the United States was moving in a neoliberal direction anyway and that German pressures were therefore redundant is certainly worthy of contemplation. But we need to be careful here not to turn this hypothetical thought experiment into an impossible abstraction. We cannot detach the national political economy of the United States from its international environment; this broader context needs to be an integral part of our analyses of foreign economic policy. Simply put, there is no world in which Germany does not exist. While we can debate the causal weight of its actions, we cannot make them disappear from the equation entirely. The more precise question to ask is therefore whether the Volcker Shock would have happened even if the German state had chosen not to exert this pressure, or perhaps even stepped up its support for the dollar. Framed in this way, it becomes clear that the answer cannot be found in a purely "internalist" mode of reasoning. Outside and indeed well before the Volcker Shock, this book has argued, the German state had profoundly restructured the external terrain, foreclosing alternative courses of action and delimiting the available policy options. The argument of this chapter that the most immediate political pressures Volcker responded to came from the German state and central bank rather than *haute finance* does not reduce the origins of neoliberalism to this final impetus. On the contrary, in keeping with the lens of uneven and combined development, it opens up this critical turning point to a more fine-grained and full-scale investigation of how external pressures interacted with societal demands to generate such a harsh and hugely influential anti-inflationary program.

A Tale of Two Monetarisms

This chapter has argued that the US abandoned Keynesian demand management in favor of monetary conservatism under the political and exchange-rate pressures of Germany in particular. To get serious on inflation, we have noted, was not enough, however (Harvey 2005: 23–24). To restore international competitiveness, and, incidentally, offer a general rather than particularistic way out of the global crisis, the income share of workers also had to be reduced. And to do that, it was understood, the source of their organized strength needed to be targeted. In this respect, the Volcker Shock did not simply replicate, in hothouse fashion, Germany's turn to "monetarism," but endowed it with a distinctive dimension of top-down class warfare that would become characteristic for the neoliberal projects constructed simultaneously in the US and the UK (Panitch and Gindin 2012: 171).

The reasons why Volcker's Fed and the Reagan administration ultimately chose to go on the offensive had to do with the radically different international and domestic context in which monetarist remedies were applied. In Germany, the Bundesbank's war on inflation had sustained the competitive advantage of its export economy and secured the assent of industrial capital and trade unions.[57] The unique structural orientation of the German economy toward the world market, and the zero-sum character of its crisis response, however, meant that this stabilization strategy could not be copied over to produce the same results. In the US, the situation was far worse and demanded more drastic measures. Because the monetarist program sought to *restore* rather than, as in the German case, *maintain* price stability, business confidence, and international competitiveness, it could never hope to sustain the embedded liberal compromise but rather depended on terminating it.

Hence the United States, with Volcker, and the United Kingdom, under Thatcher, embarked on a program that sought not simply to squeeze out inflation but to break the strength of organized labor (Panitch and Gindin 2008: 31). The real significance of this radical course of action was long lost on German officials, who doubted whether Volcker would deliver on his promise in the year Carter ran for reelection, and who were reluctant to criticize an anti-inflationary politics that they had been pushing onto the US for years.[58] It was only with the victory of Reagan and his trickle-down economics that they realized the scale of the "grand experiment" the US was conducting. Shocked to learn that their American partner "wishes for a recession as soon as possible," and seeing Reagan cut social spending amidst skyrocketing interest rates, they finally understood that the true target was not inflation but the postwar settlement between capital and labor itself.[59]

The odds of success for this "all-or-nothing" strategy, Schmidt was told by his G5 deputy Horst Schulmann, were less than 50 percent.[60] And either way, there was a shared sense among German state and central bank officials that Germany could not follow the American path. One important difference was that in Germany, as opposed to the US and the UK, "stability does not have to be regained."[61] From the standpoint of German society, there was never the need, as Schmidt's Political-Economic Paper had indeed ruled out in 1974, to "go as far as to cause a 'stability crisis' of employment for the sake of price stability."[62] This position was reiterated in 1981 when the Keynesian minority speaker of the Central Bank Council and "social conscience" of the Bundesbank (Marsh 1992: 67) Kurt Nemitz pointed out that they could not use the recession as an instrument of economic policy in the way that the Americans did.[63] And he was not alone. Following the Americans, Emminger's successor Karl Otto Pöhl argued, would amount to "throwing down the gauntlet in front of large groups of society."[64] Small and medium-sized enterprises were bound to suffer, some concluded, and the number of bankruptcies would increase, others predicted.[65] The economic advantages were of course seen as well. A high-interest rate regime would accelerate the structural adjustment process, benefitting profit-making, solvent enterprises while pushing uncompetitive firms out of the market.[66] And yet the structural power of labor was simply too strong for such a strategy to be tried. "To make do without a social safety net and generous unemployment insurance is impossible," Pöhl concluded. "Then the unemployed would be very difficult to bear politically." In the United States, he feared, "[t]hose 9–10 million unemployed could someday lead to an explosion."[67] In this respect, the attack on the welfare state that characterized the Thatcher-Reagan counterrevolution did not make any significant inroads into the Bundesbank in the early 1980s. And, as Schulmann summed up the position of the German government, "for us, after all, the preservation of the social consensus is a key factor of our economic policy."[68]

The German state, of course, was anything but an impartial arbitrator between capital and labor. The supposedly inflationary wage increases were, in essence, understood to be the "cardinal problem" of the entire world of industrial societies.[69] The share of working people in the wealth of society was deemed to be prohibitively large. And yet since the early 1970s, the managers of the German state and the owners of capital had been put on the defensive by the radical demands (including expanded social security, an extended codetermination, and investment controls) of the trade union base, the Young Socialists, and the SPD left (Webber 1983: 66–67). Under these conditions, the Bundesbank president Klasen had concluded in 1971, a "modified appeasement" of trade union demands would be unavoidable. Only in the long term, he wrote to Otto Andreas Friedrich—president of the BDA (Federation of German Employers' Associations) and logistician of Hitler's rearmament effort—might it be possible to forge a common sense of austerity that instilled in "the man on the street" the idea that one cannot consume more than one produces, and that could drive a wedge between the masses and their functionaries.[70] Even as employers had been able to resist the most ambitious reforms, and as confrontation under Brandt gave way to a more cooperative tripartite crisis management under Schmidt (Webber 1983), neither the German state nor its capitalist class dared to take on the unions directly.[71] As the IMF recognized in its 1978 Article IV consultations with Germany, any improvement in the profit situation of enterprises required "a reduction in the rate of rise of real wages (and in some cases . . . a reduction in real wages). . . . Most countries, how-ever,—and Germany seems to be no exception—find it difficult to induce a behavior of wages which will, by itself, allow an improvement in profits and then in turn investment and employment."[72] While its low-inflation re-gime gave differential opportunities to dominant export interests, Germany could not provide a solution to the systemic loss of profitability. Only the United States, with Volcker, and the United Kingdom, under Thatcher, would be prepared to go further, and chart a general path out of the crisis of postwar capitalism.

Fueling the Neoliberal Revolution

The key argument of this book has been that Germany helped to shape the global balance of power and intellectual climate that enabled the neoliberal experiment in the US and the UK. To highlight the role of Germany in preparing the ground for the counterrevolution that took place under Rea-gan and Thatcher is not to diminish the significance, but rather to sharpen the understanding, of what was ultimately "achieved" during their incum-bencies. The truly radical nature of what was done to working people un-der their governments only becomes apparent if we do not assume that the 1970s were simply a period of continuous ideological preparation, capital-ist class mobilization, or systematic hegemonic reconstruction.

There is little doubt that in this period of economic uncertainty, neolib-eral ideas gained prominence and ruling elites organized domestically and internationally to defend capitalism against popular-democratic forces (Gill 1990; Blyth 2002: 155). What allowed the counterrevolution to take place, however, was not simply the strength and coherence on the part of capital, but also the weakness and isolation on the part of labor and its advocates (Schmidt 2011; Jones 2012: 271). German state managers contributed considerably to this disorganization of progressive forces, without being themselves committed to neoliberal ideas or the restoration of capitalist class domination. It was enough for the German state to remain in the center for the pendulum to swing violently to the right. The fact that the main alternatives, with the exception of Mitterrand's ill-fated Keynesian *course solitaire*, had already been ruled out helps explain why Reagan and Thatcher were able to pursue so radical an agenda with only a modicum of consent.[73]

Even so, the victory of neoliberalism was far from inevitable when Thatcher and Reagan assumed office in May 1979 and January 1981 (Jones 2012: 253–254). Rather than follow "an ideologically consistent agenda," they had to rely on a combination of fortunate events and popular measures to consolidate their power (Bulpitt 1986: 34; see also Jones 2012: 271). While the neoliberal projects pursued in the United States and the United Kingdom ran parallel and mutually reinforced each other, and while the long-term goal of defeating organized labor was the same, the tactics differed according to the obstacles they confronted and the opportunities that presented themselves along the way.

In Britain, the militancy of trade unions had made them the prime target of Thatcher's neoliberal program. Plans for legally curtailing their power had been developed as early as 1977, even before the frustrations of voters with the Winter of Discontent put Thatcher into power (Bulpitt 1986: 34; Prasad 2006: 100, 106). Even then, it was not until the miner's strike of 1984 that the Thatcher government would launch a carefully orchestrated, full frontal attack (Jones 2012: 256–257; Evans 2013: 39). Until then, Thatcher had followed a more cautious course of action that built on those elements of neoliberalism—such as the sale of council houses—that promised the broadest electoral appeal and attracted the least opposition, including from within the conservative party (Bulpitt 1986; Hay 1992; Prasad 2006: 141; Evans 2013: 35).

In the United States, organized labor was targeted through a recessionary war on inflation launched by the Federal Reserve. Its success was measured—as Treasury Secretary Donald Regan explained—by the concessionary wages that unions had been forced to accept.[74] In addition to the disciplining force of unemployment, the American state also directly confronted the labor movement (Blyth 2002: 182). Reagan's dismissal of 11,400 striking air traffic controllers and their replacement by military personnel in 1981 sent a powerful signal that an assault on labor was not only desirable but feasible. Business owners not only felt confident to take harsher measures against unions, they were empowered to do so by Reagan's subversion of the National Labor Relations Board (Stein 2010: 267; Blyth 2002: 182–183). In Volcker's assessment, the defeat of the air controllers' strike was "the most important single action of the administration in helping the anti-inflation fight" (Volcker 1994: 162, quoted in Stein 2010: 267). This victory did "even more to break the morale of labor," he noted, than the "breaking of the pattern of wage push in the auto industry" (Volcker, quoted in Panitch and Gindin 2012: 171–172). And across the Atlantic, as one Downing Street official confirmed, it strengthened the resolve of Thatcher to take on the miners, whose defeat in 1984–1985 marked the final victory over the working class in the Anglo-American world (Jones 2012: 267; McCartin 2011: 330).

Neoliberal ideology can certainly explain why Thatcher and Reagan were willing to risk this confrontation. But their ability to remain in power and sustain their attack on organized labor and the welfare state until its "successful" conclusion also depended on favorable international circumstances. Crafting his neoliberal reforms upon voters' preferences, Reagan had combined a deregulation drive started under Carter with enormous income tax cuts and massive military expenditures, while using the resulting deficits as an excuse for gutting welfare programs and social regulation (Prasad 2006: 43–44, 48–49, 61, 63). Amidst a recession, by 1982 his approval ratings had dropped to 35 percent (Stein 2010: 267). What made this experiment workable was a peculiar policy mix of high interest rates and deficit spending that now funneled global capital into the US (Helleiner 1994: 148; Stein 2010: 268–269).

Crucially, according to Greta Krippner, this was "an inadvertent discovery rather than the culmination of a carefully executed plan to draw the world's savings to U.S. financial markets" (2011: 87, see also 92; see also Newstadt 2008). Initially, the Federal Reserve had sought to limit the inflow of foreign funds as they threatened to frustrate its efforts to tighten the money supply (Helleiner 1994: 135–139). It was only because capital was absorbed by a newly deregulated, highly profitable, and rapidly expanding financial sector that its inflationary impact was lessened, as Martin Konings (2007: 55) points out. And it is only in retrospect that "the Fed found, to its surprise, that the ongoing expansion of money and credit no longer resulted in high rates of inflation" (54).

The FOMC minutes make clear that even though the Federal Reserve was concerned about the influx of foreign capital, it felt compelled to maintain high interest rates in order to countervail the extremely loose fiscal policy of the Reagan administration (Stein 2010: 266). What Volcker had feared from the outset would be an "inevitable collision" between Reagan's fiscal laxity and the Fed's monetary restraint turned out to be a boon (Silber 2012: 206). The opposition between Volcker's monetarism and Reagan's much maligned "voodoo economics" produced the peculiar policy mix of monetary stringency and fiscal stimulus that created and sustained the attractive investment climate of a strong dollar and high interest rate (Krippner 2011: 96).

The Reagan administration, too, remained skeptical and only belatedly recognized the potential advantages of foreign capital investment (Krippner 2011: 95). Not only did the massive inflow of funds help to offset the trade and current account deficits; the Reagan administration also learned that it could afford to run federal deficits because foreign investors—now private rather than central bank agents, with Japanese investors at the forefront (Murphy 1996: 129–134, 144–145; Brenner 2006: 189)—seemed to have developed an insatiable appetite for US Treasury bonds (Krippner 2011: 87).

On a much larger scale than Thatcher, who had used the North Sea oil revenue to finance income tax reductions, the US government was able to finance both its massive tax cuts and military expenditures through the sale of Treasury bonds. While the Volcker Shock radically disinflated the world economy between 1979 and 1982, the subsequent fiscal and military expansion, as well as financial deregulation, helped the US economy stage a more vibrant recovery than its core capitalist rivals (Gill 1989: 33).

Global capital inflows, in short, both *enabled* and subsequently *rewarded* the neoliberal counterrevolution, providing a critical measure of electoral support and economic dynamism while organized labor and the welfare state were being directly attacked and systematically undermined. The result of this experiment was to strengthen immeasurably, but rather inadvertently, the unilateral capacity of the United States. Rather than simply provide a new lease on life for a declining hegemon, it gave rise to a historically novel form of capitalism that involved three unexpected transformations: despite the predictions of hegemonic decline and geopolitical fragmentation, the role of the US became more central and the system of global governance more tightly integrated. Despite the social and international challenges to global capitalism that dominated in the first half of the 1970s, the rule of transnational capital was ultimately strengthened at the expense of organized labor. And despite popular-democratic aspirations for post-Keynesian and socialist modes of life, neoliberal ideas have today become deeply ingrained in the mentality of individuals.

Conclusion

The knock-on consequences of the Volcker Shock—the outcome of incessant pressure on the US to commit to an anti-inflationary program—would ultimately pull German policymakers in a similar direction. For at the core of Germany's exit strategy lay a critical contradiction. The relative success of its crisis management was premised not only on building and extending a zone of stability in a world of inflation, but, most important, on maintaining lower rates of inflation than its international competitors. In the aftermath of the first oil shock, Germany had benefitted from a relatively more restrictive credit policy. But similar successes could not be expected if all countries pursued a restrictive course.[75] As one American critic pointedly put the question, "[W]hat would have happened if all countries had pursued policies similar to those of Germany in 1973–74? Wasn't your success at least in part a result of the fact that other countries went 'the expansionist way'?"[76] This meant that the German model could not be generalized without undermining the key to the success of Germany's growth strategy. It could command the consensus of the dominant export interests and the incorporated trade unions because, and as long as, it maintained this crucial comparative advantage in price stability. The deflationary program that Germany had pursued therefore turned out to be not only irreproducible but self-defeating. For as soon as other state elites mustered the political will to apply the lessons of monetary restraint and fiscal prudence, the limitations and indeed fragility of the German model became apparent. Germany's anti-inflationary path out of the crisis had had the side-effect of turning the DM into the world's second reserve currency, notwithstanding the efforts of its monetary technicians to limit or at least manage its international attractiveness. With the US, Britain, and Japan registering similar successes at coping with stagflation, this position of the DM was thrown into question and became a liability.[77] German monetary authorities now found themselves bound to follow the US and UK interest rate hikes in order to maintain the confidence of investors in the DM as a hard currency and to stem capital outflows even at the expense of the domestic economy.[78]

When German interest rates reached a postwar record in May 1980 and the economy went into recession, the Schmidt government briefly opened up to the French plea for collectively bringing down interest rates (Marsh 2009: 91). The opposition of the Bundesbank and the election of a socialist government in France ensured that Schmidt would remain isolated until his government was overturned. Ironically, "Helmut Schmidt, a prime instigator of the American credit squeeze, finished up as yet another victim" (91). Whereas in the US and the UK the interest rate hike formed part of a domestic project designed to defeat organized labor and dismantle welfare state regulation, Germany followed suit because of international pressures generated by this Anglo-American program. High interest rates were adopted with hesitation and continued to be compensated for by a generous welfare state and increasing levels of public indebtedness. The coming-into-power of Kohl in 1982 was, in this respect, a mere changing of the guard. The "neoliberal turn" of German society he had promised did not begin until his electoral defeat fifteen years later (Prasad 2006: 163). And yet, under Schmidt's social-liberal government, the German state had contributed significantly to neoliberalism's global emergence. And in turn, the final chapter will demonstrate, neoliberal globalization has since reshaped the international and European context in which German policymakers, to this day, seek to maintain parts of their social model.

CHAPTER 7

Deflecting Neoliberalism

Power and Purpose in Germany's Eurocrisis Management

THIS BOOK HAS ARGUED that the German state helped create the international and social conditions for neoliberalism to emerge. Having revealed its particular contribution as the unwitting architect of neoliberal globalization, we have opened up a new avenue to address the puzzle of German power that has confounded academic and policy debates for over a decade since the global financial crisis first reached European shores: why has the German state failed to provide enlightened leadership in what is still Europe's darkest moment in peacetime, and why has it imposed a program of neoliberal austerity that has deepened the economic and political divisions within the EU?

This chapter starts off by asking how the German political economy was transformed by the global rise of neoliberalism and how this change fed into Germany's approach to the eurocrisis. Given the multilinearity inscribed in the capitalist development even of the core, the chapter argues that we should not assume a convergence on an Anglo-American paradigm but should remain open to the very different outlook and interests that continue to inform German policymakers—even as Germany's so-called "coordinated" form of capitalism is dissolving, and even as the German state has moved to the forefront of neoliberal restructuring within the EU. The first part of this chapter draws out the connections between the two episodes of crisis management in order to specify these determinants. If we bear in mind that German policymakers developed extensive foreign

economic strategies during the crisis decade of the 1970s in order to preserve the embedded liberal compromise between export-oriented capital
and cooperative trade unions, we can better understand the reasons for
why they prescribed neoliberal policies in the 2010s. The second part of
this chapter argues that, when German crisis management is placed in the
context of a wider world of uneven development, a remarkable fit between
Germany's export orientation and the late industrialization of China and
other emerging market economies comes into view. In the long run, this
combination is changing the significance of the eurozone for the German
growth model from sales market to supply zone. The neoliberal restructuring of the eurozone thus offers an opportunity for German business to cut
the costs of inputs and compete internationally, and for privileged strata
of German labor to continue to partake in its export success. In the short
term, however, the divergence in national growth rates between the US,
the EU, and China has exposed Germany to sudden changes in interest rate
differentials that threaten to disrupt its exports to emerging markets and to
deepen eurozone debt beyond repayment. This amplifies the pressures for
neoliberal austerity beyond what German policy or corporate elites would
otherwise consider viable, and produces the predicament of German primacy as a transformative and yet destabilizing force within the EU.

The German *Wende* and the Fate of the German Model

The decisive victory over the working classes in the United States and the
United Kingdom created a novel and intensely competitive form of capitalism. This new model of economy and polity derived its advantage from
its ability to dispose of, and do without, the compensation and protection
that had hitherto been considered indispensable for buying the allegiance
of labor and for maintaining social cohesion and political stability. It is in
this sense that one may speak of a "transnational learning process" that,
rather than guided by economic ideas or institutionalized interactions
(McNamara 1998; Mourlon-Druol 2010; 2012), was shaped by practical results and that had started with the relative success of German state
managers in combating inflation. From the German vantage point, the
experiment involved the inversion of what the political left had demanded
in the early 1970s. Rather than "test the weight of the financial burden
which the private sector economy could be made to carry," as a former
politician of the SPD had put it (Jochen Steffen, cited in Webber 1983:

66), neoliberal politicians now sought to probe the carrying capacity of society in the interest of private enterprise.[1] In this respect, the neoliberal program of Thatcher and Reagan had not only a disciplinary intent but also a demonstration effect. Their reelections proved not only that organized labor could be taken on and defeated, but also that such class confrontation could be politically stabilized and could serve to restart the capitalist engine.

Approached from the perspective of advanced unevenness, we can see that the advent of neoliberalism opened up yet another developmental gap within the industrialized core. The great unwinding of the embedded liberal compact rewarded the US and the UK as the countries that had been the first to take organized labor head on. It rendered the economic success of the capitalistically developed societies contingent upon the degree to which they could follow, or otherwise cope with, the Anglo-American example. The crucial question that emerges from this is how German policy elites have interpreted and responded to this challenge, and how the German political economy has changed as a result.

In contrast to the neoliberal revolution under Reagan and Thatcher, the "intellectual and ethical change" announced by the incoming Kohl government (Leaman 2009: 30) never actually materialized (Menz 2005: 33). This is remarkable because there was a shared sense among ruling elites even then of the structural problems facing *Modell Deutschland*. Though presented as a partisan "free market" pamphlet, the infamous memorandum by economics minister Lambsdorff that led his liberal party to topple Schmidt was echoed within the SPD leadership. In fact, the counterpaper drawn up by the social-democratic finance minister Lahnstein concurred on many of the fundamental issues and indeed anticipated the reform drive of welfare cuts and labor market flexibilization under Schröder twenty years later: rising wage costs had rendered some sectors uncompetitive, social spending had grown disproportionately, and an underlying market economy had been overburdened by social regulations and public interventions (Abelshauser 2005: 442–443, 446). The question of why Germany nevertheless did not follow the Anglo-American example deserves some consideration. Many reasons have been cited: divisions within the new governing coalition, opposition from the social wing of the Christian Democratic Union, and a federalized and therefore unwieldy state apparatus ruled out from the start the implementation of a neoliberal program (Webber 1992: 152–153; Zohlnhöfer 2001; Prasad 2006: 164).

From a class-based perspective, the most significant difference from the Anglo-American experience is that the unified bloc of financial and industrial capital characteristic of the German political economy since the late nineteenth century, and the export-oriented alliance with organized labor forged after 1945, remained intact. Not only did the institutionalized strength of labor and its party-political representation put a roadblock in the way of a neoliberal transformation of society (Herrigel 1996: 287), there was not even a social constituency that would have supported such a program. In fact, employers showed little interest in abandoning the consensual model of industrial relations, as Lambsdorff observed not long after Kohl assumed power (Abelshauser 2005: 447; Wood 1997: 26, cited in Kinderman 2005: 435). Instead, they sought to improve their position within the existing regime of wage negotiations (van der Wurff 1993: 176–177). And rather than being attacked as in the US and the UK, trade unions and work councils continued to be actively involved in what Esser (1982) termed a "crisis management coalition" that was widely supported by public authorities, employers' associations, and economic research institutes. The ruling consensus was to postpone or soften structural adjustments as far as possible while accepting rising public indebtedness, and to otherwise turn to "an anti-protectionist and 'offensive' adaptation that would build on West Germany's position of strength within the international economy to secure old markets and open up new ones" (Esser and Fach with Dyson 1983: 108). At least initially, Reagan's spending spree stimulated global demand and opened up possibilities for German exporters. As providers of high-quality capital goods, many of them could expect to benefit from an intensified form of capitalist competition in as far as cost-saving pressures compelled some industries to upgrade to more advanced, labor-saving technologies (Beck 2015: 259).

The key to understanding the transformation of the German model is thus to be found in the gradual unraveling of *Germany Inc.* from the late 1980s onward. Led by Deutsche Bank, German finance has been lured onto international markets by the profits and pressures of Anglo-American investment banks. In an effort to globalize their operations, the leading German banks have withdrawn from the corporate network of cross-shareholdings and interlocking directorates that afforded a measure of coordination and protection against short-term profit considerations and hostile takeovers (Streeck 2009: 77; Deeg 2010; Allen 2010: 133; Windolf 2014).[2] Deprived of reliable long-term investors, German companies have in turn become more susceptible to Anglo-Saxon-style shareholder demands that have further eroded the established corporate governance structures.[3] Along with the traditional ties between finance and industrial capital, the consensual capital-labor relations have also suffered considerable strain. The collapse of the Soviet bloc has enabled German manufacturers to relocate production to low-cost locales in Central and Eastern Europe and thus strengthened their bargaining position vis-à-vis labor. The threat of moving abroad has empowered employers to circumvent the institutions of collective bargaining and to exact significant concessions that have eroded wage levels and working conditions (Streeck 2016: 58). Since the mid-1990s, German employers have also felt compelled and empowered to advocate liberal economic reforms (Kinderman 2005: 445). Whereas in the early 1990s there still seemed to be a consensus among political and economic elites that the existing structures could cope with the pressures of neoliberal globalization (though no clear sense of how they would adapt), ten years later an employer-sponsored think tank declared that "[t]he so-called German model, developed in the 1970s, has long ceased to be a model worth emulating" (Initiative Neue Soziale Marktwirtschaft 2003, quoted in Kinderman 2005: 432).

The so-called "Hartz IV" welfare state and labor market reforms introduced by the Schröder government mark the highpoint of this transformation (Hassel and Schiller 2010). The reforms ruptured relations between the governing Red-Green coalition and their social-democratic, trade-union, and working-class constituency. Combining, and reducing, unemployment and social benefits has led to an enormous increase in income inequality and old-age poverty. And the decline in unemployment often praised as a German recovery has come at the expense of a massive expansion of the part-time and low-wage sector as workers are compelled to take on precarious jobs in order to avoid punitive benefit cuts.

The multiple sclerosis of the Rhineland variety of capitalism sketched above has been discussed in a burgeoning body of comparative political economy scholarship (Menz 2005; Thelen 2014; Streeck 2016: 56). And yet the long-standing debate over the fortunes of the German model cannot explain the key puzzle at the heart of this book. The question is not simply whether the German state may or may not succumb to the pressures of neoliberal globalization, but why it has brought them to bear on other countries within the EU. To explain what appears to be an astounding *volte face* of the German state from defender of Rhineland capitalism to the principal enforcer of neoliberalism since the eurocrisis, a series of conceptual shifts are necessary.

First of all, we need to break with the misleading assumption that the erosion of *Modell Deutschland* simply lays bare an essential market mechanism that had been buried underneath an institutional superstructure. Neoliberalism, this book suggests, cannot be reduced to an Anglo-American bid to free "the market" from its various impediments and encumbrances. In fact, once we realize that the US and the UK, far from immovable movers, were driven toward a decisive break with embedded liberalism by a combination of different crisis management strategies, this essentialist conception of neoliberalism gives way to a processual and open-ended view. While it began with an organized assault on the working class in these two countries, it has since morphed into a far broader palette of policies that are united only in so far as they take aim at the social protections, political representation, and economic benefits of working people. Rather than simply a reversion to an earlier, purer form of capitalism, the dismantling of these rights can take many different and sometimes novel forms. Second, as a consequence, it is wrong to think of neoliberalism in Germany as simply repeating the same movement started by Reagan and Thatcher. We need to open ourselves to the possibility that the German political economy may have (d)evolved in qualitatively different ways rather than slavishly followed in the footsteps of the putative Anglo-American prime mover. Paying close attention to this difference, the remainder of this chapter shows, is crucial for understanding precisely how and why German state managers have responded to the eurocrisis. Third, and most crucially, even where and when we find that specific developments in Germany mirror those in the US or the UK, we cannot conclude from this that the same dynamics are at play. Much of the critical scholarship tends to assume that, in as far as Germany stands at the heart of a neoliberal Europe today, it must be driven by economic ideas, social forces, or considerations of statecraft similar to those of its neoliberal peers. As a consequence, the real motives that have guided German crisis managers remain underexplored and unexplained.

From the alternative vantage point taken in this book, some striking continuities move into view.[4] With the global turn toward neoliberalism, the welfare promises of the German social market economy have been significantly scaled back. But its dependence on exports has only deepened further, rising from 17.6 percent of gross domestic product (GDP) in 1978 to 26.5 percent in 1998, before surging to an all-time high of 47.4 percent in 2018.[5] Upon closer inspection, these staggering proportions form part of a longer-term trajectory. Unique among the advanced industrialized countries, the German political economy has defied the secular decline of its manufacturing base in the new era of neoliberal globalization (Vihriälä and Wolff 2013: 48, 60; Fratzscher 2018: 41). And, on a longer time scale still, it has retained a remarkably stable share of the value of global merchandise exports—for well over a century. This resilience stands in stark contrast to the steady decline of the US share from its peak in 1948.[6] And it is even more extraordinary in the face of the Chinese late-industrializing giant, which has sextupled its share of global manufacturing output since 1990 (Baldwin 2016: 90).

Some of the institutions of Germany's social market economy such as collective bargaining or unionization have also been weakened (Streeck 2009). And yet a rump of the original social compromise between capital and labor within Germany's export-oriented manufacturing core has remained (Beck and Scherrer 2010). In fact, although on far less favorable terms for labor, the Great Recession has reinforced elements of this bargain (Lehndorff 2016: 189). As part of a "crisis corporatism," trade unions and work councils have made work time concessions in exchange for job guarantees (Urban 2012; Solty 2016: 39–40). A recent labor consultancy study finds that employees have refrained from asking for higher wages while trade unions have focused on other benefits such as better pensions and training—supposedly so as not to endanger Germany's hard-earned competitiveness (Jones 2017). In export-driven sectors, meanwhile, the connection between entrepreneurial success and material rewards for labor continues to hold. While overall real wages stagnated for much of the 2000s, they increased "in the chemical and metal industries; sub-sectors that were particularly oriented towards exports between the years 2000 and 2012" (Becker 2015: 242). And even the punitive Hartz IV reforms, while undoubtedly shifting the German model from welfare toward workfare and significantly reducing the number of its beneficiaries, has left intact the workplace privileges of permanent employees. Indeed, the reforms may even have served to sustain this productivist core: the creation of a large pool of temporary low-wage workers deprived of job security and welfare state and pension benefits has allowed German industry to save costs by reducing the number of core employees and to respond more flexibly to the ebb and flow of world market demand (Hall 2015: 48).

Last, the deepening export orientation of German capitalism, and the persistent if circumscribed capital-labor compromise based upon it, also support a long-standing macroeconomic policy consensus broadly shared by research institutes, the business press, employers' associations, and trade unions. Reaching back to 1951, a sustained and growing trade surplus continues to be seen by these actors as a measure of success for private investment and public policy decisions that is defended vigorously against outside criticism (Beck 2015: 153).

Against this backdrop, this chapter proposes to approach the fate of the German model not as an academic debate but as a first-order governance problem. Because this practical challenge first emerged during the crisis of the 1970s, this decade provides an important precedent for how German policymakers have approached the eurocrisis and its aftermath: now as then, German crisis managers are concerned with maintaining a productivist bargain that continues to depend on Germany's export prowess but which has since come under considerable strain. Far from suggesting that the German model is alive and well, it is precisely its dissolution that motivates Germany's policymakers today. The task is therefore to explore this long-run continuity and the similarities and differences between these two episodes of German crisis management.

German Primacy and the Future of Europe

Such a historically broadened perspective sheds new light on the problem of German primacy in Europe today: the glaring contrast between the widespread calls, and seeming potential, for benevolent German leadership on the one hand, and the harsh reality of a German-led austerity agenda on the other. In principle, the new Germany that emerged from the Cold War—secure within its extended borders, favorably placed within an enlarged European Union, and enjoying a decade of strong economic growth—seems to be in a unique position to outline a comprehensive vision for Europe in the wake of the eurocrisis and after the coronavirus pandemic. And yet it has repeatedly failed to do so over the past decade and instead insisted on a punitive program of fiscal cuts, structural reforms, and privatization schemes that critics argue has proven to be socially disastrous, politically divisive, and economically unsustainable—so much so that some have questioned whether it makes sense even from a narrow German point of view (Blyth 2013a; 2013b; Matthijs 2016).

Despite evidence to the contrary, many officials and observers have repeatedly pinned their hopes on the current or next German government to assume responsibility for stabilizing global and European trade flows, pulling the eurozone out of the recession through a program of domestic reflation or offering less onerous financial assistance—if not as an express act of European solidarity than at least in Germany's enlightened self-interest of keeping the eurozone together. In the case of Greece in 2015, the assumption that, if push came to shove, "Chancellor Merkel was unlikely to decide to sacrifice Europe" (Galbraith 2016: 113) had fatal consequences for the anti-austerity politics of the newly elected Syriza government. Contrary to this expectation, this critical "test of German leadership" (Galbraith 2016: 43) backfired, as German officials were fully prepared to have Greece crash out of the eurozone lest it submit to another round of neoliberal austerity.

The first step in resolving this puzzle lies in recognizing just how deep the currents run that have pushed the German state in this direction, and how unlikely future governments are to change course. Ever since the 1950s, German policymakers have repeatedly confronted, and rejected, international criticism of their economy's excessive export orientation.[7] Moreover, they already turned down propositions to act as the driver of demand-led growth in the 1970s—under conditions, it should be noted, that were far more favorable to a coordinated rebalancing, and progressive reorganization, of the global political economy. Even though Social Democrats were in government, and despite a strong political left and organized labor movement as well as widespread social and international demands for redistribution, German state managers would not cede to calls for a global reflation for fear that this would undermine their own anti-inflationary path out of the crisis (Cesaratto and Stirati 2010: 79).

Mobilizing the master concept of "hegemony" to compare the defective exercise of German power in contemporary Europe to the successful leadership of the United States after 1945—though immensely popular—is conceptually and historically flawed. It uses the yardstick of a different time and place when Keynesian macroeconomic stabilization was still widely considered be a genuine policy option (Hillebrand 2015), and it ignores the critical transition from embedded to neoliberal capitalism that—because it radically reshaped the global policy environment—provides a far more fruitful vista onto Germany's approach to the eurocrisis. It also overlooks that, in the 1970s, Germany's strategy of crisis management already pointed in a decidedly "post-hegemonic" direction. To be sure, *within* German society, the low-inflation model based on reciprocal wage and price restraint had offered advantages to, and gained the support of, both dominant exporters and incorporated trade unions. The international extension of this model, however, could not offer the same opportunities and did not entail a similar degree of consent. At least initially, the German model was adopted not because of any shared understanding among political (and economic) elites of the preferable solution to the crisis but under the immediate impression, and indeed pressure, of Germany's practical achievements.[8] The problems of wage-push inflation were certainly recognized, but the political and economic costs of disciplining labor through monetary tightening seemed prohibitively high. Only in Germany, where relative price stability translated into export competitiveness, could monetary restraint stabilize the social-democratic bargain. The extension of the German anti-inflationary project via the snake and the EMS, however, contained a compulsive element, offering exchange-rate stability while forcing adhering countries to follow the macroeconomic example of Germany. And last, even when and where an anti-inflationary program had gained the support of financial and industrial circles (Moss 2000: 265), the model of monetary and fiscal prudence could not be replicated without undermining the Keynesian compromise.

The German solution, to be sure, involved constructing, extending, and maintaining a zone of stability in a highly inflationary global environment. But this was only the necessary and not the sufficient condition for Germany's economic success. For the model to work, Germany had not only to keep down inflation but to maintain *lower* rates of inflation than its competitors. This competitive element meant that Germany's was an inherently particularistic mode of crisis management that turned out to be self-limiting when exported to other state-society complexes.

The parochialism already apparent in the German response to the postwar crisis of capitalism has become even more pronounced in the wake of the eurocrisis. Given the creeping degradation of the German model of consensual industrial relations and the deepening export dependence of the German economy, its political administrators have found it near impossible to pursue anything other than the proven remedy of a concerted export drive. A shift toward domestic reflation—which some have insisted is the only viable solution to the structural imbalances that plague the eurozone (Pettis 2013)—not only contradicts this objective, it also threatens to weaken the underlying class compromise that this focus on exports is meant to sustain. Germany's international competitiveness—based on the suppression of internal demand, the containment of wages, and the maintenance of price stability—ultimately requires compliant unions and work councils that are willing to moderate their demands. A program of public investment unduly strengthens organized labor and "threatens the wage coordination on which exports are based" (Hall 2015: 55), thus undermining both German economic success and social cohesion. The vulnerability of this uniquely export-dependent productivist arrangement explains the remarkable consensus among Germany's incumbent and prospective state managers (with the exception of *Die Linke*, of any party-political affiliation) to defend Germany's trade surplus and refuse a program of internal demand stimulation. In the words of the Bundesbank president Jens Weidmann, "[I]t would be absurd to discuss measures aimed at artificially weakening Germany's competitiveness in order to reduce current account surpluses vis-à-vis the other euro-area countries" (Deutsche Bundesbank 2015).[9]

Overall, then, Germany is unlikely to rebalance its economy no matter what government is voted into power. But while it may never play the kind of leadership role that many politicians and observers have demanded of it (for example, Hein and Truger 2010)—not least in the face of the virus-induced recession (for example, Borelli and Karnitschnig 2020)—past experience suggests that it is not going to withdraw from the European project either, as others have feared (for example, Young and Semmler 2011). In the context of the 1970s crisis, after all, German state managers also renounced an inward-looking and self-reliant course of action. They instead chose a "flight forward," elaborating a grand strategy that gave impetus to the further monetary and economic integration of Europe, while limiting decisively the leeway for solidaristic alternatives. The onset of the global financial crisis of 2008 coincided with a remarkable recovery of the German model of capitalism from twenty years of economic malaise. And today's coronavirus pandemic comes after a decade of booming exports, rising tax revenue, and low borrowing costs for the German state. In a situation in which its material capabilities massively outweigh those of most of its eurozone partners, we can expect Germany to project its monetary and financial influence in ways that are likely to be as transformative as those of the 1970s, but—as the experience of the eurocrisis suggests—probably even more socially regressive.

With the deepening integration of the European Union since the 1990s, German crisis managers have had an ever more elaborate apparatus of supervision and sanction at their disposal. The shock of the global financial meltdown and the ad hoc organization of bailouts and austerity cuts through the triumvirate ("troika") of European Commission, European Central Bank (ECB), and IMF have only further strengthened this capacity. For instance, the pledge of one fifth of its gold reserves that Italy had to make in 1974 in order to receive $5 billion in German financial assistance (Piller 2011) cannot match the finesse of the troika-mandated transfer of Greek public property to an independent trust fund tasked to fire-sell them in order to service state debt. And the political and financial pressure that the G7 and the German-American entente are said to have brought to bear on the Italian government to exclude the PCI pales in comparison to the coordinated attack on the Greek banking system after the "Greek Spring" of 2015 put the anti-austerity Syriza party into office (Varoufakis 2017).

Many observers have noted that, in sharp contrast to the burdens of Germany's fascist past that impeded previous generations of German politicians, the political scruples about deploying this interventionist arsenal have also subsided. But more important still is that the target of these interventions has also clearly changed: Germany's eurocrisis managers have sought to induce not simply monetary restraint and fiscal rectitude but far-reaching structural reforms. Germany's insistence on mass layoffs during the summer 2015 showdown with the Syriza government was only one item in a much larger list of demands imposed or suggested by the troika under so-called memoranda of understanding signed with the debtor economies. It included raising the working time and the retirement age, weakening collective bargaining and employment protection, and extending part-time and temporary agency work, and it demonstrates that creditors have sought to reengineer social relations in deficit countries on an unprecedented scale and in a qualitatively new way (Clauwaert and Schömann 2012; Schulten and Müller 2013; Picot and Tassinari 2014). The precise conditions that will ultimately be attached to the coronavirus rescue program have yet to be negotiated, but the next section explains why it is unlikely that German policy elites will let this opportunity pass.

German Manufacturing and Neoliberal Restructuring

There is no better term to capture the content of this social reconfiguration than the much maligned category of "neoliberalism." But to subsume what is happening under this label is not to explain why it is being done. To understand how and why German policymakers have been dead set on a program of structural reform, we need to recognize their ongoing attempts to reproduce an institutionalized set of class relations within a new world-historical context of uneven and combined development.

This context is marked, first and foremost, by the rise of a new generation of capitalist late industrializers, spearheaded by China. The commercial challenge posed by Chinese companies breaking into and controlling global value chains, and the trade war launched by the United States under Trump to neutralize this threat, have fast come to dominate the agenda of German policy and corporate elites. But over the past two decades, Sino-German relations have been characterized far less by competition than by a profound complementarity. Pulled in by the massive Chinese demand for high-tech capital and luxury consumer goods (Südekum 2018: 50–51), Germany's exports have skyrocketed from about US$11 billion to $108 billion since China's accession to the World Trade Organization in 2001, making China its third largest export destination, after the United States and France.[10] The eurozone as a whole still absorbs the majority of German exports. But as Etienne Schneider (2017) has calculated, the overall share of its six largest economies declined from 41 to 31 percent of total German exports between 1995 and 2015. The eurocrisis, moreover, sapped the ability of European markets to absorb German exports and increased the importance of other outlets. While Germany's net exports to the eurozone halved between 2007 and 2011, a growing trade surplus with the rest of the world more than compensated for this loss (Jannsen and Kooths 2012: 6–7; Fratzscher 2018: 40). This diminished importance of the euro area contrasts markedly with the massive scale of opportunity that China and other major emerging markets represent, given that German manufactures are "almost perfectly suited to the needs of rapidly growing economies" (Hübner 2015: 399; Bartlett and Roller 2010: 3). Over the past ten years, Germany alone has accounted for half of all manufacturing goods that the EU sends to China.[11] Germany also consistently leads the rest of the EU in terms of foreign direct investment (FDI) into China, reaching a record 50 percent of the EU total in 2018 (Rhodium Group 2019).

Notwithstanding the geopolitical and geoeconomic rivalries that loom on the horizon today, China's rise has generated a momentous regional diversification of German trade and investment beyond the postwar growth poles of Western Europe and North America. This shift connects to the original postwar vision, developed in the first half of the twentieth century and elevated to state policy under Erhard after the Second World War (Gross 2015; Neebe 2004), that Germany could prosper as the workshop of a newly industrializing world (Abelshauser 2016: 508–509). This vision could only ever be partially fulfilled in the context of the Cold War division of the world market, the inward-looking character of European integration, and the limitations of these national development projects themselves. In a new century shaped by the ascent of China, however, that opportunity presents itself on a vastly extended scale, and in a situation in which, as the Siemens CEO Joe Kaeser argues, "[o]ur national economy is saturated in large parts, which is why we need to think about how to sustain our export model" (Mahler and Deckstein 2017).

Under these conditions, trading with (and investing in) the Chinese giant offers more than enormous profits (Hansakul and Levinger 2014: 5).[12] As long as Chinese competition can be held at bay, it helps to ensure the viability of a particular national political economy that "can function as long as there are waves of industrialization in new countries that require capital goods made in Germany" (Boyer 2015: 217). These prospects, raised powerfully by a tidal wave of capitalist late development, go a long way—if not the full distance—toward explaining the neoliberal agenda that the German state has pursued since the eurocrisis.

The growing weight of global rather than European markets helps us understand why the German state has refused to offer more generous financial assistance to its indebted partners, even though this threatens to undermine European demand (Hübner 2015: 405). We have seen that, already in the 1970s, German state managers had concluded that the advantages of such a stimulus for their manufacturers would be offset by the spendthrift behavior it would encourage and the global inflationary pressures this would fuel. Insisting on monetary and fiscal restraint instead, they resolved—as Schmidt reportedly said about Italy—to "give only as much help which enables it to be with his head out of the water, not on the beach" (De Cecco 1976, quoted in Celi and others 2018: 247). The increasing importance of China for the vitality of the German export model has shifted this cost-benefit calculation further in favor of austerity. Not only does the demand from China and other emerging market economies offset potential losses within Europe, it also changes the standing of the eurozone within Germany's crisis management. Given the structural fit between the Chinese giant and the German export model, the European home market enters the equation not so much as a vital outlet but as a regional springboard for German exports. And this shift, we shall see, explains why German policymakers have insisted not only on painful cuts but on a deeper structural adjustment—at a level of detail and complexity unimaginable to Schmidt when he concluded that "in Europe, we have to accomplish a precise division of labour" (De Cecco 1976, quoted in Celi and others 2018: 247).]

The comparison with Central and Eastern Europe after the collapse of the Soviet Union offers a glimpse of what is involved. The EU accession process opened up the postcommunist economies to foreign direct investment and allowed German corporations to extend their manufacturing networks from the Benelux countries, northern Italy, and Austria to their traditional markets in the East (Becker 2015: 238; Bohle 2018: 242). The attraction for German manufacturers clearly lies in the lower wages, weaker unions, and more pliable workers' rights that these new economies offer, with the result that "lower-value parts of the production process are hived off to cheaper locations" (Bruff 2015: 117).

The spatial reorganization of German industry is by no means limited to the Visegrád economies, however. Today, two-thirds of all trade in the EU take place within supply chains (Nordström and Flam 2018: 1). Since 2000, Germany has further consolidated its position at the center of a manufacturing hub-and-spoke system, serving as the key production partner of virtually all other EU member states (Stöllinger and others 2018: 3, 31–32; Baldwin and Lopez-Gonzalez 2015).[13] And although surpassed by Central and Eastern Europe in 2005, Southern Europe still constitutes the second most important offshoring destination for German manufacturers (Marin, Veugelers, and Feliu 2017: 117).

The lead role of German manufacturers in European and global supply chains has been widely credited for their strong export performance despite intensified competition from emerging market economies (Gräf and others 2013: 9; Vihriälä and Wolff 2013: 68). And in the wake of the eurocrisis, their ability to parcel out and optimize production across this new industrial landscape has become even more important. The Association of German Chambers of Commerce and Industry (DIHK), which regularly surveys German companies about their investment plans, notes that cost considerations have returned as an important driver of FDI, as German companies seek out cheaper energy and labor abroad (DIHK 2014: 3, 15–16). Economic upheavals and unemployment have created a suitable pool of highly skilled workers across the EU that German companies are keen to tap into (22). The structural reforms and recovery of the crisis countries, meanwhile, have led to "a renaissance of Europe in the eyes of German investors" (7). Offering lower unit labor costs than at home, a common currency and favorable exchange rate, and well-established business networks, the eurozone has reemerged as Germany's premier manufacturing base (DIHK 2017: 3, 13).

Intended to shape public opinion and official decision making, these surveys cannot claim to offer an objective account of the drivers of foreign direct investment. There is some evidence to support the shift in business sentiment invoked in these reports, however. Between 2010 and 2017, the stock of German FDI in the manufacturing sectors of the EU South grew faster than in the EU East, and well above the average rate of growth for the EU as a whole.[14] Approached as a commentary on public policy, moreover, these surveys give us a sense of the kinds of reforms German business would like to see implemented.

It is from this perspective that the neoliberal reforms—such as fire sales of public assets, wage cuts, and labor market reforms—which German elites have exacted from deficit countries starts to make some sense. From the standpoint of capital, these structural reforms promise to lower costs for German manufacturers producing in or sourcing inputs from the targeted economies and raise the competitiveness of German exports in global markets. Accordingly, one of the DIHK reports praises Spain for raising the retirement age, freezing public sector wages, and increasing the number of workdays while concluding that there is further potential for reform, especially in France and Italy (2015: 13–14). Greece, it should be noted, goes unmentioned—a sign perhaps of its status as an outlier within the German production networks and a pariah under the Syriza government. For German business, then, calls on deficit countries to improve their "competitiveness" have nothing to do with meeting German competition or following the German example; they are quite patently about creating favorable conditions for German investment.

The official mind of German crisis management is of course less transparent. But the longer-term view taken in this book suggests that German policymakers also appreciate the advantages that this structural adjustment of the eurozone holds out. In a century shaped by the rise of China, the creation of a regional low-cost environment from which German manufacturers can supply the world does not only preserve their competitive advantage. It also promises to reproduce the particular social bargain which German policy elites constructed after 1945 and managed to preserve during the 1970s. Although it has narrowed significantly since then, this compromise still brings together leading manufacturers and a privileged segment of skilled workers who contribute to and draw material benefits from Germany's world market position.

This is made possible by the fact that, unlike their US counterparts, German corporations tend to relocate only low-skill and labor-intensive parts of production, while retaining "company head offices, research and development and activities that require highly qualified, highly specialized and well paid staff" (Gräf and others 2013: 12). Rather than extricate themselves completely, they seek to offset the rigidities of the German social partnership (Dörrenbächer 2004; Boyer 2015: 215). In contrast to the United States, the internationalization of German industry has not lead to the wholesale transfer of manufacturing jobs, in part because German workers have been able to use work councils and codetermination laws to strike more reciprocal bargains at the company level (Kwon 2012). On the contrary, the deepening trade with China and Central and Eastern Europe is held to have added some 444,000 manufacturing jobs between 1990 and 2010 (Südekum 2018: 49). On the whole, it is estimated that in 2011, 6.2 million jobs in Germany depended on German exports beyond the EU—an increase from 1995 of 114 percent (Arto and others 2015: 192). There is, in other words, a distinctive *complementarity* between foreign investment and domestic production that sets Germany apart from its neoliberal peers and that can shed some light on its preference for neoliberal austerity (Kwon 2012). Similar to the bifurcation of the domestic labor market under Hartz IV, the geographical dispersion of low-skill and labor-intensive portions of the production process serves as an auxiliary to Germany's manufacturing sector and supports the symbiosis of export success and domestic stabilization.

Although this neoliberal restructuring caters primarily to the parochial interests of the German state and capital, it has been advocated by some as a general solution to Europe's economic woes. German employers have been keen to point out that the demand of German industry for intermediate and investment goods sustains 3.4 million jobs across the EU (VBW 2017)—a clear indication, in their view, that Germany's booming exports benefit rather than hurt its European partners (Beise 2017). The Kiel Institute for the World Economy, a prestigious think tank that helped design the Maastricht criteria for the euro, provides another illuminating example. In a 2012 study, two of its lead analysts concluded that Germany's global exporters can play a constructive role in rebalancing intra-European trade (Jannsen and Kooths 2012: 368, 372). All that is required is that firms from

European deficit countries, rather than strike out on their own, integrate into the global value chains dominated by German exporters as "a short-cut to target foreign markets that would otherwise remain beyond their scope" (372). More prominently, the Siemens CEO has trotted out a similar line. Asked about foreign criticism of the German export model, he replied that "the trick will be also to let partner countries participate adequately in the creation of value through a transfer of know-how and local production" (Mahler and Deckstein 2017).

Seen in this view, measures such as wage and pension cuts, work time increases, and the restriction of job security that German officials have demanded from crisis-ridden partners can be seen—and justified in their minds—as advancing a particular kind of economic integration that claims to offer a collective, though arguably elusive, road toward recovery (Bellofiore, Garibaldo, and Halevi 2010: 144; Heine and Sablowski 2016). It might appear impossible that a program of internal deflation within the eurozone could possibly bring down costs to a level low enough to meet the competition of East Asian producers. Given that wages in China have been rapidly rising, however, this possibility does not seem quite as remote. Although it is not integrated into German supply chains, average hourly wages in Greece have been cut by more than half (from €8.50 in 2009 to €4.10 in 2016; data from Euromonitor International 2017a). And in Portugal, where German corporations such as Volkswagen, Bosch, and Continental have significant investments (Silva 2015: 207), stagnating wages in the manufacturing sector are gradually converging with those in China (€3.20 vs. €4.10) (Euromonitor International 2017b).

None of this is to deny that there are serious tensions and contradictions that have characterized the German approach. Chief among them is the threat—posed again by the coronavirus pandemic—that the eurozone might collapse under the crushing weight of neoliberal austerity, which has diminished the growth expectations and impoverished the populations of Southern deficit countries at a rate unprecedented in peacetime Europe. Even if we assume that German policy elites are indifferent to the humanitarian crisis they have caused, such a fragmentation cannot possibly be in their interest. And yet, in the confrontations with Greece in 2011 and 2015—a country that had to shoulder the harshest austerity despite lying outside of the German industrial supply chain—this scenario became a very real possibility.

The final piece of the puzzle then is why German policymakers should have so vehemently insisted on a program of austerity despite the considerable costs and risks associated with this strategy. To find the answer, we need to shift from the long-term developments to the short-term fluctuations in the world economy that confronted German policymakers at the height of the eurocrisis. As I lay out in greater detail elsewhere (Germann 2018), a large part of the pressures that pushed German policymakers in this direction arose from their precarious position between divergent postcrisis trajectories of the US, the EU, and emerging markets such as China. While the United States experienced a modest recovery from 2011, Europe remained mired in recession for longer. As a consequence, the Federal Reserve officially ended its purchase of Treasury and mortgage-backed securities in October 2014 and began to raise interest rates one year later—the same year that the ECB had just started—in the context of a continuing slump and yet against German opposition—to launch an equivalent program of "quantitative easing."

The worst-case scenario on the minds of German authorities in that moment was a reprise of the Volcker Shock. This danger has receded for now, as the Federal Reserve has gone over to cutting interest rates in order to counter the effects of the US-China trade war and the massive recession brought on by the pandemic. But even a cautious departure of the Fed from the ultra-low interest rates, it was feared at the time, might trigger a destabilizing influx of capital into the US and drain the world economy of liquidity (Belke 2014: 7). Bundesbank officials repeatedly cautioned that "one thing is certain: interest rates will rise again at some point" (Dombret 2014a) and recited the old slogan that "when the United States sneezes, the world catches a cold" (Dombret 2014b)—describing a situation likely to be faced again in the not-too-distant future. Germany's political economy is doubly exposed to the repercussions of such a monetary shift. On the one hand, Germany's economic recovery, and the vitality of its social model in general, have been staked on the continuous demand from emerging market economies for its exports. A sudden outflow of capital or rising debt-servicing costs could disrupt the rapid and potentially overheated economic development of the late-industrializing giants on which Germany so critically depends. At present, to be sure, such a disruption seems more likely to be caused by the fallout of the coronavirus pandemic, which has seen investors scramble to exit emerging markets and pile into US dollars. In May 2013, however, the so-called "taper tantrum" gave a worrying indication of how emerging markets could react to the Federal Reserve tightening its monetary policy (Bruff 2015: 122). On the other hand, as the eurozone's central economy and one of its largest creditors, Germany has an enormous stake in ensuring the sustainability of public and private debt. In the context of faltering economic growth, however, the eurozone found it impossible to deleverage. Between 2007 and 2015, its ratio of total debt to GDP increased by 70 percentage points, compared to only 16 and 30 percentage points in the US and the UK, respectively (my calculations, based on Dobbs and others 2015: 4). While Germany has since returned to precrisis levels, the eurozone as a whole has seen an increase in its public debt to GDP from 65.9 in 2007 to 84.1 percent in 2019.[15]

The growing divergence in the pace of indebtedness has raised the question of how to manage the service of debt and retain the confidence of investors in the event of a monetary shift. As the Bundesbank chief Jens Weidmann (2017) put the point most forcefully, ultra-low interest rates have created an "illusion of sustainability" that will dissolve once interest rates rise again. The danger is that the ECB might be caught off guard and compelled to reverse its overly lax monetary course, on which a virus-hit eurozone depends more vitally than ever. Axel Weber, the former Bundesbank president who resigned from his post over his opposition to the ECB's bond purchases, has warned that "[e]merging markets will not be the only ones to suffer" and concluded that "European policy makers need to enact further reforms and need to work on generating dynamics, even harder than if US monetary policy were to stay on the same course" (quoted in Riecher 2013). In view of this scenario, German officials have complained that the unorthodox steps taken by the ECB since the onset of the eurocrisis merely "bought time" that has since been squandered (Schäuble 2015; compare Streeck 2014).

Overall, then, the threat of a change in global interest rates, and the sense that time is running out, has pushed German elites further down a path of austerity than they would otherwise have considered desirable or feasible. Confronted with the potential disruption of emerging market demand for German exports and the risk that eurozone debt may deepen beyond repayment, German officials have seen austerity not simply as a golden opportunity to restructure the eurozone in support of its crumbling class compromise but as an urgent necessity that appears to be without alternative.

These accelerated international pressures for reform help explain why even a country of marginal importance to Germany's production network like Greece became the battleground over the harshest austerity measures imposed anywhere. It complements accounts which argue that Greece was primarily important for its demonstration effect, especially after a radical left-wing and anti-austerity party was voted into power in 2015. One of the most compelling analyses along these lines comes from Yanis Varoufakis (2017), who served as finance minister under the new government of Alex Tsipras. His fascinating first-person account of the negotiations with Greece's creditors identifies a faction around German finance minister Schäuble that was dead set on moving Greece toward a "timeout" from the eurozone (see also Traynor 2015). The explicit aim of excluding an "unreformable" country like Greece was to commit the remaining members to fiscal restraint and structural reform.[16] In addition to the other crisis countries, Italy and France in particular were the principal target (Varoufakis 2017: 381). We now know that the Merkel government rejected Schäuble's plan and that the Syriza government ultimately gave in to more austerity for yet another bailout rather than risk an uncoordinated exit. An open question, however, is why the Merkel government refused to move even an inch from an austerity program that some of its chief proponents had long recognized would turn Greece into a bottomless hole (Varoufakis 2017: 415). After all, if the Syriza leadership had not surrendered to the troika's demands, this inflexibility would have produced the very Grexit situation that Merkel had sought to avoid. Perhaps Merkel believed that this scenario, while far from an intended or desired outcome, could nevertheless be contained. More plausible than her buying Schäuble's confidence that the financial and political fallout from Grexit could be managed, however, is that she agreed with his assessment of the dire situation. Varoufakis reported that Schäuble was convinced that there are fatal flaws in the monetary union that can only be fixed through a hardening of the currency bloc (409), that the European social model cannot withstand the cost competition of emerging economies such as China and India, and that painful adjustments are inevitable (211–212). There is no doubt that Schäuble was isolated in his favorable view of Grexit as a step in the grand plan for restructuring the EU (Varoufakis 2015; Varoufakis 2017), which I have argued above involves not only the institutional reorganization of the EU but also the structural reconfiguration of its member states around a German manufacturing center. But his strong sense that time is running out, and his desperate conclusion that "the only way I can hold this thing together, the only way I can hold this thing together, is by greater discipline" (quoted in Varoufakis 2017: 409) seems to be more widely shared. It rules out any departure from austerity even when its damaging and even counterproductive effects are becoming apparent.

The point clearly is not to explain every twist and turn in the ongoing euro-saga. What is crucial is that the aims and objectives, the biases and blindspots, as well as the limits and possibilities of German crisis management cannot be gleaned from the prevailing accounts of neoliberalism that are ultimately derived from the Anglo-American prime mover. The state-centered view of Germany as a regional semi-hegemon, too weak to offer anything other than neoliberal austerity, has already been considered and rejected. It remains, then, to submit the ideational and class-based interpretations to critical scrutiny and conceptual revision.

Dis-Ordo in the Eurozone

Perhaps the most popular reading of Germany's role in the eurocrisis proposes that its state managers have been under the spell of a homegrown variety of neoliberalism that they now seek to implement abroad (Blyth 2013a; Dyson 2010; Dullien and Guérot 2012; Art 2015). In this view, German crisis management follows an "ordoliberal" rulebook written into the constitution of its postwar political economy and enshrined in the European monetary union (Blyth 2013a: 142). While there are more benign interpretations of its actions (Meiers 2015), many argue that Germany's ruthless pursuit of austerity within the eurozone is based on the belief that a strong, market-making authority is necessary to instill in economic actors the values of stable prices and financial prudence. According to this narrative, German officials falsely believe that a specific set of policies that worked for Germany can offer a general solution for the eurozone's economic woes. As aptly summarized by Mark Blyth, "Germany and the [European Commission] want everyone else to be German" (Blyth 2013a: 102). The crisis presents an opportunity "to remake the system in Germany's image" (Art 2015: 196–197). At the same time, their steadfast commitment to ordoliberalism is said to make them blind to the negative consequences of their actions. The painful retrenchment in the deficit countries is seen as just atonement for their sins of profligacy and indebtedness (Matthijs 2016: 387). The resulting spiral of debt and deflation is seen as a necessary sacrifice even as it goes against Germany's own interests in keeping the eurozone together and getting its money back (Blyth 2013b: 738).[17]

Much of this book has questioned the explanatory value of a grand narrative centered on any such system of ideas. It has argued that there is a world of difference between ordoliberalism in theory and the social market economy as it came into existence after 1945 (compare Berghahn and

Young 2013). Most notable is the absence, and even the explicit rejection, within ordoliberal thought of social policy and welfare provisions as well as corporatist forms of labor relations (Hien 2013: 350). Both were of course core components of the reconstitution of the German political economy. In addition, this book has shown just how critical Germany's inherited export orientation—never a serious concern of ordoliberal authors—came to be to the construction of a new kind of consensual capitalist social relations that replicated the Fordist politics of productivity without a Keynesian macroeconomics. The preference for price stability and monetary and fiscal constraint that German state officials and central bankers emphasized throughout the postwar period needs to be seen in this context: as attempts to nourish and sustain this particular class constellation and to safeguard, in the words of economics and finance minister Karl Schiller, "the external economic underpinning of domestic stability policy" (quoted in Dyson and Featherstone 1999: 280).

Unless we fudge the issue and pretend that they are one and the same, we are forced to recognize that the story of ordoliberal thought within the actually existing social market economy is one of waning rather than increasing influence, as numerous scholars have shown. This dispels the notion that ordoliberalism has been present or latent in the German economy "until it became the design principle behind the euro project" (Blyth 2013a: 101). Those who point to the Bundesbank as the safe haven of ordoliberalism and model of the ECB forget that the very existence of a central bank controlling the money supply was rejected in principle by the founding father of ordoliberalism, Walter Eucken, as an impermissible form of political intervention (Feld, Köhler, and Nienteidt 2015: 6). The political independence of the Bundesbank was the product of chance and politics and *not* of ordoliberal ideas (Bibow 2009). Its postwar operation, even when and where it prioritized price stability,[18] never followed ordoliberal prescriptions in either principle or practice (Richter 1999; Feld, Köhler, and Nienteidt 2015: 8). In as far as its decision in 1974 to target the money supply was influenced by neoliberal ideas, these were supplied by Friedman and adapted to a purpose of social stabilization fundamentally at odds with the attack on organized labor that neoliberalism came to be associated with. Mindful of this historical record, even some of those who utilize the concept have acknowledged that "even in Germany this tradition had been relegated to obscurity for much of the last 40 years" (Biebricher 2013: 339).

Bringing "ordoliberalism" back in as the governing paradigm of German policymakers in the eurozone would require that we demonstrate that it has indeed experienced an "unlikely renaissance" (Biebricher 2013: 339). Given that there is no straight line leading from Erhard to Schäuble, we cannot assume that Germany's increasing economic and political weight will automatically elevate ordoliberalism to a European level. It may be possible and illuminating to investigate how ordoliberal ideas have moved from the margins to the mainstream. But what is crucial is that the demonstrable discontinuity severs the explanatory link between the positions German policymakers put forward today and what they are supposed to have "always wanted," courtesy of their supposed ordoliberal orientation (Art 2015; Biebricher 2013: 339–340).

Last, and most crucial, the account above demonstrates that German crisis management cannot be said to follow an ordoliberal blueprint. It is not about an ideologically misguided attempt to transplant a particular model that worked well in Germany onto Southern deficit countries. Rather than seeing Germany's European policy as an extension of its domestic economic program, rooted in the same peculiar way of seeing the world, the argument developed here allows us to draw a distinction between what German policymakers are trying to do abroad and at home. *Pace* Blyth, Germany does *not* "want everyone else to be German." The specificities of the German model, we recall, rests at its core on a social compromise of wage restraint in exchange for job security that is sustained through the export of German goods and relies on effective demand generated outside. The monetary and fiscal restraint associated with ordoliberalism is a means to this end rather than an end in itself. Even though we can find similar policies in Germany's austerity program, the aim is very different. The structural adjustment policies imposed on European deficit countries do not aim to spread this mode of industrial relations (Hall 2015: 55). The neoliberal reforms Germany advocates abroad do not aim to create replica "Germanies." Instead of structurally similar competitors, the new political economies that are envisioned and constructed in Southern Europe are the *opposite* from the corporatist and welfarist model associated with Germany (Hassel 2015: 125). And in as much as their structural adjustment creates opportunities for German firms to successfully transnationalize their production, they are not only contrasting with but complementary to the German export-dependent social model.

We have seen that a conceptually tight definition of ordoliberalism as a coherent school of thought leads to the recognition of its marginality. There is nothing wrong in principle with a more encompassing conception of Germany's distinct economic culture. An insightful story of European monetary integration can be told, for instance, as several iterations of the "economist" versus "monetarist" debate—the vexing question, reaching back to the early 1960s and preoccupying minds at Maastricht, of whether economic convergence must *precede* the permanent alignment of exchange rates and the introduction of a common currency—as officials from German and Dutch governments and central banks have insisted—or whether it would *follow from* such monetary coordination and unification—as French and Belgian representatives have argued instead. We certainly find a consistent preference for the former, "economistic" position on the part of many German (as well as Dutch) state managers over the past four decades—many more, in fact, than could plausibly be said to be influenced by an ordoliberal tradition, given that the position was shared by a staunch Social Democrat like Willy Brandt and an arch-Keynesian like Karl Schiller.

The related risk is that, at the hands of scholars perplexed by the misuse of German power in the eurocrisis, "ordoliberalism" has been expanded into a laundry list of all the issues that Germany's crisis managers are pushing for: monetary restraint, budget cuts, an independent central bank, legalistic procedures, a trade surplus, competitive markets, and so on.[19] This may or may not be a useful shorthand for the German negotiating stance, but the fundamental issue is that it does not provide an explanation for *why* German policymakers want these things. And as long as we are uncertain about the true motives behind Germany's demands, we cannot fully assess why they are doing what they are doing and whether they are actually getting what they want.

The institutional reconfiguration of the EU is a case in point for the scholarly confusion induced by positing ordoliberalism as an explanatory device. While scholars who diagnose the contemporary ordoliberal transformation of Europe have identified a number of institutional innovations, they differ profoundly on which of these correspond with or contradict ordoliberal thinking. Biebricher, for instance, cites two institutional innovations. One of them is the European Stability Mechanism (ESM), with its ruthlessly austerian and regularly supervised conditionality criteria that recipient countries need to meet in order to get financial assistance. Another is the Macroeconomic Imbalance Procedure (MIP), in which the European

Commission monitors the economic performance of member states and initiates disciplinary proceedings if they fall short on any one of a series of targets. The MIP supposedly "offers everything in terms of economic governance that the ordoliberals ever dreamed of" (Biebricher 2013: 347). And yet when we turn elsewhere, we find the ESM described not as the culmination of ordoliberalism but as a concession made by the Merkel government that was "anathema to ordoliberal hardliners within Germany" (Art 2015: 205). To confuse matters further, an in-house review by three luminaries of the actually existing ordoliberal school, meanwhile, cites the ESM and the ECB's bond-buying program as evidence "that German economic policy largely responded pragmatically to the challenges offered by the crisis" and suggest it "may have followed ordoliberal thinking rather too little than too much" (Feld, Köhler, and Nientiedt 2015: 1, 18). Art, however, goes further. Even though he thinks Germany has now got the kind of union it has always wanted, the ECB's bond purchases constitute nothing less than "a dramatic violation of ordoliberal orthodoxy" (2015: 209). And the MIP is said to have broadened the remit of the EU to scrutinize and potentially penalize not only deficit but also surplus countries (Jabko 2013: 360)—a move that goes against decades of steadfast German opposition to assuming responsibility for global and regional imbalances and that has been fiercely attacked in a report by the "ordoliberal" Kiel Institute for the World Economy, commissioned for the German economics ministry (IfW 2014).

This confounding difference in scholarly opinion reflects a simple truth. As Wade Jacoby (2014: 72) has pointed out, ordoliberal ideas can be found on all sides of the political debate over the course of European monetary integration—leading one proponent to conclude that "all mainstream political parties in Germany are to some extent guided by 'ordoliberalism'" (Matthijs 2016: 376). While from today's vantage point of German dominance the EMU might seem to some the crowning achievement of ordoliberalism, we also find numerous ordoliberals who have consistently argued against its construction. Many of them have seen the eurocrisis as confirmation that the move toward a single currency was premature. But while some use ordoliberal ideas to advocate strengthening the EMU, others have called for removing crisis countries or even for a return to the DM (Jacoby 2014: 73–74). This leveraging of ordoliberal arguments in favor of and against the euro should come as no surprise. After all, as this book has shown, economic ideas have been deployed tactically by political actors to legitimate their preferred policies and criticize those of others (see also

Young 2014). And yet its ubiquitous presence renders ordoliberalism of little use in explaining which policy options Germany's decision-making elites would favor, and why. In sum, it should be clear that as long as we rely on ordoliberalism as our compass, we cannot make heads or tails of where either Germany or the EU are going.

The Class Character of Germany's European Strategy

The narrative of an elite drive toward a neoliberal Europe also needs to be reconsidered. After all, the global financial and European debt crises have revealed significant ideological and policy divisions—both within Europe's ruling classes and between them and their American partners. On the polarizing question of a temporary Grexit proposed by the German finance minister during the 2015 negotiations, for instance, the eurozone was sharply divided: officials from Germany, Slovakia, Finland, and the Netherlands were open to Schäuble's proposal, while France, Spain, and Italy remained vigorously opposed (Traynor 2015). Disagreements, however, are not limited to a standoff between a frugal Northern core and the spendthrift "Latin" countries of the union. Anglo-American elites in fact have been the harshest critics of Germany's handling of the eurocrisis. Luminaries of the economics profession such as Jeffrey Sachs, Joseph Stiglitz, and Paul Krugman have lambasted Germany's approach as "unwise and highly unprofessional" (Sachs 2015), a charade of blaming the victim (Stiglitz 2016), or "a grotesque betrayal of everything the European project was supposed to stand for" (Krugman 2015). One might expect these infamous converts from neoliberalism to be lone voices amongst the organic intellectuals of the transnational capitalist class, but in reality it is German economists who are disconnected (Soll 2015; Silvia 2011).[20] More important still than this left-leaning intelligentsia are dissenting voices from within the inner circles of the Atlantic ruling class. The former governor of the Bank of England and long-time executive at Goldman Sachs Mark Carney has criticized the competitive race to the bottom induced by "internal devaluation" and called for relaxing the stringent fiscal constraints championed by Germany (Elliott 2015). The IMF's (and now the ECB's) Christine Lagarde has warned that any new Greek "rescue" program must fail without debt relief (Nasr 2017). And former US Treasury Secretary Jacob Lew has warned that a Greek exit from the eurozone—Schäuble's preferred plan—could spell disaster for the world economy (Khan and Holehouse 2015).

A US treasury secretary warning of financial Armageddon over a country with the GDP of Oregon, a G7 central banker calling for greater fiscal latitude, an IMF director urging debt forgiveness—it is hard to see how Germany's position lines up with a transnational neoliberal consensus, let alone one that has been designed by financial elites. And indeed, leading scholars writing in this tradition have recognized that "the crisis is also a reflection of the *absence* of a unified European elite" (Cafruny 2015: 65) and a case in point for the, at best, incomplete process of transnational class formation.

One may well hold on to the belief that private planning groups and policy forums play a critical role in the efforts of state and corporate elites to negotiate political differences, cultivate a collective outlook, and arrive at a common position, and likewise, that a class analysis is urgently needed in order to disentangle the medley of factions and forces that vie over how, and in whose interest, the eurozone crisis ought to be managed. After all, despite the sensationalist reports of a fever-pitched battle of "Germany versus Greece," these interests clearly do not neatly coincide with national borders.

And yet, the key point remains that the substantive disagreements and indeed struggles over the modalities of European crisis management within the upper echelons of policy coordination challenge the image of a gradual progression of like-minded, globally oriented elites toward a neoliberal utopia. The image, to be sure, can point to significant and broadly parallel processes of class recomposition and transformation within Germany. But the same image creates the paradox that German elites, long considered to trail behind the emerging consensus, appear to have overshot the target and surpassed the point of supposed convergence with their Anglo-American brethren in their zeal to structurally adjust the European periphery.

An alternative view would be to suggest that the German state enacts not the general will of a transnational elite but the parochial interests of a national fraction of capital. To some extent, the account above has indeed invoked a domestic constituency whose interests *are* taken into account by Germany's crisis managers. And yet the methodological points made in previous chapters, and the empirical picture I have painted here, is more complex than the rather monolithic view of a state projecting its power in the service of national capital would suggest.

It is true that the German political economy is marked by a peculiar— historically grown and remarkably persistent—coalition of interests that brings banks and firms, workers, and employers into various cooperative arrangements partly overseen by state officials and institutions. However, the cohesion of this bloc cannot be taken for granted. It is itself the product of a continuing political process that involves the coordinating role of the German state. As such, it is the consequence rather than the cause of Germany's crisis management. The assumption of an identity of interests between policymakers and social actors—whether structurally produced or instrumentally crafted—does not hold. Germany's crisis managers are called into action not by the solidity of this bloc and its ability to make its wishes heard, but by its potential fragmentation and the corresponding threat that the latent antagonism between capital and labor may come to the fore. And last but not least, this chapter has demonstrated that international pressures intervene to widen the gap between what social actors want and what state officials do. The exposed position of the German economy between uneven growth cycles and potentially divergent interest rate policies has pushed the austerity path of its state administrators beyond the cost-benefit calculations of any conceivable domestic constituency.

More important still, the notion that the German state favors the mercantilism of a national capital fraction or—if we drop the Marxist emphasis on class—its selfish national economic interest, neglects that the vision which informs the strategy is significantly broader in conception and potential appeal. This is not at all to suggest that Germany pursues a project of hegemony after all, given that the main thrust of this book has been to question the applicability of the term. And yet, although it may at first seem to be little more than a convenient rationalization of German self-interest, it is worth pondering the question of who might derive benefits from the structural adjustment of the eurozone. Germany's crisis management, it turns out, may well speak to a wider and more complex constellation of social forces that is in need of critical investigation. Seen from the bottom up, the "crisis corporatism" that a core of Germany's skilled labor force is actively involved in, and the privileges it derives from the hierarchical redivision of labor within the eurozone, may limit its solidarity with working people across Europe who face corresponding attacks on their social and economic security. From the perspective of capital, meanwhile, the possibility of subordinate integration into a German-centered global export drive is likely to appeal primarily to small and medium-sized suppliers of intermediate goods rather than to larger European export firms. Compared to domestic producers, the most internationally oriented fractions of capital may find such a subsidiary role to German capital unattractive. For while they are normally considered to be the principal agents and beneficiaries of neoliberal change, they may have world market aspirations of their own that define them as competitors rather than partners in such a project.

Conclusion

This chapter has argued that the uses and abuses of German power in Europe today build upon a self-interested strategy first devised to manage the end of golden-age capitalism in the 1970s. The German state, this book has shown, was deeply implicated in the global rise of neoliberalism—a regressive form of capitalism that has since boomeranged back upon Germany and significantly eroded the domestic class compromise that its actions were meant to sustain. And yet, rather than being pushed down the Anglo-American road by the pressures of neoliberal globalization, German policymakers have held on to the belief that Germany's economic prosperity and social stability can be secured through the international orientation and competitiveness of its manufacturing sector. The decisive difference, and the key to appreciating German primacy in Europe, lies in the new world-historical context in which these objectives are being pursued. The extraordinary Chinese demand for customized capital and luxury consumer goods made in Germany over the past two decades informs the long-term vision of a neoliberal Europe structurally adjusted to support the global position of German manufacturers. And the perceived threat, currently suspended but still looming on the horizon, of US interest rates rising out of step with economic conditions in Europe and emerging markets has hardened the German stance on austerity during the fever-pitched policy battles that mark the eurocrisis.

Conclusion

THE PANDEMIC OF 2020 has struck a European continent still reeling from the aftershocks of the global financial and European debt crisis. It has brought on an even worse recession that is likely to increase the hardship already suffered by tens of millions and widen the inequalities between the "northern core" and "southern periphery" of the eurozone. And it has caught out Europe's governing elites, who have long been divided over how to address the financial instabilities and macroeconomic imbalances that, as the virus reminds us, might yet destroy the European project.

At the heart of this predicament stands a reinvigorated and inexorable Germany. It is the one country that has amassed sufficient political weight and fiscal capacity to mobilize a comprehensive response the economic devastation caused by the virus. And yet it is the same country that, for the past decade, has insisted on an austerity agenda that has prolonged rather than resolved the eurocrisis and deepened rather than bridged the rift between EU member states.

This book has set out to understand how a country long thought to be irrevocably European and committed to a more social market economy could have emerged at the helm of a parochial program of structural adjustment within Europe. Its guiding premise has been that this seemingly inexplicable turn needs to be situated in the wider context—and social and international history—of neoliberal globalization.

To do this properly, we cannot conceive of neoliberalism simply as a force radiating outward from the Anglo-American core and engulfing the German political economy from the 1990s onward. Instead, we need to travel back to its point of origin and consider how far, and why, German policymakers were themselves implicated in its inception. This longer view, and shift in focus, reveals that the pragmatic attempts of German policymakers to defend the postwar social compact between capital and labor at home against global inflation and protectionism contributed significantly, but not deliberately, to the erosion of the embedded liberal international order and the neoliberal counterrevolution.

This argument has far-reaching consequences not only for how we think about Germany's approach to the eurocrisis and coronavirus but also about neoliberal globalization more broadly. First and foremost, my argument challenges the most commonly accepted narratives, which cast the rise of neoliberalism as an Anglo-American imposition, as a project of globalizing elites, or as a shift in economic paradigms. The point here is not to suggest that Germany, rather than the US, is alone responsible for neoliberalism. It is instead to insist that the role played by German state elites is significant enough that it is now impossible to tell the story of the global rise of neoliberalism without reference to the peculiar German contribution. Given that Germany is indispensable to the overall story and yet defies the three main explanatory models we have encountered in this book, we need to rethink their utility more broadly. The most important implication is that we need to broaden our analysis to include other state-society complexes, and allow for the possibility that they followed the United States and the United Kingdom in a neoliberal direction—or indeed led the way—along very different paths and for very different reasons than the geopolitical calculations, social pressures, or beliefs usually attributed to US decisions.

This expanded conception helps to make sense of an otherwise inexplicable shift in Germany's position from the defender of Rhineland capitalism to enforcer of neoliberal discipline in Europe. Today as in the 1970s, German policymakers are keen to preserve an export-dependent compromise between manufacturing firms and skilled workers. The critical difference is that these efforts have taken place in a novel context in which German exporters dominate a European production network that is geared toward global and emerging markets, and China in particular. Under these conditions, German policymakers have imposed neoliberal reforms in order to create favorable conditions for German production and investment in the targeted countries. The structural adjustments demanded of European deficit countries are thus an extension and intensification of the means and objectives that defined Germany's response to this 1970s crisis. Austerity abroad has offered avenues for German manufacturers to "nearshore" parts of their production across Europe, while securing high-skilled and relatively well-paid jobs in Germany. The Janus-faced character of Germany's crisis management, already apparent in its self-centered response during the 1970s, thus reached full maturity in the 2010s. Since the eurocrisis, German policymakers have advanced a particular kind of European economic integration that aims to prop up Germany's ailing social model by dismantling the last remnants of the embedded liberal compromise across the eurozone—an agenda likely to resurface in the negotiations over the terms and conditions of a common coronavirus response.

The peculiar interests and ideas that have informed this approach cannot be captured by the prevailing ideational, state-centered, or class-based accounts—modeled as they are on the forces presumed to have led the US and the UK down a neoliberal path. First, what studies of ordoliberalism tend to miss is that German policy elites have not sought to create replica "Germanies" according to a single ideological blueprint, but ancillary, flexibilized economies that support a hard core of manufacturing industries headquartered in Germany. Second, however, while this self-interested strategy targets social provisions and consensual industrial relations in the EU, it does not quite amount to a narrowly conceived mercantilist strategy. Nor can it be explained as the failings of a deficient hegemon, as countless comparisons with the leadership of the US after 1945 have suggested. Crucially, the German vision of European economies occupying lower rungs of a regional value chain ladder offers opportunities to individual European suppliers, albeit on the backs of working people in these countries. Nominally, the aim of serving global markets presents this program of internal deflation as the route toward a wider eurozone recovery. And last, as a consequence, the social forces supporting such a project of European integration, or postpandemic reconstruction, through subordination to German capital are likely to be more diverse and complex than the thesis of a transnational capitalist class with a coherent outlook and interest can accommodate.

The principal aim of this book has been to better understand where German primacy is taking the EU. Nevertheless, rethinking the genesis of neoliberalism through the eyes of German policy elites also sheds light on the deeper character and broader postpandemic trajectory of this particular form of capitalism. The notion that neoliberal globalization has proceeded unevenly is of course far from new (Harvey 2005: 116; Peck, Theodore, and Brenner 2010; 2012; Ban 2016). But this book has argued that comparing its multiple national paths and local variations to an Anglo-American prime mover is unhelpful. Nor is it useful to think of neoliberalism as a uniform and universalizing *project* advanced by economic elites, dominant states, or influential intellectuals. To capture the critical contribution of the German state, it proved more fruitful to approach the making of neoliberalism as a complex and continuous *process*, driven by a plurality of actors for diverse reasons and to unexpected effects. At the center of this process stands not "the market" in the abstract, but a concrete and increasingly contested social relation between capital, labor, and the state as embodied in the embedded liberal compromise established primarily in the Cold War West after 1945.[1] The one-sided termination of the postwar social contract under Reagan and Thatcher, this book has demonstrated, was the combined product of attempts by several states to resolve the postwar crisis of welfare state capitalism. And once accomplished, the historical defeat and demotion of organized labor would recast the same interactive dynamic around the problem of what to do with a postwar compromise that for the very first time appeared not only outmoded, uncompetitive, and burdensome but also, in principle and in practice, expendable. In this regard, neoliberalism designates a new era of capitalism, marked by the epochal reversal of the social, economic, and political rights that working people had wrought from property owners and invested in the postwar welfare state. It did not, however, replace the central political question of that bygone era—how to organize the consent of the wage-dependent majority—with an equivalent program of state building or market making. In its place emerged instead an assemblage of diverse, retrograde, and innovative policies, practices, and techniques that in a variety of ways seek to remove and remold the participation and protection of laboring classes in their workplace, lifeworlds, and imagined communities. Neoliberalism, therefore, does not have a single essence but a historical anchor point around which conflicting interests, competing strategies, and negotiated compromises have continued to evolve.

While this labor-centered definition militates against a general theory, as opposed to a multitrack history, of neoliberalism, it provides a perspective that can help us overcome the persistent impasse produced by the "strange non-death of neoliberalism" (Crouch 2011). The fact that neoliberalism survived the Great Recession of 2008 runs against the grain of much of critical IPE, which has staked its grand narrative of the fall of free market capitalism in the 1930s and its resurrection in the 1970s on the assumption that major crises transform ruling regimes, class coalitions, and belief systems. This book contends that this story appears out of sync today primarily because of the way in which the previous turning point has been conceptualized.

Guided by the notion that it was a change of economic paradigms, a shift in the social balance of forces, or a hegemonic power play that brought neoliberalism into being, critical scholars have expected a world beyond neoliberalism to arrive in an analogous manner. Accordingly, at the height of the 2008 global financial crisis, many hailed the comeback of Keynes as the intellectual inspiration that would foment a new macroeconomic consensus—only to find that "[t]he Master . . . had returned only for a few months" (Streeck 2013: 727). Partly at the hands of the German state, the new consensus quickly fractured, leading its critics to ponder neoliberalism's remarkable ideological staying power (for example, Farrell and Quiggin 2012). Others have pinned their hopes not on a revolution in ideas but on the resistance of progressive forces—ranging from social movements like Occupy Wall Street and the community governments of the Kurdish fighters of Rojava to the leadership bids of "old school" socialists such as Bernie Sanders and Jeremy Corbyn. And while so far the anticapitalist left has not been able to decisively turn the tables, still others argue that the long game is playing out in the arena of geopolitics, where the rise of late-industrializing powers is seen by some as providing a neodevelopmentalist model that may dislodge the neoliberal Washington Consensus from its pedestal (Arrighi 2007; Brand and Sekler 2009; for nuanced evaluations of this thesis, see Schmalz and Ebenau 2012; Gray and Murphy 2013; Bond and Garcia 2015).

While these are certainly all critical developments to watch out for, there is a serious risk that thinking of an emerging postneoliberal future in such Manichean terms leads to exaggerated expectations that are bound to be disappointed. Put simply, the kind of social and world order change that we imagine it will take to displace neoliberalism is unlikely to occur because it never generated neoliberalism in the first place. The reverse danger is that the absence of a comprehensive counterproject is mistaken as *prima facia* evidence of the staying power of neoliberalism (for example Drezner 2014: 143). The end result is a conceptual dead end, in which we can no longer think beyond the current "culmination of the neoliberal era" (Hall and Lamont 2013: 21). Short of a fundamental, but implausible, shift that some now attribute to the pandemic, we are left with ever more iterations, inflections, and modifications of the original design. As Paul Heideman (2014) aptly expresses this deadlock: "What comes after neoliberalism? More neoliberalism, apparently."

Reminding ourselves of how neoliberalism actually came into the world is key to avoiding this trap. The shift from embedded to neoliberal capitalism, the German experience suggests, did not take the form of a contestation of coherent blocs of ideas, social forces, or states, neatly aligned along a Keynesian-neoliberal divide. Those supposedly "on the sidelines," it turns out, had a crucial role to play in shaping the process and outcome. Turning away from the image of a tug-of-war between two towering giants is just as important today, when some have, once again, declared the end of neoliberalism (for example, Lent 2020). It allows us to interrogate the strengths and weaknesses of neoliberalism and its potential rivals on their own terms rather than as mirror images of each other (Schmidt 2011), and directs our attention to less pronounced sources of transformation, unexpected developments, and unlikely agents of change.

The final, intellectual-theoretical contribution of this book is toward a critical IPE that is sensitive to the counterintuitive interests and idiosyncratic ideas of decision-making elites in the advanced capitalist world and to the specific configurations of social and international forces that act upon them. To study this socially and internationally contextualized elite agency, the book has used the lens of uneven and combined development to illuminate the twin dilemmas faced by policymakers in formulating effective foreign economic strategies amidst competing domestic demands and in an international milieu in which their preferences meet and potentially collide with those of their foreign counterparts. Added to the problem of how to arbitrate between different societal interests is the problem of how to get other state elites to pursue compatible and complementary policies. This second dimension of "the international" as a superordinate sphere of multiple polities and conflicting sovereign wills far exceeds the classical anarchy problématique of realism (Rosenberg 2006). Among the advanced industrialized economies of the North Atlantic, the existential threat to survival posed by the absence of a central authority has receded into the background. Instead, the terrain that policymakers have to navigate is much more fundamentally shaped by the coexistence of differently constituted and situated national political economies with divergent cycles of boom, bust, and recovery. This "advanced unevenness" poses lateral pressures and opportunities that combine with domestic conditions and structure the choices state actors have and the strategies they deploy. It also offers policy elites a differential calculus of success and failure relative to the policies and performance of their peers. The result is a historically contingent but intelligible and theorizable dynamic of patterned interactions in which the strategic and creative choices that some actors make to deal with the problems they confront reshape the range of options available to others. Not only do the ultimate outcomes defy the original intentions of even the most powerful players in the system, they also cannot simply be read off the domestic context of each of the actors.

This book has argued that, in a closely circumscribed and strictly demilitarized sense of the term, policy "conflicts" between the advanced capitalist states and their strategies to influence their contemporaries mattered profoundly for how the crisis of the 1970s played out. What we see at work here is not a realist "geoeconomics" *avant la lettre*, however. For the critical difference is that such tensions and tactics are not called forth by the incessant pressures of international anarchy that, blocked by military dependence on the US during the Cold War, somehow found a commercial outlet. The pressures that confront policymakers then as now, and which they seek to bring to bear on their counterparts, emerge instead from a dynamic, integrated, and yet uneven capitalist world economy that is constantly shifting shape.

That the old core of this world economy is in serious trouble was apparent even before the pandemic called forth divergent national responses. Trump's economic war against a rapidly rising China has Germany caught in the firing line, and Britain's fractious departure from the EU is only one of the forces tearing at its seams. The scenario of a "secular stagnation" that policymakers have feared could stoke distributive struggles now seems relatively benign compared to the threat of another global recession.[2] And the pandemic shock in turn pales in comparison to a looming ecological catastrophe that seems irresolvable within the confines of capitalism.

The liberal triumphalism that once celebrated neoliberal globalization as humanity's destiny has collapsed, and a paralyzing realism now predicts the cataclysms of the past to return. To rescue the future from these worn-out narratives, it is vital to attend to the policy conflicts that divide those in power, without assuming that they spring from and tend toward anarchy. History does not revolve around some timeless essence. But it reminds us that revolutions can seize upon splits within the ranks of ruling classes, and thus outlines the task for a critical IPE in the short time available to us.

Notes

Introduction

1. For ease of reading, this book uses "Germany" synonymously with the Federal Republic of Germany (FRG) even though another Germany—the German Democratic Republic—existed to its east for much of the time period under consideration.

2. The data series "Exports: Value Goods for Germany" is provided by the Organization for Economic Co-Operation and Development (OECD) and was retrieved from the Federal Reserve Bank of St. Louis (Federal Reserve Economic Data). fred.stlouisfed.org/series/XTEXVA01DEA188S (accessed 6 May 2020).

3. The list of politicians and pundits that have called for benevolent German leadership includes contemporaries as far apart as business magnate and philanthropist George Soros, the former IMF director Christine Lagarde, Greece's former renegade finance minister Yanis Varoufakis, and the emeritus director of Germany's prestigious Max Planck Institute for the Study of Societies, Wolfgang Streeck.

4. In the words of Harvard historian Charles Maier (2012), "Germany is today the country on whose farsightedness the European project hinges."

5. For some notable exceptions, see Streeck (2014; 2017) and Kundnani (2014).

6. The academic literature on "neoliberalism" is enormous. For an accessible primer, see Harvey (2005). For fascinating intellectual histories that approach neoliberalism as a belief-system centered on "the market," see Mirowski and Plehwe (2009); Jones (2012); and Burgin (2012). For accounts that rethink this focus,

see, among others, Bruff (2016); Slobodian (2018); and Knafo et al. (2019). For studies that have shaped my view of neoliberalism as a new phase of capitalist globalization, see especially Gill (1992; 1995); Gowan (1999); Duménil and Lévy (2004); and Panitch and Gindin (2012). For perspectives on neoliberalism from the Global South that seek to overcome not just the Anglo-American but the wider Eurocentric bias of much of the academic scholarship (my own work included), see Prashad (2012); and Connell and Dados (2014). My quest to understand the role of the German state in the global rise of neoliberalism leads me to adopt a historically situated, labor-centered definition of "neoliberalism," understood as a range of regressive and innovative policy measures and techniques devised from the late 1970s onward which reversed the social, political, and economic rights that working people—principally, though not exclusively, in the wealthy, industrialized economies of the West (Helleiner 2003)—had wrought from capitalist property owners after 1945 (Panitch and Gindin 2012: 15). The advantage of this working definition is that it fully historicizes neoliberalism so that it no longer simply describes a generic belief in free markets. For while such market fundamentalism infused the political projects of Reagan and Thatcher, it does not exhaust the phenomenon. Its substantive focus, as opposed to the rhetoric or beliefs of some of its proponents, is not to "de-regulate" markets but to contain democracy—the limited forms which actually exist(ed) and the bolder visions which have yet to be realized. Although this book does not pursue this line of inquiry, this approach to neoliberalism can be used to broaden the view from the waged majority in the Global North to the world's majority in the Global South, whose struggles for self-determination, national development, and global justice were defeated at the same time (Prashad 2012; Slobodian 2018; Getachew 2019).

7. Indicative of this scholarly consensus over the past three decades are Paterson and Smith (1981); Zysman (1984); Gourevetich (1986); Albert (1993); Crouch and Streeck (1997); Coates (2000); Hall and Soskice (2001); Streeck and Yamamura (2001); and Schmidt (2002). For much of the 1990s and 2000s, however, the prevailing story has been one of progressive decline, dominated by the question of how much of the German social market economy has been lost or might persist (for example, Streeck 2009). Those who have stressed continuity over convergence on an Anglo-American free market model point to the recent revival of Germany's economic power, which they attribute to the persistence of many of its distinctive institutions (for example, Reisenbichler and Morgan 2012; Rinne and Zimmermann 2012; Hassel 2014).

8. For an in-depth analysis of the Hartz IV (or Agenda 2010) labor market and social security reforms introduced by the Red-Green coalition government in the 2000s, see Hassel and Schiller (2010).

9. The literature on ordoliberalism is fast expanding. For recent edited

volumes that canvas a range of perspectives, see Beck and Kotz (2017); Biebricher and Vogelmann (2017); and Hien and Joerges (2018). For a nuanced assessment, see Dyson (2017); for important critiques, see Jacoby (2014); Young (2014; 2017); and Cafruny and Talani (2019).

10. For a comparative political economy perspective on Germany's export-led growth model in the context of the eurocrisis, see, for example, Stockhammer (2016). For a longer view of Germany's postwar recovery and export orientation, see especially Beck (2015).

11. The series is available at https://history.state.gov/historicaldocuments/ ebooks (accessed 22 February 2019).

12. The cabinet minutes are available at http://www.bundesarchiv.de/cocoon /barch/0/k/index.html (accessed 7 August 2017).

Chapter 1

1. On this point, see especially van Apeldoorn, Bruff, and Ryner (2010).

2. A similar case for international historiography has been made by Granieri (2004: 228).

3. Broadly speaking, while some critical IPE scholars continue to see the 1970s as the beginning of the end of US hegemony and the transition toward an unstable interregnum (for example, Callinicos 2009), others interpret the period as a shift from a nationally anchored to a globally integrated capitalist order (for example, Robinson 2004).

4. These interpretive models are not mutually exclusive, and many empirical accounts draw on more than one (for example, Helleiner 1994; Gowan 1999; Blyth 2002).

5. Ruggie, it is true, "wrote just as Ronald Reagan and Margaret Thatcher were beginning to implement their very different visions of a smaller role in capitalism for state power" (Keohane 2012: 126). He and his interlocutors might be forgiven for failing to see that it was the *embeddedness*, rather than the *liberality* of the capitalist world economy that was fundamentally at stake. And yet critical IPE scholars had early on understood that the "[i]nternational forces undermining embedded liberalism" did not emanate from the economic nationalism of the left, as the more skeptical Robert Keohane (1984b: 26) believed, but from the transnational neoliberalism of the right (for example, Cox 1981). Moreover, Ruggie (2008: 4) has repeatedly reasserted his view that the "embedded liberalism" compromise had been sustained throughout the 1970s since its key components—liberal multilateralism and domestic interventionism—were preserved. Only in 1996 did he begin to raise concerns about "the future fate of the embedded liberalism compromise" (1996: 80) and call for a renewal of the underlying social bargain (94). And only in the face of the 2008 global financial meltdown did he conclude

that "the domestic political coalitions on which the compromise rested . . . have weakened or, as in the case of the United States, almost unraveled altogether" (2008: 4). By contrast, this book argues that the turbulences of the 1970s are best understood as the definitive crisis of embedded liberalism, involving a confrontation of social forces and culminating in the one-sided termination of the capital-labor compact in the Anglo-American world. This dissolution, it will be argued, had profoundly transformative (though not disruptive) implications for the international system. It is only in view of this crisis and transformation, frequently (though, it is argued, mistakenly) understood as the "challenge from a rejuvenated classical liberalism" (Richardson 1997: 13), that the concept of "embedded liberalism" can illuminate what was truly unique—in the sense of unprecedented and irretrievable—about the postwar synthesis of social and international order under American hegemony.

6. Richard Saull's (2007: 138) interpretation of this period holds that "the political-military leverage the US continued to hold over two of its major economic protagonists at this time—West Germany and Japan—meant that it could afford to sacrifice intra-western co-operation and harmony in the economic sphere knowing full well that the ruling classes in Bonn and Tokyo would only go so far in challenging US hegemony and their protectorate status in the Cold War."

7. For an important critique of the prevailing view that neoliberalism originated first in the Global North and was only then imposed upon the Global South, see Connell and Dados (2014). For a discussion of some of the antecedents of neoliberalism located in the Global South, see also Veltmeyer, Petras, and Vieux (1997: 60–62). For an insightful analysis of the classical Chilean case, which insists on a much deeper, capitalist transformation of social property relations than can be captured by the concept of neoliberalism, see Clark (2017).

8. Although in Gowan's empirical account there is some room for contradictions to emerge (Panitch 2000: 14).

9. The former spokesman of the board of Deutsche Bank and president of the Bundesbank Karl Klasen noted that one ought to "assess realistically the ability and willingness of many entrepreneurs to negatively dissociate themselves from ideologies or even to positively transcend them. . . . It is to be hoped that the ship has not listed too heavily yet" (Klasen to Günther von Berenberg-Gossler, 28 May 1974, BBk HA B 330/8374).

10. Ehmke to Schmidt, 20 October 1980, personal-confidential, AdsD HSA 6818.

11. As Ingo Schmidt (2011: 476) points out, this only works as an explanation for the subsequent rise of neoliberalism if one ignores that their ability to translate ideas into actual policies depends on the position of other groups in society.

12. For dissenting views, see, for example, Berghahn and Young (2013); and Young (2017).

13. For a skeptical view of Wolfgang Schäuble's ordoliberal credentials, see Rahtz (2017: 109–110, 121). For a nuanced assessment of ordoliberalism as in part an "invented tradition," see Dyson (2017).

14. See, for instance, the argument by Eric Helleiner (1994: 15) that "the ideological shift to neoliberalism took place at varying rates of speed and degrees of intensity in different countries."

Chapter 2

1. See the review by Stephanie Mudge (2008: 705), who notes that "a tendency to focus on politics in Anglo-liberal countries . . . likely misses most of the 'action'."

2. For a critique of the divide between this literature and critical IPE, see Bruff and Ebenau (2014). For an emerging rapprochement via the concepts of dependency and imperialism, see Ebenau, Bruff, and May (2015).

3. For notable exceptions, see Streeck and Yamamura (2001).

4. For a sympathetic but substantive critique of the comparative-institutionalist literature and a far-reaching alternative that aims to relocate institutional dynamics in the structures of capitalism and the agency of social forces, see Streeck (2009: 1–29).

5. It is here that the ostensibly equal standing between the two organizational models represented by the German and the Anglo-American models must be called into question. In its most influential rendition of coordinated and liberal market economies (Hall and Soskice 2001), the former is said to involve a high degree of institutionalized cooperation between capital, labor, and the state that may be possible to sustain but is difficult to achieve. By contrast, the latter is seen as the default setting once these nonmarket institutions unravel: an arms-length relationship of multiple buyers and sellers that is more readily available. For this reason, too, systemic change tends to be seen as a one-way street in which it is easier for coordinated market economies to liberalize than for liberal market economies to organize (for example, Panitch and Gindin 2003: 9). Neoliberal change, even in its most far-reaching and reflexive accounts (Streeck 2009; 2013), is conceptualized as the reversion to a primordial market logic that—while allowed to reign freely in Anglo-American economies—was temporarily restrained by Germany and other coordinated market economies. The possibility that neoliberalism is something genuinely novel and the prospect that something qualitatively different might emerge outside of the Anglo-American center are inconceivable.

6. Although Hall (2018: 10–11) notes that the global and European financial crises have drawn attention to the interdependence of national varieties of capitalism.

7. A full list can be found at http://www.unevenandcombined.com (accessed 26 February 2019). For critiques, see, for example, Teschke (2014); and Rioux (2015).

8. For significant advances toward an agency-centered conception of foreign policy, if in critical distance to the framework of uneven and combined development, see Teschke (2019: 128–129); Teschke and Wyn-Jones (2017); and Teschke and Cemgil (2014).

9. For the debate on the "scope conditions" of U&CD, see, inter alia, Ashman (2009); Allinson and Anievas (2009); and Rosenberg (2009).

10. For accounts that examine the First World War and the interwar period through the lens of uneven and combined development, see Green (2012); Anievas (2014); and Tooze (2015).

11. I use this concept to refer to deliberate and concerted efforts across several agencies of the state in pursuit of a set of broadly shared and primarily macroeconomic objectives. This working definition draws on the more comprehensive discussion of "grand strategy" as a "grand plan" by Silove (2017).

Chapter 3

1. In this crucial respect, Britain's global rule "was not hegemony in a fundamentally Gramscian sense" (Gill 1993b: 43; see also Lacher and Germann 2012).

2. Gerschenkron's (1962) original thesis that universal banking—a system in which banks are "able to both extend credits to firms and underwrite and own shares in them" (Deeg 2003: 88)—developed as a functional solution to the problem of capital mobilization has been qualified by a number of economic and financial historians. For an overview of and contribution to this literature, see Deeg (2003). For a comprehensive revisionist account of the development of German banking in the long nineteenth century, see Hughes (2016).

3. A more concise version of the historical narrative of this section and its immediate application to Germany's role in the eurocrisis is contained in Germann (2018).

4. According to Wehler (1985: 33), the "experience of the depression was to make the necessary readjustment to market conditions extremely difficult."

5. For a classic critique of the German model, see Giersch, Paqué, and Schmieding (1992).

6. For a comprehensive overview of the literature and important exceptions, see Fear (2005).

7. While he fought monopolies at home, Erhard himself believed that "agreements in the export economy can hardly be damaging to the domestic market" (quoted in Wünsche 2015: 398).

8. Though not, it should be noted, a member of the Freiburg School.

9. Titled *Kriegsfinanzierung und Schuldenkonsolidierung* (War Finance and Debt Consolidation), the working paper was one in a series of memoranda that Erhard had been tasked to develop for the *Reichsgruppe Industrie* since 1942. For a critical appraisal and documentary evidence of the lead role of Erhard in these postwar planning circles, see, inter alia, Brackmann (1993), Roth (1995; 1998; 1999a; 1999b), and Wünsche (2015).

10. Among these contributions, Germany increased its foreign aid, repaid $587 million in postwar debts, eased trade restrictions against American poultry, and revalued the DM by 5 percent (Gavin 2004: 66). The US also used the off-set negotiations to obstruct a common European monetary policy (Zimmermann 2002: 140–141).

11. Developed at a moment when the military commitment of the United States to Western Europe appeared more insecure than ever before (Niedhardt 2010: 33), Brandt's alternative "de-militarized" conception of security conflicted with, rather than complemented, American objectives in important respects (Kieninger 2017: 285). For the US, détente was to be limited to the military sphere, to remain the prerogative of the two superpowers, and to stabilize but essentially continue the systemic conflict (Lippert 2011: 18; Hanhimäki 2004). For Germany, détente was to encompass the full range of economic, political, cultural, and scientific exchanges and, through a system of complex interdependence, transcend the Cold War in favor of a pan-European security system (Kieninger 2017: 285).

12. The so-called *Abendland* (occidental) conception of Europe emerged in the interwar period in response to the danger of communism looming in the East as well as the perils of liberal democracy imported from the West and embodied in the Weimar Republic (Conze 2005a: 208). Europe, as imagined by members of the *Abendland* movement, was a culturally defined association of national-conservative elites, anchored in orthodox Catholicism and made up of the hierarchically organized, authoritarian-corporatist societies (207). Unsurprisingly, the idea of Europe as *Abendland*, with its explicit rejection of modernity and invocation of an idealized, prepolitical, monarchical, and clerical past, found many of its proponents within the nobility, particularly from southern Germany and with attachment to the Habsburg monarchy and the Austro-Hungarian Empire (more so than to the protestant Prussia of the Hohenzollern) (Conze 2005b: 63). After 1945, the *Abendland* conception held that the European continent ought to stay clear of Eastern barbarism and Western decadence, renovate its Christian foundations, and restore its former world status.

13. Other scholars who have applied the term to West German foreign policy after the Second World War and beyond the Cold War are Kohler-Koch (1991); Rittberger (1992); and Senghaas (1994). Hans Maull's (1990, 2013) conception

of Germany as a "civilian power" also captures some of these elements (see also Schrade 1997).

14. The European Economic Community (EEC) was established with the Treaty of Rome (1958) as one of three European Communities, which also included the European Coal and Steel Community and the European Atomic Energy Community. The EEC is often referred to as "European Community," a name it did not officially receive until it was incorporated into the European Union (EU) under the Maastricht Treaty (1993). I use EEC in order to distinguish it from the European Communities it was originally a part of and from the European Community it became in 1993. With the Lisbon Treaty (2009), both were fully absorbed into the EU.

15. For an illuminating comparison between the European conceptions of Erhard, Röpke, and Müller-Armack, see Warneke (2013: 167–190).

16. This ultra-imperialist vision, though not representative of all of German business, was developed in a series of high-level meetings between German and French industrialists initiated by Adenauer in March 1953. The guiding idea was that the European economy could be rendered "crisis-proof" by mitigating competition at home and instead jointly exploiting the raw material supplies and outlet markets of Africa in particular, where European corporations would not get in the way of their international competitors (Rhenisch 1999: 79–80).

Chapter 4

1. To be sure, the shift toward a floating nonsystem after 1973 did not demolish Bretton Woods *in toto*. But because its constituent principles—stable exchange rates, macroeconomic policy space, and restrictions on capital flows—formed a coherent whole, the removal of any one of these elements could not but weaken the overall logic of this monetary framework (compare Obstfeld and Taylor 2004: 29; Eichengreen 2008: 1; Helleiner 1995: 324).

2. For a revisionist account of how the classical gold standard functioned historically, rather than in the minds of postwar monetary architects, see Knafo (2006; 2013).

3. Viewed through the lens of the infamous "policy trilemma," the choice of the architects of Bretton Woods was to constrain capital mobility in favor of fixed exchange rates and monetary autonomy (Obstfeld and Taylor 2004: 37–38; Schmelzer 2010: 48). The policy trilemma holds that policymakers can only attain two of the following three possible policy preferences: fixed exchange rates, capital mobility, and monetary autonomy (compare Obstfeld and Taylor 2004: 29).

4. What was being negotiated, however, was not a reembedding of the market into society in the way Polanyi (1957) had hoped for. Full employment, welfare state provision, and mass consumerism served instead to further entrench capitalist

economies and rationalities by channeling working-class resistance into institutionalized bargaining for higher wages and compensation (Lacher 1999; Lacher 2007).

5. Without consultation with its allies, the US administration under President Nixon closed the gold window, imposed an import surcharge, and ceased to support the dollar in foreign exchange markets, thus throwing the international monetary system into disarray.

6. According to Gowan (1999: 20–21), for instance, the US had decided to move toward a pure dollar standard at the end of the 1960s, saw the international monetary crisis of 1971 as an opportunity to push this through, entered into IMF G-20 negotiations simply in order to buy time and wait for a crisis to develop, and encouraged an oil price hike at least in part in order to drown the system in a flood of petrodollars.

7. Höcherl to Kiesinger, 20 March 1968, private-confidential, BAK B 136/3335. The information was said to come from an "unimpeachable" source within Samuel Montagu, one of the major bullion trading houses in the London market that have traditionally handled the transactions of central banks (Warwick-Ching 1993: 252).

8. Compare Loriaux (1991: 189), who criticizes the depiction of France from within the framework of hegemonic stability theory: "If we return to Kindleberger's thesis, it is unclear that there is a theoretically useful place for a 'spoiler' in a world ordered by a hegemon that has turned 'predatory'."

9. In light of a worsening US balance-of-payments position, French officials knew very well that their policies were pushing the United States toward declaring inconvertibility. They had sought to prepare for such an event since the sterling troubles of 1966. Their goal, then, seems to have been to commit the United States to internal adjustment and international reform—even at the risk of an end to gold conversions. See the French policy documents discovered by Michelle Frasher Rae (2003: 103–104) and published in her book *Transatlantic Politics and the Transformation of the International Monetary System* (Frasher 2014).

10. Zimmermann notes that Blessing soon came to think that sending the letter had been a mistake and that Germany should have been "more rigorous toward the U.S. We simply should have aggressively converted the dollars we accumulated to gold until they were driven to despair" (quoted in Zimmermann 2002: 226).

11. Emminger (1986: 35; quoted in Herr and Voy 1990: 18, fn. 17) noted that as early as 1956 the *Economist* had called for German reflation to redress balance-of-payments imbalances.

12. The Kennedy administration urged Germany not to convert surplus dollars into US Treasury gold. Nevertheless, "there was always the possibility that

West Germany could turn in dollars for gold if relations with the United States soured" (Gavin 2004: 66).

13. Weinstock, "Grundsätzliche Überlegungen zur gegenwärtigen währungspolitischen Diskussion," 9 September 1971, BAK B 136/7355, p. 9.

14. Brandt to Birrenbach, 22 July 1971, BAK B 136/6220, pp. 1–2, quoted in Lippert (2011: 94).

15. West German officials were uncertain how to interpret the press conference of de Gaulle, but that he had demanded a return to the classical gold standard was ruled out as unlikely. It was assumed that de Gaulle's more general statements had been specified and complemented by Giscard d'Estaing, and that the previous CRU (collective reserve unit) proposal was contained therein ("Fragen des internationalen Währungssystems," 18 February 1965, BAK B 136/3322, p. 3).

16. De Gaulle's verbal attacks were understood to be little more than a populist appeal to the concerns of French businessmen and the general population over an impending American "takeover"—one that, it was noted, nevertheless echoed the unrest within German industrial circles ("Fragen des internationalen Währungssystems," 18 February 1965, BAK B 136/3322, pp. 5–6).

17. "Pressekonferenz von Präsident de Gaulle am 4.2.1965," 12 February 1965, BAK B 136/3322, p. 7.

18. Blessing to Erhard, "Betreff: Vorschlag von Geheimrat Vocke zur Währungsreform," 22 February 1965, confidential, BAK B 136/3322, p. 4.

19. Although from the French perspective the repeated US pressure of troop reductions brought to bear on the Germans was evident. As one French official noted, "Every time there was a meeting of Europeans to concert their [monetary] policies, the State Department announced, as if by chance, that to reduce the U.S. deficit, a possible reduction of U.S. forces in Germany was under consideration. Thus, the Germans told us: We have no chance, we have to support the American position" (quoted in Zimmermann 2002: 140–141).

20. According to Zimmermann (2002: 243), "the Blessing letter . . . robbed the FRG of the option to initiate a change [in the dollar-gold system]."

21. "Schreiben von Herrn Geheimrat Dr. Vocke an den Herrn Bundeskanzler vom 16.2.1965," 4 March 1965, BAK B 136/3322, pp. 6–7.

22. Ibid.

23. French policy documents from 1966 cited in Rae (2003: 103–104).

24. "Ergänzende Aufzeichnung für die deutsch-französischen Konsultationen am 5./6. Juli 1971, Betr.: Ergebnisse der Wirtschafts- und Finanzministerkonferenz und der anschließenden Ratstagung am 1./2. Juli 1971 in Brüssel über währungspolitische Fragen," 2 July 1971, BAK B 136/3323, p. 4.

25. "Zum 38. Treffen der Wirtschafts- und Finanzminister der EWG am

26./27. April 1971. Zu TO-Punkt 4b: Internationale Währungsfragen; hier: Andere Fragen," 23 April 1971, BAK B 102/84100, pp. 3, 10.

26. German government documents from April 1971 note that the Netherlands and Belgium had in previous months converted dollar holdings of 325 and 650 million, respectively, in gold, SDRs, and swap agreements ("covered," that is, to be paid back in gold or SDRs). Switzerland had taken similar measures in the amount of $325 million, while Great Britain used its accumulated dollar reserves to pay off debts. Other countries tried to invest part of their reserves in DM. See "Zum 38. Treffen der Wirtschafts- und Finanzminister der EWG am 26./27. April 1971. Zu TO-Punkt 4b: Internationale Währungsfragen; hier: Andere Fragen," 23 April 1971, BAK B 102/84100, p. 6.

27. The notion that a British request for $3 billion in gold prompted Nixon to close the gold window, mentioned in several memoir accounts and the secondary literature (for a list, see Nichter 2008: 113, fn. 269), has not gone uncontested. Basosi (2011: 104, fn. 19), who did extensive research in the US archives for his 2006 monograph *Il governo del dollaro*, claims that "[n]o evidence has ever been found of such a request." He holds that the more plausible account is that Britain asked for a guarantee on the dollar holdings of the Bank of England, but denies that this forced Nixon's hand. For him, Nixon's plan needs to be put in the larger context of contingency planning since 1969. There may be little to argue with his correction of this factual detail, but his interpretation needs to be challenged on two counts. First, the transcripts of the Nixon tapes, partly transcribed in Nichter (2008: 114-119), show very clearly that the administration felt under enormous pressure because of dwindling gold reserves and incoming requests (including figures that put the sum total of requests received in the first half of August at an estimated $3.694 billion in gold (Nichter 2008: 115)), independent of where they came from and what their details. And second, while Basosi is perfectly right to argue that we need to see Nixon's program in a larger context, the *proper* context is the persistent pressure that US allies had exercised prior to and after the Nixon administration had come into office and started to develop its plans.

28. "Zum 38. Treffen der Wirtschafts- und Finanzminister der EWG am 26./27. April 1971. Zu TO-Punkt 4b: Internationale Währungsfragen; hier: Andere Fragen," 23 April 1971, BAK B 102/84100, pp. 3, 10.

29. Ibid.

30. The following sections of this chapter expand on material first published in Germann (2014b).

31. Memorandum by von Bismarck-Osten, 6 May 1971, quoted in Zimmermann (2008: 166).

32. Poullain to Brandt, 25 August 1971, BBk HA B 330/8399, p. 1.

33. Central Bank Council Meeting Minutes, 5 May 1971, BBk HA B 330/6158/1, pp. 5–6.

34. US Treasury, "Contingency," 8 May 1971, FRUS 2001, doc. 152, p. 425.

35. "Ihre wirtschaftspolitischen Gespräche in den USA, hier: Freigabe des DM-Wechselkurses," 4 June 1971, BAK B 136/3323, p. 2.

36. "Deutsch-amerikanische Devisenausgleichsverhandlungen; hier: handels- und währungspolitisches Wohlverhalten der Bundesrepublik gegenüber den USA," 28 May 1971, BAK B 136/3323, p. 6.

37. "Positionspapier für die Währungsgespräche: Neuordnung des internationalen Währungssystems," 2 September 1971, BAK B 102/132970, p. 4.

38. Ibid. West German monetary authorities were particularly concerned about the inflationary pressures that seemed to result from the US abusing this privilege. The aim of the allies, and Germany was no different here, was to impose discipline and gain influence over American fiscal and monetary policy (compare Kreile 2006: 161).

39. The automatism of monetary policy devised by Friedman fulfilled this premise but was based on Keynesian monetary theory. Friedman also rejected central bank independence.

40. Nor should the institutional autonomy of the Bundesbank be credited for this shift. The Bundesbank itself only gained its independence, from the government as much as from the export interests of banks and industry, through the decision to float the DM (Johnson 1998: 53, 59, 101; compare von Hagen 1999: 411).

41. Helleiner (2005: 36–37) comes to a similar conclusion in the case of Canada. Neoliberal ideas, he argues, cannot explain why Canadian policymakers favored floating over fixed exchange rates for much of the Bretton Woods era.

42. While Jeffry Frieden (1996: 111) famously predicted internationally operating economic agents to favor fixed exchange rates under conditions of economic openness, he recognized that American banks and firms in the early 1970s "emphasized opposing protection and getting capital controls removed" and came to see dollar devaluation as "the lesser of two evils" (124). Frieden recognized that his model of exchange rate preferences only partially fit what he considered a period of transition from a closed to an open economy (124).

43. For a number of revealing examples of the fierceness of exchange-rate lobbying in West Germany, see the excellent archival research by Kinderman (2008: 856–861).

44. Foreign Trade Advisory Council Meeting Protocol, 17 December 1968, BAK 102/85139, p. 3.

45. Münchmeyer to Schiller, 3 June 1971, BAK B 102/85141; Zahn to

Klasen, 9 June 1971, BBk HA B 330/8412; Semler to Klasen, 13 July 1971, BBk HA B 330/8403, p. 9.

46. Semler to Klasen, 10 May 1971, BBk HA B 330/8403, p. 8.

47. von der Lippe, 12 July 1971, BBk HA B 330/8403, p. 1.

48. Foreign Trade Advisory Council Meeting Protocol, 17 May 1971, BAK B 102/85141, p. 6.

49. Otto A. Friedrich, president of the Bundesvereinigung der Deutschen Arbeitgeberverbände (BDA, Confederation of German Employers' Associations), Otto Wolff von Amerongen, president of the Deutscher Industrie- und Handelskammertag (DIHK, Association of German Chambers of Commerce and Industry), and Hans-Günther Sohl, president of the Bundesverband der Deutschen Industrie (BDI, Federation of German Industries).

50. Sohl to Klasen, 23 November 1971, BBk HA B 330/8404, p. 2, as well as the attached memorandum.

51. Willink to Klasen, 13 August 1971, BBk HA B 330/8411, p. 1.

52. Poullain to Brandt, 25 August 1971, BBk HA B 330/8399, p. 2.

53. Ratjen to Klasen, 5 February 1971, BBk HA B 330/8400.

54. Semler to Klasen, 20 October 1970, BBk HA B 330/8403; von der Lippe, 22 October 1970, BBk HA B 330/8403.

55. Central Bank Council Meeting Minutes, 1 September 1971, BBk HA B 330/6163/2, p. 3; von der Lippe, 12 July 1971, BBk HA B 330/8403; Zahn to Klasen, 26 May 1971, BBk HA B 330/8412, p. 3. The Bundesbank representatives rejected these concerns as an "unduly pessimistic attitude" (Central Bank Council Meeting Stenographic Transcript, 1 September 1971, BBk HA B 330/6163/2, p. 12).

56. Mommsen to Schmidt, 13 March 1973, AdsD HSA 6115, p. 1.

57. Gray (2007: 296) argues that "West Germans proved uniquely willing to accept a loss of competitive advantage in order to improve the overall functioning of the system."

58. Foreign Trade Advisory Council Meeting Protocol, 12 November 1971, BAK B 102/85143, p. 9.

59. Schmidt, 15 April 1974, AdsD HSA 10071 (hereafter "Political-Economic Paper"), p. 18.

60. Individual sectors such as the chemical industry and mechanical engineering may have taken a hit, but whether this had to do with a stronger DM or with other negative factors such as the economic slowdown of its trading partners, the restrictive measures of the Nixon administration, or a rise in production and especially wage costs was not at all clear ("Exportsituation im Maschinenbau," 27 December 1971, BAK B 102/90765, p. 2; Mesenberg, "Vorschlag einer Gedankenskizze zur Einführung des Themas 'Die handelspolitische Situation im Lichte

der währungspolitischen Entwicklung," 9 November 1971, BAK B 102/85143, p. 3).

61. Geberth, "Betr.: Probleme der Exportfinanzierung—Vorschläge Düren-Gutachten," 29 March 1973, BAK B 102/139769, p. 4.

62. Mesenberg, "Vorschlag einer Gedankenskizze zur Einführung des Themas 'Die handelspolitische Situation im Lichte der währungspolitischen Entwicklung'," 9 November 1971, BAK B 102/85143, p. 4.

63. The increasing disconnect between the external value of the DM and trade patterns was revealed in June 1974, when the Bundesbank realized just how little of an effect the exchange rate actually had had on the volume and direction of trade flows. (See the comments made by Bundesbank official Tüngeler in a meeting of the Foreign Economic Trade Council, Foreign Economic Advisory Council Meeting Protocol, 26 June 1974, BAK B 102/139773, p. 7.

64. Semler to Klasen, 13 July 1971, BBk HA B 330/8403, p. 2.

65. Hankel to Schiller, 11 June 1970, BAK B 136/3323, p. 1.

66. "Aufzeichnung über Möglichkeiten, den Devisenumtausch im Rahmen spekulativer Bewegungen zu verteuern," 29 May 1969, BAK B 130/3323, p. 2; Helleiner (1994: 103) presents similar figures for the February 1973 currency crisis.

67. "Anwendbarkeit des §23 AWG," 3 May 1971, BAK B 102/84100, p. 2; "Beurteilung der devisen- und konjunkturpolitischen Lage durch das Direktorium der Deutschen Bundesbank," 11 June 1970, BAK B 136/3323, p. 2.

68. König, "Protokoll der Besprechung mit Firmenchefs über Kreditaufnahme im Ausland und Kurssicherung von Exportforderungen am 19. Juli 1972 im Hause der Bundesbank," 24 July 1972, BBk HA B 330/8383, p. 1.

69. "Gespräch Bundesbank-Kreditwirtschaft am 30. Juli 1971 über die kreditwirtschaftliche Situation," 1 July 1971, BAK B 136/3323, p. 4.

70. König, "Protokoll der Besprechung mit Firmenchefs über Kreditaufnahme im Ausland und Kurssicherung von Exportforderungen am 19. Juli 1972 im Hause der Bundesbank," 24 July 1972, BBk HA B 330/8383, p. 1.

71. "Betr.: Landesbank Rheinland-Pfalz," 28 September 1976, AdsD HSA 7383, pp. 1, 3; Schmidt to Poullain, 18 October 1972, AdsD HSA 5952, p. 2.

72. Klasen to Classen, 7 March 1972, BBk HA B 330/8380, p. 2.

73. "Anwendbarkeit des §23 AWG," 3 May 1971, BAK B 102/84100, p. 2.

74. Emminger to Petersen, 28 August 1973, BBk HA N2 K 728.

75. For classic analyses of inflation as a distributive conflict, see Crouch (1978); and Goldthorpe (1978).

76. Bauer to Klasen, 25 February 1971, BBk HA B 330/8473.

77. Ibid.

78. Grünewald to Schmidt, 12 April 1979, AdsD HSA 7308.

79. Foreign Economic Advisory Council Meeting Protocol, 26 June 1974, BAK B 102/139773, p. 7.

80. Foreign Economic Advisory Council Meeting Protocol, 22 March 1976, BAK B 102/226513, p. 12.

Chapter 5

1. As noted by the chairman of the Federal Reserve, Paul Volcker.

2. For concerns over protectionist forces gaining ground with the election of Nixon, see, inter alia, the memorandum of the German-American Chamber of Commerce, "Die handelspolitischen Aussichten der nächsten Monate," 11 November 1968, BAK B 102/85129.

3. "Political-Economic Paper." A "defused" (*entschärfte*) version of the paper was sent to finance ministers Giscard d'Estaing und Wim Duisenberg.

4. "Political-Economic Paper," p. 30. Throughout the 1970s, the German chancellor had repeatedly warned publicly of a return of beggar-thy-neighbor policies and a coming "struggle for the world product" (e.g. Schmidt 1974). In retrospect, he concluded that what had been avoided in the 1970s was nothing less than "open economic warfare, one against the other" (1988: 67).

5. "Funktionen und Verwendungsmöglichkeiten der Devisenreserven der Deutschen Bundesbank," 20 February 1976, BAK B 102/269506, p. 2.

6. One policy document divided the various proposals into three groups: (a) the direct or indirect investment in stockpiles of petroleum and other resources; (b) international aid measures such as development aid or foreign currency loans; and (c) domestic social policy. In the mid- to late 1970s, the first two were the most intensely debated; compare "Funktionen und Verwendungsmöglichkeiten der Devisenreserven der Deutschen Bundesbank," 20 February 1976, BAK B 102/269506, pp. 2–3.

7. See, for instance, the interviews with James Akins, top energy specialist of the US State Department and ambassador to Saudi Arabia, in Oppenheim (1976) and with the former Saudi Arabian oil minister Ahmed Yamani in the *Guardian* (2001).

8. Apel to Schmidt, 9 January 1974, AdsD HSA 8999, p. 2.

9. Compare Otmar Emminger, "Ausführungen des Bundeskanzlers über die Verwendung von Währungsreserven (Stichworte)," 10 August 1977, confidential, BBk N2 K 319, p. 3.

10. Due to differences between importing and processing industries (Foreign Economic Advisory Council Meeting Protocol, 9 April 1976, BAK B 102/226514, p. 12 [Mommsen]), opposition from the central bank, and a general aversion to state intervention, none of these plans would see the light of day.

11. The third idea was supported by domestic refineries (Kaffka to Schmidt, 24 May 1974, AdsD HSA 6170, p. 2) but opposed by the Ruhr industries ("Political-Economic Paper," p. 67).

12. "Funktionen und Verwendungsmöglichkeiten der Devisenreserven der Deutschen Bundesbank," 20 February 1976, BAK B 102/269506, p. 3.

13. Kaffka to Schmidt, 24 May 1974, personal-confidential, AdsD HSA 6170, p. 1.

14. Wolfram to Schmidt, 21 June 1978, AdsD HSA 7314.

15. See the letter from Hellmuth Buddenberg, chairman of Deutsche BP, to Schmidt, 25 November 1978, AdsD HSA 7314, pointing out that the decision of the government would have "immediate repercussions on the upcoming investment decisions of Deutsche BP."

16. After a meeting of the head of British Petroleum David Steel with the chancellor (*Der Spiegel* 1978: 60), Callaghan personally intervened on behalf of British Petroleum in December 1978, urging Schmidt in an aide memoire to instruct his economics minister to override the veto of the cartel office; Callaghan to Schmidt, 5 December 1978, AdsD HSA 7314: "The Prime Minister has been following the progress of the deal and the Chairman of BP, Sir David Steel, has told him of the importance which his company attaches to it. The Prime Minister agrees. . . . The Prime Minister therefore hopes that Chancellor Schmidt will do what he can to bring the deal to a successful conclusion."

17. The particular vulnerability of West Germany did not escape the attention of US policymakers. See, for example, CIA, "The Arab Oil Cutback and Higher Prices: Implications and Reactions," 19 October 1973, secret, p. 3. http://www. foia.cia.gov/sites/default/files/document_conversions/1699355/1973-10-19E.pdf (accessed 17 June 2013).

18. Foreign Economic Advisory Council Meeting Protocol, 11 February 1977, BAK B 102/226516, appendix 3, Mommsen, "Sitzung des Außenwirtschaftsbeirates am 11. February 1977," p. 6: "There is, after all, a whole series of industrialized countries that can calmly await raw material agreements because they are themselves large producers of raw materials and because their extractive economy is integrated with their industry."

19. "Political-Economic Paper," p. 33.

20. For a useful assessment of the IR literature on "grand strategy" and its much-neglected economic dimension, see Silove (2017).

21. Helmut Schmidt, "Erwägungen für 1977," final version, 10 April 1977, AdsD HSA 6567 (hereafter "Marbella Paper"), pp. 22–27.

22. See, for example, Irmler, "Vermerk: Gespräch Bundeskanzler Schmidt in Bonn am 16. Oktober 1975," 20 October 1975, strictly confidential, BBk HA N2 K 319, p. 2.

23. In a telling sign of how closely connected policy elites thought the international and domestic challenges to capitalism to be, consider the analogy drawn by one of the members of the Bundesbank's executive board. Given how little of an impact the much more pronounced domestic struggles had had on the distribution of wealth *within* capitalist societies, he reasoned, the efforts of developing countries to obtain a greater share of the world social product were unlikely to bear fruits (Schlesinger, "Alternativen im internationalen Verteilungskampf, der durch die Erdölpreissteigerung ausgelöst wurde," 8 February 1974, BBk HA B 330/25959, p. 2.

24. Flendorffer, "Verlagerung der deutschen Devisenreserven," 16 July 1975, BAK B 102/269506, pp. 3, 5; "Funktionen und Verwendungsmöglichkeiten der Devisenreserven der Deutschen Bundesbank," 20 February 1976, BAK B 102/269506, pp. 4–5.

25. "Verwendung der Devisenreserven der Deutschen Bundesbank," 2 December 1976, BAK B 102/269506, p. 2.

26. "In most cases this means: no direct bilateral currency credits, but the interposition of international institutions (IMF, and so on) with the possibility of economic policy [*wirtschaftspolitische*] conditions" (Bundesbank Board of Directors, "Zur Frage des Einsatzes der Währungsreserven der Bundesbank," 12 October 1977, BBk HA 9661, p. 8).

27. "Marbella Paper," final version, p. 5.

28. "Funktionen und Verwendungsmöglichkeiten der Devisenreserven der Deutschen Bundesbank," 20 February 1976, BAK B 102/269506, p. 4; Flendorffer, "Verlagerung der deutschen Devisenreserven," 16 July 1975, BAK B 102/269506, p. 4.

29. "Verwendung der Devisenreserven der Deutschen Bundesbank," 2 December 1976, BAK B 102/269506, p. 3.

30. "Verwendung von Devisenreserven unter außenpolitischen Gesichtspunkten," 31 March 1976, BAK B 102/342476, pp. 2–3.

31. As Lankowski (1982a: 344) observed, "Germany therefore used its vast foreign exchange reserves to support regimes willing to introduce austerity measures aimed at reducing public expenditure." *Pace* Lankowski, however, this was not done "in the hope that this would directly affect the price level and therewith the ability to import."

32. "Political-Economic Paper," p. 63.

33. Ibid., p. 21.

34. Ibid., p. 63.

35. Kurth to Schmidt, "Beabsichtigtes fernmündliches Gespräch zwischen dem Herrn BK und Präsident Giscard d'Estaing; hier: Ankoppelung des Schweizer Franken an die Mini-Währungsschlange, Bezug: Vorlage von Herrn AL IV vom 19. März 1975," n.d., AdsD HSA 6582.

36. This paragraph draws on the research of Tobias Straumann (2010), who challenges the traditional comparative-institutionalist argument (compare Katzenstein 1985; Scharpf 1991) that the corporatist structure of smaller European states allowed them to pursue a tight monetary policy and to negotiate the wage restraint necessary to maintain a hard-currency peg.

37. McNamara (1998: 157) agrees that because of their small size and exposed external position, "[p]olicy emulation may not be the best way to characterize their behavior."

38. "Political-Economic Paper," p. 20.

39. Ibid., p. 63.

40. Thanks are due to Herman Schwartz for his feedback on an early version of this chapter and for sharing the quote with me.

41. Parboni (1981: 138) and Basosi (2011: 109) speak of an economically conservative US-German entente.

42. Nixon to Kissinger, 10 March 1973, FRUS 2009, doc. 31, p. 119.

43. FRUS 2009, Editorial Note, pp. 123, 126. For a comprehensive analysis, see Trachtenberg (2011: 19–23).

44. Memo from Hormats to Scowcroft, 17 March 1976, FRUS 2009, doc. 130, p. 465.

45. Ibid.

46. "The International Monetary Situation," Memo by Simon, FRUS 2009, doc. 132, p. 470.

47. "Aufzeichnung über das Gespräch des Bundeskanzlers mit Secretary Simon (Treasury) und Chairman Burns (FED) am 9. Juni 1975, 9–10.15 Uhr im kleinen Kabinettsaal," 13 June 1975, BBk HA N2 K 322.

48. Memorandum of Conversation, Schmidt/Genscher, Ford/Kissinger/Scowcroft, 27 July 1975, National Security Adviser's Memoranda of Conversation Collection, GFPL), pp. 5–6. https://www.fordlibrarymuseum.gov/library/document/0314/1553186.pdf (accessed 12 November 2019).

49. As Simon summed up the discussions at Puerto Rico in preparation for a meeting with Chancellor Schmidt: "It was understood that countries in structural deficit need to adopt corrective economic and financial policies." Memo from Simon to Ford, 13 July 1976. GFPL. William Simon Papers. Series II: Internal Memoranda.

50. "Economic Stabilization of Western Europe," Memorandum of Conversation, 26 March 1976, FRUS 2009, doc. 133, p. 476.

51. For an account that focuses on the lead role and belief system of Schmidt in shaping German-American stabilization efforts, see Bernardini (2017).

52. "Economic Storm Warnings," Memo from Hormats to Ford, 17 March 1976, FRUS 2009, doc. 130, p. 467.

53. "The International Monetary Situation," Memo by Simon, FRUS 2009, doc. 132, p. 470. The argument of Harvey (2005: 73) that the fiscal crisis in New

York City served as a blueprint for structural adjustment programs in the 1980s is reflected in the assessment of US policymakers, who likened the situation of Italy and Britain to that of New York City as having lived beyond their means ("Economic Stabilization of Western Europe," Memorandum of Conversation, 26 March 1976, FRUS 2009, doc. 133, p. 476).

54. The strategic thinking of Germany and the United States converged on the creation of a multilateral instrument for enforcing adjustment and held that addressing the economic problems was central to countering the political threat of communism (conversation between German government and US Administration, 27 July 1975, p. 219, cited in Bernardini [2011: 329]).

55. Bernardini (2011: 326, citing Schmidt to Rumor, 23 July 1974, AdsD HSA 6549) notes that "Schmidt urged Rumor to adopt 'German solutions' to cope with economic turmoil, and especially to curb inflation that was undermining every effort to restore economic stability."

56. "Aufzeichnung des Ministerialdirektors van Well," 11 May 1976, quoted in Bernardini (2011: 317).

57. "Rambouillet II; Lebanon; Djibouti; Nuclear Non-proliferation," Memorandum of Conversation, 18 May 1976, FRUS 2009, doc. 138, p. 491.

58. "The International Monetary Situation," Memo by Simon, FRUS 2009, doc. 132, p. 473; Pöhl, "Betr.: Besprechung mit Yeo, de la Rosière und Mitchell am 10./11. April 1976," 14 April 1976, AdsD DHS 5, p. 4.

59. Yeo to Ford, 24 June 1976, FRUS 2009, doc. 146, p. 523.

60. For accounts of this history and some possible answers to this question, see Goodman (1992: 159); Sassoon (1996: 572–592); Simonazzi and Vianello (1998: 109); Brogi (2011: 322); and Bernardini (2011: 336).

61. Ehmke to Brandt, "Betr.: Rom-Besuch vom 20.-25. Juli 1978," n.d., AdsD HSA 6818, p. 3. This supports the argument by Gruber (2000: 183) that Italy would have preferred the status quo ante but felt compelled to enter the EMS because of the high costs of exclusion.

62. Statement by Schmidt, Central Bank Council Meeting Minutes, 30 November 1978, BBk HA N2 269, p. 69. Marsh (2009) was the first to discover the transcript of Schmidt's visit to the Central Bank Council in the personal papers of Otmar Emminger. An English translation has been made available at http://www.margaretthatcher.org/document/111554 (accessed 18 September 2012).

63. As argued, for instance, by Harmon (1997: 228–229).

64. Pöhl, "Betr.: Besprechung mit Ed Yeo (Undersecretary), de la Rosière (Directeur du Trésor), Sir Derek Mitchell (Secretary) und Staatssekretär Karl Otto Pöhl am 19.3.1976 in London, sowie bilaterale Besprechung mit Yeo am 21.3.1976 in Bonn," 23 March 1976, AdsD DHS 5, p. 1.

65. Ibid.

66. The British offers included concessions in the Common Agricultural Policy (CAP) and the offset agreement, as well as the sale of BP Burma oil (Pöhl, "Vermerk über das Gespräch mit Schatzkanzler Denis Healey," 9 November 1976, confidential, AdsD DHS 5, p. 2).

67. Callaghan to Schmidt, 10 November 1976, secret and personal, AdsD DHS 5, p. 1; Schmidt to Callaghan, 16 November 1976, AdsD DHS 5.

68. Pöhl to Schmidt, 8 October 1976, personal-confidential, AdsD DHS 5.

69. Pöhl, "Betr.: Besprechung mit de la Rosière, Yeo, Mitchel und Pöhl am 19./20.7.1976 in Paris; hier: Eventuelle Kredithilfe für Italien," 23 July 1976, AdsD DHS 5, p. 2.

70. See Jones (2012: 379, fn. 77), who quotes a telephone conversation between Schmidt and Callaghan on 2 November 1976.

71. Pöhl to Schmidt, 8 October 1976, personal-confidential, AdsD DHS 5, pp. 1–2.

72. Pöhl to Schmidt, 18 October 1976, strictly confidential, personal-confidential, AdsD DHS 5, pp. 2, 4; Hiss, "Aufzeichnung des Telefongesprächs des Bundeskanzlers mit Präsident Ford am 24. November 1976, 15.30 Uhr," 24 November 1976, AdsD DHS 5; Pöhl, "Ergebnisvermerk: Betr.: Besprechung des Herrn Bundeskanzlers mit Under-Secretary Yeo, Weitere Teilnehmer: BM Dr. Apel, StS Pöhl," 3 November 1976, AdsD DHS 5.

73. Foreign Economic Advisory Council Meeting Protocol, 11 February 1977, BAK B 102/226516, p. 11.

74. See, for instance, the observation by Kissinger: "If the British are smart, it could be in their interest to be pressured into agreement on conditions, so that they can say that the only reason they imposed stringent conditions on the British economy is because of those American SOBs. This is better for Callaghan than having to deal with the unions himself" ("Economic Summit at Puerto Rico," Memorandum of Conversation, 4 June 1976, FRUS 2009, doc. 140, p. 498.

75. Ibid.

76. Emminger to Simon, 17 February 1977, BBk HA N2 K734.

77. Though see Howarth (2016: 89), who points to support from big business and the *Conseil National du Patronat Français* in particular.

78. Statement by Schmidt, Central Bank Council Meeting Minutes, 30 November 1978, BBk HA N2 269, p. 8.

79. Emminger, "Währungspolitische Fortschritte in Europa: Möglichkeiten— Probleme," 29 March 1978, BBk HA N2 K712, p. 1.

80. Statement by Schmidt, Central Bank Council Meeting Minutes, 30 November 1978, BBk HA N2 269, p. 3. See also Celi et al. (2018: 241), who note that the EMS was of particular importance for Germany's mature industrial sectors.

81. Pöhl to Schmidt, 21 March 1978, BBk HA N4 1, p. 3: "It is . . . in our interest that other currencies are also used for transaction, investment and reserve purposes as much as possible."

82. Pöhl, "Zur währungspolitischen Lage," 16 December 1977, BBk HA N4 1, p. 6.

83. Concerns that an electoral victory of the French left might lead to a breakup of the European Economic Community are mentioned in "Vermerk über das Gespräch des Herrn Bundeskanzlers mit BM Matthöfer, BM Graf Lambsdorff und Präsident Emminger am 1.3.1978," 6 March 1978, BBk HA N2 K324, p. 2.

84. Sohl to Schmidt, 7 December 1976, AdsD HSA 7307, p. 1.

85. Emminger, "Währungspolitische Fortschritte in Europa: Möglichkeiten— Probleme," 29 March 1978, BBk HA N2/K712, p. 1.

86. Statement by Schmidt, Central Bank Council Meeting Minutes, 30 November 1978, BBk HA N2 269, pp. 8, 71.

87. Such as in Germany, where conservative newspapers like the *Frankfurter Allgemeine* and *Welt* had repeatedly sided with the Bundesbank's anti-inflationary, hard-currency course (Marsh 1992: 175). Statement by Schmidt, Central Bank Council Meeting, 30 November 1978, verbatim record, BBk HA N2/269, pp. 9–10, 64.

88. Central Bank Council Meeting Minutes, 4 March 1982, BBk HA B 330/11366/2, p. 11.

89. As Schmidt was paraphrased in an internal memorandum to President Ford. Memo by Sisco to Ford, 27 April 1976, "Your Meeting with FRG Opposition Leader Kohl, May 4, 3:00pm," p. 13. GFPL, Presidential Country Files for Europe and Canada, Box 5, Germany (10).

Chapter 6

1. "Politische Aspekte des heutigen Währungsmechanismus," 16 December 1963, BAK B 136/3322.

2. Flendorffer, "Verlagerung der deutschen Devisenreserven," 16 July 1975, BAK B 102/269506; "Anlage von Rohstoffreserven," Central Bank Council Meeting Minutes, p. 3. The idea of repurposing the Bundesbank's currency reserves was dropped by the government in early 1979 (compare Central Bank Council Meeting Minutes, 29 March 1979, BBk HA B 330/9663).

3. Irmler, "Vermerk: Gespräch Bundeskanzler Schmidt in Bonn am 16. Oktober 1975," 20 October 1975, strictly confidential, BBk HA N2 K 319, p. 2: "The chancellor wants to induce the United States to greater participation in a responsible 'global management.' The currency reserves of the Bundesbank were not to be considered 'tied up in the US as a matter of course.' . . . Whether the

Bundesbank's currency reserves invested in the US could be used as leverage was discussed, but the opinions of the Bundesbank and chancellor are deeply divided."

4. Emminger, "Ausführungen des Bundeskanzlers über die Verwendung von Währungsreserven (Stichworte)," 10 August 1977, confidential, BBk HA N2 K 319, p. 3: "If we collect our foreign exchange reserves from [Treasury Secretary] Blumenthal, we remove them from the purview of the American authorities and the US will have to get the money elsewhere, for example on the capital market. Our investment in dollars means that everything is at the American disposal."

5. Bundesbank Board of Directors, "Zur Frage des Einsatzes der Währungsreserven der Bundesbank," 12 October 1977, BBk HA 9661, p. 8.

6. Flendorffer, "Verlagerung der deutschen Devisenreserven," 16 June 1975, BAK B 102/269506, pp. 2, 4; "Verwendung der Devisenreserven der Deutschen Bundesbank," 2 December 1976, BAK B 102/269506, pp. 1–2.

7. Statement by Schmidt, Central Bank Council Meeting Minutes, 30 November 1978, BBk HA N2 269, p. 69.

8. For divergent interpretations of what caused this reversal—unfortunate circumstances or the mobilization of business and ideological entrepreneurs—see Biven (2002); and Blyth (2002).

9. Memorandum of Conversation, 27 June 1976, FRUS 2009, doc. 148, pp. 541–542.

10. Lahnstein to Matthöfer, "Betr.: Treffen der G5-deputies in Paris," 16 June 1978, confidential, AdsD DHS 11, p. 2.

11. By keeping the price of oil below world levels, the US encouraged the consumption and import of petroleum that weighed down on the balance of trade and the foreign exchange rate of the dollar and thwarted international attempts to reduce the costs by conserving energy (Putnam and Henning 1989: 56).

12. "Zum Staatsbesuch von Präsident Carter vom 14.7.-15.7.1978," 26 June 1978, BBk HA N2 K286.

13. Central Bank Council Meeting Minutes, 10 August 1978, B 330/9084/1, part II, (Emminger), p. 7.

14. Schmidt to Emminger, 17 July 1978, BBk HA N2 K 286, p. 2.

15. Statement by Schmidt, Central Bank Council Meeting Minutes, 30 November 1978, BBk HA N2 269, p. 7.

16. Central Bank Council Meeting Protocol, 13 and 14 December 1978, BBk HA B 330/9657, pp. 13, 18. Emminger reminded his colleagues of having committed to a restrictive course of action in a subsequent meeting in mid-January (Central Bank Council Meeting Protocol, 18 January 1979, BBk HA B 330/9659, p. 12).

17. Central Bank Council Meeting Protocol, 18 January 1979, BBk HA B 330/9659, p. 14.

18. Central Bank Council Meeting Protocol, 15 March 1979, BBk HA B 330/9662, p. 3.

19. Ibid., pp. 3–5.

20. Ibid., p. 17; for the endorsement of the Bundesbank's policies by the chancellor, see Central Bank Council Meeting Protocol, 31 May 1979, BBk HA B 330/10140, p. 3.

21. Central Bank Council Meeting Protocol, 15 March 1979, BBk BA B 330/9662, p. 16.

22. Ibid., p. 5.

23. The following two sections build on archival material and expand upon arguments first made in Germann (2014a).

24. Central Bank Council Meeting Minutes, 10 August 1978, BBk HA B 330/9084/1, part II, p. 1.

25. Statement by Schmidt, Central Bank Council Meeting Minutes, 30 November 1978, BBk HA N2 269, p. 7.

26. Foreign Economic Advisory Council Protocol, 17 November 1978, BAK B 102/226521 (Gleske), p. 5; see also Eichengreen (2011, 185, fn. 41): "Some argue that the shift was no coincidence—that, in a telling sign of how a country's policies can be influenced by foreign powers that hold its debts, veiled threats from OPEC about dumping the dollar compelled Carter to attach a higher priority to fighting inflation and shift from Miller to Volcker."

27. CIA National Foreign Assessment Center, "Changing Power Relations Among OECD States," 22 October 1979, p. 4. The document is cited in Basosi (2010: 14). An online version is available at http://www.margaretthatcher.org /document/C28E73FAD72D4604BD1BF3A26BDA1E30.pdf (accessed 24 September 2012).

28. Statement by Schmidt, Central Bank Council Meeting Minutes, 30 November 1978, BBk HA N2 269, p. 9.

29. Central Bank Council Meeting Minutes, 15 June 1978, BBk HA B 330/9082/2, part I, (Pöhl), p. 5.

30. "Note on Interventions in the Snake, 9.3. 1978," BBk HA N2 K 732, p. 1.

31. Statement by Schmidt, Central Bank Council Meeting Minutes, 30 November 1978, BBk HA N2 269, p. 70. This possibility had been recognized in the contingency plans of American strategists over a decade earlier, which had warned that "[i]nstead of submissively accommodating themselves to the U.S. Plan X offensive, . . . the Eurobloc members might also choose to adopt an aggressive posture," including "a deliberate program of pushing the dollar lower and lower" ("Contingency Plan X: A Proposal to Force Major Surplus Countries to Support

the Dollar at Present Parities or to Allow a Relative Appreciation of Their Currencies," pp. 38–39, cited in Gavin [2004: 169]).

32. Statement by Schmidt, Central Bank Council Meeting Minutes, 30 November 1978, BBk HA N2 269, pp. 69–70.

33. Data on US and German foreign exchange interventions (net purchases and sales of dollars) are presented in Bordo, Humpage, and Schwartz (2010) and available from the website of the Federal Reserve Bank of St. Louis at https://research.stlouisfed.org (accessed 14 February 2018).

34. "Internationale Währungsfragen, USA-Reise von BM Dr. Lambsdorff," 31 January 1979, BAK B 102/269501, p. 2.

35. Central Bank Council Meeting Protocol, 15 March 1979 (28 March 1979), BBk HA B 330/9662, pp. 14, 16; Central Bank Council Meeting Protocol, 31 May 1979 (15 June 1979), BBk HA B 330/10139, p. 8.

36. Central Bank Council Meeting Minutes, 28 June 1979, BBk HA B 330/10141/1, p. 3; Emminger, "Telefongespräch mit Paul Volcker am 25. Juni 1979," 25 June 1979, BBk HA N2 K 322, p. 1.

37. In his memoirs, Schmidt (1989: 265, quoted in Biven 2002: 117) described the situation in more diplomatic terms: "[W]e could meet the request only to a limited degree because we took the risk of inflation in our own country seriously; every mark spent in support of the dollar bloated the German money supply." But the serious implications of the German position for US policy were recognized as early as August 1978, when Acting Treasury Secretary Carswell told Carter, "In any event, the German monetary authorities are reluctant to have us continue to intervene in marks until we have taken more fundamental U.S. domestic measures. They are providing almost no dollar support themselves. Thus, little more can be done with strictly monetary measures other than a tightening of the domestic money supply" (Memo from Carswell to Carter, 30 August 1978, FRUS 2013, doc. 158, pp. 497–498).

38. Schulmann to Schmidt, "Ihr Telefongespräch mit Präsident Carter, hier: Währungsfragen," 21 September 1979, AdsD HSA 6587, p. 1.

39. Transcript of FOMC Meeting, 18 September 1979, p. 3. http://www.federalreserve.gov/monetarypolicy/files/FOMC19790918meeting.pdf (accessed 4 February 2013).

40. The data have been compiled by Michael Bordo, Owen Humpage, and Anna Schwartz and published at http://www.clevelandfed.org/research/data/fx-intervention/index.cfm (accessed February 4, 2012). At the time of completing this book, the dataset is no longer hosted on this website. However, it has been digitally archived by and can be accessed through the Internet Archive (https://archive.org/web).

41. Solomon, "US/German Monetary Cooperation—Talking Points," 27 September 1979, quoted in Marsh (2009: 89).

42. Central Bank Council Meeting Minutes, 4 October 1979, BBk HA B 330/10146, p. 17.

43. "Vermerk über das Gespräch des Herrn Bundeskanzlers mit Secretary Miller und Chairman Volcker im Überseeclub Hamburg am 29. September 1979, von 12.00 bis 14.15 Uhr," 1 October 1979, BBk HA N2/K322, p. 11. Remarkably, the editors of the *Foreign Relations of the United States* series conclude that "[n]o memorandum of conversation of the meeting was found" in the US archives (Memo from Miller to Carter, 26 September 1979, FRUS 2013, doc. 227, p. 661, fn. 3).

44. Ibid., p. 5.

45. Central Bank Council Meeting Minutes, 18 October 1979, BBk HA B 330/10147, p. 4.

46. Transcript of FOMC Meeting, 6 October 1979, p. 6. http://www.federal reserve.gov/monetarypolicy/files/FOMC19791006meeting.pdf (accessed 14 February 2019). Two pertinent lines of the transcript were also redacted.

47. Ibid., p. 7.

48. Ibid., p. 4.

49. Ibid., p. 7.

50. Fed economist Stephen Axilrod, tasked in mid-September 1979 to outline the monetarist change in the Fed's operating procedures, recalls that "it was . . . a deteriorating trend in markets generally that was continuing into late summer and early fall, especially in the foreign exchange market, that clearly signalled the need for a paradigm shift in domestic monetary policy" (Axilrod 2005: 238).

51. The connection of Volcker to international planning bodies that promoted a neoliberal agenda is tenuous. He was *not* part of the Shadow Open Market Committee. The *Lobster* argued that there is evidence he attended a meeting of the Pinay Circle in Washington, but this was in December 1979.

52. Foreign Economic Advisory Council Meeting Protocol, 4 September 1979, BAK B 102/226523 (Wolff von Amerongen), p. 4.

53. Central Bank Council Meeting Minutes, 17 April 1980, BBk HA B 330/10651, p. 3.

54. Volcker to Emminger, 27 November 1979, BBk HA N2 K 322, p. 1.

55. Central Bank Council Meeting Protocol, 29 May 1980, BBk HA B 330/10655, p. 3; Central Bank Council Meeting Minutes, 29 May 1980, BBk HA B 330/10655, p. 2.

56. Central Bank Council Meeting Minutes, 12 June 1980, BBk HA B 300/10666, p. 4.

57. In Germany, Emminger argued, the support of all social groups and the majority of the population was indispensable for an effective stabilization policy. See Emminger, "Geldpolitik und Wahrungsstärke—Geldmengenziel als Wundermittel?" first draft, 28 May 1977, BBk HA N2 K 731, p. 4.

58. Central Bank Council Meeting Minutes, 2 October 1980, BBk HA B 330/10665 (Schöllhorn), p. 7.

59. As said by the German G5 deputy Horst Schulmann about his US counterpart Beryl Sprinkle (Schulmann, "Betr.: G5D am 8. 9. 1981 in Paris," 14 September 1981, AdsD DHS 11, p. 1). See also Schulmann, "Betr.: Treffen der G-5 Deputies in London am 19.2.1981," 23 February 1981, AdsD DHS 11, p. 9.

60. Schulmann to Schmidt, "Betr.: Deutsch-französische Haltung in Wirtschaftsfragen im Vorfeld des Europäischen Rates vor Maastricht; hier: Sondierungsgespräch mit GS Wahl und MP Barre in Paris am 12.3.1981," n.d., AdsD DHS 23, p. 1.

61. Schulmann, "Betr.: Treffen der G-5 Deputies in London am 19.2.1981," 23 February 1981, AdsD DHS 11, p. 7.

62. "Political-Economic Paper," p. 55.

63. Central Bank Council Meeting Minutes, 5 February 1981, BBk HA B 330/11164, part II, p. 6; Central Bank Council Meeting Minutes, 17 December 1981, BBk HA B 330/11364/1, p. 8.

64. Central Bank Council Meeting Minutes, 5 February 1981, BBk HA B 330/11164, part II (Pöhl), pp. 1–2, 6.

65. Central Bank Council Meeting Minutes, 19 March 1981, BBk HA B 330/11167, part I, pp. 15 and 17.

66. Ibid., pp. 19–20.

67. Central Bank Council Meeting Minutes, 3 June 1982, BBk HA B 330/11370/1, pp. 19–20.

68. Schulmann, "Betr.: Treffen der G-5 Deputies in London am 19.2.1981," 23 February 1981, AdsD DHS 11, p. 9.

69. "Political-Economic Paper," p. 52.

70. Klasen to Friedrich, 30 April 1971, BBk HA B 330/8383.

71. Klasen to Berenberg-Gossler, 28 May 1974, BBk HA B 330/8374.

72. IMF, "Germany—1978 Article IV Consultation Discussions: Some Preliminary Remarks," AdsD DHS 11, pp. 4–5.

73. In this sense, the neoliberal order that emerged in the 1980s and 1990s is best described as "post-hegemonic."

74. Regan, quoted in Schulmann, "Betr.: G-5 M Treffen am 17.01.1982 in Versailles," AdsD DHS 11, p. 1.

75. "Bericht über die Sitzung des Wirtschaftspolitischen Ausschusses (EPC)

der OECD am 20. und 21. November 1980," 24 November 1980, BBk HA B 330/10669, p. 7.

76. R. Solomon to Emminger, 25 June 1979, BBk HA N2 K 737.

77. Central Bank Council Meeting Minutes, 11 December 1980, BBk HA B 330/11161, (Kloten), p. 7: "If successful, this anti-inflationary policy would mean that the potential for an appreciating DM will increasingly melt away. In this case, we could not hope that the DM will assume a stronger position in foreign exchange markets. The Japanese now manage to deal with their problem; and it now looks as if the Americans and the British will succeed as well. We are not sure about the French."

78. Pöhl to Schmidt, 16 June 1980, BBk HA N1 4: "In my view, the implications of this situation for our economic policy are clear. We need to pursue a policy that reduces the current account deficit. A decrease in domestic demand is going to help us in this. Our level of interest rates needs to be attractive enough to draw in foreign capital in order to compensate at least partially for the current account and capital account deficit. After all, we cannot raise any doubts abroad as to our resolve to do everything we can to ensure that the DM will remain a 'hard currency.' Only in this way can we nip expectations of devaluation in the bud. This plan may temporarily come into conflict with our internal economic wants and needs, such as an economic slowdown. Nevertheless, I believe we need to see it through at almost any cost if we want to maintain the strong economic position of the FRG. It needs no special emphasis that such a plan is incompatible with a reprise of the 'locomotive theory.'"

Chapter 7

1. Ehmke to Schmidt, 20 October 1980, personal-confidential, AdsD HSA 6818.

2. For an analysis that sees German banks as the victims of Germany's export success and the growing ability of German firms to self-finance, see Braun and Deeg (2019). For an analysis that predates the internationalization of German banks to the 1960s and re-conceptualizes it as central to both the making and unmaking of the German model, see Beck (2019).

3. See Vitols (2004) for a nuanced assessment of how this process led to distinctive outcomes rather than the wholesale adoption of Anglo-American practices.

4. The following paragraphs modify and expand on material first published in Germann (2018).

5. See the time series "Exports of Goods and Services (% of GDP)," based on national accounts data from the World Bank and Organisation for Economic Co-Operation and Development (OECD) and available at https://data.worldbank .org/indicator/NE.EXP.GNFS.ZS?locations=DE (accessed 20 May 2020).

6. My calculations indicate that Germany's share of the value of world merchandise exports stood at 10.9 percent in 1900 and 8 percent in 2018. They are based on a report by the Statistical Office of the United Nations (1962) that drew on the international trade statistics of the League of Nations, and a contemporary dataset ("Merchandise: Total Trade and Share, Annual, 1948–2016") from UNCTADstat (https://unctadstat.unctad.org).

7. In an op-ed for the *Frankfurter Allgemeine Zeitung* titled "The German Locomotive Is Moving Fast Enough," Kenneth Rogoff (2014) notes that "German frugality has been a subject of contention in global macro-debates for much of the past six decades."

8. Statement by Schmidt, Central Bank Council Meeting Minutes, 30 November 1978, BBk HA N2 269, p. 9: "That is to say, these countries have ultimately adopted the German example of stabilization politics since May 1973 not because they or their political leaders like it. Not because they have realized that this is better in principle, but because they have had to experience in practice that we have fared better with it."

9. The economics ministry is reported to have studied a range of measures that might balance Germany's trade surplus. Its preference appears to be to encourage private investment rather than commit to public investment. A reduction of value-added tax in order to boost internal demand was dismissed as having only a negligible impact (Creutzburg 2017).

10. My calculations, based on the most recent release of UN Comtrade data (https://comtrade.un.org) at the time of writing (2019).

11. UN Comtrade. To measure exports in "manufactured goods," I use the Standard International Trade Classification (SITC) of the United Nations, Rev. 3, (5–8).

12. The enormous potential of China was emphasized by German business elites vis-à-vis the German state in the early 1950s (Bernardini 2018: 30).

13. In advanced manufacturing, Germany increased its share of regional value chain trade from 31.5 percent to 36.6 percent between 2000 and 2014, far above the single-digit figures of all other EU members. In 2014, about 40 percent of this trade was oriented toward global demand (Stöllinger et al. 2018: 27, 81).

14. Comparable data on German foreign direct investment disaggregated by selected host countries and sectors is available from 2010 and published annually by the German Central Bank: https://www.bundesbank.de/de/statistiken/aussen wirtschaft/direktinvestitionen/-/bestandsangaben-772320 (accessed 27 January 2020). "EU South" refers to Portugal, Italy, and Spain, as figures for Greece are not available at this level of detail. "EU East" refers to the Visegrád countries and Rumania.

15. Eurostat, "General Government Gross Debt," https://ec.europa.eu/euro-stat/databrowser/view/sdg_17_40/default/table?lang=en (accessed 20 May 2020).

16. Considering the eurozone to be unsustainable, Schäuble confided in Varoufakis that "the only way I can keep this thing together, the only way I can hold this thing together, is by greater discipline. Anyone who wants the euro must accept discipline. And it will be a much stronger eurozone if it is disciplined by Grexit" (Varoufakis 2017: 409).

17. Matthijs (2016) admits that there are multiple versions of ordoliberalism represented by different parts of German policy elites. This raises the question of why the most self-defeating course of action won out over more moderate alternatives. This in turn reveals the circular reasoning at work whereby explanans and explanandum are conflated. Why did "Germany . . . stick to a narrow version of its ordoliberal ideas, despite evidence that the resulting policies were systematically doing damage in material terms" (2016: 384)? In keeping with the demands of an *ideational* explanation, the only possible answer is that German policy elites were guided by harsh ordoliberal ideas.

18. In the 1940s and 1950s, price stability was only one of several goals that the German central bank pursued, and in the 1960s, when Keynesian ideas dominated the agenda, monetary policy aimed to support full employment (Richter 1999: 19–20).

19. For an especially comprehensive list, see Meiers (2015), who adds a focus on external surpluses.

20. The image of a coherent Anglo-Saxon bloc colliding with German economics may be misleading. For a qualification, see Braunberger (2015).

Conclusion

1. The countries of the Global South were largely excluded from the postwar project of embedded liberalism (for example, Steffek 2006; Connell and Dados 2014: 123). Most of them were still under colonial rule when this international order was negotiated. And even where and when they had achieved formal independence, many of them were deprived of the resources and autonomy to provide the forms of economic intervention and social protection that were needed at the domestic level in order to cushion the adverse effects of multilateral economic liberalization (Ruggie 2003: 94). Recognizing from the outset that "[t]he main problem with embedded liberalism is that it only works for industrialized countries" (Steffek 2006: 53), they originally envisioned and repeatedly asked for more far-reaching forms of global redistribution, regulation, and reform—most prominently in the movement for a New International Economic Order (Steffek 2006; Getachew 2019). These postcolonial demands for global justice came under attack at the same time as the more limited—in scope and aspiration—embedded liberal

compromise. A truly global history of the origins of neoliberalism that connects these experiences is beyond the reach of this book, but recent work along these lines centers on the 1970s as the watershed moment and the attack on democracy as its common denominator (Prashad 2012: 12; Slobodian 2018; Getachew 2019).

2. This fear is aptly captured in the title of the IMF's April 2016 World Economic Outlook, "Too Slow for Too Long" (IMF 2016).

References

Archival Sources

AdsD—Archiv der sozialen Demokratie (Archive of Social Democracy), Bonn
    DHS—Depository Horst Schulmann
HSA—Helmut Schmidt Archive
BAK—Bundesarchiv (Federal Archives), Koblenz
    B 102—Federal Ministry of Economics
    B 136—Federal Chancellery
BBk HA—Bundesbank, Historisches Archiv (German Federal Bank, Historical Archives), Frankfurt
    B 330—German Federal Bank
    N2—Personal papers, Otmar Emminger
    N4—Personal papers, Karl Otto Pöhl
FRUS—Foreign Relations of the United States, http://history.state.gov/historicaldocuments

    2001. *Foreign Relations of the United States, 1969–1976, Volume III, Foreign Economic Policy; International Monetary Policy, 1969–1972*, ed. Bruce Duncombe and David Patterson. Washington, DC: US Government Printing Office.

    2009. *Foreign Relations of the United States, 1969–1976, Volume XXXI, Foreign Economic Policy, 1973–1976*, ed. Kathleen Rasmussen and Edward Keefer. Washington, DC: US Government Printing Office.

    2013. *Foreign Relations of the United States, 1977–1980, Volume III, Foreign Economic Policy*, ed. Kathleen Rasmussen and Adam Howard. Washington, DC: US Government Printing Office.

GFPL—Gerald R. Ford Presidential Library, Ann Arbor, Michigan

Other Sources

Abdelal, Rawi. 2007. *Capital Rules: The Construction of Global Finance*. New York: Harvard University Press.

Abelshauser, Werner. 1987. "Freiheitlicher Korporatismus im Kaiserreich und in der Weimarer Republik." In *Die Weimarer Republik als Wohlfahrtsstaat: Zum Verhältnis von Wirtschafts- und Sozialpolitik in der Industriegesellschaft*, ed. Werner Abelshauser, 147–170. Stuttgart: Franz Steiner.

———. 2001. "Umbruch und Pertinenz: Das deutsche Produktionsregime in historischer Perspektive." *Geschichte und Gesellschaft* 27 (4): 503–523.

———. 2005. *Deutsche Wirtschaftsgeschichte seit 1945*. Munich: C.H. Beck.

———. 2006. "Der 'Rheinische Kapitalismus' im Kampf der Wirtschaftskulturen." In *Gibt es einen deutschen Kapitalismus? Tradition und globale Perspektiven der sozialen Marktwirtschaft*, ed. Volker Berghahn and Sigurt Vitols, 186–199. Frankfurt: Campus.

———. 2016. "Deutsche Wirtschaftspolitik zwischen europäischer Integration und Weltmarktorientierung." In *Das Bundeswirtschaftsministerium in der Ära der Sozialen Marktwirtschaft: Wirtschaftspolitik in Deutschland, 1917–1990, Volume IV*, ed. Werner Abelshauser, 482–581. Munich: De Gruyter.

Abse, Tobias. 2005. "Italy's Long Road to Austerity and the Paradoxes of Communism." In *Monetary Union in Crisis: The European Union as a Neo-Liberal Construction*, ed. Bernard Moss, 249–265. New York: Palgrave Macmillan.

Albert, Michel. 1993. *Capitalism Against Capitalism*. London: Whurr.

Allen, Christopher. 1989. "The Underdevelopment of Keynesianism in the Federal Republic of Germany." In *The Political Power of Economic Ideas: Keynesianism Across Nations*, ed. Peter Hall, 263–289. Princeton, NJ: Princeton University Press.

———. 2005. "'Ordoliberalism' Trumps Keynesianism: Economic Policy in the Federal Republic of Germany and the EU." In *Monetary Union in Crisis: The European Union as a Neo-Liberal Constitution*, ed. Bernard Moss, 199–221. New York: Palgrave Macmillan.

———. 2010. "Ideas, Institutions and Organized Capitalism: The German Model of Political Economy Twenty Years After Unification." *German Politics and Society* 28 (2): 130–150.

Allinson, Jamie, and Alexander Anievas. 2009. "The Uses and Abuses of Uneven and Combined Development: An Anatomy of a Concept." *Cambridge Review of International Affairs* 22 (1): 47–67.

Amable, Bruno. 2003. *The Diversity of Modern Capitalism*. Oxford: Oxford University Press.

Anievas, Alex. 2014. *Capital, the State, and War: Class Conflict and Geopolitics in the Thirty Years' Crisis, 1914–1945*. Ann Arbor: University of Michigan Press.

Anievas, Alexander, and Kerem Nişancıoğlu. 2015. *How the West Came to Rule: The Geopolitical Origins of Capitalism*. London: Pluto.

Aronson, Jonathan David. 1977. *Money and Power: Banks and the World Monetary System*. London: Sage.

Arrighi, Giovanni. 1994. *The Long Twentieth Century: Money, Power, and the Origins of Our Times*. New York: Verso.

———. 2005a. "Hegemony Unravelling 1." *New Left Review* 32 (March-April): 23–80.

———. 2005b. "Hegemony Unravelling 2." *New Left Review* 32 (May-June): 83–116.

———. 2007. *Adam Smith in Beijing: Lineages of the 21st Century*. London: Verso.

Art, David. 2015. "The German Rescue of the Eurozone: How Germany Is Getting the Europe It Always Wanted." *Political Science Quarterly* 130 (2): 181–212.

Arto, Iñaki, José Rueda-Cantuche, Antonio Amores, Erik Dietzenbacher, Nuno Sousa, Letizia Montinari, and Anil Markandya. 2015. *EU Exports to the World: Effects on Employment and Income*. Luxembourg: Publications Office of the European Union.

Ashman, Sam. 2009. "Capitalism, Uneven and Combined Development and the Transhistoric." *Cambridge Review of International Affairs* 22 (1): 29–46.

Axilrod, Stephen. 2005. "Commentary." *Federal Reserve of St. Louis Review* 87 (2, Part 2): 237–242.

Babb, Sarah. 2013. "The Washington Consensus as Transnational Policy Paradigm: Its Origins, Trajectory and Likely Successor." *Review of International Political Economy* 20 (2): 268–297.

Baker, Andrew. 1999. "Nebuleuse and the 'Internationalization of the State' in the UK? The Case of HM Treasury and the Bank of England." *Review of International Political Economy* 6 (1): 79–100.

Baldwin, Richard. 2016. *The Great Convergence: Information Technology and the New Globalization*. Cambridge, MA: Belknap.

Baldwin, Richard, and Javier Lopez-Gonzalez. 2015. "Supply-Chain Trade: A Portrait of Global Patterns and Several Testable Hypotheses." *The World Economy* 38 (11): 1682–1721.

Ban, Cornell. 2016. *Ruling Ideas: How Global Neoliberalism Goes Local*. Oxford: Oxford University Press.

Barker, Colin. 1978. "A Note on the Theory of Capitalist States." *Capital & Class* 4: 118–129.

———. 2006. "Beyond Trotsky: Extending Combined and Uneven Development." In *100 Years of Permanent Revolution: Results and Prospects*, ed. Bill Dunn and Hugo Radice, 72–87. London: Pluto.

Barrow, Clyde. 1993. *Critical Theories of the State: Marxist, Neo-Marxist, Post-Marxist*. Madison: University of Wisconsin Press.

———. 2008. "Ralph Miliband and the Instrumentalist Theory of the State: The (Mis)Construction of an Analytic Concept." In *Class, Power and the State in Capitalist Society: Essays on Ralph Miliband*, ed. Paul Wetherly, Clyde Barrow, and Peter Burnham, 84–108. London: Palgrave.

Bartlett, David, and Christian Roller. 2010. "German Exporters Amid the Global Recovery." *RSM International Talking Points*, July. http://www.rsmsingapore .sg/res_pub/German-Exporters-Amid-the-Global-Recovery-July2010.pdf (accessed 31 January 2016).

Basosi, Duccio. 2006. *Il governo del dollaro: Interdipendenza economica e potere statunitense negli anni di Richard Nixon, 1969–1973*. Florence: Polistampa.

———. 2010. "Principle or Power? Jimmy Carter's Ambivalent Endorsement of the European Monetary System, 1977–1979." *Journal of Transatlantic Studies* 8 (1): 6–18.

———. 2011. "The US, Western Europe and a Changing Monetary System." In *Europe in the International Arena During the 1970s: Entering a Different World*, ed. Antonio Varsori and Guia Migani, 99–116. Brussels: P.I.E. Peter Lang.

Beck, Mareike. 2019. *German Banking and the Rise of Financial Capitalism*. PhD diss., University of Sussex, Brighton, UK.

Beck, Stefan. 2015. *Vom Fordistischen zum Kompetitiven Merkantilismus*. Marburg: Metropolis.

Beck, Stefan, and Christoph Scherrer. 2010. "The German Economic Model Emerges Reinforced from the Crisis." *Global Labour Column*. http://column. global-labour-university.org/2010/08/german-economic-model-emerges. html (accessed 10 March 2016).

Beck, Thorsten, and Hans-Helmut Kotz, eds. 2017. *Ordoliberalism: A German Oddity?* London: CEPR Press.

Becker, Joachim. 2015. "German Neo-Mercantilism: Contradictions of a (Non-) Model." In *The German Model: Seen by Its Neighbours*, ed. Brigitte Unger, 237–250. London: SE.

Beise, Marc. 2017. "Jobs für Europa." *Süddeutsche Zeitung*, 15 June. http://www .sueddeutsche.de/wirtschaft/prognos-studie-jobs-fuer-europa-1.3546316 (accessed 2 October).

Belke, Ansgar. 2014. "Exit Strategies and Their Impact on the Euro Area: A Model Based View." *Ruhr Economic Papers* 467. http://www.rwi-essen.de /media/content/pages/publikationen/ruhr-economic-papers/ REP_14_467.pdf (accessed 25 March 2016).

Bellofiore, Riccardo, Francesco Garibaldo, and Joseph Halevi. 2010. "The Global Crisis and the Crisis of European Neomercantilism." In *Socialist Register 2011:*

The Crisis This Time, ed. Leo Panitch, Greg Albo, and Vivek Chibber, 120–147. London: Merlin.

Berghahn, Volker. 1986. *The Americanisation of West German Industry, 1945–1973.* Leamington Spa: Berg.

———. 1996. "German Big Business and the Quest for a European Economic Empire in the Twentieth Century." In *The Quest for Economic Empire: European Strategies of German Big Business in the Twentieth Century*, ed. Volker Berghahn, 1–34. Providence, RI: Berghahn Books.

———. 2006. "Das 'deutsche Kapitalismus-Modell' in Geschichte und Geschichtswissenschaft." In *Gibt es einen deutschen Kapitalismus? Tradition und globale Perspektiven der sozialen Marktwirtschaft*, ed. Volker Berghahn and Sigurt Vitols, 25–59. Frankfurt: Campus.

———. 2010a. "Ludwig Erhard, die Freiburger Schule und das 'Amerikanische Jahrhundert'." *Freiburg Discussion Papers on Constitutional Economics* 10 (1). http://hdl.handle.net/10419/51547 (accessed 23 April 2020).

———. 2010b. "The Debate on 'Americanization' Among Economic and Cultural Historians." *Cold War History* 10 (1): 107–130.

Berghahn, Volker, and Brigitte Young. 2013. "Reflections on Werner Bonefeld's 'Freedom and the Strong State: On German Ordoliberalism' and the Continuing Importance of the Ideas of Ordoliberalism to Understand Germany's (Contested) Role in Resolving the Eurozone Crisis." *New Political Economy* 18 (5): 768–778.

Bergsten, C. Fred, and C. Randall Henning. 1996. *Global Economic Leadership and the Group of Seven.* Washington, DC: Institute for International Economics.

Bernanke, Ben, and Ilian Mihov. 1997. "What Does the Bundesbank Target?" *European Economic Review* 41 (6): 1025–1053.

Bernardini, Giovanni. 2011. "The FRG and the Resistable Rise of the 'Historic Compromise' in Italy, 1974–1978." In *Europe in the International Arena During the 1970s: Entering a Different World*, ed. Antonio Varsori and Guia Migani, 317–338. Brussels: P.I.E. Peter Lang.

———. 2017. "Helmut Schmidt, the 'Renewal' of European Social Democracy, and the Roots of Neoliberal Globalization." In *Contesting Deregulation: Debates, Practices and Developments in the West Since the 1970s*, ed. Knud Andersen and Stefan Müller, 111–124. New York: Berghahn Books.

———. 2018. "Between Economic Interests and Political Constraints: The Federal Republic of Germany and the People's Republic of China During the Early Cold War." In *Roads to Reconciliation: People's Republic of China, Western Europe, and Italy During the Cold War, 1949–1971*, ed. Guido Samarani, Carla Meneguzzi Rostagni, and Sofia Graziana, 79–98. Venice: Edition Ca'Foscari.

Beyer, Andreas, Vitor Gaspar, Christina Gerberding, and Otmar Issing. 2008. "Opting Out of the Great Inflation: German Monetary Policy After the Breakdown of Bretton Woods." National Bureau of Economic Research Working Paper 14596. http://www.nber.org/papers/w14596 (accessed 23 September 2017).

Bibow, Jörg. 2004. "Investigating the Intellectual Origins of Euroland's Macroeconomic Policy Regime: Central Banking Institutions and Traditions in West Germany After the War." *The Levy Economics Institute of Bard College Working Paper Series* 406 (May).

———. 2009. "On the Origin and Rise of Central Bank Independence in West Germany." *European Journal of the History of Economic Thought* 16 (1): 155–190.

Biebricher, Thomas. 2013. "Europe and the Political Philosophy of Neoliberalism." *Contemporary Political Theory* 12 (4): 338–349.

Biebricher, Thomas, and Frieder Vogelmann. 2017. "Introduction." In *The Birth of Austerity: German Ordoliberalism and Contemporary Neoliberalism*, ed. Thomas Biebricher and Frieder Vogelmann, 1–22. New York: Rowman & Littlefield.

Bieler, Andreas, and Adam David Morton. 2001. *Social Forces in the Making of the New Europe: The Restructuring of European Social Relations in the Global Political Economy*. London: Palgrave.

Biven, W. Carl. 2002. *Jimmy Carter's Economy: Policy in an Age of Limits*. Chapel Hill: University of North Carolina Press.

Blackbourn, David, and Geoff Eley. 1984. *The Peculiarities of German History: Bourgeois Society and Politics in Nineteenth Century Germany*. New York: Oxford University Press.

Block, Fred. 1977. *The Origins of International Economic Disorder: A Study of United States International Monetary Policy from World War II to the Present*. Berkeley: University of California Press.

———. 1978. "Marxist Theories of the State in World Systems Analysis." In *Social Change in the Capitalist World System*, ed. Barbara Hockey Kaplan, 27–37. Beverly Hills, CA: Sage.

———. 1980. "Beyond Relative Autonomy: State Managers as Historical Subjects." In *Socialist Register 1980*, ed. Ralph Miliband and John Saville, 227–241. London: Merlin.

Blyth, Mark. 2002. *Great Transformations: Economic Ideas and Institutional Change in the Twentieth Century*. Cambridge, MA: Cambridge University Press.

———. 2013a. *Austerity: The History of a Dangerous Idea*. Oxford: Oxford University Press.

———. 2013b. "Austerity as Ideology: A Reply to My Critics." *Comparative European Politics* 11 (6): 737–751.

Bohle, Dorothee. 2018. "European Integration, Capitalist Diversity and Crises Trajectories on Europe's Eastern Periphery." *New Political Economy* 23 (2): 239–253.

Bond, Patrick, and Ana Garcia. 2015. *BRICS: An Anti-Capitalist Critique*. London: Pluto.

Bonefeld, Werner. 2012. "Freedom and the Strong State: On German Ordoliberalism." *New Political Economy* 17 (3): 1–24.

———. 2013. "Adam Smith and Ordoliberalism: On the Political Form of Market Liberty." *Review of International Studies* 39 (2): 233–250.

Booth, Alan, Joseph Melling, and Christoph Dartmann. 1997. "Institutions and Economic Growth: The Politics of Productivity in West Germany, Sweden, and the United Kingdom, 1945–1955." *The Journal of Economic History* 57 (2): 416–444.

Bordo, Michael, Owen Humpage, and Anna Schwartz. 2010. "US Intervention and the Early Dollar Float, 1973–1981." Federal Reserve Bank of Cleveland Working Paper 10–23. https://www.clevelandfed.org/en/newsroom-and -events/publications/working-papers/working-papers-archives/2010-work ing-papers/wp-1023-us-intervention-and-the-early-dollar-float-1973-1981 .aspx (accessed 23 September 2017).

Bordo, Michael, Dominique Simard, and Eugene White. 1994. "France and the Breakdown of the Bretton Woods International Monetary System: 1960–1968." *IMF Working Paper* 94/128. http://econpapers.repec.org/paper/ nbrnberwo/4642.htm (accessed 23 September 2017).

Borelli, Silvia Sciorilli, and Matthew Karnitschnig. 2020. "Italy's Future Is in German Hands." *Politico*, 2 April. https://www.politico.eu/article/coronavirus -italy-future-germany (accessed 20 May 2020).

Boyer, Robert. 2015. "The Success of Germany from a French Perspective: What Consequences for the Future of the European Union?" In *The German Model: Seen by Its Neighbours*, ed. Brigitte Unger, 201–236. London: SE.

Brackmann, Michael. 1993. *Vom Totalen Krieg zum Wirtschaftswunder: Die Vorgeschichte der westdeutschen Währungsreform 1948*. Essen: Klartext.

Brand, Ulrich, and Nicola Sekler. 2009. "Postneoliberalism: Catch-All Word or Valuable Analytical and Political Concept? Aims of a Beginning Debate." *Development Dialogue* 51: 5–13.

Braun, Benjamin, and Richard Deeg. 2019. "Strong Firms, Weak Banks: The Financial Consequences of Germany's Export-Led Growth Model." *German Politics* (26 December): 1–24.

Braun, Hans-Joachim. 1990. *The German Economy in the Twentieth Century*. London: Routledge.

Braunberger, Gerald. 2015. "Gespräche mit Ökonomen (9): Es gibt keinen An-gelsächsischen Block gegen Deutschland." *Frankfurter Allgemeine Zeitung*, 23 July. http://blogs.faz.net/fazit/2015/07/23/gespraeche-mit-oekonomen-es-gibt-keinen-angelsaechsischen-block-gegen-deutschland-6151 (accessed 2 November 2017).

Brenner, Robert. 2006. *The Economics of Global Turbulence: The Advanced Capitalist Economies from Long Boom to Long Downturn, 1945–2005*. London: Verso.

Brogi, Alessandro. 2011. *Confronting America: The Cold War Between the United States and the Communists in France and Italy*. Chapel Hill: University of North Carolina Press.

Bromley, Simon. 2003. "Reflections on Empire, Imperialism and United States Hegemony." *Historical Materialism* 11 (3): 17–68.

Bruff, Ian. 2011. "What About the Elephant in the Room? Varieties of Capitalism, Varieties in Capitalism." *New Political Economy* 16 (4): 481–500.

———. 2015. Germany and the Crisis: Steady as She Goes? In *The Future of Capitalism after the Financial Crisis: The Varieties of Capitalism Debate in the Age of Austerity*, ed. Richard Westra, Dennis Badeen, and Robert Albritton, 114–131. London: Routledge.

———. 2016. "Neoliberalism and Authoritarianism." In *The Handbook of Neoliberalism*, ed. Simon Springer, Kean Birch, and Julie MacLeavy, 107–117. New York: Routledge.

Bruff, Ian, and Matthias Ebenau. 2014. "Critical Political Economy and the Critique of Comparative Capitalisms Scholarship on Capitalist Diversity." *Capital & Class* 38 (1): 3–15.

Bruun, Hans Henrik. 2007. *Science, Values and Politics in Max Weber's Methodology*. Aldershot: Ashgate.

Bryant, Ralph, and Edith Hodgkinson. 1989. "Problems of International Cooperation." In *Can Nations Agree? Issues in International Economic Cooperation*, 1–11. Washington, DC: The Brookings Institution.

Buchheim, Christoph. 1999. "The Establishment of the Bank Deutscher Länder and the West German Currency Reform." In *Fifty Years of the Deutsche Mark: Central Bank and the Currency in Germany Since 1948*, ed. Deutsche Bundesbank, 55–96. Oxford, UK: Oxford University Press.

———. 2001. "Die Unabhängigkeit der Bundesbank: Folge eines amerikanischen Oktrois?" *Vierteljahreshefte für Zeitgeschichte* 49 (1): 1–30.

Bührer, Werner. 1990. "Erzwungene oder freiwillige Liberalisierung? Die USA, die OEEC und die Westdeutsche Außenhandelspolitik, 1949–1952." In *Vom Marshallplan Zur EWG: Die Eingliederung der Bundesrepublik in die Westliche Welt*, ed. Ludolf Herbst, Werner Bührer, and Hanno Sowade, 139–162. Munich: Oldenbourg.

Bulmer, Simon, and William Paterson. 2013. "Germany as the EU's Reluctant Hegemon." *Journal of European Public Policy* 20 (10): 1387–1405.

Bulpitt, Jim. 1986. "The Discipline of the New Democracy: Mrs Thatcher's Domestic Statecraft. *Political Studies* 34 (1): 19–39.

Burgin, Angus. 2012. *The Great Persuasion: Reinventing Free Markets Since the Depression.* Cambridge, MA: Harvard University Press.

Burk, Kathleen, and Alec Cairncross. 1992. *Goodbye, Great Britain: The 1976 IMF Crisis.* Avon, UK: Bath Press.

Buzan, Barry, and George Lawson. 2015. *The Global Transformation: History, Modernity and the Making of International Relations.* Cambridge, UK: Cambridge University Press.

Cafruny, Alan. 2015. "The European Crisis and the Rise of German Power." In *Asymmetric Crisis in Europe and Possible Futures*, ed. Johannes Jäger and Elisabeth Springler, 61–77. London: Routledge.

Cafruny, Alan, and Magnus Ryner, eds. 2003. *A Ruined Fortress? Neoliberal Hegemony and Transformation in Europe.* Lanham, MD: Rowman & Littlefield.

Callinicos, Alex. 2009. *Imperialism and Global Political Economy.* Cambridge, UK: Polity.

Cafruny, Alan, and Leila Simona Talani. 2019. "German Ordoliberalism and the Future of the EU." *Critical Sociology* 45 (7–8): 1011–1022.

Calleo, David. 1982. *The Imperious Economy.* Cambridge, MA: Harvard University Press.

Cameron, David. 1996. "Exchange Rate Politics in France, 1981–1983: The Regime-Defining Choices of the Mitterrand Presidency." In *The Mitterrand Era: Policy Alternatives and Political Mobilization in France*, ed. Anthony Daley, 56–82. London: Palgrave.

Carnoy, Martin. 1984. *The State and Political Theory.* Princeton, NJ: Princeton University Press.

Celi, Giuseppe, Andrea Ginzburg, Dario Guarascio, and Annamaria Simonazzi. 2018. *Crisis in the European Monetary Union: A Core-Periphery Perspective.* London: Routledge.

Cesaratto, Sergio, and Antonella Stirati. 2010. "Germany and the European and Global Crises." *International Journal of Political Economy* 39 (4): 56–86.

Clark, Timothy David. 2017. "Rethinking Chile's 'Chicago Boys': Neoliberal Technocrats or Revolutionary Vanguard?" *Third World Quarterly* 38 (6): 1350–1365.

Clarke, Simon. 1987. "Capitalist Crisis and the Rise of Monetarism." In *Socialist Register 1987: Conservatism in Britain and America: Rhetoric and Reality*, ed. Ralph Miliband, Leo Panitch, and John Saville, 393–427. London: Merlin.

Clauwaert, Stefan, and Isabelle Schömann. 2012. "The Crisis and National Labour Law Reforms: A Mapping Exercise." *European Trade Union Institute Working Paper* 4. http://www.etui.org/%20Publications2/Working-Papers/The-crisis-and-national-labour-law-reforms-a-mapping-exercise (accessed 31 August 2017).

Clift, Ben, and Jim Tomlinson. 2008. "Negotiating Credibility: Britain and the International Monetary Fund, 1956–1976." *Contemporary European History* 17 (4): 545–566.

Coates, David. 2000. *Models of Capitalism: Growth and Stagnation in the Modern Era.* London: Polity.

Cockett, Richard. 1995. *Thinking the Unthinkable: Think Tanks and the Economic Counter-Revolution, 1931–83.* London: Fontana.

Cohen, Benjamin. 2008. *International Political Economy: An Intellectual History.* Princeton, NJ: Princeton University Press.

Cohen, Roger. 2015. "The German Question Redux." *New York Times,* 13 July 2015. https://www.nytimes.com/2015/07/14/opinion/roger-cohen-the-german-question-redux.html (accessed 23 September 2017).

Connell, Raewyn, and Nour Dados. 2014. "Where in the World Does Neoliberalism Come From? The Market Agenda in Southern Perspective." *Theory & Society* 43: 117–138.

Conze, Vanessa. 2005a. "Abendland gegen Amerika! 'Europa' als antiamerikanisches Konzept im westeuropäischen Konservatismus, 1950–1970: Das CEDI und die Idee des 'Abendlandes'." In *Antiamerikanismus im 20. Jahrhundert: Studien zu Ost- und Westeuropa,* ed. Jan Behrends, Árpád von Klimó, and Patrice Poutrus, 204–224. Bonn: Dietz.

———. 2005b. *Das Europa der Deutschen: Ideen von Europa in Deutschland zwischen Reichstradition und Westorientierung, 1920–1970.* Munich: Oldenbourg.

Cowie, Jefferson. 2010. *Stayin' Alive: The 1970s and the Last Days of the Working Class.* New York: New Press.

Cox, Robert. 1981. "Social Forces, States and World Orders: Beyond International Relations Theory." *Millennium: Journal of International Studies* 10 (2): 126–155.

———. 1983. "Gramsci, Hegemony and International Relations: An Essay in Method." *Millennium: Journal of International Studies* 12 (2): 162–175.

Creutzburg, Dietrich. 2017. "Wirtschaftsministerium prüft Senkung der Mehrwertsteuer." *Frankfurter Allgemeine Zeitung,* 11 June. http://www.faz.net/aktuell/wirtschaft/wirtschaftspolitik/gegen-exportueberschuss-wirtschaftsministerium-prueft-senkung-der-mehrwertsteuer-15056837.html (accessed 31 August 2017).

Crotty, James, and Gerald Epstein. 1996. "In Defence of Capital Controls." In *Socialist Register 1996: Are There Alternatives?,* ed. Leo Panitch, 118–149. London: Merlin.

Crouch, Colin. 1978. "Inflation and the Political Organization of Economic Interests." In *The Political Economy of Inflation*, ed. Fred Hirsch and John Goldthorpe, 217–239. London: Martin Robertson.

———. 2011. *The Strange Non-Death of Neoliberalism.* London: Polity.

Crouch, Colin, and Wolfgang Streeck, eds. 1997. *Political Economy of Modern Capitalism: Mapping Convergence and Diversity.* London: Sage.

Crozier, Michel, Samuel Huntington, and Jåoji Watanuki. 1975. *The Crisis of Democracy: Report on the Governability of Democracies to the Trilateral Commission.* New York: New York University Press.

Culpepper, Pepper. 2015. "Structural Power and Political Science in the Post-Crisis Era." *Business & Politics* 17 (3): 391–409.

Darwin, John. 2009. *The Empire Project: The Rise and Fall of the British World-System, 1830–1970.* Cambridge, UK: Cambridge University Press.

De Cecco, Marcello. 1976. "L'economia tedesca e il bastone americano." *La Repubblica,* 22 July.

Deeg, Richard. 2003. "On the Development of Universal Banking in Germany." In *The Origins of National Financial Systems: Alexander Gerschenkron Reconsidered,* ed. Douglas Forsyth and Daniel Verdier, 87–104. London: Routledge.

———. 2010. "Industry and Finance in Germany Since Unification." *German Politics and Society* 28 (2): 116–129.

Delhaes-Guenther, Linda. 2003. *Erfolgsfaktoren des westdeutschen Exports in den 1950er und 1960er Jahren.* Dortmund: Gesellschaft für Westfälische Wirtschaftsgeschichte.

Deppe, Frank, David Salomon, and Ingar Solty. 2011. *Imperialismus.* Cologne: PapyRossa.

Der Spiegel. 1978. "Fusionen: Alles beim alten." *Der Spiegel* 40 (2 October): 60–65. https://www.spiegel.de/spiegel/print/d-40605656.html (accessed 4 May 2020).

Deubner, Christian. 1984. "Change and Internationalization in Industry: Toward a Sectoral Interpretation of West German Politics." *International Organization* 38 (3): 501–535.

Deutsche Bundesbank. 2015. "Weidmann: Do Not Artificially Weaken German Competitiveness." https://www.bundesbank.de/Redaktion/EN/Topics/2015/2015_04_20_weidmann_do_not_artificially_weaken_german_competitiveness.html (accessed 2 September 2017).

Devine, Pat. 2007. "The 1970s and After: The Political Economy of Inflation and the Crisis of Social Democracy." In *Reading Karl Polanyi for the Twenty-First Century: Market Economy as a Political Project,* ed. Ayşe Buğra and Kaan Ağartan, 33–47. New York: Palgrave Macmillan.

Dickhaus, Monika. 1996. *Die Bundesbank im Westeuropäischen Wiederaufbau: Die*

Internationale Währungspolitik der Bundesrepublik Deutschland 1948 bis 1958. Munich: Oldenbourg.

DIHK [Deutscher Industrie- und Handelskammertag (Association of German Chambers of Commerce and Industry)]. 2014. "Auslandsengagement steigt—besonders in Europa." Berlin. https://www.ihk-krefeld.de/de/media/pdf/international/auslandsinvestitionen-in-der-industrie-fruehjahr-2014.pdf (accessed 6 February 2020).

———. 2015. "Europa punktet erneut: Kostendruck wieder wichtiger: Auslandsinvestitionen in der Industrie." Berlin. http://www.dihk.de/ressourcen/downloads/auslandsinvestitionen-15.pdf (accessed 30 January 2016).

———. 2017. "Auslandsinvestitionen 2017 so hoch wie nie zuvor." Berlin. https://www.ihk-nuernberg.de/de/media/PDF/International/publikationen/dihk-auslandsinvestitionen-20172.pdf (accessed 6 February 2020).

Dixon, Keith. 2000. *Die Evangelisten des Marktes. Die britischen Intellektuellen und der Thatcherismus.* Konstanz: Universitätsverlag Konstanz.

Dobbs, Richard, Susan Lund, Jonathan Woetzel and Mina Mutafchieva. 2015. "Debt and (Not Much) Deleveraging." *McKinsey Global Institute Report*, 1 February. http://www.mckinsey.com/global-themes/employment-and-growth/debt-and-not-much-deleveraging (accessed 10 April 2016).

Dombret, Andreas. 2014a. "What Is Going on in Europe? The View from Within." Speech at the New York Stock Exchange, 26 March. https://www.bundesbank.de/Redaktion/EN/ Reden/2014/2014_03_26_dombret.html (accessed 30 January 2016).

———. 2014b. "The 'Too Big to Fail' Problem and the Roots of International Cooperation." Speech at a reception to bid farewell to Winfried Liedtke, financial attaché, and to welcome his successor, Thomas Notheis, Beijing, 29 October. https://www.bundesbank.de/Redaktion/EN/Reden/2014/2014_10_28_dombret.html (accessed 12 May 2015).

Dörrenbächer, Christoph. 2004. "Fleeing or Exporting the German Model? The Internationalization of German Multinationals in the 1990s." *Competition and Change* 8 (4): 443–456.

Drezner, Daniel. 2014. *The System Worked: How the World Stopped Another Great Depression.* New York: Oxford University Press.

Duchêne, François, Kinhide Mushakoji, and Henry Owen. 1974. "The Crisis of International Cooperation." *Trilateral Commission Task Force Report* 2. New York: Trilateral Commission.

Dullien, Sebastian, and Ulrike Guérot. 2012. "The Long Shadow of Ordoliberalism: Germany's Approach to the Euro Crisis." *European Council of Foreign Relations Policy Brief.* London.

Duménil, Gérard, and Dominique Lévy. 2004. *Capital Resurgent: Roots of the Neoliberal Revolution.* Cambridge, MA: Harvard University Press.

———. 2005. "From Prosperity to Neoliberalism: Europe Before and After the Structural Crisis of the 1970s." 10 May. http://www.cepremap.fr/membres /dlevy/dle2002d.pdf (accessed 23 September 2017).

Dyson, Kenneth. 2010. "Norman's Lament: The Greek and Euro Area Crisis in Historical Perspective." *New Political Economy* 15 (4): 597–608.

———. 2017. "Ordoliberalism as Tradition and Ideology." In *Ordoliberalism: Law and the Rule of Economics*, ed. Josef Hien and Christian Joerges, 87–100. Oxford: Hart.

Dyson, Kenneth, and Kevin Featherstone. 1999. *The Road to Maastricht*. London: Oxford University Press.

Ebenau, Matthias, Ian Bruff, and Christian May. 2015. *Comparative Capitalisms Research: Critical and Global Perspectives*. London: Palgrave.

Eichengreen, Barry. 2000. "From Benign Neglect to Malign Preoccupation: US Balance of Payments Policy in the 1960s." In *Economic Events, Ideas, and Policies: The 1960s and After*, ed. George Perry and James Tobin, 185–242. Washington, DC: The Brookings Institution.

———. 2004. "Review of Francis Gavin. 'Gold, Dollars, and Power: The Politics of International Monetary Relations, 1958–1971'." *The American Historical Review* 109 (5): 1542–1543.

———. 2007. *Global Imbalances and the Lessons of Bretton Woods*. Cambridge, MA: MIT Press.

———. 2008. *Globalizing Capital: A History of the International Monetary System*. 2nd ed. Princeton, NJ: Princeton University Press.

———. 2011. *Exorbitant Privilege: The Rise and Fall of the Dollar and the Future of the International Monetary System*. New York: Oxford University Press.

Eicker-Wolf, Kai. 2003. *Vom hydraulischen Keynesianismus zur Radikalen Politischen Ökonomie*. Marburg: Marburger Institut für Wirtschafts- und Politikforschung.

Elliott, Larry. 2015. "Bank of England Governor Attacks Eurozone Austerity." *Guardian*, 28 January. https://www.theguardian.com/business/2015 /jan/28/bank-england-governor-attacks-eurozone-austerity (accessed 11 June 2017).

Emminger, Otmar. 1986. *D-Mark, Dollar, Währungskrisen*. Stuttgart: Deutsche Verlags-Anstalt.

Engdahl, F. William. 2004. *A Century of War: Anglo-American Oil Politics and the New World Order*. London: Pluto.

Epstein, Gerald, and Arjun Jayadev. 2005. "The Rise of Rentier Incomes in OECD Countries: Financialization, Central Bank Policy and Labor Solidarity." In *Financialization and the World Economy*, ed. Gerald Epstein, 46–76. Cheltenham, UK: Edward Elgar.

Erker, Paul. 1999. "Einleitung: Industrie-Eliten im 20. Jahrhundert." In *Deutsche

Unternehmer zwischen Kriegswirtschaft und Wiederaufbau: Studien zur Erfahrungsbildung von Industrie-Eliten, ed. Paul Erker and Toni Pierenkemper, 1–18. Munich: Oldenbourg.

Esser, Josef. 1982. *Gewerkschaften in der Krise*. Frankfurt: Suhrkamp.

Esser, Josef, and Wolfgang Fach, with Kenneth Dyson. 1983. "'Social Market' and Modernization Policy: West Germany." In *Industrial Crisis: A Comparative Study of the State and Industry*, ed. Kenneth Dyson and Stephen Wilks, 102–127. Oxford: Martin Robertson.

Euromonitor International. 2017a. "Wage per Hour." http://euromonitor.com (accessed 2 October 2017).

———. 2017b. "Wage per Hour in Manufacturing." http://euromonitor.com (accessed 2 October 2017).

Evans, Eric. 2013. *Thatcher and Thatcherism*. 3rd ed. London: Routledge.

Farrell, Henry, and John Quiggin. 2012. "Consensus, Dissensus and Economic Ideas: The Rise and Fall of Keynesianism During the Economic Crisis." Unpublished manuscript, 9 March. http://www.henryfarrell.net/Keynes.pdf (accessed 31 August 2017).

FAZ (Frankfurter Allgemeine Zeitung). 2017. "Staatsschulden sinken auf weniger als 2 Billionen Euro." *Frankfurter Allgemeine Zeitung*, 29 June. http://www.faz.net/aktuell/wirtschaft/wirtschaftspolitik/erstmals-seit-jahren-staatsschulden-sinken-auf-weniger-als-2-billionen-euro-15082689.html (accessed 7 August 2017).

Fear, Jeffrey. 2005. *Organizing Control: August Thyssen and the Construction of German Corporate Management*. Cambridge, MA: Harvard University Press.

———. 2006. "Streaming Knowledge: A Hidden History of Codetermination: The Schmalenbach Society and the Dinkelbach School of German Management." *Harvard Business School Working Paper Series* 6 (42).

Feld, Lars, Ekkehard Köhler, and Daniel Nienteidt. 2015. "Ordoliberalism, Pragmatism and the Eurozone Crisis: How the German Tradition Shaped Economic Policy in Europe." *CESifo Working Papers* 5368. Munich: Center for Economic Studies.

———. 2017. "The 'Dark Ages of German Macroeconomics' and Other Alleged Shortfalls in German Economic Thought." In *Ordoliberalism: A German Oddity?*, ed. Thorsten Beck and Hans-Helmut Kotz, 41–52. London: CEPR Press.

Fleming, Sam, and Mehreen Khan. 2020. "Brussels Warns Coronavirus Crisis Threatens Eurozone's Stability." *Financial Times*, 6 May. https://www.ft.com/content/147044ea-a019-49cb-8cb1-d8660a63c7ec (accessed 11 May 2020).

Fourcade-Gourinchas, Marion, and Sarah Babb. 2002. "The Rebirth of the Liberal Creed: Paths to Neoliberalism in Four Countries." *American Journal of Sociology* 108 (3): 533–579.

Franzese, Robert, and Peter Hall. 2000. "Institutional Dimensions of Coordinating Wage Bargaining and Monetary Policy" In *Unions, Employers, and Central Banks: Macroeconomic Coordination and Institutional Change in Social Market Economies*, ed. Torben Iversen, Janus Pontusson, and David Soskice, 173–204. New York: Cambridge University Press.

Frasher, Michelle. 2014. *Transatlantic Politics and the Transformation of the International Monetary System*. London: Routledge.

Fratzscher, Marcel. 2018. *The Germany Illusion: Between Economic Euphoria and Despair*. New York: Oxford University Press.

Frieden, Jeffry. 1996. "Economic Integration and the Politics of Monetary Policy in the United States." In *Internationalization and Domestic Politics*, ed. Robert Keohane and Helen Milner, 108–136. Cambridge, UK: Cambridge University Press.

———. 2006. *Global Capitalism: Its Fall and Rise in the Twentieth Century*. New York: W.W. Norton.

Friedman, Milton. 1963. *Inflation: Causes and Consequences*. Bombay: Asia Publishing House.

———. 1983. "What Could Reasonably Have Been Expected from Monetarism: The United States." Paper presented at the Mont Pelerin Society meeting in Vancouver, Canada, 29 August. http://0055d26.netsolhost.com/friedman/pdfs/other_academia/MP.08.29.1983.pdf (accessed 24 August 2013).

Galbraith, James. 2016. *Welcome to the Poisoned Chalice: The Destruction of Greece and the Future of Europe*. London: Yale University Press.

Gallagher, John, and Ronald Robinson. 1953. "The Imperialism of Free Trade." *The Economic History Review* 6 (1): 1–15.

Gamble, Andrew. 1979. "The Free Economy and the Strong State." In *Socialist Register 1979*, ed. Ralph Miliband and John Saville, 1–25. London: Merlin.

Garavini, Giuliano, and Francesco Petrini. 2011. "Continuity or Change? The 1973 Oil Crisis Reconsidered." In *Europe in the International Arena During the 1970s: Entering a Different World*, ed. Antonio Varsori and Guia Migani, 211–230. Brussels: P.I.E. Peter Lang.

Garber, Peter. 1993. "The Collapse of the Bretton Woods Fixed Exchange-Rate System." In *A Retrospective on the Bretton Woods System: Lessons for International Monetary Reform*, ed. Michael Bordo and Barry Eichengreen, 461–494. Chicago: University of Chicago Press.

Gavin, Francis. 2004. *Gold, Dollars, and Power: The Politics of International Monetary Relations, 1958–1971*. Chapel Hill: University of North Carolina Press.

Geiger, Tim. 2008. *Atlantiker gegen Gaullisten: Außenpolitischer Konflikt und innerparteilicher Machtkampf in der CDU/CSU 1958–1969*. Munich: Oldenbourg.

Germann, Julian. 2014a. "German 'Grand Strategy' and the Rise of Neoliberalism." *International Studies Quarterly* 58 (4): 706–716.

———. 2014b. "State-Led or Capital-Driven? The Fall of Bretton Woods and the German Currency Float Reconsidered." *New Political Economy* 19 (5): 769–789.

———. 2018. "Beyond 'Geo-Economics': Advanced Unevenness and the Anatomy of German Austerity." *European Journal of International Relations* 24 (3): 590–613.

Gerschenkron, Alexander. 1962. *Economic Backwardness in Historical Perspective: A Book of Essays*. Cambridge, MA: Belknap.

———. 1966 [1945]. *Bread and Democracy in Germany*. New York: H. Fertig.

Getachew, Adom. 2019. *Worldmaking After Empire: The Rise and Fall of Self-Determination*. Princeton, NJ: Princeton University Press.

Giersch, Herbert, Karl-Heinz Paqué, and Holger Schmieding. 1992. *The Fading Miracle: Four Decades of Market Economy in Germany*. Cambridge, MA: Cambridge University Press.

Gill, Stephen. 1989. "American Perceptions and Policies." In *Atlantic Relations: Beyond the Reagan Era*, ed. Stephen Gill, 14–39. New York: St. Martin's Press.

———. 1990. *American Hegemony and the Trilateral Commission*. New York: Cambridge University Press.

———. 1992. "Economic Globalization and the Internationalization of Authority: Limits and Contradictions." *Geoforum* 23 (3): 269–283.

———. ed. 1993a. *Gramsci, Historical Materialism, and International Relations*. New York: Cambridge University Press.

———. 1993b. "Epistemology, Ontology and the Italian School." In *Gramsci, Historical Materialism and International Relations*, 21–48. Cambridge, UK: Cambridge University Press.

———. 1995. "Globalisation, Market Civilisation, and Disciplinary Neoliberalism." *Millennium: Journal of International Studies* 24 (3): 399–423.

———. 1999. "Structural Changes in Multilateralism: The G-7 Nexus and the Global Crisis." In *Innovation in Multilateralism*, 113–165. Tokyo: United Nations University Press.

———. 2008. *Power and Resistance in the New World Order*. 2nd ed. New York: Palgrave Macmillan.

Gill, Stephen, and David Law. 1989. "Global Hegemony and the Structural Power of Capital." *International Studies Quarterly* 33 (4): 475–499.

Gill, Stephen, and Ingar Solty. 2013. "Die organischen Krisen des Kapitalismus und die Demokratiefrage." *Juridikum: Zeitschrift für Kritik, Recht, Gesellschaft* 1: 51–65.

Gilpin, Robert. 1975. *U.S. Power and the Multinational Corporation: The Political Economy of Foreign Direct Investment*. New York: Basic Books.

———. 1981. *War and Change in World Politics*. New York: Cambridge University Press.

———. 1987. *The Political Economy of International Relations*. Princeton, NJ: Princeton University Press.

———. 2000. *The Challenge of Global Capitalism: The World Economy in the Twenty-First Century*. Princeton, NJ: Princeton University Press.

Goldthorpe, John. 1978. "The Current Inflation: Towards a Sociological Account." In *The Political Economy of Inflation*, ed. Fred Hirsch and John Goldthorpe, 186–214. London: Martin Robertson.

Goodman, John. 1992. *Monetary Sovereignty: The Politics of Central Banking in Western Europe*. Ithaca, NY: Cornell University Press.

Gourevitch, Peter. 1986. *Politics in Hard Times: Comparative Responses to International Economic Crises*. Ithaca, NY: Cornell University Press.

Gowa, Joanne. 1983. *Closing the Gold Window: Domestic Politics and the End of Bretton Woods*. Ithaca, NY: Cornell University Press.

———. 1984. "State Power, State Policy: Explaining the Decision to Close the Gold Window." *Politics & Society* 13 (1): 91–117.

Gowan, Peter. 1999. *The Global Gamble: Washington's Faustian Bid for World Dominance*. London: Verso.

———. 2001. "Explaining the American Boom: The Roles of 'Globalisation' and United States Global Power." *New Political Economy* 6 (3): 359–374.

———. 2002. "A Calculus of Power." *New Left Review* 16 (July-August): 47–67.

———. 2003. "The American Campaign for Global Sovereignty." In *Socialist Register 2003: Fighting Identities*, ed. Leo Panitch and Colin Leys, 1–27. London: Merlin.

———. 2013. "Economics and Politics Within the Capitalist Core and the Debate on the New Imperialism." *Journal of Global Faultlines* 1 (1): 5–33.

Gräf, Bernhard, Jochen Möbert, Heiko Peters, and Stefan Schneider. 2013. "Focus Germany: Structural Improvements Support Exceptional Position." *Deutsche Bank Research* (1 July). Frankfurt: Deutsche Bank.

Gramsci, Antonio. 1971. *Selections from the Prison Notebooks*. New York: International Publishers.

Granieri, Ronald. 2004. *The Ambivalent Alliance: Konrad Adenauer, the CDU/CSU, and the West, 1949–1966*. New York: Berghahn Books.

Gray, Kevin, and Craig Murphy. 2013. "Introduction: Rising Powers and the Future of Global Governance." *Third World Quarterly* 34 (2): 183–193.

Gray, William Glenn. 2007. "Floating the System: Germany, the United States, and the Breakdown of Bretton Woods, 1969–1973." *Diplomatic History* 31 (2): 295–323.

———. 2010. "Toward a 'Community of Stability'? The Deutsche Mark Between European and Atlantic Priorities, 1968–1973." In *The Strained Alliance:*

US-European Relations from Nixon to Carter, ed. Matthias Schulz and Thomas Schwartz, 145–167. New York: Cambridge University Press.

Green, Jeremy. 2012. "Uneven and Combined Development and the Anglo-German Prelude to World War I." *European Journal of International Relations* 18 (2): 345–368.

Greider, William. 1987. *Secrets of the Temple: How the Federal Reserve Runs the Country*. New York: Simon & Schuster.

Gross, Stephen. 2015. *Export Empire: German Soft Power in Southeastern Europe, 1890–1945*. New York: Cambridge University Press.

Gruber, Lloyd. 2000. *Ruling the World: Power Politics and the Rise of Supranational Institutions*. Princeton, NJ: Princeton University Press.

Grunenberg, Nina. 2008. *Die Wundertäter: Netzwerke der deutschen Wirtschaft, 1942–1966*. Munich: Siedler.

The Guardian. 2001. "Saudi Dove in the Oil Slick," 14 January. http://www.theguardian.com/business/2001/jan/14/globalrecession.oilandpetrol (accessed 20 August 2013).

Guerrieri, Paolo, and Pier Carlo Padoan. 1988. "International Cooperation and the Role of Macroeconomic Regimes." In *The Political Economy of International Cooperation*, ed. Paolo Guerrieri and Pier Carlo Padoan, 1–27. New York: Croom Helm.

Halevi, Joseph. 2019. "From the EMS to the EMU and . . . to China." *Institute for New Economic Thinking Working Papers* 102. https://www.ineteconomics.org/uploads/papers/WP_102-Halevi.pdf (accessed 31 January 2020).

Hall, Peter. 1989. *The Political Power of Economic Ideas: Keynesianism Across Nations*. Princeton, NJ: Princeton University Press.

———. 1992. "The Movement from Keynesianism to Monetarism: Institutional Analysis and British Economic Policy in the 1970s." In *Structuring Politics: Historical Institutionalism in Comparative Analysis*, ed. Sven Steinmo, Kathleen Thelen, and Frank Longstreth, 90–113. New York: Cambridge University Press.

———. 1993. "Policy Paradigms, Social Learning, and the State: The Case of Economic Policymaking in Britain." *Comparative Politics* 25 (3): 275–296.

———. 2015. "The Fate of the German Model." In *The German Model: Seen by Its Neighbours*, ed. Brigitte Unger, 43–62. London: SE.

———. 2018. "Varieties of Capitalism in Light of the Euro Crisis." *Journal of European Public Policy* 25 (1): 7–30.

Hall, Peter, and Michèle Lamont. 2013. "Introduction." In *Social Resilience in the Neoliberal Era*, ed. Peter Hall and Michèle Lamont, 1–34. New York: Cambridge University Press.

Hall, Peter, and David Soskice, eds. 2001. *Varieties of Capitalism: The Institutional Foundations of Comparative Advantage*. Oxford: Oxford University Press.

Hamilton, Arran, and Michael Oliver. 2007. "Downhill from Devaluation: The Battle for Sterling, 1968–72." *The Economic History Review* 60 (3): 486–512.

Hancké, Bob, ed. 2009. *Debating Varieties of Capitalism: A Reader*. London: Oxford University Press.

Hanhimäki, Jussi. 2004. *The Flawed Architect: Henry Kissinger and American Foreign Policy*. New York: Oxford University Press.

Hansakul, Syetarn, and Hannah Levinger. 2014. "China-EU Relations: Gearing Up for Growth." *Deutsche Bank Research* (31 July). Frankfurt: Deutsche Bank.

Harmon, Mark. 1997. *The British Labour Government and the 1976 IMF Crisis*. Basingstoke, UK: Macmillan.

Harvey, David. 2005. *A Brief History of Neoliberalism*. New York: Oxford University Press.

Hassel, Anke. 2014. "The Paradox of Liberalization: Understanding Dualism and the Recovery of the German Political Economy." *British Journal of Industrial Relations* 52 (1): 57–81.

———. 2015. "The German Model in Transition." In *The German Model: Seen by its Neighbours*, ed. Brigitte Unger, 105–134. London: Social Europe.

Hassel, Anke, and Cristof Schiller. 2010. *Der Fall Hartz IV: Wie es zur Agenda 2010 kam und wie es weitergeht*. Frankfurt: Campus.

Hawley, James. 1983. "Interests, State Foreign Economic Policy and the World System: The Case of the U.S. Capital Controls, 1961–1974." In *Foreign Policy and the Modern World System*, ed. Pat McGowan and Charles W. Kegley Jr., 223–254. Beverly Hills, CA: Sage.

———. 1984. "Protecting Capital from Itself: US Attempts to Regulate the Eurocurrency System." *International Organization* 38 (1): 131–165.

———. 1987. *Dollars and Borders: U.S. Government Attempts to Restrict Capital Flows, 1960–1980*. New York: M.E. Sharpe.

Hay, Colin. 1992. "Housing Policy in Transition: From the Post-War Settlement Towards 'Thatcherite' Hegemony." *Capital & Class* 16 (1): 27–64.

Heidemann, Paul. 2014. "Bulletproof Neoliberalism." *Jacobin*, 6 January. https://www.jacobinmag.com/2014/06/bulletproof-neoliberalism (accessed 30 April 2020).

Hein, Eckhard, and Achim Truger. 2010. "Finance-Dominated Capitalism in Crisis: The Case for a Keynesian New Deal at the European and the Global Level." *Institute for International Political Economy Berlin Working Paper* 6. http://www.ipe-berlin.org/fileadmin/downloads/working_paper/ipe_work ing_paper_06.pdf (accessed 23 September 2017).

Heine, Frederic, and Thomas Sablowski. 2016. "Monetary Union Unravelling? Trade and Capital Relations, Causes of the Crisis and Development Perspectives of the Euro Area." Berlin: Rosa Luxemburg Stiftung.

Heisenberg, Dorothee. 1999. *The Mark of the Bundesbank: Germany's Role in European Monetary Cooperation*. Boulder, CO: Lynne Rienner.

Helleiner, Eric. 1994. *States and the Reemergence of Global Finance: From Bretton Woods to the 1990s*. Ithaca, NY: Cornell University Press.

———. 1995. "Explaining the Globalization of Financial Markets: Bringing States Back In." *Review of International Political Economy* 2 (2): 315–341.

———. 2003. "The Southern Side of 'Embedded Liberalism': America's Unorthodox Money Doctoring During the Early Post-1945 Years." In *Money Doctors: The Experience of International Financial Advising, 1850–2000*, ed. Marc Flandreu, 249–275. London: Routledge.

———. 2005. "A Fixation with Floating: The Politics of Canada's Exchange Rate Regime." *Canadian Journal of Political Science/Revue Canadienne de Science Politique* 38 (1): 23–44.

Henning, C. Randall. 1994. *Currencies and Politics in the United States, Germany, and Japan*. Washington, DC: Peterson Institute.

———. 1998. "Systemic Conflict and Regional Monetary Integration: The Case of Europe." *International Organization* 52 (3): 537–573.

Herr, Hansjörg, and Klaus Voy. 1990. *Währungskonkurrenz und Deregulierung der Weltwirtschaft*. Marburg: Metropolis.

Herrigel, Gary. 1996. *Industrial Constructions: The Sources of German Industrial Power*. New York: Cambridge University Press.

Hetzel, Robert. 2002. "German Monetary History in the Second Half of the Twentieth Century: From the Deutsche Mark to the Euro." *Federal Reserve Bank of Richmond Economic Quarterly* 88 (2): 29–64.

———. 2008. *The Monetary Policy of the Federal Reserve: A History*. Cambridge, MA: Cambridge University Press.

Hickson, Kevin. 2005. *The IMF Crisis of 1976 and British Politics*. London: I.B. Tauris.

Hien, Josef. 2013. "The Ordoliberalism That Never Was." *Contemporary Critical Theory* 12 (4): 349–358.

Hien, Josef, and Christian Joerges, eds. 2018. *Ordoliberalism: Law and the Rule of Economics*. Oxford: Hart.

Hillebrand, Rainer. 2015. "Germany and Its Eurozone Crisis Policy: The Impact of the Country's Ordoliberal Heritage." *German Politics and Society* 33 (1/2): 6–24.

Hirsch, Joachim. 1995. *Der nationale Wettbewerbsstaat: Staat, Demokratie und Politik im globalen Kapitalismus*. Berlin: Edition ID-Archiv.

Hiscox, Michael. 2005. "The Domestic Sources of Foreign Economic Policy." In *Global Political Economy*, ed. John Ravenhill, 50–83. London: Oxford.

Hoffmeyer, Erik. 1993. *The International Monetary System: An Essay in Interpretation.* New York: North-Holland.

Hollingsworth, J. Rogers, and Robert Boyer. 1997. *Contemporary Capitalism: The Embeddedness of Institutions.* New York: Cambridge University Press.

Holmwood, John, and Alexander Stewart. 1991. *Explanation and Social Theory.* New York: St. Martin's Press.

Holtfrerich, Carl-Ludwig. 1999. "Monetary Policy Under Fixed Exchange Rates, 1948–1970." In *Fifty Years of the Deutsche Mark: Central Bank and the Currency in Germany Since 1948,* ed. Deutsche Bundesbank, 307–401. Oxford: Oxford University Press.

———. 2008. "Monetary Policy in Germany Since 1948: National Tradition, International Best Practice or Ideology?" In *Central Banks as Economic Institutions,* ed. J. P. Touffut, 23–51. Cheltenham, UK: Edward Elgar.

Holtham, Gerald. 1989. "German Macroeconomic Policy and the 1978 Bonn Summit." In *Can Nations Agree? Issues in International Economic Cooperation,* 141–177. Washington, DC: The Brookings Institution.

Höpner, Martin, and Alexander Spielau. 2018. "Better Than the Euro? The European Monetary System (1979–1998)." *New Political Economy* 23 (2): 160–173.

Howarth, David. 2016. "Raymond Barre: Modernizing France Through European Monetary Cooperation." In *Architects of the Euro: Intellectuals in the Making of European Monetary Union,* ed. Kenneth Dyson and Ivo Maes, 75–92. London: Oxford University Press.

Hudson, Michael. 1972. *Super Imperialism: The Economic Strategy of American Empire.* New York: Holt, Rinehart and Winston.

———. 1977. *Global Fracture: The New International Economic Order.* New York: Harper & Row.

———. 2003. *Super Imperialism: The Economic Strategy of American Empire.* 2nd ed. London: Pluto.

Hughes, Matthieu. 2016. *The Peculiarities of Universal Banking: Politics, Economic and Social Struggle in the Making of German Finance.* PhD diss., University of Sussex, Brighton, UK.

Hübner, Kurt. 2015. "Europeanisation and Globalisation as Drivers of the German Growth Model." In *Routledge Handbook of German Politics & Culture,* ed. Sarah Colvin, 391–408. London: Routledge.

IfW [Institut für Weltwirtschaft (Institute for the World Economy)]. 2014. "Das europäische Verfahren zur Vermeidung und Korrektur makroökonomischer Ungleichgewichte: Auswertung der bisherigen Erfahrung und mögliche Reformansätze." Study commissioned by the Federal Ministry for Economics and Energy. Kiel: IfW.

IMF [International Monetary Fund]. 2016. "Too Slow for Too Long." *World Economic Outlook* (April 2016). http://www.imf.org/external/pubs/ft /weo/2016/01/index.htm (accessed 18 April 2016).

———. 2020 [1944]. *Articles of Agreement.* https://www.imf.org/external /pubs/ft/aa/pdf/aa.pdf (accessed 24 April 2020).

Initiative Neue Soziale Marktwirtschaft. 2003. *Ein Reformbündnis schmieden.* Cologne: INSM.

Isaac, Jeffrey. 1987. *Power and Marxist Theory.* Ithaca, NY: Cornell University Press.

Iversen, Torben. 1999. *Economic Institutions: The Politics of Macroeconomics and Wage Bargaining in Advanced Democracies.* New York: Cambridge University Press.

Jabko, Nicolas. 2013. "Re-Problematizing Neoliberalism." *Contemporary Political Theory* 12 (4): 359–364.

Jacoby, Wade. 2014. "The Politics of the Eurozone Crisis: Two Puzzles Behind the German Consensus." *German Politics and Society* 32 (2): 70–85.

James, Harold. 1996. *International Monetary Cooperation Since Bretton Woods.* Washington, DC: International Monetary Fund.

———. 2017. "Rule Germania." In *Ordoliberalism: A German Oddity?*, ed. Thorsten Beck and Hans-Helmut Kotz, 25–30. London: CEPR Press.

Jannsen, Nils, and Stefan Kooths. 2012. "German Trade Performance in Times of Slumping Euro Area Markets." *Intereconomics: Review of European Economic Policy* 6: 368–372.

Johnson, Peter Andrew. 1998. *The Government of Money: Monetarism in Germany and the United States.* Ithaca, NY: Cornell University Press.

Jones, Claire. 2017. "German Wage Growth Low as Workers Look Beyond Pay Packets." *Financial Times,* 11 June. https://www.ft.com/content/a34ebea0 -4b66-11e7-a3f4-c742b9791d43 (accessed 15 August 2017).

Jones, Daniel Stedman. 2012. *Masters of the Universe: Hayek, Friedman, and the Birth of Neoliberal Politics.* Princeton, NJ: Princeton University Press.

Jones, Eric. 2005. "The 'Monetarist' Turn in Belgium and the Netherlands." In *Monetary Union in Crisis: The European Union as a Neoliberal Construction,* ed. Bernard Moss, 233–248. New York: Palgrave Macmillan.

Kaltenthaler, Karl. 1998. *Germany and the Politics of Europe's Money.* Durham, NC: Duke University Press.

Katzenstein, Peter, ed. 1978. *Between Power and Plenty: Foreign Economic Policies of Advanced Industrial States.* Madison: University of Wisconsin Press.

———. 1985. *Small States in World Markets: Industrial Policy in Europe.* Ithaca, NY: Cornell University Press.

Katzenstein, Peter, and Stephen Nelson. 2013. "Worlds in Collision: Uncertainty and Risk in Hard Times." In *Politics in the New Hard Times*, ed. Miles Kahler and David Lake, 233–252. Ithaca, NY: Cornell University Press.

Kemp, Tom. 1985. *Industrialization in Nineteenth-Century Europe*. 2nd ed. London: Longman.

Keohane, Robert. 1984a. *After Hegemony: Cooperation and Discord in the World Political Economy*. Princeton, NJ: Princeton University Press.

———. 1984b. "The World Political Economy and the Crisis of Embedded Liberalism." In *Order and Conflict in Contemporary Capitalism*, ed. John Goldthorpe, 15–38. Oxford: Oxford University Press.

———. 2012. "Twenty Years of Institutional Liberalism." *International Relations* 26 (2): 125–138.

Keohane, Robert, and Joseph Nye. 1977. *Power and Interdependence: World Politics in Transition*. Boston: Little, Brown.

Khan, Mehreen, and Matthew Holehouse. 2015. "Europeans Told to Bring Greece Back from the Brink and Avoid Descent into 'Uncontrolled Grexit'." *Telegraph*, 8 July. http://www.telegraph.co.uk/finance/economics/11727607/Europes-creditors-told-to-avoid-descent-into-uncontrolled-Grexit.html (accessed 2 October 2017).

Kieninger, Stephan. 2017. "Between Power Politics and Morality: The United States, the Long Détente, and the Transformation of Europe, 1969–1985." In *The Long Détente: Changing Concepts of Security and Cooperation in Europe, 1950s–1980s*, ed. Oliver Bange and Poul Villaume, 281–313. Budapest: CEU.

Kinderman, Daniel. 2005. "Pressure from Without, Subversion from Within: The Two-Pronged German Employer Offensive." *Comparative European Politics* 3: 432–463.

———. 2008. "The Political Economy of Sectoral Exchange Rate Preferences and Lobbying: Germany from 1960–2008, and Beyond." *Review of International Political Economy* 15 (5): 851–880.

Kindleberger, Charles. 1973. *The World in Depression, 1929–1939*. Berkeley: University of California Press.

———. 1976. "Systems of International Economic Organization." In *Money and the Coming World Order*, ed. David Calleo, 15–40. New York: New York University Press.

Kirshner, Jonathan. 1997. *Currency and Coercion: The Political Economy of International Monetary Power*. Princeton, NJ: Princeton University Press.

Kluth, Andreas. 2020. "Why Germany Will Never Be Europe's Leader." *Bloomberg*, 30 April. https://www.bloomberg.com/opinion/articles/2020-04-30/coronavirus-crisis-why-germany-will-never-be-europe-s-leader (accessed 11 May 2020).

Knafo, Samuel. 2006. "The Gold Standard and the Origins of the Modern International Monetary System." *Review of International Political Economy* 13 (1): 78–102.

———. 2010. "Critical Approaches and the Legacy of the Agent/Structure Debate in International Relations." *Cambridge Review of International Affairs* 23 (3): 493–516.

———. 2013. *The Making of Modern Finance: Liberal Governance and the Gold Standard.* London: Routledge.

Knafo, Samuel, Sahil Dutta, Richard Lane, and Steffan Wyn-Jones. 2019. "The Managerial Lineages of Neoliberalism." *New Political Economy* 24 (2): 235–251.

Kocka, Jürgen. 1988. "German History Before Hitler: The Debate About the German Sonderweg." *Journal of Contemporary History* 23 (1): 3016.

———. 1998. "Nach dem Ende des Sonderwegs. Zur Tragfähigkeit eines Konzepts." In *Doppelte Zeitgeschichte*, ed. Arnd Bauerkämper, 364–375. Göttingen: Dietz.

Kohler-Koch, Beate. 1991. "Deutsche Einigung im Spannungsfeld internationaler Umbrüche." *Politische Vierteljahresschrift* 32 (4): 605–620.

Konings, Martijn. 2007. "The Institutional Foundations of US Structural Power in International Finance: From the Re-emergence of Global Finance to the Monetarist Turn." *Review of International Political Economy* 15 (1): 35–61.

Krasner, Stephen. 1976. "State Power and the Structure of International Trade." *World Politics* 28 (3): 317–347.

———. 1985. *Structural Conflict: The Third World Against Global Liberalism.* Berkeley: University of California Press.

Kreile, Michael. 1977. "West Germany: The Dynamics of Expansion." *International Organization* 31 (4): 775–808.

———. 2006. "The Search for a New Monetary System: Germany's Balancing Act." In *The Strategic Triangle: France, Germany and the United States in the Shaping of the New Europe*, ed. Helga Haftendorn, Stephen F. Szabo, Samuel F. Wells Jr., and Georges-Henri Soutou, 149–170. Baltimore: Johns Hopkins University Press.

Krippner, Greta. 2011. *Capitalizing on Crisis: The Political Origins of the Rise of Finance.* New York: Harvard University Press.

Krugman, Paul. 2015. "Killing the European Project." *New York Times Opinion Pages*, 12 July. https://krugman.blogs.nytimes.com/2015/07/12/killing-the-european-project (accessed 6 February 2020).

Kundnani, Hans. 2011. "Germany as a Geo-Economic Power." *Washington Quarterly* 34 (3): 31–45.

———. 2014. *The Paradox of German Power.* London: Hurst.

Kurzer, Paulette. 1993. *Business and Banking: Political Change and Economic Integration in Western Europe.* Ithaca, NY: Cornell University Press.

Kwon, Hyeong-ki. 2012. "Politics of Globalization and National Economy: The German Experience Compared with the United States." *Politics & Society* 40 (4): 581–607.

Lacher, Hannes. 1999. "Embedded Liberalism, Disembedded Markets: Reconceptualising the Pax Americana." *New Political Economy* 4 (3): 343–360.

———. 2002. "Making Sense of the International System: The Promises of Contemporary Marxist Theories of International Relations." In *Historical Materialism and Globalization,* ed. Mark Rupert and Hazel Smith, 147–164. New York: Routledge.

———. 2005. "International Transformation and the Persistence of Territoriality: Toward a New Political Geography of Capitalism." *Review of International Political Economy* 12 (1): 26–52.

———. 2006. *Beyond Globalization: Capitalism, Territoriality, and the International Relations of Modernity.* New York: Routledge.

———. 2007. "The Slight Transformation: Contesting the Legacy of Karl Polanyi." In *Reading Karl Polanyi for the Twenty-First Century: Market Economy as a Political Project,* ed. Ayşe Buğra and Kaan Ağartan, 49–66. New York: Palgrave Macmillan.

Lacher, Hannes, and Julian Germann. 2012. "Before Hegemony: Britain, Free Trade, and Nineteenth-Century World Order Revisited." *International Studies Review* 14 (1): 99–124.

Lankowski, Carl. 1982a. *Germany and the European Communities: Anatomy of a Hegemonial Relation.* PhD diss., Columbia University, New York.

———. 1982b. "Modell Deutschland and the Internationalization of the West German State in the 1970s." In *The Political Economy of West Germany: Modell Deutschland,* ed. Andrei Markovits, 90–115. New York: Praeger.

Lapavitsas, Costas, and Heiner Flassbeck. 2015. *Against the Troika: Crisis and Austerity in the Eurozone.* London: Verso.

Layne, Christopher. 2006. *The Peace of Illusions: American Grand Strategy from 1940 to the Present.* Ithaca, NY: Cornell University Press.

Leaman, Jeremy. 2001. *The Bundesbank Myth: Towards a Critique of Central Bank Independence.* London: Palgrave.

———. 2009. *The Political Economy of Germany Under Chancellors Kohl and Schröder: Decline of the German Model?* New York: Berghahn Books.

Lehndorff, Steffen. 2016. "Internal Devaluation and Employment Trends in Germany." In *Unemployment, Internal Devaluation and Labour Market Deregulation in Europe,* ed. Martin Myant, Sotiria Theodoropoulou, and Agnieszka Piasna, 169–196. Brussels: European Trade Union Institute (ETUI).

Lent, Jeremy. 2020. "Coronavirus Spells the End of the Neoliberal Era. What's Next?" *Open Democracy*, 12 April. https://www.opendemocracy.net/en/transformation/coronavirus-spells-the-end-of-the-neoliberal-era-whats-next (accessed 23 May 2020).

Lindblom, Charles Edward. 1977. *Politics and Markets: The World's Political Economic Systems*. New York: Basic Books.

———. 1982. "The Market as Prison." *Journal of Politics* 44: 324–336.

Lindlar, Ludger, and Carl-Ludwig Holtfrerich. 1997. "Geography, Exchange Rates and Trade Structures: Germany's Export Performance Since the 1950s." *European Review of Economic History* 1: 217–246.

Lindsey, David, Athanasios Orphanides, and Robert Rasche. 2005. "The Reform of October 1979: How It Happened and Why." *Federal Reserve Bank of St. Louis Review* 87 (2, Part 2): 187–235.

Lippert, Werner. 2011. *The Economic Diplomacy of Ostpolitik: Origins of NATO's Energy Dilemma*. New York: Berghahn Books.

Loriaux, Michael Maurice. 1991. *France After Hegemony: International Change and Financial Reform*. Ithaca, NY: Cornell University Press.

Ludlam, Steve. 1992. "The Gnomes of Washington: Four Myths of the 1976 IMF Crisis." *Political Studies* 40 (4): 713–727.

Ludlow, N. Piers. 2013. "The Real Years of Europe? US-West European Relations During the Ford Administration. *Journal of Cold War Studies* 15 (3): 136–161.

Luger, Stan. 2000. *Corporate Power, American Democracy, and the Automobile Industry*. New York: Cambridge University Press.

Lundestad, Geir. 1986. "Empire by Invitation? The United States and Western Europe, 1945–1952." *Journal of Peace Research* 23 (3): 263–277.

Madrick, Jeff. 2011. *Age of Greed: The Triumph of Finance and the Decline of America, 1970 to the Present*. New York: Random House.

Mahler, Armin, and Dinah Deckstein. 2017. "Das wird die Schicksalsfrage der deutschen Wirtschaft." Interview with Siemens CEO Joe Kaeser. *Der Spiegel*, 23 September. https://www.spiegel.de/spiegel/joe-kaeser-ueber-digitalisierung-schicksalsfrage-der-wirtschaft-sein-a-1169382.html (accessed 30 January 2020).

Maier, Charles. 1977. "The Politics of Productivity: Foundations of American International Economic Policy After World War II." *International Organization* 31 (4): 607–633.

———. 2012. "Europe Needs a German Marshall Plan." *New York Times*, 9 June. http://www.nytimes.com/2012/06/10/opinion/sunday/europe-needs-a-german-marshall-plan.html (accessed 7 August 2017).

Manow, Philip. 2001a. "Welfare State Building and Coordinated Capitalism in Japan and Germany." In *The Origins of Nonliberal Capitalism: Germany and*

Japan in Comparison, ed. Wolfgang Streeck and Kozo Yamamura, 94–120. Ithaca, NY: Cornell University Press.

———. 2001b. "Ordoliberalismus als ökonomische Ordnungstheologie." *Leviathan* 29 (2): 179–198.

Marin, Dalia, Reinhilde Veugelers, and Justine Feliu. 2017. "A Revival of Manufacturing in Europe? Recent Evidence About Reshoring." In *Remaking Europe: The New Manufacturing as an Engine for Growth*, ed. Reinhilde Veugelers, 102–124. Brussels: Bruegel.

Markovits, Andrei, ed. 1982. *The Political Economy of West Germany: Modell Deutschland*. New York: Praeger.

Marsh, David. 1992. The Bundesbank: The Bank That Rules Europe. London: Heinemann.

———. 2009. *The Euro: The Politics of the New Global Currency*. New Haven, CT: Yale University Press.

Marx, Karl. 1990. *Capital: A Critique of Political Economy, Volume I*. London: Penguin.

Mastanduno, Michael. 2009. "System Maker and Privilege Taker: U.S. Power and the International Political Economy." *World Politics* 61 (1): 121–154.

Matin, Kamran. 2013. *Recasting Iranian Modernity: International Relations and Social Change*. London: Routledge.

Matthiesen, Max. 1987. *Die staatliche Einwirkung zur Sicherung der Energieversorgung und ihre Grenzen*. Berlin: Duncker & Humblot.

Matthijs, Matthias. 2011. *Ideas and Economic Crises in Britain from Attlee to Blair, 1945–2005*. London: Routledge.

———. 2016. "Powerful Rules Governing the Euro: The Perverse Logic of German Ideas." *Journal of European Public Policy* 23 (3): 375–391.

Matthijs, Matthias, and Mark Blyth. 2011. "Why Only Germany Can Fix the Euro." *Foreign Affairs*, 17 November. https://www.foreignaffairs.com /articles/germany/2011-11-17/why-only-germany-can-fix-euro (accessed 22 April 2020).

Matusow, Allen. 1998. *Nixon's Economy: Booms, Busts, Dollars, and Votes*. Lawrence: University Press of Kansas.

———. 2003. "Richard Nixon and the Failed War Against the Trading World." *Diplomatic History* 27 (5): 767–772.

Maull, Hanns. 1990. "Germany and Japan: The New Civilian Powers." *Foreign Affairs* 69 (5): 91–106.

———. 2013. "'Zivilmacht': Karrier eines Begriffs." Valedictory address, University of Trier, 3 May. https://www.uni-trier.de/fileadmin/fb3/POL/Mitar beiter/Maull_ Hanns_W/Abschiedsvorlesung_Rev.pdf (accessed 30 January 2016).

———. 2015. "Foreign Policy: From 'Civilian Power' to 'Trading State'?" In *The*

Routledge Handbook of German Politics & Culture, ed. Sarah Colvin and Mark Taplin, 409–424. London: Routledge.

McCartin, Joseph. 2011. *Collision Course: Ronald Reagan, the Air Traffic Controllers, and the Strike That Changed America*. New York: Oxford University Press.

McFarland, Victor. 2012. "Review of Linda Qaimmaqami and Edward C. Keefer, eds. *Foreign Relations of the United States, 1969–1976, Volume XXXVI, Energy Crisis, 1969–1974*." http://h-diplo.org/FRUS/PDF/FRUS19.pdf (accessed 10 March 2020).

McMichael, Philip. 1990. Incorporating Comparison Within a World-Historical Perspective: An Alternative Comparative Method. *American Sociological Review* 55 (June): 385–397.

———. 2000. "World-Systems Analysis, Globalization, and Incorporated Comparison." *Journal of World-Systems Research* 6 (3): 668–690.

McNally, David. 2011. *Global Slump: The Economics and Politics of Crisis and Resistance*. Oakland, CA: PM Press.

McNamara, Kathleen. 1998. *The Currency of Ideas: Monetary Politics in the European Union*. Ithaca, NY: Cornell University Press.

Meiers, Franz-Josef. 2015. *Germany's Role in the Euro Crisis*. Heidelberg: Springer.

Meltzer, Allan. 2009. *A History of the Federal Reserve, Volume 2*. Chicago: University of Chicago Press.

Menz, Georg. 2005. "*Auf Wiedersehen*, Rhineland Model: Embedding Neoliberalism in Germany." In *Internalizing Globalization: The Rise of Neoliberalism and the Decline of National Varieties of Capitalism*, ed. Susanne Soederberg, Georg Benz, and Philip Cerny, 33–48. New York: Palgrave Macmillan.

Miliband, Ralph. 1969. *The State in Capitalist Society*. London: Merlin Press.

———. 1973. "Poulantzas and the Capitalist State." *New Left Review* 82: 83–92.

Milward, Alan. 1984. *The Reconstruction of Western Europe, 1945–1951*. Berkeley: University of California Press.

———. 1986. "Entscheidungsphasen der Westintegration." In *Westdeutschland, 1945–1955: Unterwerfung, Kontrolle, Integration*, ed. Ludolf Herbst, 231–245. Munich: Oldenbourg.

Mirowski, Philip. 2008. "Review of David Harvey, *A Brief History of Neoliberalism*." *Economics and Philosophy* 24 (1): 111–117.

Mirowski, Philip, and Dieter Plehwe. 2009. *The Road from Mont Pèlerin: The Making of the Neoliberal Thought Collective*. Cambridge, MA: Harvard University Press.

Moran, Andrew. 2011. "More Than a Caretaker: The Economic Policy of Gerald R. Ford." *Presidential Studies Quarterly* 41 (1): 39–63.

Moravcsik, Andrew. 1998. *The Choice for Europe: Social Purpose and State Power from Messina to Maastricht.* Ithaca, NY: Cornell University Press.

Moss, Bernard. 2000. "The European Community as Monetarist Construction: A Critique of Moravcsik." *Journal of European Area Studies* 8 (2): 247–265.

———. 2005. "Socialist Challenge: Class Politics in France." In *Monetary Union in Crisis: The European Union as a Neo-Liberal Constitution*, ed. Bernard Moss, 121–144. New York: Palgrave Macmillan.

Mourlon-Druol, Emmanuel. 2010. "The Victory of the Intergovernmental Method? The Emergence of the European Council in the Community's Institutional Set-Up, 1974–1977." In *The Road Europe Travelled Along: The Evolution of the EEC/EU Institutions and Policies*, ed. Daniela Preda and Daniele Pasquinucci, 27–40. Brussels: P.I.E. Peter Lang.

———. 2012. *A Europe Made of Money: The Emergence of the European Monetary System.* Ithaca, NY: Cornell University Press.

Mudge, Stephanie Lee. 2008. "What Is Neo-Liberalism?" *Socio-Economic Review* 6 (4): 703–731.

Murphy, R. Taggart. 1996. *The Weight of the Yen: How Denial Imperils America's Future and Ruins an Alliance.* New York: W. W. Norton.

Nasr, Joseph. 2017. "Greece Needs Debt Restructuring, Interest Rate Cuts: IMF's Lagarde." *Reuters*, 22 February. http://www.reuters.com/article/us -eurozone-greece-imf-idUSKBN1612CI (accessed 11 June 2017).

Neebe, Reinhard. 1990. "Optionen westdeutscher Außenwirtschaftspolitik, 1949–1953." In *Vom Marshallplan zur EWG: Die Eingliederung der Bundesrepublik in die Westliche Welt*, ed. Ludolf Herbst, Werner Bührer, and Hanno Sowade, 163–202. Munich: Oldenbourg.

———. 1991. *Überseemärkte und Exportstrategien in der westdeutschen Wirtschaft 1945 bis 1966: Aus den Reiseberichten von Dietrich Wilhelm von Menges.* Stuttgart: Steiner.

———. 1996. "German Big Business and the Return to the World Market After World War II." In *The Quest for Economic Empire: European Strategies of German Big Business in the Twentieth Century*, ed. Volker Berghahn, 95–122. Providence, RI: Berghahn Books.

———. 2004. *Weichenstellung für die Globalisierung: Deutsche Weltmarktpolitik, Europa und Amerika in der Ära Ludwig Erhard.* Cologne: Böhlau.

Neikirk, William. 1987. *Volcker, Portrait of the Money Man.* Chicago: Congdon & Weed.

Newstadt, Eric. 2008. "Neoliberalism and the Federal Reserve." In *American Empire and the Political Economy of Global Finance*, ed. Leo Panitch and Martijn Konings, 90–118. New York: Palgrave Macmillan.

Nicholls, Anthony James. 1994. *Freedom with Responsibility: The Social Market Economy in Germany, 1918–1963*. Oxford: Clarendon Press.

Nichter, Luke. 2008. *Richard Nixon and Europe: Confrontation and Cooperation, 1969–1974*. PhD diss., Bowling Green State University, Ohio.

Niedhardt, Gottfried. 2010. "US Détente and German Ostpolitik: Parallels and Frictions." In *The Strained Alliance: US-European Relations from Nixon to Carter*, ed. Matthias Schulz and Thomas Schwartz, 23–44. New York: Cambridge University Press.

Nitzan, Jonathan, and Shimshon Bichler. 2009. *Capital as Power: A Study of Order and Creorder*. London: Routledge.

Nölke, Andreas. 2016. "Economic Causes of the Eurozone Crisis: The Analytical Contributions of Comparative Capitalism." *Socio-Economic Review* 14 (1): 141–161.

Nordström, Håkan, and Harry Flam. 2018. "Production Integration in the European Union." *CESifo Working Papers* 6944. Munich: Center for Economic Studies.

Nützenadel, Alexander. 2005. *Stunde der Ökonomen: Wissenschaft, Politik und Expertenkultur in der Bundesrepublik 1949–1974*. Göttingen: Vandenhoeck & Ruprecht.

Obstfeld, Maurice, and Alan Taylor. 2004. *Global Capital Markets: Integration, Crisis, and Growth*. Cambridge: Cambridge University Press.

O'Connor, James. 1973. *The Fiscal Crisis of the State*. New York: St. Martin's Press.

Odell, John. 1982. *US International Monetary Policy: Markets, Power, and Ideas as Sources of Change*. Princeton, NJ: Princeton University Press.

Offe, Claus. 1984. *Contradictions of the Welfare State*. Cambridge, MA: MIT Press.

Oppenheim, V. H. 1976. "The Past: We Pushed Them." *Foreign Policy* 25 (4): 24–57.

Ötsch, Walter Otto, Stephan Pühringer, and Katrin Hirte. 2018. *Netzwerke des Marktes: Ordoliberalismus als Politische Ökonomie*. Wiesbaden: Springer.

Overbeek, Henk. 1990. *Global Capitalism and National Decline: The Thatcher Decade in Perspective*. London: Unwin Hyman.

———. 1993. "Atlanticism and Europeanism in British Foreign Policy." In *Restructuring Hegemony in the Global Political Economy: The Rise of Transnational Neo-Liberalism in the 1980s*, ed. Henk Overbeek and Kees van der Pijl, 110–133. London: Routledge.

———. 2008. *Rivalität und ungleiche Entwicklung: Einführung in die Internationale Politik aus der Sicht der Internationalen Politischen Ökonomie*. Wiesbaden: VS Verlag.

Overbeek, Henk, and Bob Jessop, eds. 2019. *Transnational Capital and Class Fractions: The Amsterdam School Perspective Revisited*. London: Routledge.

Overbeek, Henk, and Kees van der Pijl. 1993. "Restructuring Capital and

Restructuring Hegemony: Neo-Liberalism and the Unmaking of the Post-War Order." In *Restructuring Hegemony in the Global Political Economy: The Rise of Transnational Neo-Liberalism in the 1980s*, ed. Henk Overbeek and Kees van der Pijl, 1–57. London: Routledge.

Painter, David. 2012. "Oil and the American Century." *Journal of American History* 99 (1): 24–39.

Panitch, Leo. 1994. "Globalization and the State." In *Socialist Register 1994: Between Globalism and Nationalism*, ed. Ralph Miliband and Leo Panitch, 60–93. London: Merlin.

———. 2000. "The New Imperial State." *New Left Review* 2: 5–20.

———. 2002. "The Impoverishment of State Theory." In *Paradigm Lost: State Theory Reconsidered*, ed. Stanley Aronowitz and Peter Bratsis, 89–104. London: University of Minnesota Press.

Panitch, Leo, and Sam Gindin. 2003. "American Imperialism and Eurocapitalism." *Studies in Political Economy* 71/72: 7–38.

———. 2008. "Finance and American Empire." In *American Empire and the Political Economy of Global Finance*, ed. Leo Panitch and Martijn Konings, 17–47. New York: Palgrave Macmillan.

———. 2012. *The Making of Global Capitalism: The Political Economy of American Empire*. London: Verso.

Parboni, Riccardo. 1981. *The Dollar and Its Rivals*. London: Verso.

———. 1988. "U.S. Economic Strategies Against Western Europe: From Nixon to Reagan." *Geoforum* 19 (1): 45–54.

Paterson, William, and Gordon Smith, eds. 1981. *The West German Model: Perspectives on a Stable State*. London: Frank Cass.

Peck, Jamie, Nik Theodore, and Neil Brenner. 2010. "Postneoliberalism and Its Malcontents." *Antipode* 41: 94–116.

———. 2012. "Neoliberalism Resurgent? Market Rule After the Great Recession." *South Atlantic Quarterly* 111 (2): 265–288.

Petersen, Tore. 2009. *Richard Nixon, Great Britain and the Anglo-American Alignment in the Persian Gulf and Arabian Peninsula: Making Allies Out of Clients*. East Sussex, UK: Sussex Academic Press.

Pettis, Michael. 2013. *The Great Rebalancing: Trade, Conflict, and the Perilous Road Ahead for the World Economy*. Princeton, NJ: Princeton University Press.

Picot, Georg, and Arianna Tassinari. 2014. "Liberalization, Dualization, or Recalibration? Labor Market Reforms Under Austerity: Italy and Spain, 2010–2012." *Nuffield College Working Paper Series in Politics*. https://www.nuffield.ox.ac.uk/Research/Politics%20Group/Working%20papers/Documents/PicotTassinari%20Labor%20market%20reforms%20under%20austerity%20.pdf (accessed 31 August 2017).

Piller, Tobias. 2011. "Wie Deutschland früher half: Der Goldkredit an Italien."

Frankfurter Allgemeine Zeitung, 8 September. http://www.faz.net/artikel /C30638/wie-deutschland-frueher-half-der-goldkredit-an-italien-30498777 .html (accessed 2 September 2017).

Polanyi, Karl. 1957. *The Great Transformation: The Political and Economic Origins of Our Time*. Boston: Beacon.

Pollard, Syndey. 1981. *Peaceful Conquest: The Industrialization of Europe, 1760–1970*. London: Oxford University Press.

Poulantzas, Nicos. 1973. *Political Power and Social Classes*. London: New Left Books.

Prasad, Monica. 2006. *The Politics of Free Markets: The Rise of Neoliberal Economic Policies in Britain, France, Germany, and the United States*. Chicago: University of Chicago Press.

———. 2012. "The Popular Origins of Neoliberalism in the Reagan Tax Cut of 1981." *Journal of Policy History* 24 (3): 351–383.

Prashad, Vijay. 2012. *The Poorer Nations: A Possible History of the Global South*. London: Verso.

Przeworski, Adam, and Michael Wallerstein. 1988. "Structural Dependence of the State on Capital." *American Political Science Review* 82 (1): 11–29.

Ptak, Ralf. 2004. *Vom Ordoliberalismus zur Sozialen Marktwirtschaft: Stationen des Neoliberalismus in Deutschland*. Opladen: Leske + Budrich.

———. 2009. "Neoliberalism in Germany: Revisiting the Ordoliberal Foundations of the Social Market Economy." In *The Road from Mont Pelerin: The Making of the Neoliberal Thought Collective*, ed. Philip Mirowski and Dieter Plehwe, 98–138. Cambridge, MA: Harvard University Press.

Putnam, Robert. 1988. "Diplomacy and Domestic Politics: The Logic of Two-Level Games." *International Organization* 42 (3): 427–460.

Putnam, Robert, and Nicholas Bayne. 1984. *Hanging Together: The Seven-Power Summits*. Cambridge, MA: Harvard University Press.

Putnam, Robert, and C. Randall Henning. 1989. "The Bonn Summit of 1978: A Case Study in Coordination." In *Can Nations Agree? Issues in International Economic Cooperation*, 12–140. Washington, DC: The Brookings Institution.

Rae, Michelle Frasher. 2003. *International Monetary Relations Between the United States, France, and West Germany in the 1970s*. PhD diss., Texas A&M, College Station, Texas.

Rahtz, Joshua. 2017. "The Soul of the Eurozone." *New Left Review* 104 (March-April): 107–131.

Reichart, Alexandre. 2015. "French Monetary Policy, 1981–1985: A Constrained Policy Between Volcker Shock, the EMS and Macroeconomic Imbalances." *The Journal of European Economic History* 44 (1): 11–46.

Reisenbichler, Alexander, and Kimberly J. Morgan. 2012. "From 'Sick Man' to

'Miracle': Explaining the Robustness of the German Labor Market During and After the Financial Crisis, 2008–2009." *Politics & Society* 40 (4): 549–579.

Rhenisch, Thomas. 1999. *Europäische Integration und industrielles Interesse. Die deutsche Industrie und die Gründung der Europäischen Wirtschaftsgemeinschaft.* Stuttgart: Steiner.

Rhodium Group. 2019. "People's Republic of China—European Union Direct Investment, 4Q 2018 and Full Year 2018 Update." *Rhodium Group CrossBorder Monitor* (16 January).

Richardson, James. 1997. "Contending Liberalisms: Past and Present." *European Journal of International Relations* 3 (1): 5–33.

Richter, Rudolf. 1999. *Deutsche Geldpolitik 1948–1998.* Tübingen: Mohr Siebeck.

Riecher, Stefan. 2013. "UBS's Weber Says Fed's Tapering Negatively Affects Europe." *Bloomberg*, 15 July. https://www.bloomberg.com/news/articles /2013-07-15/ubs-s-weber-says-fed-s-tapering-negatively-affects-europe (accessed 11 July 2017).

Rinne, Ulf, and Klaus Zimmermann. 2012. "Another Economic Miracle? The German Labor Market and the Great Recession." *IZA Journal of Labor Policy* 1 (3).

Rioux, Sébastien. 2015. "Mind the (Theoretical) Gap: On the Poverty of International Relations Theorising of Uneven and Combined Development." *Global Society* 29 (4): 481–509.

Rittberger, Volker. 1992. "Nach der Vereinigung: Deutschlands Stellung in der Welt." *Leviathan* 20 (2): 207–229.

Rittershausen, Johannes. 2007. "The Postwar West German Economic Transition: From Ordoliberalism to Keynesianism." *IWP Discussion Paper* 2007/1. Cologne: Institute for Economic Policy. http://hdl.handle.net/10419/57975 (accessed 23 September 2017).

Robinson, William. 2001. "Social Theory and Globalization: The Rise of a Transnational State." *Theory and Society* 30 (2): 157–200.

———. 2004. *A Theory of Global Capitalism: Production, Class, and State in a Transnational World.* Baltimore: Johns Hopkins University Press.

Rogers, Chris. 2009a. "From Social Contract to 'Social Contrick': The Depoliticisation of Economic Policy-Making Under Harold Wilson, 1974–1975." *The British Journal of Politics & International Relations* 11 (4): 634–651.

———. 2009b. "The Politics of Economic Policy Making in Britain: A Reassessment of the 1976 IMF Crisis." *Politics & Policy* 37 (5): 971–994.

———. 2013. "Crisis, Ideas, and Economic Policy-Making in Britain During the 1970s Stagflation." *New Political Economy* 18 (1): 1–20.

Rogoff, Kenneth. 2014. "The German Locomotive Is Moving Fast Enough." *Frankfurter Allgemeine Zeitung*, 24 June. http://blogs.faz.net/fazit/2014/06/24 /german-locomotive-moving-fast-enough-4185 (accessed 3 October 2017).

Rosecrance, Richard. 1986. *The Rise of the Trading State: Commerce and Conquest in the Modern World*. New York: Basic Books.

Rosenberg, Justin. 2006. "Why Is There No International Historical Sociology?" *European Journal of International Relations* 12(3): 307–340.

———. 2009. "Basic Problems in the Theory of Uneven and Combined Development: A Reply to the CRIA Forum." *Cambridge Review of International Affairs* 22 (1): 107–110.

———. 2017. "Escaping from the Prison of Political Science." In *What's the Point of International Relations?*, ed. Jan Selby, Rorden Wilkinson, and Synne Dyvik, 219–230. London: Routledge.

Rosenberg, Justin, and Chris Boyle. 2019. "Understanding 2016: China, Brexit and Trump in the History of Uneven and Combined Development." *Journal of Historical Sociology* 32 (1): e1–e58.

Roth, Karl Heinz. 1995. "Das Ende eines Mythos: Ludwig Erhard und der Übergang der deutschen Wirtschaft von der Annexions- zur Nachkriegsplanung (1939–1945). I. Teil: 1939 bis 1943." *1999* 10 (4): 53–93.

———. 1998. "Das Ende eines Mythos: Ludwig Erhard und der Übergang der deutschen Wirtschaft von der Annexions- zur Nachkriegsplanung (1939–1945). Teil II: 1943 bis 1945." *1999* 13 (1): 92–123.

———. 1999a. "Das Ende eines Mythos: Ludwig Erhard und der Übergang der deutschen Wirtschaft von der Annexions- zur Nachkriegsplanung (1939–1945). Teil II: 1943 bis 1945. Fortsetzung und Schluss." *1999* 14 (1): 73–91.

———. 1999b. "Wirtschaftliche Vorbereitungen auf das Kriegsende und Nachkriegsplanungen." In *Geschichte der deutschen Kriegswirtschaft, Volume III*, ed. Dietrich Eichholtz, 509–611. Munich: Saur.

Rudolph, Karsten. 2004. *Wirtschaftsdiplomatie im Kalten Krieg: Die Ostpolitik der westdeutschen Großindustrie, 1945–1991*. New York: Campus Verlag.

Ruggie, John Gerard. 1982. "International Regimes, Transactions, and Change: Embedded Liberalism in the Postwar Economic Order." *International Organization* 36 (2): 379–415.

———. 1991. "Embedded Liberalism Revisited: Institutions and Progress in International Economic Relations." In *Progress in Post-War International Relations*, ed. Emanuel Adler and Beverly Crawford, 201–234. New York: Columbia University Press.

———. 1996. "Globalization and the Embedded Liberalism Compromise: The End of an Era?" In *Internationale Wirtschaft, nationale Demokratie: Herausforderungen für die Demokratietheorie*, ed. Wolfgang Streeck, 79–98. Frankfurt: Campus.

———. 2003. "Taking Embedded Liberalism Global: The Corporate Connection." In *Taming Globalization: Frontiers of Governance*, ed. David Held and Mathias Koenig-Archibugi, 93–129. Cambridge, UK: Polity.

———. 2008. "Introduction: Embedding Global Markets." In *Embedding Global Markets: An Enduring Challenge*, ed. John Gerard Ruggie, 1–12. Burlington, VT: Ashgate.

Rupert, Mark. 1995. *Producing Hegemony*. Cambridge, MA: Cambridge University Press.

Ryner, Magnus, and Alan Cafruny. 2017. *The European Union and Global Capitalism: Origins, Development and Crisis*. London: Palgrave.

Sachs, Jeffrey. 2015. "Germany, Greece, and the Future of Europe." *Huffington Post*, 28 July. https://www.huffpost.com/entry/germany-greece-and-the-future -of-europe_b_7886494?guccounter=1 (accessed 6 February 2020).

Sargent, Daniel. 2015. *A Superpower Transformed: The Remaking of American Foreign Relations in the 1970s*. London: Oxford University Press.

Sassen, Saskia. 1991. *The Global City: New York, London, Tokyo*. Princeton, NJ: Princeton University Press.

Sassen, Saskia. 2008. *Territory, Authority, Rights: From Medieval to Global Assemblages*. Princeton, NJ: Princeton University Press.

Sassoon, Donald. 1996. *One Hundred Years of Socialism: The West European Left in the Twentieth Century*. New York: New Press.

Saull, Richard. 2007. *The Cold War and After: Capitalism, Revolution and Superpower Politics*. London: Pluto.

Scharpf, Fritz. 1984. "Economic and Institutional Constraints of Full-Employment Strategies: Sweden, Austria, and West Germany, 1973–1982." In *Order and Conflict in Contemporary Capitalism*, ed. John Goldthorpe, 257–290. Oxdord, UK: Clarendon Press.

———. 1991. *Crisis and Choice in European Social Democracy*. Ithaca, NY: Cornell University Press.

———. 2000. "Economic Changes, Vulnerabilities, and Institutional Capabilities." In *Welfare and Work in the Open Economy: From Vulnerability to Competitiveness*, ed. Fritz Scharpf and Vivien Schmidt, 21–124. Oxford, UK: Oxford University Press.

Schäuble, Wolfgang. 2015. "German Priorities and Eurozone Myths." *New York Times*, 16 April.

Schmalz, Stefan, and Matthias Ebenau. 2012. "After Neoliberalism? Brazil, India, and China in the Global Economic Crisis." *Globalizations* 9 (4): 487–501.

Schmelzer, Matthias. 2010. *Freiheit für Wechselkurse und Kapital: Die Ursprünge neoliberaler Währungspolitik und die Mont Pèlerin Society*. Marburg: Metropolis.

Schmidt, Helmut. 1974. "The Struggle for the World Product: Politics Between Power and Morals." *Foreign Affairs* 52 (3): 437–451.

———. 1988. "Prospects for International Cooperation." In *International Economic Cooperation*, ed. Martin Feldstein, 65–74. Chicago: University of Chicago Press.

———. 1989. *Men and Power: A Political Retrospective*. New York: Random House.

———. 1996. *Weggefährten: Erinnerungen und Reflexionen*. Berlin: Siedler.

Schmidt, Ingo. 2011. "There Were Alternatives: Lessons from Efforts to Advance Beyond Keynesian and Neoliberal Economic Policies in the 1970s." *WorkingUSA* 14 (4): 473–498.

Schmidt, Vivien. 2002. *The Futures of European Capitalism*. Oxford: Oxford University Press.

Schneider, Etienne. 2017. "Germany in the European Core-Periphery Constellation." Paper presented at the 8th Annual IIPPE Conference in Political Economy, Berlin, 13–15 September. http://iippe.org/8th-annual-conference-in-political-economy (accessed 6 February 2020).

Schrade, Christina. 1997. "Machtstaat, Handelsstaat, Zivilstaat? Deutsche Entwicklungspolitik nach dem Ende des Ost-West-Konflikts." *Zeitschrift für Internationale Beziehungen* 4 (2): 255–294.

Schulten, Thorsten, and Torsten Müller. 2013. "A New European Interventionism? The Impact of the New European Economic Governance on Wages and Collective Bargaining." In *Social Developments in the European Union 2012*, ed. David Natali and Bart Vanhercke, 181–213. Brussels: ETUI, OSE.

Schwarz, Hans-Peter. 1994. *Die Zentralmacht Europas*. Hamburg: Siedler.

Senghaas, Dieter. 1994. "Deutschland ist ein 'Handelsstaat'." *Eichholz Brief/ Zeitschrift zur politischen Bildung* 31 (2): 30–39.

Sewell, William. 2012. "Economic Crises and the Shape of Modern History. *Public Culture* 24 (2): 303–327.

Shonfield, Andrew. 1965. *Modern Capitalism: The Changing Balance of Public and Private Power*. London: Oxford University Press.

Silber, William. 2012. *Volcker: The Triumph of Persistence*. New York: Bloomsbury.

Silove, Nina. 2017. "Beyond the Buzzword: The Three Meanings of 'Grand Strategy'." *Security Studies* 27 (1): 27–57.

Silva, Joaquim Ramo. 2015. "Foreign Direct Investment in the Context of the Financial Crisis and Bailout: Portugal." In *Foreign Investment in Eastern and Southern Europe After 2009: Still a Lever of Growth?*, ed. Béla Galgóczi, Jan Drahokoupil, and Magdalena Bernaciak, 171–207. Brussels: ETUI.

Silvia, Steven. 2011. "Why Do German and US Reactions to the Financial Crisis Differ?" *German Politics and Society* 29 (4): 68–77.

Simonazzi, Annamaria, and Fernando Vianello. 1998. "Italy Towards European Monetary Union (and Domestic Disunion)." In *The Single Currency in National Perspective: A Community in Crisis?*, ed. Bernhard Moss and Jonathan Michie, 105–124. London: Macmillan.

Sinn, Hans-Werner. 2016. "Europe's Secret Bailout." *Project Syndicate*, 28 November. http://www.hanswernersinn.de/en/PS_28112016 (accessed 7 August 2017).

Sklair, Leslie. 2001. *The Transnational Capitalist Class*. Malden, MA: Blackwell.

Skocpol, Theda. 1980. "Political Response to Capitalist Crisis: Neo-Marxist Theories of the State and the Case of the New Deal." *Politics & Society* 10 (2): 155–201.

Slobodian, Quinn. 2018. *Globalists: The End of Empire and the Birth of Neoliberalism*. Cambridge, MA: Harvard University Press.

Smith, Neil. 2004. *American Empire: Roosevelt's Geographer and the Prelude to Globalization*. Berkeley: University of California Press.

———. 2005. *The Endgame of Globalization*. New York: Routledge.

Sobel, Andrew. 2012. *Birth of Hegemony: Crisis, Financial Revolution, and Emerging Global Networks*. Chicago: University of Chicago Press.

Soll, Jacob. 2015. "Germany's Destructive Anger." *New York Times*, 15 July. http://www.nytimes.com/2015/07/15/opinion/germanys-destructive-anger.html (accessed 14 March 2016).

Solty, Ingar. 2016. *Exportweltmeister in Fluchtursachen: Die neue deutsche außenpolitik, die Krise und linke Alternativen*. Berlin: Rosa Luxemburg Stiftung.

Spahn, Heinz-Peter. 1990. "Währungssicherung und außenwirtschaftliches Gleichgewicht: Prinzipien der 'Geschäftspolitik' der Bundesbank und volkswirtschaftliche Aufgaben der Geldpolitik." In *Geldpolitik und ökonomische Entwicklung: Ein Symposium*, ed. Hajo Riese and Heinz-Peter Spahn, 45–59. Regensburg: Transfer-Verlag.

———. 2005. "Wie der Monetarismus nach Deutschland kam: Zum Paradigmenwechsel der deutschen Geldpolitik in den frühen 1970er Jahren." *Hohenheimer Diskussionsbeiträge* 285.

Spaulding, Robert Mark Jr. 1996. "'Reconquering Our Old Position': West German Osthandel Strategies of the 1950s." In *The Quest for Economic Empire: European Strategies of German Big Business in the Twentieth Century*, ed. Volker Berghahn, 95–122. Providence, RI: Berghahn Books.

Spiro, David. 1999. *The Hidden Hand of American Hegemony: Petrodollar Recycling and International Markets*. Ithaca, NY: Cornell University Press.

Staack, Michael. 2000. *Handelsstaat Deutschland. Deutsche Außenpolitik in einem neuen internationalen System*. Paderborn: Schöningh.

Steffek, Jens. 2006. *Embedded Liberalism and Its Critics: Justifying Global Governance in the American Century*. London: Palgrave.

Stein, Judith. 2010. *Pivotal Decade: How the United States Traded Factories for Finance in the Seventies*. New Haven, CT: Yale University Press.

Stiglitz, Joseph. 2016. "The Problem with Europe Is the Euro." *The Guardian*, 10 August. https://www.theguardian.com/business/2016/aug/10/joseph-stiglitz-the-problem-with-europe-is-the-euro (accessed 6 February 2020).

Stockhammer, Engelbert. 2016. "Neoliberal Growth Models, Monetary Union and the Euro Crisis. A Post-Keynesian Perspective." *New Political Economy* 21 (4): 365–379.

Stokes, Raymond. 1988. "German Energy in the U.S. Post-War Economic Order, 1945–1951." *Journal of European Economic History* 17 (3): 621–639.

Stöllinger, Roman, Doris Hanzl-Weiss, Sandra Leitner, and Robert Stehrer. 2018. "Global and Regional Value Chains: How Important, How Different?" *WIIW Research Report* 427 (April). Vienna: Vienna Institute for International Economic Studies.

Stolper, Gustav. 1940. *German Economy, 1870–1940.* New York: Reynal & Hitchcock.

Strange, Susan. 1980. "Germany and the World Monetary System." In *West Germany: A European and Global Power,* ed. Wilfrid Kohl and Georgio Basevi, 45–62. Lexington, KY: Lexington Books.

———. 1986. *Casino Capitalism.* Oxford: Blackwell.

Straumann, Tobias. 2010. *Fixed Ideas of Money: Small States and Exchange Rate Regimes in Twentieth-Century Europe.* New York: Cambridge University Press.

Streeck, Wolfgang. 1991. "On the Institutional Conditions of Diversified Quality Production." In *Beyond Keynesianism: The Socio-Economics of Production and Employment,* ed. Egon Matzner and Wolfgang Streeck, 21–61. London: Edward Elgar.

———. 2001. "Introduction: Explorations into the Origins of Nonliberal Capitalism in Germany and Japan." In *The Origins of Nonliberal Capitalism: Germany and Japan,* ed. Wolfgang Streeck and Kozo Yamamura, 1–38. Ithaca, NY: Cornell University Press.

———. 2009. *Re-Forming Capitalism: Institutional Change in the German Political Economy.* New York: Oxford University Press.

———. 2011. "The Crises of Democratic Capitalism." *New Left Review* 71 (September-October): 5–29.

———. 2013. "Will Expansion Work? On Mark Blyth, Austerity: The History of a Dangerous Idea." *Comparative European Politics* 11 (6): 722–728.

———. 2014. *Buying Time: The Delayed Crisis of Democratic Capitalism.* London: Verso.

———. 2015. "German Hegemony: Unintended and Unwanted." *Eurozine,* 23 September. http://www.eurozine.com/german-hegemony-unintended-and -unwanted (accessed 7 August 2017).

———. 2016. "Von Konflikt ohne Partnerschaft zu Partnerschaft ohne Konflikt: Industrielle Beziehungen in Deutschland." *Industrielle Beziehungen* 23 (1): 47–60.

———. 2017. "Playing Catch Up." *London Review of Books* 39 (9): 26–28.

Streeck, Wolfgang, and Kathleen Ann Thelen, eds. 2005. *Beyond Continuity: Institutional Change in Advanced Political Economies.* New York: Oxford University Press.

Streeck, Wolfgang, and Kozo Yamamura, eds. 2001. *The Origins of Nonliberal Capitalism: Germany and Japan*. Ithaca, NY: Cornell University Press.

Südekum, Jens. 2018. "The China Shock and the Rise of Robots: Why Germany Is Different." In *Explaining Germany's Exceptional Recovery*, ed. Dalia Marin, 47–54. London: CEPR Press.

Teschke, Benno. 2003. *The Myth of 1648: Class, Geopolitics, and the Making of Modern International Relations*. London: Verso.

———. 2008. "Marxism." In *Oxford Handbook of International Relations*, ed. Christian Reus-Smit and Duncan Snidal, 163–187. Oxford: Oxford University Press.

———. 2014. "IR Theory, Historical Materialism and the False Promise of International Historical Sociology." *Spectrum: Journal of Global Studies* 6 (1): 1–66.

———. 2019. "The Social Origins of 18th Century British Grand Strategy: A Historical Sociology of the Peace of Utrecht." In *The 1713 Peace of Utrecht and Its Enduring Effects*, ed. Alfred H. A. Soons, 120–155. Leiden: Brill.

Teschke, Benno, and Can Cemgil. 2014. "The Dialectic of the Concrete: Reconsidering Dialectic for IR and Foreign Policy Analysis." *Globalizations* 11 (5): 605–625.

Teschke, Benno, and Steffan Wyn-Jones. 2017. "Marxism in Foreign Policy." In *Oxford Research Encyclopedia of Politics*, ed. Cameron Thies. Oxford: Oxford University Press. http://oxfordre.com/politics/view/10.1093/acrefore/9780190228637.001.0001/acrefore-9780190228637-e-372 (accessed 26 February 2019).

Thelen, Kathleen. 2014. *Varieties of Liberalization and the New Politics of Social Solidarity*. New York: Cambridge University Press.

Thompson, E. P. 1978. *The Poverty of Theory and Other Essays*. London: Merlin Press.

Tietmeyer, Hans. 1988. "Comment." In *Economic Policy Coordination: Proceedings of an International Seminar Held in Hamburg*, moderated by Wilfried Guth, 135–141. Washington, DC: International Monetary Fund.

Tipton, Frank. 2003. *A History of Modern Germany Since 1815*. London: Continuum.

Tooze, Adam. 2015. "Capitalist Peace or Capitalist War? The July Crisis Revisited." In *Cataclysm 1914: The First World War and the Making of the Modern World Politics*, 66–95. Leiden: Brill.

———. 2003. "The Question of Realism." *Security Studies* 13 (1): 156–194.

———. 2011. "The French Factor in U.S. Foreign Policy During the Nixon-Pompidou Period, 1969–1974." *Journal of Cold War Studies* 13 (1): 4–59.

Traynor, Ian. 2015. "Three Days That Saved the Euro." *The Guardian*, 22 October. https://www.theguardian.com/world/2015/oct/22/three-days-to-save-the-euro-greece (accessed 15 August 2017).

Treaster, Joseph. 2004. *Paul Volcker: The Making of a Financial Legend*. Hoboken, NJ: Wiley.

Trebilcock, Clive. 1981. *The Industrialisation of the Continental Powers, 1780–1914*. London: Macmillan.

Trotsky, Leon. 1969. *The Permanent Revolution and Results and Prospects*. New York: Pathfinder.

———. 1992 [1932]. *The History of the Russian Revolution*. New York: Pathfinder.

———. 2016 [1907]. *1905*. Chicago: Haymarket Books.

Truman, Edwin. 2004. "A Critical Review of Coordination Efforts in the Past." In *Macroeconomic Policies in the World Economy*, ed. Horst Siebert, 267–310. Heidelberg: Springer.

———. 2005. "Reflections." *Federal Reserve Bank of St. Louis Review* 87 (2, Part 2): 353–357.

United Nations. 1962. "International Trade Statistics, 1900–1960. Statistical Office of the United Nations." Draft paper. https://unstats.un.org/unsd/trade/data/tables. asp#historical (accessed 12 July 2017).

Urban, Hans-Jürgen. 2012. "Crisis Corporatism and Trade Union Revitalisation in Europe." In *A Triumph of Failed Ideas: European Models of Capitalism in the Crisis*, ed. Steffen Lehndorff, 219–241. Brussels: ETUI.

van Apeldoorn, Bastiaan. 2002. *Transnational Capitalism and the Struggle Over European Integration*. London: Routledge.

van Apeldoorn, Bastiaan, Ian Bruff, and Magnus Ryner. 2010. "The Richness and Diversity of Critical IPE Perspectives: Moving Beyond the Debate on the 'British School'." In *International Political Economy: Debating the Past, Present and Future*, ed. Nicola Philips and Catherine Weaver, 215–222. New York: Routledge.

van der Pijl, Kees. 1984. *The Making of an Atlantic Ruling Class*. London: Verso.

———. 1989. "Ruling Classes, Hegemony, and the State System: Theoretical and Historical Considerations." *International Journal of Political Economy* 19 (3): 7–35.

———. 2006. *Global Rivalries from the Cold War to Iraq*. London: Pluto.

———. 2007. "Capital and the State System: A Class Act." *Cambridge Review of International Affairs* 20 (4): 619–637.

van der Wurff, Richard. 1993. "Neo-Liberalism in Germany? The 'Wende' in Perspective." In *Restructuring Hegemony in the Global Political Economy: The Rise of Transnational Neo-Liberalism in the 1980s*, ed. Henk Overbeek and Kees van der Pijl, 162–187. London: Routledge.

Varoufakis, Yanis. 2015. "Dr Schäuble's Plan for Europe: Do Europeans Approve?" 17 July. https://www.yanisvaroufakis.eu/2015/07/17/dr-schaubles

-plan-for-europe-do-europeans-approve-english-version-of-my-article-in-die
-zeit (accessed 15 August 2017).

———. 2017. *Adults in the Room: My Battle with Europe's Deep Establishment.*
London: Bodley Head.

VBW [Vereinigung der Bayerischen Wirtschaft (Bavarian Industry Association)].
2017. "Importance of the German Economy for Europe: A VBW Study Prepared by Prognos AG." Munich.

Veltmeyer, Henry, James Petras, and Steve Vieux. 1997. *Neoliberalism and Class
Conflict in Latin America.* London: Macmillan.

Vihriälä, Erkki, and Guntram Wolff. 2013. "Manufacturing as a Source of Growth
for Southern Europe: Opportunities and Obstacles." In *Manufacturing Europe's Future,* ed. Reinhilde Veugelers, 48–72. Brussels: Bruegel.

Vitols, Sigurt. 2004. "Changes in Germany's Bank-Based Financial System: A Varieties of Capitalism Perspective." *WZB Discussion Papers* (March). Berlin: Wissenschaftszentrum Berlin für Sozialforschung. https://www.econstor.eu/bitst
ream/10419/51230/1/38574787X.pdf (accessed 4 May 2020).

Volcker, Paul. 1994. "Monetary Policy." In *American Economic Policy in the 1980s,*
ed. Martin Feldstein. 145–151. Chicago: University of Chicago Press.

Volcker, Paul, and Toyoo Gyohten. 1992. *Changing Fortunes: The World's Money
and the Threat to American Leadership.* New York: Times Books.

von Hagen, Jürgen. 1999. "A New Approach to Monetary Policy, 1971–1978." In
*Fifty Years of the Deutsche Mark: Central Bank and the Currency in Germany Since
1948,* ed. Deutsche Bundesbank, 403–438. Oxford, UK: Oxford University Press.

Wadbrook, William. 1972. *West German Balance-of-Payments Policy: The Prelude
to European Monetary Integration.* New York: Praeger.

Wagner, Rene. 2020. "Germany Ran World's Largest Current Account Surplus
in 2019: Ifo." *Reuters,* 3 February. https://uk.reuters.com/article/us-ger-
many-economy-currentaccount-exclus/exclusive-germany-ran-worlds-largest
-current-account-surplus-in-2019-ifo-idUKKBN1ZW0UZ (accessed 6 May
2020).

Waltz, Kenneth. 1979. *Theory of International Politics.* Menlo Park, CA:
Addison-Wesley.

Warneke, Sara. 2013. *Die europäische Wirtschaftsintegration aus der Perspektive
Wilhelm Röpkes.* Berlin: De Gruyter.

Warwick-Ching, Tony. 1993. *The International Gold Trade.* Cambridge, UK:
Woodhead.

Wass, Douglas. 2008. *Decline to Fall: The Making of British Macro-Economic Policy
and the 1976 IMF Crisis.* New York: Oxford University Press.

Webb, Michael, and Stephen Krasner. 1989. "Hegemonic Stability Theory: An
Empirical Assessment." *Review of International Studies* 15 (2): 183–198.

Webber, Douglas. 1983. "A Relationship of 'Critical Partnership'? Capital and the Social-Liberal Coalition in West Germany." In *Capital and Politics in Western Europe*, ed. David Marsh, 61–86. London: Frank Cass.

———. 1992. "Kohl's *Wendepolitik* After a Decade." *German Politics* 1 (2): 149–180.

Wehler, Hans-Ulrich. 1985. *The German Empire, 1871–1918*. New York: Berg.

Weidmann, Jens. 2017. "Feuerwehr oder Brandbeschleuniger: Notenbanken am Scheideweg?" Dinner speech at the financial market meeting of the CDU Economic Council, Berlin, 26 January. https://www.bundesbank.de/Redaktion /DE/Reden/2017/2017_01_26_weidmann.html (accessed 18 April 2017).

Wigger, Angela. 2017. "Debunking the Myth of the Ordoliberal Influence on Post-War European Integration." In *Ordoliberalism: Law and the Rule of Economics*, ed. Josef Hien and Christian Joerges, 161–178. Oxford: Hart.

Williamson, John. 1977. *The Failure of World Monetary Reform, 1971–1974*. New York: New York University Press.

Windolf, Paul. 2014. "The Corporate Network in Germany, 1896–2010." In *The Power of Corporate Networks: A Comparative and Historical Perspective*, ed. Thomas David and Gerarda Westerhuis, 66–88. New York: Routledge.

Winkler, Heinrich August. 2000. *Germany: The Long Road to the West*. New York: Oxford University Press.

Wolf, Holger. 1995. "Post-War Germany in the European Context: Domestic and External Determinants of Growth." In *Europe's Post-War Recovery*, ed. Barry Eichengreen, 323–352. New York: Cambridge University Press.

Wolf, Martin. 2016. "Germany Is the Eurozone's Biggest Problem." *Financial Times*, 10 May.

Wolfe, Alan. 1977. *The Limits of Legitimacy: Political Contradictions of Contemporary Capitalism*. New York: Free Press.

Wood, Ellen. 1981. "The Separation of the Economic and the Political in Capitalism." *New Left Review* 1 (127): 66–95.

Wood, Stewart. 1997. "Weakening Codetermination? Works Council Reform in West Germany in the 1980s." *Wissenschaftszentrum Berlin für Sozialforschung Discussion Paper* FSI97-302.

Woolley, John. 1984. *Monetary Politics: The Federal Reserve and the Politics of Monetary Policy*. Cambridge: Cambridge University Press.

Wünsche, Horst Friedrich. 2015. *Ludwig Erhards Soziale Marktwirtschaft: Wissenschaftliche Grundlagen und politische Fehldeutungen*. Reinbek: Lau.

Young, Brigitte. 2014. "German Ordoliberalism as Agenda Setter for the Euro Crisis: Myth Trumps Reality." *Journal of Contemporary European Studies* 22 (3): 276–287.

———. 2017. "Is Germany's and Europe's Crisis Politics Ordoliberal and/or Neoliberal?" In *German Ordoliberalism and Contemporary Neoliberalism*, ed. Thomas Biebricher and Frieder Vogelmann, 221–238. London: Rowman & Littlefield.

Young, Brigitte, and Willi Semmler. 2011. "The European Sovereign Debt Crisis: Is Germany to Blame?" *German Politics & Society* 29 (1): 1–24.

Zimmermann, Hubert. 2001. "The Fall of Bretton Woods and the Emergence of the Werner Plan." In *From the Werner Plan to the EMU: A European Political Economy in Historical Light*, ed. Lars Magnusson and Bo Stråth, 49–72. Brussels: P.I.E. Peter Lang.

———. 2002. *Money and Security: Troops, Monetary Policy, and West Germany's Relations with the United States and Britain, 1950–1971*. New York: Cambridge University Press.

———. 2008. "West German Monetary Policy and the Transition to Flexible Exchange Rates, 1969–1973." In *Orderly Change: International Monetary Relations Since Bretton Woods*, ed. David M. Andrews, 155–176. Ithaca, NY: Cornell University Press.

———. 2010. "Unraveling the Ties That Really Bind: The Dissolution of the Transatlantic Monetary Order and the European Monetary Cooperation, 1965–1973." In *The Strained Alliance: US-European Relations from Nixon to Carter*, ed. Matthias Schulz and Thomas Schwartz, 125–144. New York: Cambridge University Press.

Zohlnhöfer, Reimut. 2001. *Die Wirtschaftspolitik der Ära Kohl: Eine Analyse der Schlüsselentscheidungen in den Politikfeldern Finanzen, Arbeit und Entstaatlichung, 1982–1998*. Opladen: Leske + Budrich.

Zysman, John. 1984. *Governments, Markets and Growth: Financial Systems and the Politics of Industrial Change*. Ithaca, NY: Cornell University Press.

Index

pound sterling, 86, 120, 128–131;
float, 127–128
power: structural, 49–50, 100, 102.
See also hegemony
Prasad, Monica, 32
price stability *See* inflation
"productive capital," *vs.* "money capital," 24–26
profits, 23, 65, 69–70, 103–104,
157–158
protectionism and economic nationalism, 60, 63, 108–113; Britain,
126, 128, 130–132; German
strategy *vs.*, 116–118
Prussia, 60
Puerto Rico summit, 142
Putnam, Robert, 141–142, 144

quantitative easing, 182–183

Reagan, Ronald, 10, 122, 127, 152,
154–161, 166–167
realism, 13–14, 16–20, 46–47, 55,
199–200
Regan, Donald, 159
Reichsbank, 69
relationality, 55
relative autonomy, 49–52, 105
rentier theory, 23–24, 153–154. *See
also* class-based interpretations
reserves, 84, 86, 114, 139, 147–148
Robinson, Ronald, 73
Rogers, Chris, 127, 129
Rogers, William, 131
Rojava, 198
Röpke, Wilhelm, 68
Rosecrance, Richard, 72, 113
Ruggie, John Gerard, 19, 81
Rumor, Mariano, 124
Russia, 40

Sachs, Jeffrey, 190
Sachverständigenrat, 103

Sanders, Bernie, 198
Schacht, Hjalmar, 111
Schäuble, Wolfgang, 119, 184, 187,
190
Schiller, Karl, 94–97, 186, 188
Schlecht, Otto, 104, 131
Schmidt, Helmut, 13, 15, 28, 46,
177; defeating alternatives,
109–110, 113–117, 121, 124,
130; defeating alternatives, France,
134–136; disciplining the US,
139–144, 156–157, 162–163;
from benign neglect to Volcker
Shock, 146–148, 150; unwinding
Bretton Woods, 95, 98, 103
Schneider, Etienne, 176
Schröder, Gerhard, 26, 166, 168
Schulmann, Horst, 13, 156–157
Schwarz, Hans-Peter, 72
Second World War, 64, 112
seignorage, 9, 82–83
selection bias, 20
Siemens, 177, 181
Simon, William, 121–122, 131–132
Slovakia, 190
snake *See* European Exchange Rate
Agreement
Social Democrats, 25–26, 95–96; defeat of Left, 113–115, 117, 124;
disciplining the US, 141, 157;
eurocrisis, 165–166, 172
social forces, 14, 16, 23–24, 27, 192
social market economy, 8, 21, 41;
embedded liberalism, 66–71,
74, 77; eurocrisis, 169–170,
185–186. *See also* varieties of
capitalism
socialists, 68, 108, 113–114, 123,
198; Britain, 126–127, 130–132;
France, 133, 135
societies, differences between, 41–42
Solomon, Anthony, 148
Soviet Union, 85, 111

Lightning Source UK Ltd.
Milton Keynes UK
UKHW010233061120
372905UK00002B/29